GROWING UP
ISSUES AFFECTING AMERICA'S YOUTH

ISSN 1939-084X

GROWING UP
ISSUES AFFECTING AMERICA'S YOUTH

Melissa J. Doak

INFORMATION PLUS® REFERENCE SERIES
Formerly Published by Information Plus, Wylie, Texas

GALE
CENGAGE Learning

Detroit • New York • San Francisco • New Haven, Conn • Waterville, Maine • London

Growing Up: Issues Affecting America's Youth

Melissa J. Doak

Kepos Media, Inc., Paula Kepos and Janice Jorgensen, Series Editors

Project Editors: Kathleen J. Edgar, Elizabeth Manar, Kimberley A. McGrath

Rights Acquisition and Management: Robyn Young

Composition: Evi Abou-El-Seoud, Mary Beth Trimper

Manufacturing: Cynde Lentz

For product information and technology assistance, contact us at **Gale Customer Support, 1-800-877-4253.** For permission to use material from this text or product, submit all requests online at **www.cengage.com/permissions.** Further permissions questions can be e-mailed to **permissionrequest@cengage.com**

Cover photograph: Image copyright, 2009. Used under license from Jupiterimages.

While every effort has been made to ensure the reliability of the information presented in this publication, Gale, a part of Cengage Learning, does not guarantee the accuracy of the data contained herein. Gale accepts no payment for listing; and inclusion in the publication of any organization, agency, institution, publication, service, or individual does not imply endorsement of the editors or publisher. Errors brought to the attention of the publisher and verified to the satisfaction of the publisher will be corrected in future editions.

Gale
27500 Drake Rd.
Farmington Hills, MI 48331-3535

ISBN-13: 978-0-7876-5103-9 (set)   ISBN-10: 0-7876-5103-6 (set)
ISBN-13: 978-1-4144-4862-6   ISBN-10: 1-4144-4862-7

ISSN 1939-084X

This title is also available as an e-book.
ISBN-13: 978-1-4144-7524-0 (set)
ISBN-10: 1-4144-7524-1 (set)
Contact your Gale sales representative for ordering information.

Printed in the United States of America
1 2 3 4 5 6 7 13 12 11

TABLE OF CONTENTS

PREFACE

Growing Up: Issues Affecting America's Youth is part of the *Information Plus Reference Series*. The purpose of each volume of the series is to present the latest facts on a topic of pressing concern in modern American life. These topics include the most controversial and studied social issues of the 21st century: abortion, capital punishment, care of senior citizens, crime, the environment, health care, immigration, minorities, national security, social welfare, water, women, and many more. Even though this series is written especially for high school and undergraduate students, it is an excellent resource for anyone in need of factual information on current affairs.

By presenting the facts, it is the intention of Gale, Cengage Learning to provide its readers with everything they need to reach an informed opinion on current issues. To that end, there is a particular emphasis in this series on the presentation of scientific studies, surveys, and statistics. These data are generally presented in the form of tables, charts, and other graphics placed within the text of each book. Every graphic is directly referred to and carefully explained in the text. The source of each graphic is presented within the graphic itself. The data used in these graphics are drawn from the most reputable and reliable sources, such as from the various branches of the U.S. government and from private organizations and associations. Every effort was made to secure the most recent information available. Readers should bear in mind that many major studies take years to conduct and that additional years often pass before the data from these studies are made available to the public. Therefore, in many cases the most recent information available in 2011 is dated from 2008 or 2009. Older statistics are sometimes presented as well, if they are landmark studies or of particular interest and no more-recent information exists.

Even though statistics are a major focus of the *Information Plus Reference Series*, they are by no means its only content. Each book also presents the widely held positions and important ideas that shape how the book's subject is discussed in the United States. These positions are explained in detail and, where possible, in the words of their proponents. Some of the other material to be found in these books includes historical background, descriptions of major events related to the subject, relevant laws and court cases, and examples of how these issues play out in American life. Some books also feature primary documents or have pro and con debate sections that provide the words and opinions of prominent Americans on both sides of a controversial topic. All material is presented in an even-handed and unbiased manner; readers will never be encouraged to accept one view of an issue over another.

HOW TO USE THIS BOOK

Childhood and adolescence are perhaps the most critical period in any person's life. The education one receives during this time; the environment one is raised in; and the way one is treated by family, friends, and the larger community can have lifelong impacts and consequences. This volume addresses various factors that affect youth, including family income, who cares for children, health and safety issues, educational matters, and teen sexuality and pregnancy. Also, crime, violence, and victimization are addressed, including gang violence, school violence, and crime prevention and punishment.

Growing Up: Issues Affecting America's Youth consists of 10 chapters and three appendixes. Each chapter is devoted to a particular aspect of youth in the United States. For a summary of the information covered in each chapter, please see the synopses provided in the Table of Contents. Chapters generally begin with an overview of the basic facts and background information on the chapter's topic, then proceed to examine subtopics of particular interest. For example, Chapter 3, Caring for Children, begins with a discussion of the societal changes that led to more mothers entering the workforce, creating the necessity for quality child care. It then delves into child care for school-age and preschool-age children. It discusses different types of child care programs and arrangements, ranging from Head Start and Twenty-First-Century Community Learning Centers to home-based day care providers, informal relative care, and self-care. It also examines how race, ethnicity, and poverty affect a family's child care choices—and the extremely high cost of quality child care throughout the nation. The chapter concludes with a look at the Family and Medical Leave Act. Readers can find their way through a chapter by looking for the section and subsection headings, which are clearly set off from the text. They can also refer to the book's extensive index, if they already know what they are looking for.

Statistical Information

The tables and figures featured throughout *Growing Up: Issues Affecting America's Youth* will be of particular use to readers in learning about this topic. These tables and figures represent an extensive collection of the most recent and valuable statistics on growing up in the United States, as well as related issues—for example, graphics cover the number of children without health insurance, the percentage of students who consume alcohol, the rate of teens having abortions, the number of children who participate in the National School Lunch Program, and the presence of violence at school. Gale, Cengage Learning believes that making this information available to readers is the most important way to fulfill the goal of this book: to help readers understand the issues and controversies surrounding youth in the United States and reach their own conclusions.

Each table or figure has a unique identifier appearing above it for ease of identification and reference. Titles for the tables and figures explain their purpose. At the end of each table or figure, the original source of the data is provided.

To help readers understand these often complicated statistics, all tables and figures are explained in the text. References in the text direct readers to the relevant statistics. Furthermore, the contents of all tables and figures are fully indexed. Please see the opening section of the index at the back of this volume for a description of how to find tables and figures within it.

Appendixes

Besides the main body text and images, *Growing Up: Issues Affecting America's Youth* has three appendixes. The first is the Important Names and Addresses directory.

Here, readers will find contact information for a number of organizations that study children, adolescents, and families. The second appendix is the Resources section, which can also assist readers in conducting their own research. In this section, the author and editors of *Growing Up: Issues Affecting America's Youth* describe some of the sources that were most useful during the compilation of this book. The final appendix is the index. It has been greatly expanded from previous editions and should make it even easier to find specific topics in this book.

ADVISORY BOARD CONTRIBUTIONS

The staff of Information Plus would like to extend its heartfelt appreciation to the Information Plus Advisory Board. This dedicated group of media professionals provides feedback on the series on an ongoing basis. Their comments allow the editorial staff who work on the project to make the series better and more user-friendly. The staff's top priority is to produce the highest-quality and most useful books possible, and the Information Plus Advisory Board's contributions to this process are invaluable.

The members of the Information Plus Advisory Board are:

- Kathleen R. Bonn, Librarian, Newbury Park High School, Newbury Park, California

- Madelyn Garner, Librarian, San Jacinto College, North Campus, Houston, Texas

- Anne Oxenrider, Media Specialist, Dundee High School, Dundee, Michigan

- Charles R. Rodgers, Director of Libraries, Pasco-Hernando Community College, Dade City, Florida

- James N. Zitzelsberger, Library Media Department Chairman, Oshkosh West High School, Oshkosh, Wisconsin

COMMENTS AND SUGGESTIONS

The editors of the *Information Plus Reference Series* welcome your feedback on *Growing Up: Issues Affecting America's Youth*. Please direct all correspondence to:

Editors
Information Plus Reference Series
27500 Drake Rd.
Farmington Hills, MI 48331-3535

CHAPTER 1
CHILDREN AND FAMILIES IN THE UNITED STATES

DEFINING CHILDHOOD AND ADULTHOOD

Exactly when childhood ends and adulthood begins differs among cultures and over periods of time within cultures. People in some societies believe adulthood begins with the onset of puberty, arguing that people who are old enough to have children are also old enough to assume adult responsibilities. This stage of life is often solemnized with special celebrations. In the Jewish tradition, for example, the bar mitzvah ceremony for 13-year-old boys and the bat mitzvah ceremony for 13-year-old girls commemorates the attainment of adult responsibility for observing Jewish law.

Modern American society identifies an interim period of life between childhood and adulthood known as adolescence, during which teens reach a series of milestones as they accept increasing amounts of adult responsibility. At age 16 most Americans can be licensed to drive. At 18 most young people leave the public education system and are eligible to vote. At that time they can join the military without parental permission and are tried as adults for all crimes in all states (although some states try younger people as adults, and in serious offenses such as murder, rape, or armed robbery, juveniles are sometimes tried as adults). There are contradictions in the rights and privileges conferred, however. In many states teens under the age of 18 years can marry but cannot legally access pornographic material.

In general, American society recognizes 21 as the age of full adulthood. At 21 young men and women are considered legally independent of their parents and are completely responsible for their own decisions. At that time, they are allowed to buy alcoholic beverages.

According to the Federal Interagency Forum on Child and Family Statistics, in *America's Children in Brief: Key National Indicators of Well-Being, 2010* (July 2010, http://www.childstats.gov/americaschildren/tables .asp), in 2009, 74.5 million children younger than the age of 18 years lived in the United States. This number is expected to increase to 81.7 million by 2020. However, because the country's entire population will increase, the percentage of children in the population is projected to decline, decreasing slightly from 24.3% in 2009 to 23.9% by 2020.

BIRTH AND FERTILITY RATES

Fertility is measured in a number of ways. One such measure, called the crude birthrate, is the number of live births per 1,000 women in the population, regardless of their age, in any given year. In 2006 the crude birthrate was 14.2 live births per 1,000 women. (See Table 1.1.) The crude birthrate for Hispanic women (of any race) was considerably higher (23.4) than for Asian or Pacific Islander women (16.6), non-Hispanic African-American women (16.5), Native American or Alaskan Native women (14.9), and non-Hispanic white women (11.6).

Another way to measure the number of births is the fertility rate, which is the number of live births per 1,000 women in the population between the ages of 15 and 44 years in any given year. These are the years generally considered to be a woman's reproductive age range. During the first 10 years of the baby boom that immediately followed World War II (1939–1945), fertility rates were well over 100 births per 1,000 women. (See Table 1.1.) In contrast, the fertility rate for American women in 2006 was 68.5 births per 1,000 women, only 58.1% of the 1960 fertility rate of 118 births per 1,000 women. However, some groups in American society have much higher fertility rates than the average. In 2006 the fertility rate for Hispanic women was 101.5 births per 1,000 women; non-Hispanic African-American women, 70.6; Asian or Pacific Islander women, 67.5; Native American or Alaskan Native mothers, 63.1; and non-Hispanic white women, 59.5.

TABLE 1.1

Crude birth rates, fertility rates, and birth rates by age of mother, according to race and Hispanic origin, selected years 1950–2006

[Data are based on birth certificates]

Race Hispanic origin, and year	Crude birth rate[a]	Fertility rate[b]	10–14 years	15–19 years Total	15–17 years	18–19 years	20–24 years	25–29 years	30–34 years	35–39 years	40–44 years	45–54 years[c]
All races				Live births per 1,000 women								
1950	24.1	106.2	1.0	81.6	40.7	132.7	196.6	166.1	103.7	52.9	15.1	1.2
1960	23.7	118.0	0.8	89.1	43.9	166.7	258.1	197.4	112.7	56.2	15.5	0.9
1970	18.4	87.9	1.2	68.3	38.8	114.7	167.8	145.1	73.3	31.7	8.1	0.5
1980	15.9	68.4	1.1	53.0	32.5	82.1	115.1	112.9	61.9	19.8	3.9	0.2
1985	15.8	66.3	1.2	51.0	31.0	79.6	108.3	111.0	69.1	24.0	4.0	0.2
1990	16.7	70.9	1.4	59.9	37.5	88.6	116.5	120.2	80.8	31.7	5.5	0.2
1995	14.6	64.6	1.3	56.0	35.5	87.7	107.5	108.8	81.1	34.0	6.6	0.3
2000	14.4	65.9	0.9	47.7	26.9	78.1	109.7	113.5	91.2	39.7	8.0	0.5
2004	14.0	66.3	0.7	41.1	22.1	70.0	101.7	115.5	95.3	45.4	8.9	0.5
2005	14.0	66.7	0.7	40.5	21.4	69.9	102.2	115.5	95.8	46.3	9.1	0.6
2006	14.2	68.5	0.6	41.9	22.0	73.0	105.9	116.7	97.7	47.3	9.4	0.6
Race of child:[d] White												
1950	23.0	102.3	0.4	70.0	31.3	120.5	190.4	165.1	102.6	51.4	14.5	1.0
1960	22.7	113.2	0.4	79.4	35.5	154.6	252.8	194.9	109.6	54.0	14.7	0.8
1970	17.4	84.1	0.5	57.4	29.2	101.5	163.4	145.9	71.9	30.0	7.5	0.4
1980	14.9	64.7	0.6	44.7	25.2	72.1	109.5	112.4	60.4	18.5	3.4	0.2
Race of mother:[e] White												
1980	15.1	65.6	0.6	45.4	25.5	73.2	111.1	113.8	61.2	18.8	3.5	0.2
1985	15.0	64.1	0.6	43.3	24.4	70.4	104.1	112.3	69.9	23.3	3.7	0.2
1990	15.8	68.3	0.7	50.8	29.5	78.0	109.8	120.7	81.7	31.5	5.2	0.2
1995	14.1	63.6	0.8	49.5	29.6	80.2	104.7	111.7	83.3	34.2	6.4	0.3
2000	13.9	65.3	0.6	43.2	23.3	72.3	106.6	116.7	94.6	40.2	7.9	0.4
2004	13.5	66.1	0.5	37.7	19.5	65.0	99.2	118.6	99.1	46.4	8.9	0.5
2005	13.4	66.3	0.5	37.0	18.9	64.7	99.2	118.3	99.3	47.3	9.0	0.6
2006	13.7	68.0	0.5	38.2	19.4	67.5	102.5	119.1	100.9	48.2	9.2	0.6
Race of child:[d] Black or African American												
1960	31.9	153.5	4.3	156.1	—	—	295.4	218.6	137.1	73.9	21.9	1.1
1970	25.3	115.4	5.2	140.7	101.4	204.9	202.7	136.3	79.6	41.9	12.5	1.0
1980	22.1	88.1	4.3	100.0	73.6	138.8	146.3	109.1	62.9	24.5	5.8	0.3
Race of mother:[e] Black or African American												
1980	21.3	84.7	4.3	97.8	72.5	135.1	140.0	103.9	59.9	23.5	5.6	0.3
1985	20.4	78.8	4.5	95.4	69.3	132.4	135.0	100.2	57.9	23.9	4.6	0.3
1990	22.4	86.8	4.9	112.8	82.3	152.9	160.2	115.5	68.7	28.1	5.5	0.3
1995	17.8	71.0	4.1	94.4	68.5	135.0	133.7	95.6	63.0	28.4	6.0	0.3
2000	17.0	70.0	2.3	77.4	49.0	118.8	141.3	100.3	65.4	31.5	7.2	0.4
2004	16.0	67.6	1.6	63.3	37.2	104.4	127.7	103.6	67.9	34.0	7.9	0.5
2005	16.2	69.0	1.7	62.0	35.5	104.9	129.9	105.9	70.3	35.3	8.5	0.5
2006	16.8	72.1	1.5	64.6	36.6	110.2	135.8	109.4	74.0	36.6	8.5	0.5
American Indian or Alaska Native mothers[e]												
1980	20.7	82.7	1.9	82.2	51.5	129.5	143.7	106.6	61.8	28.1	8.2	*
1985	19.8	78.6	1.7	79.2	47.7	124.1	139.1	109.6	62.6	27.4	6.0	*
1990	18.9	76.2	1.6	81.1	48.5	129.3	148.7	110.3	61.5	27.5	5.9	*
1995	15.3	63.0	1.6	72.9	44.6	122.2	123.1	91.6	56.5	24.3	5.5	*
2000	14.0	58.7	1.1	58.3	34.1	97.1	117.2	91.8	55.5	24.6	5.7	0.3
2004	14.0	58.9	0.9	52.5	30.0	87.0	109.7	92.8	58.0	26.8	6.0	0.2
2005	14.2	59.9	0.9	52.7	30.5	87.6	109.2	93.8	60.1	27.0	6.0	0.3
2006	14.9	63.1	0.9	55.0	30.7	93.0	115.4	97.8	61.8	28.4	6.1	0.4

Birth Trends

According to Frederick W. Hollmann, Tammany J. Mulder, and Jeffrey E. Kallan of the U.S. Census Bureau, in *Methodology and Assumptions for the Population Projections of the United States: 1999 to 2100* (January 13, 2000, http://www.census.gov/population/www/documentation/twps0038.pdf), the most recent study regarding U.S. population projections as of January 2011, fertility rates among racial and ethnic groups are expected to differ markedly during the 21st century. The total fertility rate refers to the average number of children a woman will give birth to during her lifetime. The total fertility rate for non-Hispanic white women is expected to rise slightly during the century but not to reach the population

TABLE 1.1

Crude birth rates, fertility rates, and birth rates by age of mother, according to race and Hispanic origin, selected years 1950–2006 [CONTINUED]

[Data are based on birth certificates]

Race Hispanic origin, and year	Crude birth rate[a]	Fertility rate[b]	Age of mother									
			10–14 years	15–19 years			20–24 years	25–29 years	30–34 years	35–39 years	40–44 years	45–54 years[c]
				Total	15–17 years	18–19 years						
			Live births per 1,000 women									
Asian or Pacific Islander mothers[e]												
1980	19.9	73.2	0.3	26.2	12.0	46.2	93.3	127.4	96.0	38.3	8.5	0.7
1985	18.7	68.4	0.4	23.8	12.5	40.8	83.6	123.0	93.6	42.7	8.7	1.2
1990	19.0	69.6	0.7	26.4	16.0	40.2	79.2	126.3	106.5	49.6	10.7	1.1
1995	16.7	62.6	0.7	25.5	15.6	40.1	64.2	103.7	102.3	50.1	11.8	0.8
2000	17.1	65.8	0.3	20.5	11.6	32.6	60.3	108.4	116.5	59.0	12.6	0.8
2004	16.8	67.1	0.2	17.3	8.9	29.6	59.8	108.6	116.9	62.1	13.6	1.0
2005	16.5	66.6	0.2	17.0	8.2	30.1	61.1	107.9	115.0	61.8	13.8	1.0
2006	16.6	67.5	0.2	17.0	8.8	29.5	63.2	108.4	116.9	63.0	14.1	1.0
Hispanic or Latina mothers[e, f]												
1980	23.5	95.4	1.7	82.2	52.1	126.9	156.4	132.1	83.2	39.9	10.6	0.7
1990	26.7	107.7	2.4	100.3	65.9	147.7	181.0	153.0	98.3	45.3	10.9	0.7
1995	24.1	98.8	2.6	99.3	68.3	145.4	171.9	140.4	90.5	43.7	10.7	0.6
2000	23.1	95.9	1.7	87.3	55.5	132.6	161.3	139.9	97.1	46.6	11.5	0.6
2004	22.9	97.8	1.3	82.6	49.7	133.5	165.3	145.6	104.1	52.9	12.4	0.7
2005	23.1	99.4	1.3	81.7	48.5	134.6	170.0	149.2	106.8	54.2	13.0	0.8
2006	23.4	101.5	1.3	83.0	47.9	139.7	177.0	152.4	108.5	55.6	13.3	0.8
White, not Hispanic or Latina mothers[e, f]												
1980	14.2	62.4	0.4	41.2	22.4	67.7	105.5	110.6	59.9	17.7	3.0	0.1
1990	14.4	62.8	0.5	42.5	23.2	66.6	97.5	115.3	79.4	30.0	4.7	0.2
1995	12.5	57.5	0.4	39.3	22.0	66.2	90.2	105.1	81.5	32.8	5.9	0.3
2000	12.2	58.5	0.3	32.6	15.8	57.5	91.2	109.4	93.2	38.8	7.3	0.4
2004	11.6	58.4	0.2	26.7	12.0	48.7	81.9	110.0	97.1	44.8	8.2	0.5
2005	11.5	58.3	0.2	25.9	11.5	48.0	81.4	109.1	96.9	45.6	8.3	0.5
2006	11.6	59.5	0.2	26.6	11.8	49.3	83.4	109.1	98.1	46.3	8.4	0.6
Black or African American, not Hispanic or Latina mothers[e, f]												
1980	22.9	90.7	4.6	105.1	77.2	146.5	152.2	111.7	65.2	25.8	5.8	0.3
1990	23.0	89.0	5.0	116.2	84.9	157.5	165.1	118.4	70.2	28.7	5.6	0.3
1995	18.2	72.8	4.2	97.2	70.4	139.2	137.8	98.5	64.4	28.8	6.1	0.3
2000	17.3	71.4	2.4	79.2	50.1	121.9	145.4	102.8	66.5	31.8	7.2	0.4
2004	15.8	67.0	1.6	63.1	37.1	103.9	126.9	103.0	67.4	33.7	7.8	0.5
2005	15.7	67.2	1.7	60.9	34.9	103.0	126.8	103.0	68.4	34.3	8.2	0.5
2006	16.5	70.6	1.6	63.7	36.2	108.4	133.2	107.1	72.6	36.0	8.3	0.5

—Data not available.

*Rates based on fewer than 20 births are considered unreliable and are not shown.

[a]Live births per 1,000 population.

[b]Total number of live births regardless of age of mother per 1,000 women 15–44 years of age.

[c]Prior to 1997, data are for live births to mothers 45–49 years of age per 1,000 women 45–49 years of age. Starting with 1997 data, rates are for live births to mothers 45–54 years of age per 1,000 women 45–49 years of age.

[d]Live births are tabulated by race of child.

[e]Live births are tabulated by race and/or Hispanic origin of mother.

[f]Prior to 1993, data from states lacking an Hispanic-origin item on the birth certificate were excluded. Rates in 1985 were not calculated because estimates for the Hispanic and non-Hispanic populations were not available.

Notes: Data are based on births adjusted for underregistration for 1950 and on registered births for all other years. Starting with 1970 data, births to persons who were not residents of the 50 states and the District of Columbia are excluded. Starting with Health, United States, 2003, rates for 1991–1999 were revised using intercensal population estimates based on the 2000 census. Rates for 2000 were computed using the 2000 census counts and starting in 2001 rates were computed using 2000-based postcensal estimates. The race groups, white, black, American Indian or Alaska Native, and Asian or Pacific Islander, include persons of Hispanic and non-Hispanic origin. Persons of Hispanic origin may be of any race. Starting with 2003 data, some states reported multiple-race data. The multiple-race data for these states were bridged to the single-race categories of the 1977 Office of Management and Budget standards for comparability with other states. Interpretation of trend data should take into consideration expansion of reporting areas and immigration. Some data have been revised and differ from previous editions of Health, United States. Data for additional years are available.

SOURCE: "Table 4. Crude Birth Rates, Fertility Rates, and Birth Rates by Age, Race and Hispanic Origin of Mother: United States, Selected Years 1950–2006," in *Health, United States, 2009: With Special Feature on Medical Technology*, Centers for Disease Control and Prevention, National Center for Health Statistics, February 2010, http://www.cdc.gov/nchs/data/hus/hus09.pdf (accessed October 15, 2010)

replacement rate (the fertility rate needed to keep the population stable, which is 2,100 births per 1,000 women). The total fertility rate for non-Hispanic African-American women will remain steady at about the population replacement rate. Native American and Asian or Pacific Islander total fertility rates are expected to decrease slightly but remain well above the population replacement rate during the 21st century. The Hispanic total fertility rate is also expected to decrease from a high of 2,920.5 births per 1,000 women during their lifetime in 1999 to 2,333.8 births per 1,000 women in 2100—a rate still well above the population replacement rate and well above the rates of other ethnic and racial groups.

As a result of these different fertility rates, the proportion of American children who are non-Hispanic white is expected to decrease from 55.3% in 2009 to 48.7% in 2025, and the proportion of children who are Hispanic is expected to increase from 22.5% in 2009 to 28.9% in 2025. (See Table 1.2.) The percentage of African-American children is expected to decrease slightly, from 15.1% in 2009 to 14% in 2025, whereas the proportion of Asian or Pacific Islander children is expected to increase slightly, from 4.4% in 2009 to 5.1% in 2025.

After 2020 Hispanic births are expected to add more people each year to the U.S. population than all other non-white racial and ethnic groups combined. The non-Hispanic white population is projected to rise from 200.9 million in 2010 to 203.3 million in 2050, an increase of 2.4 million, whereas the Hispanic population will increase by 83.1 million (due to high birthrates and continued immigration), from 49.7 million to 132.8 million. (See Table 1.3.) In 2010 non-Hispanic whites will make up 64.8% (200.9 million out of 310.2 million) of the total U.S. population, whereas Hispanics will make up 16% (49.7 million out of 310.2 million). By contrast, in 2050 non-Hispanic whites are expected to make up 46.3% (203.3 million out of 439 million) of the total U.S. population, whereas Hispanics will make up 30.3% (132.8 million out of 439 million).

As a result, the youth segment of the U.S. population is becoming more racially diverse. Between 1980 and 2009 the non-Hispanic white share of the under-18 population dropped from 74% to 55.3%. (See Table 1.2.) During this same period the non-Hispanic African-American share of this population remained stable, increasing only slightly from 15% to 15.1%. In contrast, the Asian or Pacific Islander share of the under-18 population increased from 2% in 1980 to 4.4% in 2009. The Hispanic share of the under-18 population showed the highest increase, from 9 % in 1980 to 22.5% in 2009. In other words, in 2009 more than one out of every five children in the United States was of Hispanic origin.

Evidence also suggests that racial and ethnic lines became less rigid in the United States during the last two decades of the 20th century, as people from different ethnic and racial backgrounds parented children together. In *Age: 2000* (October 2001, http://www.census.gov/prod/2001pubs/c2kbr01-12.pdf), Julie Meyer of the Census Bureau notes that people who reported in the 2000 census that they came from more than one ethnic or racial background had a significantly younger median age (half of all people below the median value and half of all people above the median value) than all single-race groups, at 22.7 years. Nearly four out of 10 (41.9%) people with a mixed ethnic or racial background were under the age of 18 years.

The number of children under the age of 18 years with a biracial background continued to increase between 2000 and 2009, from 1.8 million in 2000 to 2.5 million in 2009. (See Table 1.4.) The median age of people of two or more races was young, at 19.7 in 2009. These findings may indicate that distinctions between racial and ethnic groups in the United States will continue to blur during the 21st century.

Birth Rates during the Recession

D'Vera Cohn and Gretchen Livingston of the Pew Research Center report in "U.S. Birth Rate Decline Linked to Recession" (April 6, 2010, http://pewsocialtrends.org/2010/04/06/us-birth-rate-decline-linked-to-recession/) that even though the nation's birthrate grew annually between 2003 and 2007, it dropped off sharply in 2008. The researchers suggest that this drop was due to the economic recession that began in late 2007. Cohn and Livingston state, "There is a strong association between the magnitude of fertility change in 2008 across states and key economic indicators including changes in per capita income, housing prices and share of the working-age population that is employed across states." The birthrate continued to decline in 2009. In fact, the researchers indicate that the nation's birthrate has mirrored the U.S. economy's ups and downs since 2000.

Seeing the economic booms and busts reflected in the nation's birthrate is not new. In fact, the Great Depression and the recessions that preceded it intensified the trend toward declining birth rates between 1926 and 1935. However, Cohn and Livingston note that the economy is only one factor influencing birth rates. Others include societal acceptance of working women, the rise in women's wages, and the availability of contraception.

THE CHANGING FAMILY

Family and Household Size

The composition of households in American society changed markedly during the 20th century. Frank Hobbs and Nicole Stoops of the Census Bureau indicate in *Demographic Trends in the 20th Century* (November 2002, http://www.census.gov/prod/2002pubs/censr-4.pdf) that in 1950 families accounted for 89.4% of all households; by 2000 this number had decreased to 68.1%. The proportion of married-couple households that included at least one

TABLE 1.2

Children by race and Hispanic origin, 1980–2009 and projected 2010–50

Race and Hispanic origin[a]	1980	1981	1982	1983	1984	1985	1986	1987	1988	1989	1990	1991	1992	1993	1994	1995	1996	1997	1998	1999
White, non-Hispanic[b]	74.0	73.0	73.0	72.0	72.0	72.0	71.0	70.0	70.0	69.0	69.0	68.0	68.0	67.0	66.0	66.0	65.0	64.0	64.0	63.0
Black, non-Hispanic[b]	15.0	15.0	15.0	15.0	15.0	15.0	15.0	15.0	15.0	15.0	15.0	15.0	15.0	15.0	15.0	15.0	15.0	15.0	15.0	15.0
American Indian or Alaskan Native[b]	1.0	1.0	1.0	1.0	1.0	1.0	1.0	1.0	1.0	1.0	1.0	1.0	1.0	1.0	1.0	1.0	1.0	1.0	1.0	1.0
Asian or Pacific Islander[b]	2.0	2.0	2.0	2.0	2.0	3.0	3.0	3.0	3.0	3.0	3.0	3.0	3.0	3.0	3.0	4.0	4.0	4.0	4.0	4.0
Hispanic[d]	9.0	9.0	10.0	10.0	10.0	10.0	11.0	11.0	12.0	12.0	12.0	13.0	13.0	13.0	14.0	14.0	15.0	15.0	16.0	17.0

Race and Hispanic origin[a]	2000	2001	2002	2003	2004	2005	2006	2007	2008	2009	2010	2011	2012	2013	2014	2015	2016	2017	2018	2019
White	76.8	76.7	76.6	76.4	76.3	76.2	76.0	75.9	75.7	75.6	76.0	75.9	75.9	75.8	75.7	75.6	75.6	75.5	75.4	75.4
White, non-Hispanic[b]	61.2	60.6	59.9	59.3	58.6	58.0	57.3	56.6	55.9	55.3	55.3	54.8	54.3	53.8	53.4	52.9	52.5	52.1	51.7	51.3
Black	15.6	15.6	15.5	15.4	15.4	15.3	15.3	15.2	15.2	15.1	14.7	14.6	14.5	14.4	14.4	14.3	14.3	14.2	14.2	14.2
Asian	3.6	3.7	3.8	3.9	4.0	4.1	4.1	4.2	4.3	4.4	4.4	4.5	4.5	4.6	4.7	4.7	4.7	4.8	4.8	4.9
All other races[c]	4.0	4.1	4.2	4.2	4.3	4.4	4.5	4.6	4.7	4.9	4.9	5.0	5.1	5.2	5.3	5.3	5.4	5.5	5.6	5.6
Hispanic[d]	17.2	17.7	18.3	18.8	19.4	20.0	20.6	21.3	21.9	22.5	22.8	23.3	23.7	24.2	24.6	25.0	25.4	25.8	26.2	26.5

Race and Hispanic origin[a]	2020	2021	2022	2023	2024	2025	2026	2027	2028	2029	2030	2031	2032	2033	2034	2035	2036	2037	2038	2039
White	75.3	75.2	75.1	75.0	75.0	74.9	74.8	74.8	74.7	74.6	74.6	74.5	74.4	74.4	74.3	74.2	74.1	74.0	74.0	73.9
White, non-Hispanic[b]	50.9	50.5	50.0	49.6	49.2	48.7	48.3	47.8	47.4	46.9	46.4	45.9	45.5	45.0	44.5	44.0	43.5	43.1	42.6	42.2
Black	14.1	14.1	14.1	14.0	14.0	14.0	13.9	13.9	13.8	13.8	13.7	13.7	13.6	13.6	13.5	13.4	13.4	13.3	13.3	13.2
Asian	4.9	4.9	5.0	5.0	5.0	5.1	5.1	5.1	5.2	5.2	5.3	5.3	5.4	5.4	5.5	5.6	5.6	5.7	5.7	5.8
All other races[c]	5.7	5.8	5.9	5.9	6.0	6.1	6.1	6.2	6.3	6.4	6.4	6.5	6.6	6.7	6.7	6.8	6.9	7.0	7.0	7.1
Hispanic[d]	26.9	27.3	27.7	28.1	28.5	28.9	29.3	29.7	30.2	30.6	31.1	31.5	32.0	32.5	32.9	33.4	33.8	34.2	34.7	35.1

Race and Hispanic origin[a]	2040	2041	2042	2043	2044	2045	2046	2047	2048	2049	2050
White	73.8	73.7	73.6	73.5	73.5	73.4	73.3	73.2	73.2	73.1	73.0
White, non-Hispanic[b]	41.7	41.3	40.9	40.5	40.1	39.8	39.4	39.0	38.7	38.3	38.0
Black	13.2	13.1	13.1	13.0	13.0	13.0	12.9	12.9	12.9	12.8	12.8
Asian	5.9	5.9	6.0	6.0	6.1	6.1	6.1	6.2	6.2	6.3	6.3
All other races[c]	7.2	7.3	7.3	7.4	7.5	7.6	7.6	7.7	7.8	7.8	7.9
Hispanic[d]	35.5	35.9	36.2	36.6	36.9	37.3	37.6	37.9	38.2	38.5	38.8

[a]For race and Hispanic-origin data in this table: In 1980 and 1990, following the 1977 OMB standards for collecting and presenting data on race, the decennial census asked respondents to choose one race from the following: White, black American Indian or Alaskan Native, or Asian or Pacific Islander. The Census Bureau also offered an "Other" category. Beginning in 2000, following the 1997 OMB standards for collecting and presenting data on race, the decennial census asked respondents to choose one or more races from the following: White, black or African American, Asian, American Indian or Alaska Native, or Native Hawaiian or other Pacific Islander. In addition, a "Some other race" category was included with OMB approval. Those who chose more than one race were classified as "Two or more races." Except for the "All other races" category, all race groups discussed in this table from 2000 onward refer to people who indicated only one racial identity within the racial categories presented. (Those who were "Two or more races" were included in the "All other races" category, along with American Indians or Alaska Natives and Native Hawaiians or other Pacific Islanders.) People who responded to the question on race by indicating only one race are referred to as the race-alone population. The use of the race-alone population in this table does not imply that it is the preferred method of presenting or analyzing data. Data from 2000 onward are not directly comparable with data from earlier years. Data on race and Hispanic origin are collected separately; Hispanics may be of any race.

[b]Excludes persons in this race group who are of Hispanic origin.

[c]Includes American Indian, Eskimo and Aleut, Native Hawaiian and other Pacific Islander, and all multiple race ("Two or more races").

[d]Persons of Hispanic origin may be of any race.

SOURCE: "POP3. Racial and Ethnic Composition: Percentage of U.S. Children Ages 0–17 by Race and Hispanic Origin, 1980–2009 and Projected 2010–2050," in America's Children in Brief: Key National Indicators of Well-Being, 2010, Federal Interagency Forum on Child and Family Statistics, July 2010, http://www.childstats.gov/americaschildren/tables.asp (accessed October 15, 2010)

TABLE 1.3

Projected population of the United States, by race and Hispanic origin, 2010–50

[Resident population as of July 1. Numbers in thousands.]

Sex, race, and Hispanic origin*	2010	2015	2020	2025	2030	2035	2040	2045	2050
Population total	**310,233**	**325,540**	**341,387**	**357,452**	**373,504**	**389,531**	**405,655**	**422,059**	**439,010**
White alone, not Hispanic	200,853	203,208	205,255	206,662	207,217	206,958	206,065	204,772	203,347
Black alone	37,985	39,916	41,847	43,703	45,461	47,144	48,780	50,380	51,949
AIAN alone	2,392	2,548	2,697	2,830	2,946	3,053	3,157	3,260	3,358
Asian alone	14,083	16,141	18,308	20,591	22,991	25,489	28,064	30,704	33,418
NHPI alone	452	497	541	585	628	672	716	760	803
Two or more races	4,743	5,519	6,374	7,309	8,329	9,442	10,650	11,950	13,342
Hispanic	49,726	57,711	66,365	75,772	85,931	96,774	108,223	120,231	132,792

*Hispanics may be of any race.
Abbreviations: Black = Black or African American; AIAN = American Indian and Alaska Native; NHPI = Native Hawaiian and Other Pacific Islander
Note: The original race data from Census 2000 are modified to eliminate the "some other race" category.

SOURCE: Adapted from "Table 4. Projections of the Population by Sex, Race, and Hispanic Origin for the United States: 2010 to 2050," in *U.S. Population Projections*, U.S. Census Bureau, Population Division, August 14, 2008, http://www.census.gov/population/www/projections/summarytables.html (accessed October 15, 2010)

child under the age of 18 years had also decreased. In *America's Children in Brief*, the Federal Interagency Forum on Child and Family Statistics states that in 1980, 77% of all children lived in families headed by married couples; this percentage had dropped to 66.8% by 2009.

The American family shrank in size during the 20th century. In 1900 most households consisted of five or more people. According to the Census Bureau, in *Families and Living Arrangements* (November 2010, http://www.census.gov/population/www/socdemo/hh-fam.html), by 1960 two-person families became the most common family type and remained so until the end of the century. The proportion of one- and two-person households increased from 1960 to 2009, whereas the proportion of households with three or more people steadily decreased. In addition, the average household size declined from 3.33 people in 1960 to 2.57 in 2009. (See Table 1.5.) The family size also decreased, from 3.58 people in 1970 to 3.15 people in 2009. Shrinking household and family sizes are partly due to the aging of the population, which means that a smaller proportion of households consists of parents and their children.

Fewer "Traditional" Families

One of the more significant social changes to occur during the last decades of the 20th century was a shift away from the traditional family structure—a married couple with their own child or children living in the home. The Census Bureau divides households into two major categories: family households (defined as groups of two or more people living together related by birth, marriage, or adoption) and nonfamily households (consisting of a person living alone or an individual living with others to whom he or she is not related). As a percentage of all households, family households declined between 1970 and 2009. According to the Census Bureau, in 1970, 51.5 million (81.2%) out of 63.4

million total U.S. households were family households. (See Table 1.6.) By 2009 only 78.9 million (67.3%) out of 117.2 million households were family households. In contrast, the number of nonfamily households increased from 11.9 million (18.8%) in 1970 to 38.3 million (32.7%) in 2009.

The rise in nonfamily households is the result of many factors, some of the most prominent being:

- People are postponing marriage until later in life and are thus living alone or with nonrelatives for a longer period.

- A rising divorce rate translates into more people living alone or with nonrelatives.

- A rise in the number of people who cohabit before or instead of marriage results in higher numbers of nonfamily households.

- The oldest members of the U.S. population are living longer and often live in nonfamily households as widows/widowers or in institutional settings.

Even though family households were a smaller proportion of all households in 2009 than in 1950, they were still the majority of households. The Census Bureau divides family households into three categories: married couples with their own children, married couples without children, and other family households. This last category includes single-parent households and households made up of relatives (such as siblings) who live together or grandparents who live with grandchildren without members of the middle generation being present. Of the three categories, the "other family household" grew the most between 1970 and 2009, increasing from 6.7 million (10.6%) out of 63.4 million U.S. households in 1970 to 19.7 million (16.8%) out of 117.2 million households in 2009. (See Table 1.6.) Married couples headed 44.7

TABLE 1.4

Two or more races population, by sex and age, 2000–09

Sex and age	July 1, 2009	July 1, 2008	July 1, 2007	July 1, 2006	July 1, 2005	July 1, 2004	July 1, 2003	July 1, 2002	July 1, 2001	July 1, 2000	April 1, 2000 Estimates Base	April 1, 2000 Census
					Population estimates							
Both sexes	**5,323,506**	**5,158,692**	**4,992,741**	**4,825,157**	**4,666,223**	**4,513,706**	**4,362,968**	**4,220,880**	**4,078,120**	**3,932,871**	**3,897,722**	**3,897,680**
Under 18 years	2,491,422	2,418,754	2,344,875	2,263,978	2,187,543	2,113,551	2,040,728	1,970,806	1,901,418	1,830,481	1,813,533	1,813,503
Under 5 years	838,069	819,421	796,060	768,352	748,281	725,370	700,191	674,783	648,291	619,682	613,159	613,147
5 to 13 years	1,220,527	1,178,200	1,137,059	1,096,396	1,054,933	1,019,729	988,739	956,648	925,133	892,912	885,026	885,012
14 to 17 years	432,826	421,133	411,756	399,230	384,329	368,452	351,798	339,375	327,994	317,887	315,348	315,344
18 to 64 years	2,557,409	2,477,542	2,398,395	2,322,478	2,249,623	2,180,513	2,110,807	2,047,042	1,981,221	1,914,476	1,898,095	1,898,085
18 to 24 years	643,299	619,850	596,297	577,631	560,484	542,656	521,203	499,449	475,903	450,173	443,508	443,537
25 to 44 years	1,167,657	1,133,618	1,100,307	1,067,815	1,037,508	1,012,770	990,309	973,902	957,865	942,045	938,067	938,039
45 to 64 years	746,453	724,074	701,791	677,032	651,631	625,087	599,295	573,691	547,453	522,258	516,520	516,509
65 years and over	274,675	262,396	249,471	238,701	229,057	219,642	211,433	203,032	195,481	187,914	186,094	186,092
16 years and over	3,042,022	2,945,993	2,850,182	2,755,026	2,661,403	2,575,355	2,491,894	2,414,910	2,335,952	2,256,603	2,237,493	2,237,479
18 years and over	2,832,084	2,739,938	2,647,866	2,561,179	2,478,680	2,400,155	2,322,240	2,250,074	2,176,702	2,102,390	2,084,189	2,084,177
15 to 44 years	2,130,317	2,065,284	2,002,737	1,941,055	1,880,706	1,824,023	1,770,060	1,724,006	1,676,177	1,627,209	1,614,505	1,614,503
Median age (years)	19.7	19.6	19.6	19.7	19.7	19.7	19.7	19.8	19.8	19.8	19.8	19.8

SOURCE: Adapted from "Table 4. Annual Estimates of the Two or More Races Population by Sex and Age for the United States: April 1, 2000 to July 1, 2009," in *U.S. Census Bureau, Population Division, June 2010,* http://www.census.gov/popest/national/asrh/NC-EST2009-asrh.html (accessed October 15, 2010)

TABLE 1.5

Households by size, selected years 1960–2009

[Numbers in thousands]

Year	All households	One person	Two persons	Three persons	Four persons	Five persons	Six persons	Seven or more persons	Persons per household
2009	117,181	31,657	39,242	18,606	16,099	7,406	2,640	1,529	2.57
2000	104,705	26,724	34,666	17,172	15,309	6,981	2,445	1,428	2.62
1990	93,347	22,999	30,114	16,128	14,456	6,213	2,143	1,295	2.63
1980	80,776	18,296	25,327	14,130	12,666	6,059	2,519	1,778	2.76
1970	63,401	10,851	18,333	10,949	9,991	6,548	3,534	3,195	3.14
1960	52,799	6,917	14,678	9,979	9,293	6,072	3,010	2,851	3.33

SOURCE: Adapted from "HH-4. Households by Size: 1960 to Present," in *Families and Living Arrangements*, U.S. Census Bureau, January 2009, http://www.census.gov/population/www/socdemo/hh-fam.html (accessed October 15, 2010)

TABLE 1.6

Households by type, selected years 1940–2009

[Numbers in thousands]

Year	Total households	Family households				Nonfamily households		
		Total	Married couples	Other family		Total		
				Male householder	Female householder		Male householder	Female householder
2009	117,181	78,850	59,118	5,252	14,480	38,331	17,694	20,637
2000	104,705	72,025	55,311	4,028	12,687	32,680	14,641	18,039
1990	93,347	66,090	52,317	2,884	10,890	27,257	11,606	15,651
1980	79,108	58,426	48,180	1,706	8,540	20,682	8,594	12,088
1970	63,401	51,456	44,728	1,228	5,500	11,945	4,063	7,882
1960	52,799	44,905	39,254	1,228	4,422	7,895	2,716	5,179
1950	43,554	38,838	34,075	1,169	3,594	4,716	1,668	3,048
1940*	34,949	31,491	26,571	1,510	3,410	3,458	1,599	1,859

*Based on 1940 census.

SOURCE: Adapted from "HH-1. Households, by Type: 1940 to Present," in *Families and Living Arrangements*, U.S. Census Bureau, January 2009, http://www.census.gov/population/www/socdemo/hh-fam.html (accessed October 15, 2010)

million (70.5%) out of 63.4 million U.S. households in 1970, but only 59.1 million (50.5%) out of 117.2 million households in 2009.

One- and Two-Parent Families

Among all families with children, married two-parent families accounted for 25.8 million (87.2%) out of 29.6 million families in 1970, but only 25.8 million (66.2%) out of 38.9 million families in 2009. (See Table 1.7.) Overall, most households with children are still headed by married couples. However, the decline in the percentage of children being raised in two-parent households has been the subject of much study and attention.

In 2009, 11.6 million (29.8%) families with children out of a total of 38.9 million were maintained by a single parent, compared with 3.8 million (12.8%) out of 29.6 million in 1970. (See Table 1.7.) In 2009 mothers maintained 9.9 million families with children, whereas fathers maintained only 1.7 million; mothers headed families alone nearly six times as often as fathers did. In 1970 this figure

was close to nine times as often because there were very few single-father families.

The proportion of families headed by a single parent increased from 1980 to 2009 in all racial and ethnic groups. (See Table 1.7.) African-American children were the least likely of all racial and ethnic groups to live in two-parent households throughout this period.

The rise in single-parent families is the result of several factors, all pointing to a change in American lifestyles and values. Among these changes is an escalating divorce rate. The Census Bureau reports in *Families and Living Arrangements* that in 2010, 23.7 million (9.8%) out of 242 million Americans aged 15 years and older were divorced and had not remarried. The number of divorced individuals in 2010 was five and a half times the number of divorced individuals in 1970. In that year only 4.3 million (2.9%) out of 148.3 million Americans aged 15 years and older had divorced and not remarried.

The rise in the number of single-parent family households can also be attributed to the dramatic rise in the

TABLE 1.7

All parent/child situations, by type, race, and Hispanic origin of householder or reference person, selected years 1970–2009

[Numbers in thousands. Family groups with children[a] include all parent-child situations (two-parent and one-parent): those that maintain their own household (family households with children); those that live in the home of a relative (related subfamilies); and those that live in the home of a nonrelative (unrelated subfamilies). Data based on the Current Population Survey (CPS).]

		All family groups						
		Two-parent			One-parent			
							Maintained by	
Years	Total with children under 18[b]	Total	Married	Unmarried	Total	Mother	Father
All races							
2009[e]	38,943	27,321	25,799	1,522	11,622	9,880	1,742
2000	37,496	25,771	25,771	N/A	11,725	9,681	2,044
1990	34,670	24,921	24,921	N/A	9,749	8,398	1,351
1980	32,150	25,231	25,231	N/A	6,920	6,230	690
1970	29,626	25,823	25,823	N/A	3,803	3,410	393
White							
2009[d, e]	30,292	22,735	21,574	1,161	7,557	6,232	1,325
2000	30,079	22,241	22,241	N/A	7,838	6,216	1,622
1990	28,294	21,905	21,905	N/A	6,389	5,310	1,079
1980	27,294	22,628	22,628	N/A	4,664	4,122	542
1970	26,115	23,477	23,477	N/A	2,638	2,330	307
Black							
2009[d, e]	5,683	2,296	2,043	253	3,387	3,093	294
2000	5,530	2,135	2,135	N/A	3,395	3,060	335
1990	5,087	2,006	2,006	N/A	3,081	2,860	221
1980	4,074	1,961	1,961	N/A	2,114	1,984	129
1970	3,219	2,071	2,071	N/A	1,148	1,063	85
Hispanic origin[c]							
2009[e]	7,337	5,013	4,572	441	2,324	2,041	283
2000	5,503	3,625	3,625	N/A	1,878	1,565	313
1990	3,429	2,289	2,289	N/A	1,140	1,003	138
1980	2,194	1,626	1,626	N/A	568	526	42
1970	N/A	N/A	N/A	N/A	N/A	N/A	N/A

N/A = Not available.
[a]Family groups prior to 2007 were restricted to married couple and single-parent families and their "own" children. In 2007, unmarried two-parent families were added to the table. Unmarried two-parent family groups are opposite sex partners who have at least one joint child under 18.
[b]In 2007, the total of family groups with children under 18 does not match the total on table FG7 because of weighting.
[c]Persons of Hispanic origin may be of any race.
[d]Householder whose race was reported as only one race.
[e]Estimates produced using PELNMOM and PELNDAD, the new parent pointer variables introduced in 2007.

SOURCE: Adapted from "FM-2. All Parent/Child Situations, by Type, Race, and Hispanic Origin of Householder or Reference Person: 1970 to Present," in *Families and Living Arrangements*, U.S. Census Bureau, January 2009, http://www.census.gov/population/www/socdemo/hh-fam.html (accessed October 15, 2010)

---

number of births to unmarried women. In "Births: Final Data for 2007" (*National Vital Statistics Reports*, vol. 58, no. 24, August 9, 2010), Joyce A. Martin et al. of the Centers for Disease Control and Prevention report that 39.7% of births in 2007 were to unmarried women. (See Table 1.8.) Nonmarital birthrates differed significantly by race and ethnicity. Hispanic women had the highest birthrate among unmarried mothers in 2007, at 108.4 births per 1,000 women of childbearing age. The birthrate for unmarried African-American women in 2007 was 72.6 births per 1,000 women, and for unmarried non-Hispanic white women it was 33.3 births per 1,000 women. The rate of births to unmarried women was highest among women in their 20s; the birthrate for unmarried women aged 20 to 24 years was 80.6 births per 1,000 women, and the rate for women aged 25 to 29 was 76.9 births per 1,000 women. According to Martin et al., unmarried teen

birthrates fell 34% between 1991 and 2005, but then increased 5% between 2005 and 2007.

LIVING ARRANGEMENTS OF CHILDREN

Single-Parent Families

Many children who live in single-parent households face significant challenges that can be exacerbated by racial and ethnic inequalities. According to the Federal Interagency Forum on Child and Family Statistics, in *America's Children in Brief*, the poverty rate for African-American children in 2008 was 34.7% and for Hispanic children was 30.6%, but for non-Hispanic white children it was only 10.6%. Children who lived in minority families with a single parent were especially likely to have greatly reduced economic, educational, and social opportunities. Single parents were more likely to have a low income and less

TABLE 1.8

Number, birth rate, and percentage of births to unmarried women, by age, race, and Hispanic origin of mother, 2007

Measure and age of mother	All races[a]	White Total[b]	White Non-Hispanic	Black Total[b]	Black Non-Hispanic	American Indian or Alaska Native[b]	Asian or Pacific Islander[b]	Hispanic[c]
Number								
All ages	1,715,047	1,159,796	642,621	480,799	449,233	32,266	42,186	545,533
Under 15 years	6,121	3,478	1,247	2,439	2,306	120	84	2,355
15–19 years	380,499	256,451	140,168	109,816	103,075	8,063	6,169	122,547
15 years	18,025	11,675	4,631	5,717	5,397	362	271	7,349
16 years	40,703	26,961	11,814	12,189	11,467	914	639	15,844
17 years	71,742	48,657	24,556	20,445	19,066	1,505	1,135	25,403
18 years	108,923	73,309	41,611	31,514	29,622	2,329	1,771	33,465
19 years	141,106	95,849	57,556	39,951	37,523	2,953	2,353	40,486
20–24 years	644,553	437,313	259,920	181,560	170,396	12,212	13,468	187,659
25–29 years	389,485	261,964	141,085	109,391	101,863	6,933	11,197	127,555
30–34 years	185,501	125,862	60,198	49,783	45,918	3,165	6,691	69,061
35–39 years	86,434	59,304	31,150	22,120	20,432	1,433	3,577	29,505
40 years and over	22,454	15,424	8,853	5,690	5,243	340	1,000	6,851
Rate per 1,000 unmarried women in specified group								
15–44 years[d]	52.3	48.1	33.3	72.6	—	—	27.3	108.4
15–19 years	37.4	32.6	22.6	64.1	—	—	13.6	71.0
15–17 years	20.8	18.0	10.9	36.3	—	—	7.4	43.8
18–19 years	63.9	55.9	40.7	109.1	—	—	23.1	120.2
20–24 years	80.6	72.1	52.3	126.5	—	—	33.4	166.8
25–29 years	76.9	72.7	49.2	98.3	—	—	38.5	167.8
30–34 years	57.9	58.5	36.5	60.3	—	—	38.0	129.9
35–39 years	28.7	28.8	19.0	28.4	—	—	29.1	66.7
40–44 years[e]	6.8	6.4	4.6	7.5	—	—	10.0	15.3
Percent of births to unmarried women								
All ages	39.7	34.8	27.8	71.2	71.6	65.3	16.6	51.3
Under 15 years	98.8	98.2	99.0	99.8	99.8	99.2	97.7	97.7
15–19 years	85.5	81.5	81.0	96.7	97.1	90.0	78.9	82.5
15 years	97.7	96.8	97.6	99.7	99.9	97.6	96.1	96.2
16 years	94.1	92.0	92.8	99.1	99.4	97.0	91.0	91.4
17 years	91.0	88.1	89.0	98.6	98.9	93.8	87.6	87.6
18 years	85.7	81.7	82.4	97.0	97.4	89.5	80.0	81.3
19 years	79.6	74.7	74.4	94.5	95.0	85.9	70.7	75.8
20–24 years	59.6	53.4	49.4	84.4	85.1	72.6	42.1	61.5
25–29 years	32.2	27.5	20.9	64.2	64.8	55.8	15.7	44.3
30–34 years	19.3	16.5	10.6	47.2	47.2	44.7	7.7	34.3
35–39 years	17.3	15.0	10.3	40.5	40.3	43.7	7.7	30.8
40 years and over	20.0	17.5	13.3	39.7	39.5	45.2	10.5	32.0

—Data not available.
[a]Includes races other than white and black and origin not stated.
[b]Race and Hispanic origin are reported separately on birth certificates. Race categories are consistent with the 1977 Office of Management and Budget standards. Data for persons of Hispanic origin are included in the data for each race group according to the mother's reported race. Twenty-seven states reported multiple-race data for 2007. The multiple-race data for these states were bridged to the single-race categories of the 1977 Office of Management and Budget standards for comparability with other states.
[c]Includes all persons of Hispanic origin of any race.
[d]Birth rates computed by relating total births to unmarried mothers, ragardless of age of mother, to unmarried women aged 15–44 years.
[e]Birth rates computed by relating births to unmarried mothers aged 40 years and over to unmarried women aged 40–44 years.
Notes: For 48 States and the District of Columbia, marital status is reported in the birth registration process; for Michigan and New York, mother's marital status is inferred. Rates cannot be computed for unmarried non-Hispanic black women or for American Indian or Alaska Native women because the necessary populations are not available.

SOURCE: Joyce A. Martin et al., "Table 18. Number, Birth Rate, and Percentage of Births to Unmarried Women by Age, Race, and Hispanic Origin of Mother: United States, 2007," in "Births: Final Data for 2007," *National Vital Statistics Reports*, vol. 58, no. 24, August 2010, http://www.cdc.gov/nchs/data/nvsr/nvsr58/nvsr58_24.pdf (accessed October 15, 2010)

education and were more likely to be unemployed and to be renting a home or apartment or living in public housing. In 2008 just 9.9% of children living with married parents lived below the poverty level, whereas 43.5% of children living with an unmarried mother were.

Table 1.9 shows the dramatic differences in the proportion of children living with single parents by race and ethnic group. In 2009 children from all backgrounds were much more likely to be living with a single mother (22.8%) than a single father (3.4%), and 66.8% lived with married parents. Among African-Americans, however, the percent of children who lived with a single mother was much higher (49.8%), whereas only 35.4% lived with married parents.

Figure 1.1 shows that a larger proportion of school-age children lived with their mother as the sole adult than did children of younger ages in 2007. Seventeen percent of children aged six to 11 years and 18% of children aged 12 to 17 years lived with their mother, whereas 11% of children

TABLE 1.9

Percentage of children under age 18, by presence of married parents in household and race and Hispanic origin, selected years 1980–2009

Race and Hispanic origin,[a] and family structure	1980	1985	1990	1995	2000	2005[b]	2006[b]	2007[b]	2008[b]	2009[b]
Total										
Two parents	—	—	—	—	—	—	—	70.7	69.9	69.8
Two married parents	77.0	74.0	73.0	69.0	69.0	67.3	67.4	67.8	66.7	66.8
Mother only	18.0	21.0	22.0	23.0	22.0	23.4	23.3	22.6	22.8	22.8
Father only	2.0	2.0	3.0	4.0	4.0	4.8	4.7	3.2	3.5	3.4
No parent	4.0	3.0	3.0	4.0	4.0	4.5	4.6	3.5	3.8	4.0
White, non-Hispanic										
Two married parents	—	—	81.0	78.0	77.0	—	—	—	—	—
Mother only	—	—	15.0	16.0	16.0	—	—	—	—	—
Father only	—	—	3.0	3.0	4.0	—	—	—	—	—
No parent	—	—	2.0	3.0	3.0	—	—	—	—	—
White-alone, non-Hispanic										
Two parents	—	—	—	—	—	—	—	78.6	77.8	78.1
Two married parents	—	—	—	—	—	75.9	75.9	76.2	75.4	75.8
Mother only	—	—	—	—	—	16.4	16.0	15.3	15.5	15.3
Father only	—	—	—	—	—	4.8	4.8	3.6	4.1	3.8
No parent	—	—	—	—	—	2.9	3.2	2.5	2.6	2.8
Black										
Two married parents	42.0	39.0	38.0	33.0	38.0	—	—	—	—	—
Mother only	44.0	51.0	51.0	52.0	49.0	—	—	—	—	—
Father only	2.0	3.0	4.0	4.0	4.0	—	—	—	—	—
No parent	12.0	7.0	8.0	11.0	9.0	—	—	—	—	—
Black-alone										
Two parents	—	—	—	—	—	—	—	39.8	37.5	38.7
Two married parents	—	—	—	—	—	35.0	34.6	36.8	34.5	35.4
Mother only	—	—	—	—	—	50.2	51.2	49.8	51.1	49.8
Father only	—	—	—	—	—	5.0	4.8	3.5	3.3	3.3
No parent	—	—	—	—	—	9.8	9.4	6.8	8.1	8.2
Hispanic[c]										
Two parents	—	—	—	—	—	—	—	69.8	69.7	68.7
Two married parents	75.0	68.0	67.0	63.0	65.0	64.7	65.9	65.5	64.2	63.7
Mother only	20.0	27.0	27.0	28.0	25.0	25.4	25.0	24.5	24.1	24.9
Father only	2.0	2.0	3.0	4.0	4.0	4.8	4.1	2.1	2.4	2.5
No parent	3.0	3.0	3.0	4.0	5.0	5.1	5.0	3.6	3.9	3.9

—Not available.

[a]For race and Hispanic-origin data in this table: From 1980 to 2002, following the 1977 OMB standards for collecting and presenting data on race, the Current Population Survey (CPS) asked respondents to choose one race from the following: White, Black, American Indian or Alaskan Native, or Asian or Pacific Islander. The Census Bureau also offered an "Other" category. Beginning in 2003, following the 1997 OMB standards for collecting and presenting data on race, the CPS asked respondents to choose one or more races from the following: White, black or African American, Asian, American Indian or Alaska Native, or Native Hawaiian or other Pacific Islander. All race groups discussed in this table from 2003 onward refer to people who indicated only one racial identity within the racial categories presented. People who responded to the question on race by indicating only one race are referred to as the race-alone population. The use of the race-alone population in this table does not imply that it is the preferred method of presenting or analyzing data. Data from 2003 onward are not directly comparable with data from earlier years. Data on race and Hispanic origin are collected separately. Persons of Hispanic origin may be of any race.
[b]Beginning with March 2001, data are from the expanded CPS sample and use population controls based on Census 2000.
[c]Persons of Hispanic origin may be of any race.
Note: Prior to 2007, CPS data identified only one parent on the child's record. This meant that a second parent could only be identified if they were married to the first parent. In 2007, a second parent identifier was added to CPS. This permits identification of two coresident parents, even if the parents are not married to each other. In this table, "two parents" reflects all children who have both a mother and father identified in the household, including biological, step, and adoptive parents. Before 2007, "mother only" and "father only" included some children who lived with a parent who was living with the other parent of the child, but was not married to them. Beginning in 2007, "mother only" and "father only" refer to children for whom only one parent has been identified, whether biological, step, or adoptive.

SOURCE: Adapted from "FAM1.A. Family Structure and Children's Living Arrangements: Percentage of Children Ages 0–17 by Presence of Parents in Household, and Race and Hispanic Origin, 1980–2009," in *America's Children in Brief: Key National Indicators of Well-Being, 2010*, Federal Interagency Forum on Child and Family Statistics, July 2010, http://www.childstats.gov/americaschildren/tables.asp (accessed October 15, 2010)

two years old and younger and 14% of children aged three to five years did. By contrast, mothers of the youngest children were more likely to be living with the other parent or with another adult than were mothers of older children.

Nontraditional Families

Many single-parent families, however, are not single adult families; some single parents maintain a household with an unmarried partner. (See Figure 1.1.) In 1990 the Census Bureau sought to reflect changing lifestyles in the United States by asking for the first time whether unmarried couples maintained households together. Even though in 2000 a slight majority (52%) of U.S. households were headed by married couples, a significant number of unmarried couples also maintained households together. The Census Bureau indicates in the 2008 American Community Survey (November 13, 2009, http://www.census.gov/compendia/statab/2010/tables/10s0063.xls) that in 2008, 6.2 million unmarried

FIGURE 1.1

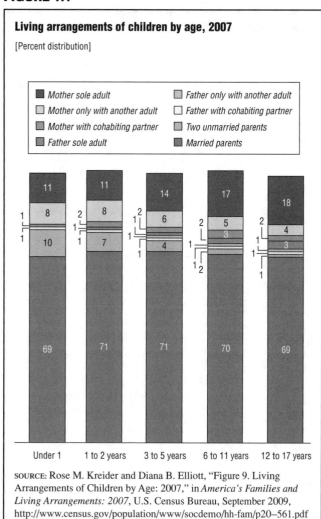

Living arrangements of children by age, 2007

[Percent distribution]

- ■ Mother sole adult
- ☐ Mother only with another adult
- ▨ Mother with cohabiting partner
- ▨ Father sole adult
- ▨ Father only with another adult
- ☐ Father with cohabiting partner
- ☐ Two unmarried parents
- ▨ Married parents

SOURCE: Rose M. Kreider and Diana B. Elliott, "Figure 9. Living Arrangements of Children by Age: 2007," in *America's Families and Living Arrangements: 2007*, U.S. Census Bureau, September 2009, http://www.census.gov/population/www/socdemo/hh-fam/p20–561.pdf (accessed October 15, 2010)

couples cohabited in the United States. Most of these couples were opposite-sex couples, but approximately 565,000 of them were same-sex couples. Rose M. Kreider of the Census Bureau reports in *Increase in Opposite-Sex Cohabiting Couples from 2009 to 2010 in the Annual Social and Economic Supplement (ASEC) to the Current Population Survey (CPS)* (September 15, 2010, http://www.census.gov/population/www/socdemo/Inc-Opp-sex-2009-to-2010.pdf) that between 2009 and 2010 the number of cohabiting couples increased by 13%. Kreider suggests that part of the motivation for couples to cohabitate was economic because of an increase in unemployment during and after the recession that lasted from late 2007 to mid-2009.

In 2008 the Census Bureau studied for the first time the percentage of unmarried mother births that were to women who were in a cohabiting relationship, and the results were published by Jane Lawler Dye in *Fertility of American Women: 2008* (November 2010, http://www.census.gov/prod/2010pubs/p20-563.pdf). Dye finds that in 2008,

425,000 mothers gave birth while living with an unmarried partner. This made up 28% of all births to unmarried women. She also notes that there was a significant relationship between the level of education and the marital status at the time of the birth of a child. Among women aged 15 to 29 years, only 30% of those with less than a high school education, 39% of high school graduates, 52.4% of those who had attended some college, and 81.8% of college graduates were married at the time of a birth. Women aged 30 years and older were significantly more likely to be married at the time a child was born.

Grandparents

Grandparents sometimes provide housing for, and sometimes reside in, the homes of their children and grandchildren. According to the Child Trends Databank (September 10, 2010, http://www.childtrendsdatabank.org/sites/default/files/59_Tab01.pdf), in 2009, 6.1% of children under the age of 18 years lived in the homes of their grandparents, and 2.1% lived with their grandparents without a parent present. These caretaking grandparents were responsible for most of the basic needs (food, shelter, and clothing) of one or more of the grandchildren living with them. Even though the percentage of children living with their grandparents had remained fairly steady since 1994, the percentage of children living with their grandparents had risen by 1% between 2006 and 2009, most likely due to the housing and economic crisis that began in 2007. Even though the economic recession ended in mid-2009, foreclosures continued throughout 2010.

The living and caretaking arrangements of grandparents and grandchildren varied by race and ethnicity in 2009. The Census Bureau explains in *America's Families and Living Arrangements: 2009* (2010, http://www.census.gov/population/www/socdemo/hh-fam/cps2009.html) that non-Hispanic white children were less likely to live with their grandparents than Hispanic, Asian-American, and African-American children—only 6.8% of non-Hispanic white children lived with their grandparents, whereas 11.6% of Hispanic children, 13.2% of Asian-American children, and 13.9% of African-American children did. However, African-American children were much more likely than other groups to be living with a grandparent with no parent present. Of all children living with their grandparents in 2004, 38% of African-American children, 23% of non-Hispanic white children, 16% of Hispanic children, and 4% of Asian-American children had no parent present in the home. (See Figure 1.2.)

The homes maintained by grandparents without parents present were more likely to experience economic hardship than families with a parent present, reflecting the often limited and fixed resources of senior citizens. In *Children's Living Arrangements and Characteristics: March 2002* (June 2003, http://www.census.gov/prod/2003pubs/p20-547.pdf), the most recent study regarding

FIGURE 1.2

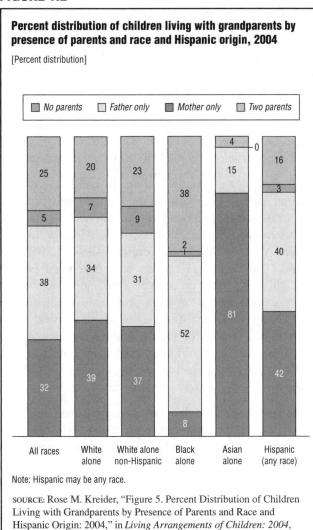

Percent distribution of children living with grandparents by presence of parents and race and Hispanic origin, 2004

[Percent distribution]

Legend: ■ No parents □ Father only ■ Mother only □ Two parents

Note: Hispanic may be any race.

SOURCE: Rose M. Kreider, "Figure 5. Percent Distribution of Children Living with Grandparents by Presence of Parents and Race and Hispanic Origin: 2004," in *Living Arrangements of Children: 2004*, U. S. Census Bureau, February 2008, http://www.census.gov/prod/2008pubs/p70–114.pdf (accessed October 15, 2010)

children's living arrangements as of January 2011, Jason Fields of the Census Bureau states that of all grandchildren in 2002, 18% lived below the poverty line, 23% were not covered by health insurance, and 9% received public assistance. Among children who lived with their grandparents with their parents absent, the numbers were much higher: 30% were below the poverty line, 36% were not covered by health insurance, and 17% received public assistance. These numbers suggest that children who live with their grandparents without a parent present are at an economic disadvantage; grandchildren's presence in their grandparents' home without an economic contribution from the middle generation appears to severely tax the economic resources of grandparents.

Foster Care and Adoption

As of January 2011, there was no comprehensive federal registry system for adoptions, which can be arranged by government agencies, private agencies, or through pri-

vate arrangements between birth mothers and adoptive parents with the assistance of lawyers. The federally funded National Center for Social Statistics collected information on all finalized adoptions from 1957 to 1975, but with the dissolution of the center, limited statistical information is now available. With the passage of the Adoption and Safe Families Act of 1997, there was a renewed effort to improve the data available about adoption. The U.S. Department of Health and Human Services, through the Adoption and Foster Care Analysis and Reporting System (AFCARS), now tracks adoptions that are arranged through the foster care system, but this represents only some of the children who are adopted by American families each year.

In *The AFCARS Report* (July 2010, http://www.acf.hhs.gov/programs/cb/stats_research/afcars/tar/report17.htm), AFCARS states that on September 30, 2009, 423,773 children were living in foster homes with foster parents. Foster parents are trained people supervised by local social service agencies who provide space in their home and care for children who have been neglected, abused, or abandoned or whose parents have surrendered them to public agencies because they are unable to care for them. According to the American Public Welfare Association, foster care is the most common type of substitute care, but children needing substitute care might also live in group homes, emergency shelters, child care facilities, hospitals, correctional institutions, or on their own. It is becoming more difficult to place children in foster care. The number of potential foster care families is down, due in part to the fact that women, the primary providers of foster care, are entering the paid labor force in greater numbers.

AFCARS reports that in fiscal year 2009, 255,418 children younger than 18 years old entered foster care, with an average age of 7.9 years. A disproportionate share of children entering foster care were African-American—25% of children entering foster care were African-American, but according to the Census Bureau, in *National Population Estimates—Characteristics* (June 2010, http://www.census.gov/popest/national/asrh/), only 16.8% of all Americans under the age of 18 years were African-American (alone or in combination) in 2009. Non-Hispanic white children were underrepresented among those entering foster care—44% were non-Hispanic white children, compared with 55.3% of all non-Hispanic white children under the age of 18 years. Hispanic and Native American or Alaskan Native children were more proportionally represented —20% entering foster care were Hispanic (compared with 22.5% of children in the general population), and 2% were Native American or Alaskan Native (compared with 1.3% of children in the general population). Asian-American children were underrepresented in foster care; only 1% of children in foster care were Asian-American, compared with 5.7% of all children in the general population.

TABLE 1.10

Children who exited foster care, fiscal year 2009

HOW MANY CHILDREN EXITED FOSTER CARE DURING FISCAL YEAR 2009? (276,266)

What were the ages of the children who exited care during fiscal year 2009?

Mean age	9.6	
Median age	8.9	
Less than 1 year	5.0%	12,409
1 year	8.0%	21,070
2 years	8.0%	21,525
3 years	7.0%	18,204
4 years	6.0%	15,674
5 years	5.0%	13,846
6 years	5.0%	12,700
7 years	4.0%	11,890
8 years	4.0%	10,860
9 years	4.0%	10,065
10 years	3.0%	9,549
11 years	3.0%	8,794s
12 years	3.0%	8,630
13 years	3.0%	9,040
14 years	4.0%	10,936
15 years	5.0%	13,621
16 years	6.0%	16,323
17 years	6.0%	17,514
18 years	10.0%	26,416
19 years	2.0%	4,213
20 years	1.0%	1,837

What were the outcomes for the children exiting foster care during fiscal year 2009?

Reunification with parent(s) or primary caretaker(s)	51%	140,061
Living with other relative(s)	8%	21,424
Adoption	20%	55,684
Emancipation	11%	29,471
Guardianship	7%	19,290
Transfer to another agency	2%	6,291
Runaway	1%	2,141
Death of child	0%	417

Note: Deaths are attributable to a variety of causes including medical conditions, accidents, and homicide.

What were the lengths of stay of the children who exited foster care during fiscal year 2009?

Mean months	22.0	
Median months	13.7	
Less than 1 month	13.0%	35,340
1–5 months	15.0%	41,459
6–11 months	18.0%	49,475
12–17 months	14.0%	38,631
18–23 months	10.0%	28,110
24–29 months	7.0%	20,673
30–35 months	5.0%	14,932
3–4 years	10.0%	28,226
5 years or more	7.0%	19,307

What was the race/ethnicity of the children who exited care during fiscal year 2009?

Alaska Native/American Indian	2%	5,389
Asian	1%	2,111
Black	27%	74,264
Hawaiian/other Pacific Islander	0%	674
Hispanic (of any race)	20%	55,200
White	43%	118,422
Unknown/unable to determine	2%	6,062
Two or more races	5%	13,573

Note: Using U.S. Bureau of the Census standards, all races exclude children of Hispanic origin. Beginning in fiscal year 2000, children could be identified with more than one race designation. Adapted from "How Many Children Exited Foster Care during FY 2009?" in *The AFCARS Report*, no. 17, U.S. Department of Health and Human Services, Administration for Children and Families, July 2010, http://www.acf.hhs.gov/programs/cb/stats_research/afcars/tar/report17.htm (accessed October 15, 2010)

A child's stay in foster care can vary from just a few days to many years. Thirteen percent of children who left foster care in fiscal year 2009 had been in care less than a month, 33% had been in care from one to 11 months, 24% had been in care from one to two years, and 29% had lived in foster care for two years or longer. (See Table 1.10.)

AFCARS states that more than half (51%) of the children who left foster care in fiscal year 2009 were reunited with their parents. (See Table 1.10.) About 8% of the children who left foster care moved to a relative's or a guardian's home. Eleven percent were emancipated, or "aged out" of the system when they turned 18 years old, and 20% of children who left foster care were adopted.

According to AFCARS, adopted children were on average younger (6.3 years) than children still in foster care (9.6 years), reflecting the preference of adoptive parents for younger children. Of those adopted children in fiscal year 2009, 29,146 were male and 28,306 were female. (See Table 1.11.) Foster parents adopted 54% of these children, relatives adopted 32%, and nonrelatives who had not fostered the child previously adopted 14%. Even though traditional families (married couples) made up two-thirds (66%) of families who adopted children from foster care, a significant share were nontraditional families—28% of adopters were single women, 3% were single men, and 2% were unmarried couples.

In 1996 the federal government began providing incentives to potential adoptive parents to move children into adoptive homes more quickly. The government provided a $5,000 tax credit for adoptive parents to cover adoption expenses; the credit was $6,000 if the adopted child had special needs. Children with special needs were defined as those with physical, mental, or emotional problems; children needing to be adopted with siblings; or children who were difficult to place because of age, race, or ethnicity. In 2002 the tax credit was increased to $10,000 to cover adoption expenses for children without special needs; adoptive parents of special-needs children, including many children from foster care, received the full amount of the tax credit regardless of incurred expenses. This tax credit has been adjusted for inflation in subsequent years and was $13,170 in 2010.

In addition, Congress passed the Adoption and Safe Families Act in 1997, providing fiscal incentives to states to move children from foster care into adoptive families more quickly. States that increased the number of adoptions of foster children (in a given year over a base year) received a standard payment of $4,000 per adopted child and an additional $2,000 for the adoption of each special-needs child and an additional $4,000 for the adoption of each child aged nine years and older.

Despite these incentives, many children who enter foster care will never have a permanent family, but instead will age out of the system. On September 30, 2009, there were 69,947 children whose parents' rights had been terminated living in foster homes. These "waiting children"

TABLE 1.11

Children adopted from the public foster care system, fiscal year 2009

What is the gender distribution of the children adopted from the public foster care system?

Male	51%	29,146
Female	49%	28,306

How old were the children when they were adopted from the public foster care system?

Mean age	6.3	
Median age	5.2	
Less than 1 year	2.0%	1,136
1 year	11.0%	6,486
2 years	15.0%	8,366
3 years	11.0%	6,543
4 years	9.0%	5,270
5 years	8.0%	4,505
6 years	7.0%	3,904
7 years	6.0%	3,478
8 years	5.0%	3,096
9 years	5.0%	2,642
10 years	4.0%	2,418
11 years	4.0%	2,042
12 years	3.0%	1,812
13 years	3.0%	1,523
14 years	2.0%	1,308
15 years	2.0%	1,091
16 years	2.0%	911
17 years	1.0%	725
18 years	0%	150
19 years	0%	24
20 years	0%	14

What percentage of the children adopted receive an adoption subsidy?

Yes	88%	50,481
No	12%	6,754

What is the racial/ethnic distribution of the children adopted from the public foster care system?

Alaska Native/American Indian	2%	923
Asian	0%	280
Black	25%	14,211
Hawaiian/other Pacific Islander	0%	120
Hispanic (of any race)	21%	11,878
White	44%	25,418
Unknown/unable to determine	2%	874
Two or more races	7%	3,754

How many months did it take after termination of parental rights for the children to be adopted?

Mean months	13.9	
Median months	10.2	
Less than 1 month	2.0%	1,373
1–5 months	23.0%	13,007
6–11 months	33.0%	18,326
12–17 months	18.0%	10,242
18–23 months	10.0%	5,364
24–29 months	5.0%	2,867
30–35 months	3.0%	1,648
3–4 years	4.0%	2,299
5 years or more	2.0%	867

What is the family structure of the child's adoptive family?

Married couple	66%	36,133
Unmarried couple	2%	1,299
Single female	28%	15,408
Single male	3%	1,567

TABLE 1.11

Children adopted from the public foster care system, fiscal year 2009 [CONTINUED]

What was the relationship of the adoptive parents to the child prior to the adoption?

Non-relative	14%	7,637
Foster parent	54%	29,417
Stepparent	0%	120
Other relative	32%	17,300

SOURCE: Adapted from "How Many Children Were Adopted with Public Agency Involvement in FY 2009?" in *The AFCARS Report*, no. 17, U.S. Department of Health and Human Services, Administration for Children and Families, July 2010, http://www.acf.hhs.gov/programs/cb/stats_research/afcars/tar/report17.htm (accessed October 15, 2010)

African-American. (See Table 1.12.) The majority (54%) of waiting children lived in foster homes with nonrelatives while waiting to be adopted.

Living Arrangements of Young Adults

A young person's transition into adult independence does not necessarily occur at age 18. The marriage age has risen since the 1950s, and, as obtaining a college education has become the norm, young people have delayed finding employment that allows them to support themselves independently of their parents. A growing number of young adults older than the age of 18 years continue to live in, or return to, their parents' home. Some young people live with their parents until their mid-20s, and others are likely to return to their parents' home at some time after moving out, especially after college or service in the military. Many young adults also share households with other young adults.

Socioeconomic experts attribute this phenomenon to the rising cost of living in the United States. Wages have not increased at the same rate as the cost of living; therefore, the same amount of money buys less than it did in previous years. Furthermore, credit markets tightened during the economic recession that lasted from late 2007 until mid-2009, which made it difficult to qualify for a mortgage and may have further delayed young people leaving home. At the same time, foreclosures skyrocketed; young adults who found themselves in foreclosure may have returned to their parents' home.

In 2009, 8.2 million young men and 6.9 million young women between the ages of 18 and 24 years lived in their parents' home. (See Table 1.13; this figure includes those who were living in college dormitories who were still counted as residing at their parents' residence.) Males in this age group were more likely (56.7%) than females (48.9%) to live with their parents. This is primarily because men tend to marry at a later age than women do. In fact, the Census Bureau notes in *Families and Living Arrangements* that the age at first marriage for both men and women has risen since 1970, when men married at an average age of

were disproportionately African-American. Whereas 16.8% of all children under the age of 18 years were African-American and 25% of children entering foster care were African-American in 2009, 30% of waiting children were

TABLE 1.12

Children waiting to be adopted on September 30, 2009

What is the gender distribution of the waiting children?

Male	53%	60,287
Female	47%	54,269

How many months have the waiting children been in continuous foster care?

Mean months	38.0	
Median months	29.0	
Less than 1 month	1%	661
1–5 months	4%	4,991
6–11 months	8%	9,206
12–17 months	13%	15,313
18–23 months	14%	15,479
24–29 months	12%	14,248
30–35 months	10%	11,015
36–59 months	22%	24,773
60 or more months	16%	18,876

What is the racial/ethnic distribution of the waiting children?

Alaska Native/American Indian	2%	1,920
Asian	0%	535
Black	30%	34,088
Hawaiian/other Pacific Islander	0%	213
Hispanic (of any race)	22%	25,231
White	38%	43,918
Unknown/unable to determine	2%	1,807
Two or more races	6%	6,807

How old were the waiting children when they were removed from their parents or caretakers?

Mean age	5.0	
Median age	4.1	
Less than 1 year	25%	28,315
1 year	9%	10,092
2 years	8%	8,800
3 years	7%	7,998
4 years	7%	7,686
5 years	7%	7,404
6 years	6%	7,150
7 years	6%	6,578
8 years	5%	6,177
9 years	5%	5,343
10 years	4%	4,718
11 years	3%	3,954
12 years	3%	3,304
13 years	2%	2,545
14 years	2%	1,792
15 years	1%	1,037
16 years	0%	450
17 years	0%	89

Where were the waiting children living on September 30, 2009?

Pre-adoptive home	14%	15,759
Foster family home (relative)	22%	25,165
Foster family home (non-relative)	54%	61,362
Group home	3%	3,980
Institution	6%	6,331
Supervised independent living	0%	128
Runaway	1%	636
Trial home visit	1%	725

How old were the waiting children on September 30, 2009?

Mean age	8.1	
Median age	7.5	
Less than 1 year	4%	4,351
1 year	9%	9,817
2 years	9%	9,953
3 years	8%	8,767
4 years	7%	7,800
5 years	6%	7,054
6 years	6%	6,515
7 years	5%	6,225
8 years	5%	6,023
9 years	5%	5,884
10 years	5%	5,635
11 years	5%	5,534
12 years	5%	5,373
13 years	5%	5,335
14 years	5%	5,547
15 years	5%	5,814
16 years	4%	5,014
17 years	3%	3,921

SOURCE: Adapted from "How Many Children Were Waiting to Be Adopted on September 30, 2009?" in *The AFCARS Report*, no. 17, U.S. Department of Health and Human Services, Administration for Children and Families, July 2010, http://www.acf.hhs.gov/programs/cb/stats_research/afcars/tar/report17.htm (accessed October 15, 2010)

23.2 years and women at 20.8 years. By 2010 men married at an average age of 28.2 years and women at 26.1 years.

Young adults who live by themselves for any length of time are unlikely to return home after experiencing independence. By contrast, those who move in with roommates or who cohabit without marrying are more likely to return to the parental home if the living situation does not work out or the relationship fails. Some young people struggle on their own only to return home for respite from financial pressures, loneliness, or because they need emotional support or security.

Even if they do not settle into careers immediately, most young adults living in their parents' home work for wages. Those young people who lived away from home and then moved back were more likely to pay rent or make some financial contribution to the household than those who never lived on their own, even if they were employed.

HOW LONG DO THEY STAY? Young men are more likely than young women to stay with their parents indefinitely. This may be because young men typically lose less of their autonomy when they return home than young women do. Young women report they have more responsibility to help around the house and more rules to obey than do their young male counterparts.

TABLE 1.13

Young adults living at home, selected years 1960–2009

[Numbers in thousands. Data based on Current Population Survey (CPS) unless otherwise specified]

Age	Male			Female		
	Total	Child of householder	Percent	Total	Child of householder	Percent
18 to 24 years						
2009	14,498	8,219	56.7	14,161	6,923	48.9
2005	14,060	7,448	53.0	13,933	6,413	46.0
2000	13,291	7,593	57.1	13,242	6,232	47.1
1990	12,450	7,232	58.1	12,860	6,135	47.7
1980 Census	14,278	7,755	54.3	14,844	6,336	42.7
1970 Census	10,398	5,641	54.3	11,959	4,941	41.3
1960 Census	6,842	3,583	52.4	7,876	2,750	34.9
25 to 34 years						
2009	20,419	3,178	15.6	20,069	1,988	9.9
2005	19,656	2,660	13.5	19,632	1,597	8.1
2000	18,563	2,387	12.9	19,222	1,602	8.3
1990	21,462	3,213	15.0	21,779	1,774	8.1
1980 Census	18,107	1,894	10.5	18,689	1,300	7.0
1970 Census	11,929	1,129	9.5	12,637	829	6.6
1960 Census	10,896	1,185	10.9	11,587	853	7.4

Note: In CPS data, unmarried college students living in dormitories are counted as living in their parent(s) home.

SOURCE: Adapted from "Table AD-1. Young Adults Living at Home: 1960 to Present," in *Families and Living Arrangements*, U.S. Census Bureau, January 2009, http://www.census.gov/population/www/socdemo/hh-fam.html (accessed October 15, 2010)

CHAPTER 2
CHILDREN, TEENS, AND MONEY

FAMILY INCOME

Almost all children are financially dependent on their parents, with their financial condition directly dependent on how much their parents earn. Carmen DeNavas-Walt, Bernadette D. Proctor, and Jessica C. Smith of the U.S. Census Bureau report in *Income, Poverty, and Health Insurance Coverage in the United States: 2009* (September 2010, http://www.census.gov/prod/2010pubs/p60-238.pdf) that real income rose throughout the 1990s and then declined in the early 21st century, especially during the economic recession that lasted from late 2007 to mid-2009. Between 2007 and 2009 real household income declined by 4.2%. The median household income (half of all households earned more and half earned less) in 2009 was $49,777, down 0.7% from the previous year. (See Table 2.1.) For married-couple families, the median household income was $71,830, down 1.2% from the previous year.

DeNavas-Walt, Proctor, and Smith find that single-parent families, particularly those headed by single mothers, fared worse than other households in 2009. Families with female heads-of-household and no husband present had a median income of $32,597, down 1.1% from the previous year, whereas male-headed households with no wife present had a median income of $48,084, 1.9% lower than the year before. (See Table 2.1.)

According to DeNavas-Walt, Proctor, and Smith, the median income varied greatly by race and ethnic group. Asian-American households had the highest median income, at $65,469, followed by non-Hispanic white households at $54,461. (See Table 2.1.) The median income for Hispanic households was $38,039, and the median income for African-American households, at $32,584, was the lowest of any reported race or ethnic group. The median income of African-American households also decreased more than any other group over the previous year, by 4.4%.

The Cost of Raising a Child

Since the 1960s the Family Economics Research Group of the U.S. Department of Agriculture (USDA) has provided estimates on the cost of rearing a child to adulthood. The estimates are calculated per child in a household with two children and are categorized by the age of the child using different family income levels. Attorneys and judges use these estimates in determining child-support awards in divorce cases as well as in cases involving the wrongful death of a parent. Public officials use the estimates to determine payments for the support of children in foster care and for subsidies to adoptive families. Financial planners and consumer educators use them in helping people determine their life insurance needs.

INCOME LEVELS. The estimated annual family expenditures for a child vary widely depending on the income level of the household. The estimated amount a family spends on a child also tends to increase as the child ages. The USDA estimates that in 2009 married-couple households that earned less than $56,670 per year spent amounts ranging from $8,570 for very young children to $9,450 for 12- to 17-year-olds. (See Table 2.2.) The estimates for middle-income, married-couple families ranged from $11,700 for the youngest children to $13,530 for 15- to 17-year-olds. The estimates for married-couple families with incomes above $98,120 ranged from $19,410 to $23,180, depending on the age of the child.

The estimated annual expenditures for single-parent families that earned less than $56,670 per year spent slightly less than those of two-parent families, most likely because their average incomes were lower ($25,130 for single-parent families and $36,250 for two-parent families). (See Table 2.3 and Table 2.2.) The USDA estimates that in 2009 these single parents spent an annual average of $7,410 to $8,980, depending on the age of the child. Single-parent families that earned $56,670 or more spent

TABLE 2.1

Median income by type of household and race and Hispanic origin of householder, 2008–09

[Income in 2009 dollars. Households and people as of March of the following year.]

| | 2008 | | 2009[a] | | Percentage change in real median income |
	Number (thousands)	Median income (dollars) Estimate	Number (thousands)	Median income (dollars) Estimate	Estimate
Characteristic					
Households					
All households	117,181	50,112	117,538	49,777	−0.7
Type of household					
Family households	78,850	62,383	78,833	61,265	−1.8
Married-couple	59,118	72,733	58,410	71,830	−1.2
Female householder, no husband present	14,480	32,947	14,843	32,597	−1.1
Male householder, no wife present	5,252	48,999	5,580	48,084	−1.9
Nonfamily households	38,331	29,964	38,705	30,444	1.6
Female householder	20,637	24,919	20,442	25,269	1.4
Male householder	17,694	35,869	18,263	36,611	2.1
Race[b] and Hispanic origin of householder					
White	95,297	52,113	95,489	51,861	−0.5
White, not Hispanic	82,884	55,319	83,158	54,461	−1.6
Black	14,595	34,088	14,730	32,584	−4.4
Asian	4,573	65,388	4,687	65,469	0.1
Hispanic (any race)	13,425	37,769	13,298	38,039	0.7

[a]Medians are calculated using $2,500 income intervals. Beginning with 2009 income data, the Census Bureau expanded the upper income intervals used to calculate medians of $250,000 or more. Medians falling in the upper open-ended interval are plugged with $250,000." Before 2009, the upper open-ended interval was $100,000 and a plug of "$100,000" was used.
[b]Federal surveys now give respondents the option of reporting more than once race. Therefore, two basic ways of defining a race group are possible. A group such as Asian may be defined as those who reported Asian and no other race (the race-alone or single-race concept) or as those who reported Asian regardless of whether they also reported another race (the race-alone-or-in-combination concept.) This table shows data using the first approach (race alone). The use of single-race population does not imply that it is the preferred method of presenting or anlayzing data. About 2.6 percent of people reported more than once race in Census 2000 Data for American Indians and Alaska Natives, Native Hawaiians and other Pacific Islanders, and those reporting two or more races are not shown separately in this table.

SOURCE: Adapted from Carmen DeNavas-Walt, Bernadette D. Proctor, and Jessica C. Smith, "Table 1. Income and Earnings Summary Measures by Selected Characteristics: 2008 and 2009," in *Income, Poverty, and Health Insurance Coverage in the United States: 2009*, U.S. Census Bureau, September 2010, http://www.census.gov/prod/2010pubs/p60–238.pdf (accessed October 22, 2010)

$15,940 to $19,460 per child, which was more than the middle-income, two-parent families.

Even though the USDA estimates that in 2009 the highest-income households spent about twice the amount on their children than the lowest-income households, this difference varied by the type of expense. For example, the estimated food expenditure for children aged 15 to 17 years in the highest-income husband-wife families was $3,040, compared with $2,030 in the lowest-income group. (See Table 2.2.) The estimated annual expense for education and child care for children aged 15 to 17 years in these high-income families ($5,940) was over seven times that for a child the same age in the lowest-income families ($830). These variations among income groups by type of expense held true for single-parent households as well. (See Table 2.3.)

AGE OF CHILD. The 2009 estimates of family expenditures on a child generally increased with the child's age, except for housing, education, and child care. (See Table 2.2 and Table 2.3.) The estimates for education, child care, and related expenses were highest for preschoolers (under the age of six years) in most income groups. Many women with children this age are in the labor force and must pay for child care. Once children enter school, the child care

costs decrease. As school-age children grow up, the need for after-school and summer care also decreases. The estimates do not include expenses related to college attendance, which typically do not occur until the child is at least 18 years old. However, higher income groups tended to spend more on education for 15- to 17-year-olds, suggesting that some disposable income in these groups is spent on providing additional educational opportunities for their children.

FUTURE COSTS. By incorporating an average annual inflation rate of 2.79% (the average annual inflation rate over the previous 20 years), the USDA also estimates the total cost of raising a child born in 2009 who will reach the age of 17 years in 2026. The total family expenses for raising a child born in 2009 are estimated to be $205,960 for the lowest-income group, $286,050 for the middle-income group, and $475,680 for the highest-income group. (See Table 2.4.)

CHILDREN IN POVERTY

Children are the largest group of poor in the United States. In 1975 they replaced the elderly as the poorest age group. (See Figure 2.1.) DeNavas-Walt, Proctor, and Smith

TABLE 2.2

Estimated annual expenditures on a child by husband-wife families, 2009

Age of child	Total expense	Housing	Food	Transportation	Clothing	Health care	Child care and education[a]	Miscellaneous[b]
Before-tax income: Less than $56,670 (Average = $36,250)								
0–2	$8,570	$2,960	$1,110	$990	$630	$590	$1,870	$420
3–5	8,630	2,960	1,210	1,030	500	560	1,760	610
6–8	8,330	2,960	1,640	1,140	560	620	780	630
9–11	9,040	2,960	1,890	1,140	570	670	1,190	620
12–14	9,450	2,960	2,040	1,250	680	1,020	810	690
15–17	9,450	2,960	2,030	1,380	720	950	830	580
Total	**$160,410**	**$53,280**	**$29,760**	**$20,790**	**$10,980**	**$13,230**	**$21,720**	**$10,650**
Before-tax income: $56,670 to $98,120 (Average = $76,250)								
0–2	$11,700	$3,890	$1,340	$1,420	$750	$790	$2,630	$880
3–5	11,730	3,890	1,430	1,470	600	750	2,510	1,080
6–8	11,650	3,890	2,010	1,570	670	880	1,540	1,090
9–11	12,420	3,890	2,290	1,580	690	940	1,940	1,090
12–14	13,090	3,890	2,470	1,680	820	1,320	1,750	1,160
15–17	13,530	3,890	2,450	1,810	890	1,240	2,210	1,040
Total	**$222,360**	**$70,020**	**$35,970**	**$28,590**	**$13,260**	**$17,760**	**$37,740**	**$19,020**
Before-tax income: More than $98,120 (Average = $171,710)								
0–2	$19,410	$7,030	$1,820	$2,160	$1,030	$920	$4,680	$1,770
3–5	19,410	7,030	1,910	2,200	870	870	4,560	1,970
6–8	19,380	7,030	2,520	2,300	950	1,010	3,590	1,980
9–11	20,230	7,030	2,850	2,310	990	1,080	3,990	1,980
12–14	21,510	7,030	3,050	2,410	1,150	1,510	4,310	2,050
15–17	23,180	7,030	3,040	2,550	1,260	1,430	5,940	1,930
Total	**$369,360**	**$126,540**	**$45,570**	**$41,790**	**$18,750**	**$20,460**	**$81,210**	**$35,040**

Estimates are based on 2005–06 Consumer Expenditure Survey data updated to 2009 dollars by using the Consumer Price Index. For each age category, the expense estimates represent average child-rearing expenditures for each age (e.g., the expense for the 3–5 age category, on average, applies to the 3-year-old, the 4-year-old, or the 5-year-old). The Total (0–17) row represents the expenditure sum of all ages (0, 1, 2, 3,...17) in 2009 dollars. The figures represent estimated expenses on the younger child in a two-child family. Estimates are about the same for the older child, so to calculate expenses for two children, figures should be summed for the appropriate age categories. To estimate expenses for an only child, multiply the total expense for the appropriate age category by 1.25. To estimate expenses for each child in a family with three or more children, multiply the total expense for each appropriate age category by 0.78. For expenses on all children in a family, these totals should be summed.
[a]Includes only families with child care and education expenses.
[b]Includes personal care items, entertainment, and reading materials.

SOURCE: Mark Lino, "Table 1. Estimated Annual Expenditures on a Child by Husband-Wife Families, Overall United States, 2009," in *Expenditures on Children by Families, 2009*, U.S. Department of Agriculture, Center for Nutrition Policy and Promotion, June 2010, http://www.cnpp.usda.gov/Publications/CRC/crc2009.pdf (accessed October 22, 2010)

state that in 2009 the poverty rate for all children younger than 18 years of age was 20.7%, or 15.5 million children, which was up from 19%, or 14.1 million children, in 2008. Children under 18 years old made up 24.3% of the total U.S. population, but they made up 33.3% of the people living below the poverty line. (For population estimates for July 1, 2009, by age, see the Census Bureau's "Population Estimates" [June 2010, http://www.census.gov/popest/national/asrh/NC-EST2009-sa.html].) Children under the age of six years are particularly vulnerable to poverty. According to DeNavas-Walt, Proctor, and Smith, in 2009 the poverty rate for families with children under the age of six years was 23.8%, which was higher than the overall rate of child poverty. In addition, over half (54.3%) of children younger than the age of six years living with a single mother were in poverty, which was more than four times the rate of poverty for children younger than the age of six years living in married-couple families (13.4%).

The child poverty rate declined between 1995 and 2000, but the rate of children living in poverty (100% of the poverty line or below) and in low-income families (100% to 200% of the poverty line) began to rise again in 2000. By 2008, 40% of children lived in low-income or poor families. (See Figure 2.2.) The economic recession that began in December 2007 and ended in mid-2009 had a significant impact on the poverty rate overall and an even larger impact on the child poverty rate. During the recession the poverty rate increased by 1.9%, and the child poverty rate increased by 2.7%. (See Table 2.5.)

However, some children were more likely to be poor than others. Hispanic and African-American children were disproportionately poor. Whereas 10.6% of non-Hispanic white children were poor, 30.6% of Hispanic children and 34.7% of African-American children were poor. (See Table 2.6.) Preschoolers were particularly likely to live in poor families (21.7%).

Another trend in child poverty emerged during the first decade of the 21st century. The Children's Defense Fund notes in *The State of America's Children 2010* (May 2010, http://www.childrensdefense.org/child-research-data-publications/data/state-of-americas-children.pdf) that the number

TABLE 2.3

Estimated annual expenditures on a child by single-parent families, 2009

Age of child	Total expense	Housing	Food	Transportation	Clothing	Health care	Child care and education[a]	Miscellaneous[b]
Before-tax income: Less than $56,670 (Average = $25,130)								
0–2	$7,410	$2,810	$1,340	$570	$400	$490	$1,290	$510
3–5	8,160	2,810	1,310	780	320	560	1,780	600
6–8	8,060	2,810	1,750	870	340	630	880	780
9–11	8,590	2,810	1,920	900	400	580	1,250	730
12–14	8,980	2,810	2,060	960	410	880	1,030	830
15–17	8,720	2,810	2,170	950	450	870	810	660
Total	**$149,760**	**$50,580**	**$31,650**	**$15,090**	**$6,960**	**$12,030**	**$21,120**	**$12,330**
Before-tax income: $56,670 or more (Average = $102,830)								
0–2	$15,940	$5,820	$1,990	$1,620	$580	$920	$3,370	$1,640
3–5	16,740	5,820	1,980	1,820	490	1,020	3,870	1,740
6–8	16,910	5,820	2,560	1,910	520	1,110	3,080	1,910
9–11	17,700	5,820	2,870	1,940	600	1,040	3,570	1,860
12–14	18,640	5,820	2,950	2,000	640	1,460	3,810	1,960
15–17	19,460	5,820	3,080	2,000	720	1,450	4,600	1,790
Total	**$316,170**	**$104,760**	**$46,290**	**$33,870**	**$10,650**	**$21,000**	**$66,900**	**$32,700**

Estimates are based on 2005–06 Consumer Expenditure Survey data updated to 2009 dollars by using the Consumer Price Index. For each age category, the expense estimates represent average child-rearing expenditures for each age (e.g., the expense for the 3–5 age category, on average, applies to the 3-year-old, the 4-year-old, or the 5-year-old). The Total (0–17) row represents the expenditure sum of all ages (0, 1, 2, 3, ...17) in 2009 dollars. The figures represent estimated expenses on the younger child in a single-parent, two-child family. For estimated expenses on the older child, multiply the total expense for the appropriate age category by 0.97. To estimate expenses for two children, the expenses on the younger child and older child after adjusting the expense on the older child downward should be summed for the appropriate age categories. To estimate expenses for an only child, multiply the total expense for the appropriate age category by 1.29. To estimate expenses for each child in a family with three or more children, multiply the total expense for each appropriate age category by 0.77 after adjusting the expenses on the older children downward. For expenses on all children in a family, these totals should be summed.
[a]Includes only families with child care and education expenses.
[b]Includes personal care items, entertainment, and reading materials.

SOURCE: Mark Lino, "Table 7. Estimated Annual Expenditures on a Child by Single-Parent Families, Overall United States, 2009," in *Expenditures on Children by Families, 2009*, U.S. Department of Agriculture, Center for Nutrition Policy and Promotion, June 2010, http://www.cnpp.usda.gov/Publications/CRC/crc2009.pdf (accessed October 22, 2010)

TABLE 2.4

Estimated annual expenditures on children born in 2009, by income group

Year	Age	Income group		
		Lowest	Middle	Highest
2009	<1	$8,570	$11,700	$19,410
2010	1	8,810	12,030	19,950
2011	2	9,050	12,360	20,510
2012	3	9,370	12,740	21,080
2013	4	9,630	13,090	21,670
2014	5	9,900	13,460	22,270
2015	6	9,830	13,740	22,860
2016	7	10,100	14,120	23,500
2017	8	10,380	14,520	24,150
2018	9	11,580	15,910	25,920
2019	10	11,900	16,350	26,640
2020	11	12,240	16,810	27,380
2021	12	13,150	18,210	29,930
2022	13	13,510	18,720	30,760
2023	14	13,890	19,240	31,620
2024	15	14,280	20,440	35,020
2025	16	14,680	21,010	36,000
2026	17	15,090	21,600	37,010
Total		**$205,960**	**$286,050**	**$475,680**

Note: Estimates are for the younger child in husband-wife families with two children and assume an average annual inflation rate of 2.79 percent.

SOURCE: Mark Lino, "Table 10. Estimated Annual Expenditures on a Child Born in 2009, by Income Group, Overall United States," in *Expenditures on Children by Families, 2009*, U.S. Department of Agriculture, Center for Nutrition Policy and Promotion, June 2010, http://www.cnpp.usda.gov/Publications/CRC/crc2009.pdf (accessed October 22, 2010)

of children living in extreme poverty (below one-half of the poverty level) increased by 1.6 million between 2000 and 2008. According to DeNavas-Walt, Proctor, and Smith, approximately 6.9 million children lived in extreme poverty in 2009.

Government Aid to Children

Many programs exist in the United States to assist families and children living with economic hardship. Some of these programs are federally operated, and others are run at the state level. In many cases the programs are mandated at the federal level and administered by the states, which can make tracking them complicated.

TEMPORARY ASSISTANCE FOR NEEDY FAMILIES. Under the Temporary Assistance for Needy Families (TANF) program, states receive a fixed amount from the federal government to provide "welfare" to residents with few federal constraints on how they manage the funds. The Administration for Children and Families (ACF) of the U.S. Department of Health and Human Services (August 2010, http://www.acf.hhs.gov/programs/ofs/data/2009/table_a1_2009.html) indicates that the total federal funds spent on TANF expenditures for fiscal year (FY) 2009 were $21.8 billion.

Under TANF each state decides what categories of children receive aid. TANF requires that an adult recipient

FIGURE 2.1

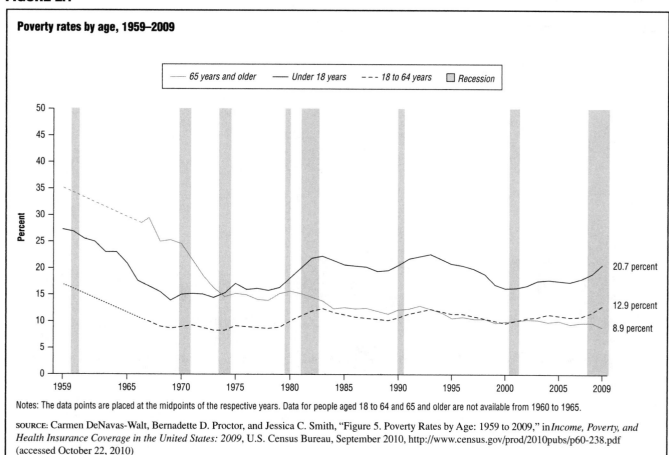

Poverty rates by age, 1959–2009

Legend: 65 years and older — Under 18 years — – – 18 to 64 years — Recession

20.7 percent
12.9 percent
8.9 percent

Percent

1959   1965   1970   1975   1980   1985   1990   1995   2000   2005   2009

Notes: The data points are placed at the midpoints of the respective years. Data for people aged 18 to 64 and 65 and older are not available from 1960 to 1965.

SOURCE: Carmen DeNavas-Walt, Bernadette D. Proctor, and Jessica C. Smith, "Figure 5. Poverty Rates by Age: 1959 to 2009," in *Income, Poverty, and Health Insurance Coverage in the United States: 2009*, U.S. Census Bureau, September 2010, http://www.census.gov/prod/2010pubs/p60-238.pdf (accessed October 22, 2010)

work in exchange for time-limited assistance. In *Temporary Assistance for Needy Families Program (TANF): Eighth Annual Report to Congress* (June 2009, http://www.acf.hhs.gov/programs/ofa/data-reports/annualreport8/TANF_8th_Report_111908.pdf), the ACF notes that in FY 2006, 33% of all TANF families and 46% of two-parent TANF families had an employed family member. The employment rate of all adult recipients that year was 21.6%, down from 23.2% the year before.

The size of families receiving public assistance was decreasing in 2006. According to the ACF, the average number of people in a TANF family was 2.3 in 2006, down from an average of 2.8 in 1996. Half of TANF families in 2006 included only one child recipient, whereas only 10% had three or more children. Nearly half (47.2%) of TANF families were child-only cases, including no adult recipients.

The amount of government assistance provided to individuals and families was down sharply during the first decade of the 21st century. The average monthly benefit per TANF recipient in 2006 was $154, down from a high of $238 (in 2006 dollars) in 1978 under the old Aid to Families with Dependent Children program. (See Figure 2.3.) Benefits included cash and work-based assistance, child care, and transportation assistance. In addition, the number

of families receiving income assistance continued to decline in 2006. (See Figure 2.4.) In response to the economic recession that lasted from late 2007 to mid-2009, Congress allocated additional contingency funds of $5 billion to help states that experienced increases in families needing TANF assistance. The Center for Law and Social Policy reports in "TANF Reauthorization" (December 2010, http://www.clasp.org/federal_policy/pages?id=0021) that Congress did not meet the deadline of September 30, 2010, to reauthorize TANF; on that day, President Barack Obama (1961–) signed into law an extension of the TANF block grant through December 3, 2010, but the bill did not include provisions for the TANF Emergency Fund. In December Congress approved a TANF extension through September 30, 2011.

The reduction in the welfare rolls and expenditures may actually harm poor children. Olivia Golden (1955–), the assistant secretary for children and families in the Department of Health and Human Services under President Bill Clinton (1946–), states in "Welfare Reform Mostly Worked" (*Orlando Sentinel*, July 24, 2005) that she believes the welfare-to-work model "mostly worked" in the sense that welfare caseloads had dropped and that most low-income parents were now working to support their families.

FIGURE 2.2

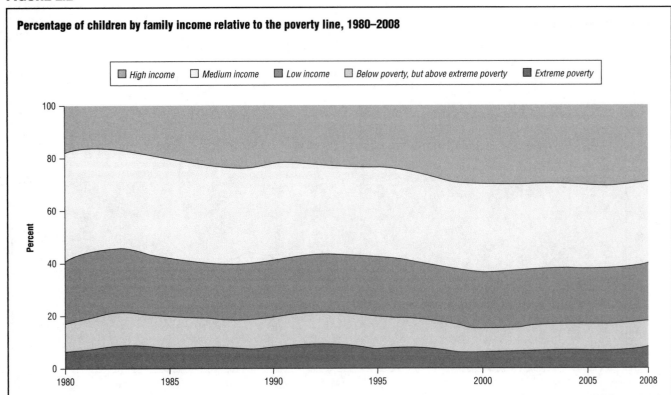

Percentage of children by family income relative to the poverty line, 1980–2008

High income ☐ Medium income ☐ Low income ☐ Below poverty, but above extreme poverty ☐ Extreme poverty

SOURCE: "Figure 4. Percentage of Related Children Ages 0–17 by Family Income Relative to the Poverty Line, 1980–2008," in *America's Children in Brief: Key National Indicators of Well-Being, 2010*, Federal Interagency Forum on Child and Family Statistics, July 2010, http://www.childstats.gov/americaschildren/eco.asp#figure4 (accessed October 15, 2010)

TABLE 2.5

Change in poverty during income years surrounding recessions, 1969–2009

[Numbers in thousands]

Recessions[a]	Income years	Change in number of people in poverty	Change in poverty rate[b]	Change in number of children in poverty	Change in child poverty rate
December 2007, trough not yet defined	2007 to 2009	6,293	1.9	2,127	2.7
March 2001 to November 2001	1999 to 2002	1,779	0.2	−147	−0.4
July 1990 to March 1991	1989[b] to 1991	3,293	1.2	1,187	1.7
January 1980 to July 1980 and July 1981 to November 1982	1978 to 1983	10,806	3.9	3,980	6.4
November 1973 to March 1975	1973 to 1975	2,904	1.2	1,462	2.7
December 1969 to November 1970	1969 to 1971	1,412	0.4	860	1.3

[a]Recessions are determined by the National Bureau of Economic Research, a private research organization.
[b]For comparability purposes, the 1989 poverty rate used in this calculation (13.1 percent) is based on data that reflect the implementation of the 1990 decennial census population controls.
Note: Income years are based on peak income year prior to or during the start of the recession and the trough income year near or after the end of the recession.

SOURCE: Carmen DeNavas-Walt, Bernadette D. Proctor, and Jessica C. Smith, "Table 5. Change in Poverty during Income Years Surrounding Recessions: 1969 to 2009," in *Income, Poverty, and Health Insurance Coverage in the United States: 2009*, U.S. Census Bureau, September 2010, http://www.census.gov/prod/2010pubs/p60–238.pdf (accessed October 22, 2010)

However, this very success brought about additional problems. She notes, "In less than a decade, welfare has faded as a means of support for impoverished families. Many of these families are working long hours despite low wages, shrinking health-insurance coverage and serious trade-offs between work and decent care for their children. Yet, neither our politics nor our policies have adjusted to our success at bringing more of these parents into the labor force."

In "Policy Basics: An Introduction to TANF" (March 19, 2009, http://www.cbpp.org/cms/index.cfm?fa=view &id=936), Liz Schott of the Center on Budget and Policy

TABLE 2.6

Percentage of children living below selected poverty levels by gender, age, and race and Hispanic origin, selected years 1980–2008

Characteristic	1980	1985	1990	1995	2000	2005	2006	2007	2008
Below 100% poverty									
All children[a]	18.3	20.7	20.6	20.8	16.2	17.6	17.4	18.0	19.0
Gender									
Male	18.1	20.3	20.5	20.4	16.0	17.4	17.2	17.9	18.8
Female	18.6	21.1	20.8	21.2	16.3	17.8	17.6	18.1	19.2
Age									
Ages 0–5	20.7	23.0	23.6	24.1	18.3	20.2	20.3	21.1	21.7
Ages 6–17	17.3	19.5	19.0	19.1	15.2	16.3	16.0	16.5	17.6
Race and Hispanic origin[b]									
White, non-Hispanic	11.8	12.8	12.3	11.2	9.1	—	—	—	—
White-alone, non-Hispanic	—	—	—	—	—	10.0	10.0	10.1	10.6
Black	42.3	43.6	44.8	41.9	31.2	—	—	—	—
Black-alone	—	—	—	—	—	34.5	33.4	34.5	34.7
Hispanic[c]	33.2	40.3	38.4	40.0	28.4	28.3	26.9	28.6	30.6
Below 50% poverty									
All children[a]	6.9	8.6	8.8	8.5	6.7	7.7	7.5	7.8	8.5
Gender									
Male	6.9	8.6	8.8	8.4	6.6	7.3	7.5	7.8	8.4
Female	6.9	8.6	8.8	8.5	6.8	8.1	7.5	7.8	8.6
Age									
Ages 0–5	8.3	10.0	10.7	10.8	8.1	9.1	9.4	9.8	10.4
Ages 6–17	6.2	7.8	7.8	7.2	6.0	7.0	6.5	6.8	7.5
Race and Hispanic origin[b]									
White, non-Hispanic	—	—	5.0	3.9	3.7	—	—	—	—
White-alone, non-Hispanic	—	—	—	—	—	4.1	4.3	4.3	4.5
Black	—	—	22.8	20.6	15.2	—	—	—	—
Black-alone	—	—	—	—	—	17.3	16.0	17.3	17.6
Hispanic[c]	—	—	14.2	16.3	10.2	11.5	10.3	11.0	12.5
Below 150% poverty									
All children[a]	29.9	32.3	31.4	32.2	26.7	28.2	28.6	29.3	30.5
Gender									
Male	29.6	32.2	31.3	31.7	26.6	28.0	28.4	29.2	30.4
Female	30.3	32.3	31.6	32.7	26.8	28.3	28.8	29.5	30.6
Age									
Ages 0–5	33.2	35.6	34.6	35.5	29.3	31.5	32.2	33.2	34.0
Ages 6–17	28.4	30.5	29.7	30.5	25.4	26.5	26.8	27.4	28.8
Race and Hispanic origin[b]									
White, non-Hispanic	—	—	21.4	20.1	16.4	—	—	—	—
White-alone, non-Hispanic	—	—	—	—	—	17.2	17.7	17.8	19.0
Black	—	—	57.9	56.8	45.7	—	—	—	—
Black-alone	—	—	—	—	—	48.8	48.1	49.0	50.5
Hispanic[c]	—	—	56.0	59.4	47.3	45.9	45.9	47.8	47.7
Below 200% poverty									
All children[a]	42.3	43.5	42.4	43.3	37.5	38.9	39.0	39.2	40.6
Gender									
Male	42.3	43.2	42.5	43.1	37.5	38.6	38.8	39.1	40.4
Female	42.4	43.7	42.3	43.5	37.6	39.3	39.2	39.3	40.8
Age									
Ages 0–5	46.8	47.1	46.0	46.7	41.0	42.4	42.9	42.9	44.0
Ages 6–17	40.3	41.6	40.5	41.5	35.9	37.3	37.1	37.3	38.8

Priorities states that the initial success of the welfare-to-work provisions of TANF can be attributed to a strong economy and strong work supports. However, as the economy slowed between 2007 and 2009 the employment of single mothers declined and child poverty grew, with a reduced safety net in place to protect children. Schott notes that "the fact that the share of eligible families receiving aid has plummeted so sharply means that the program now does significantly less to protect children from deep poverty than was once the case."

THE SUPPLEMENTAL NUTRITION ASSISTANCE PROGRAM. The Supplemental Nutrition Assistance Program (SNAP), known previously as the food stamp program, which is administered by the USDA, provides low-income households with electronic benefit cards that can be used

TABLE 2.6

Percentage of children living below selected poverty levels by gender, age, and race and Hispanic origin, selected years 1980–2008

[CONTINUED]

Characteristic	1980	1985	1990	1995	2000	2005	2006	2007	2008
Race and Hispanic origin[b]									
White, non-Hispanic	—	—	32.3	30.5	25.5	—	—	—	—
White-alone, non-Hispanic	—	—	—	—	—	26.2	26.3	26.2	27.3
Black	—	—	68.3	68.1	59.2	—	—	—	—
Black-alone	—	—	—	—	—	61.3	60.2	60.6	60.9
Hispanic[c]	—	—	69.5	72.9	62.6	60.7	61.0	60.8	62.0

— Not available.

[a]Includes children not related to the householder.

[b]For race and Hispanic-origin data in this table: From 1980 to 2002, following the 1977 OMB standards for collecting and presenting data on race, the Current Population Survey (CPS) asked respondents to choose one race from the following: White, Black, American Indian or Alaskan Native, or Asian or Pacific Islander. The Census Bureau also offered an "Other" category. Beginning in 2003, following the 1997 OMB standards for collecting and presenting data on race, the CPS asked respondents to choose one or more races from the following: White, black or African American, Asian, American Indian or Alaska Native, or Native Hawaiian or other Pacific Islander. All race groups discussed in this table from 2002 onward refer to people who indicated only one racial identity within the racial categories presented. People who responded to the question on race by indicating only one race are referred to as the race-alone population. The use of the race-alone population in this table does not imply that it is the preferred method of presenting or analyzing data. Data from 2002 onward are not directly comparable with data from earlier years. Data on race and Hispanic origin are collected separately. Persons of Hispanic origin may be of any race.

[c]Persons of Hispanic origin may be of any race.

[d]Regions: Northeast includes CT, MA, ME, NH, NJ, NY, PA, RI, and VT. South includes AL, AR, DC, DE, FL, GA, KY, LA, MD, MS, NC, OK, SC, TN, TX, VA, and WV. Midwest includes IA, IL, IN, KS, MI, MN, MO, ND, NE, OH, SD, and WI. West includes AK, AZ, CA, CO, HI, ID, MT, NM, NV, OR, UT, WA, and WY.

Notes: Related children are persons ages 0–17 who are related to the householder (or subfamily reference person) by birth, marriage, or adoption, but are not themselves householders, spouses, or reference persons. The 2004 data have been revised to reflect a correction to the weights in the 2005 Annual Social and Economic Supplement (ASEC). Data for 1999, 2000, and 2001 use Census 2000 population controls. Data for 2000 onward are from the expanded Current Population Survey (CPS) sample. The poverty level is based on money income and does not include noncash benefits, such as food stamps. Poverty thresholds reflect family size and composition and are adjusted each year using the annual average Consumer Price Index level. The average poverty threshold for a family of four was $22,025 in 2008. The levels shown here are derived from the ratio of the family's income to the family's poverty threshold.

SOURCE: Adapted from "ECON1.A. Child Poverty: Percentage of All Children and Related Children Ages 0–17 Living below Selected Poverty Levels by Selected Characteristics,1980–2008," in *America's Children in Brief: Key National Indicators of Well-Being, 2010*, Federal Interagency Forum on Child and Family Statistics, July 2010, http://www.childstats.gov/americaschildren/tables.asp (accessed October 15, 2010)

at most grocery stores, much like debit cards, in place of cash. This assistance is intended to ensure that recipients have access to a nutritious diet. It is available to households that have a gross monthly income of no more than 130% of the poverty line and a net monthly income at or below the poverty line. According to Joshua Leftin, Andrew Gothro, and Esa Eslami of the Food and Nutrition Service (FNS), in "Characteristics of Supplemental Nutrition Assistance Program Households: Fiscal Year 2009" (October 2010, http://www.fns.usda.gov/ora/menu/Published/SNAP/FILES/Participation/2009CharacteristicsSummary.pdf), almost nine out of 10 (86%) households that received SNAP benefits in 2009 lived in poverty and 41% of SNAP households lived in extreme poverty.

The amount of money a family receives on its benefit card is based on the USDA's estimate of how much it costs to provide households with nutritious, low-cost meals, called the Thrifty Food Plan. This estimate changes yearly to reflect inflation. The American Recovery and Reinvestment Act of 2009 increased SNAP maximum allotments by 13.6% starting on April 1, 2009. According to the FNS (November 2, 2010, http://www.fns.usda.gov/snap/faqs.htm), in FY 2010 the maximum monthly benefit for a family of four was $668, up from $588 before April 1, 2009. The average monthly benefit for all households in FY 2009 was $272. (See Table 2.7.) SNAP households containing children received an average of $398 in benefits per month, in part because

households with children tended to be larger (3.3 people) than households in general (2.2 people).

Joshua Leftin, Andrew Gothro, and Esa Eslami state in *Characteristics of Supplemental Nutrition Assistance Program Households: Fiscal Year 2009* (October 2010, http://www.fns.usda.gov/ora/menu/Published/SNAP/FILES/Participation/2009Characteristics.pdf) that 7.5 million (49.9%) households that received supplemental nutrition assistance in FY 2009 contained children. About three out of 10 (29.1%) SNAP households were single-parent households, and 27.2% of them were headed by single mothers.

THE SPECIAL SUPPLEMENTAL NUTRITION PROGRAM FOR WOMEN, INFANTS, AND CHILDREN. The Special Supplemental Nutrition Program for Women, Infants, and Children (WIC) provides food assistance and nutritional screening for low-income pregnant and postpartum women and their infants and children under the age of five years. This program can help women and young children with household incomes that are too high to receive SNAP benefits. In "Frequently Asked Questions about WIC" (September 8, 2009, http://www.fns.usda.gov/wic/FAQs/FAQ.HTM), the FNS explains that income eligibility guidelines for the period July 1, 2009, to June 30, 2010, required applicants to have an income at or below 185% of the poverty level and be nutritionally "at risk," meaning that to be eligible an individual must have medically or diet-based risks. The income eligibility guidelines state that

FIGURE 2.3

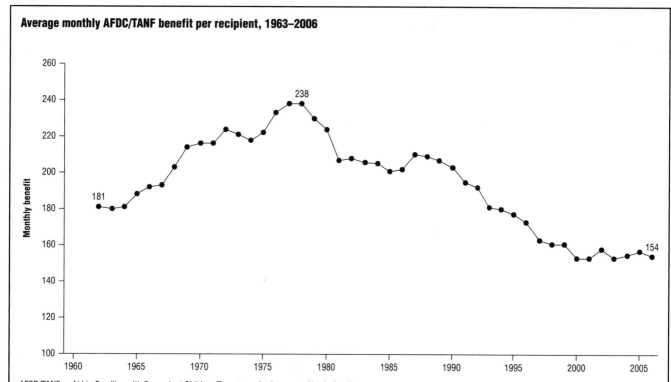

Average monthly AFDC/TANF benefit per recipient, 1963–2006

AFCD/TANF = Aid to Families with Dependent Children/Temporary Assistance to Needy Families.
Note: Comparison of trends in the average monthly AFDC/TANF benefit per recipient in constant 2006 dollars with the weighted average maximum benefit in constant 2006 dollars since 1988 indicates that the primary cause of the decline in the average monthly benefit has been the erosion of the real value of the maximum benefit due to inflation. This is due to the fact that the current value of the maximum benefits has increased less than the cost of living in most states since the late1980s.

SOURCE: Gil Crouse, Susan Hauan, and Annette Waters Rogers, "Figure TANF2. Average Monthly AFDC/TANF Benefit per Recipient in Constant 2006 Dollars," in *Indicators of Welfare Dependence, Annual Report to Congress, 2008*, U.S. Department of Health and Human Services, December 2008, http://aspe.hhs.gov/hsp/indicators08/apa.pdf (accessed October 22, 2010)

a family of one (in other words, a single, pregnant woman) could earn up to $1,670 per month and still qualify for WIC. A family of four could earn $3,400 per month and participate in WIC. Patty Connor et al. of the FNS note in "WIC Participant and Program Characteristics 2008, WIC-08-PC" (January 2010, http://www.fns.usda.gov/oane/menu/Published/WIC/FILES/PC2008Summary.pdf) that two-thirds (68.3%) of WIC participants in 2008 had household incomes below the poverty line.

According to Connor et al., in April 2008, 9.5 million women and children participated in WIC. Half (49.5%) of WIC participants were children, 25.5% were infants, and 25% were pregnant, postpartum, or breastfeeding women. Recipients receive food items or vouchers for purchases of certain items in retail stores. The WIC program is federally funded but administered by state and local health agencies. In "WIC Program Participation and Costs" (December 2, 2010, http://www.fns.usda.gov/pd/wisummary.htm), the FNS states that in FY 2009 the WIC program's estimated food cost was $4.6 billion and its estimated administrative costs were $1.8 billion, for a total cost of nearly $6.5 billion.

SCHOOL NUTRITION PROGRAMS. School nutrition programs offer food assistance to school-age children. The programs provide millions of children with nutritious food each school day. Children living in families that earn no more than 185% of the poverty level are eligible for reduced-price school meals; children living in families that earn no more than 130% of the poverty level are eligible for free school meals. The FNS reports in "Federal Cost of School Food Programs" (December 2, 2010, http://www.fns.usda.gov/pd/cncosts.htm) that in FY 2009 the U.S. government spent $12.6 billion on school nutrition programs, including the National School Lunch Program, the School Breakfast Program, and the Special Milk Program. In FY 2009, 31.3 million children took part in the National School Lunch Program. (See Table 2.8.)

CHILD SUPPORT

Children living in single-parent families are far more likely to be poor than children living in two-parent households, and the number of children living with only one parent—usually the mother—is increasing. According to Timothy S. Grall of the Census Bureau, in *Custodial Mothers and Fathers and Their Child Support: 2007* (November 2009, http://www.census.gov/prod/2009pubs/p60-237.pdf), in the spring of 2008, 13.7 million parents had custody of 21.8 million children under the age of 21 years whose other parent lived elsewhere. Mothers accounted for 82.6% of all

FIGURE 2.4

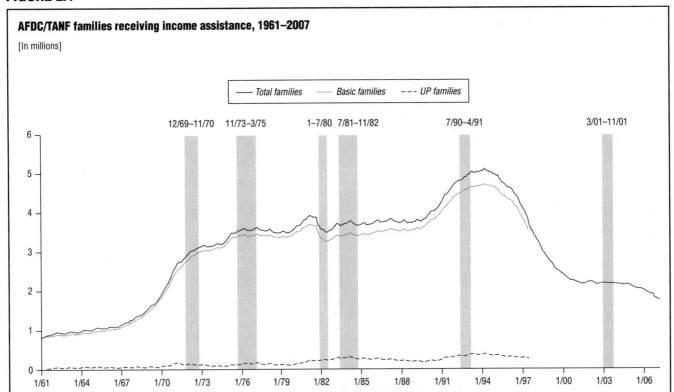

AFDC/TANF families receiving income assistance, 1961–2007

[In millions]

Note: "Basic Families" are single-parent families and "UP Families" are two-parent cases receiving benefits under AFDC Unemployed Parent programs that operated in certain states before FY 1991 and in all states after October 1, 1990. The AFDC Basic and UP programs were replaced by TANF as of July 1, 1997 under the Personal Responsibility and Work Opportunity Reconciliation Act of 1996. Shaded areas indicate NBER designated periods of recession from peak to trough. The decrease in number of families receiving assistance during the 1981–82 recession stems from changes in eligibility requirements and other policy changes mandated by OBRA 1981. Beginning in 2000, "Total Families" includes TANF and SSP families. Last data point plotted is March 2007.

AFCD/TANF = Aid to Families with Dependent Children/Temporary Assistance to Needy Families
NBER = National Bureau of Economic Research
SSP = Separate State Program

SOURCE: Gil Crouse, Susan Hauan, and Annette Waters Rogers, "Figure TANF1. AFDC/TANF Families Receiving Income Assistance," in *Indicators of Welfare Dependence, Annual Report to Congress, 2008*, U.S. Department of Health and Human Services, December 2008, http://aspe.hhs.gov/hsp/indicators08/apa.pdf (accessed October 22, 2010)

custodial parents, whereas fathers made up only 17.4% of custodial parents. These proportions have not changed significantly since 1994.

Grall indicates that 7.4 million (54%) of the 13.7 million custodial parents in 2008 had a child support agreement with the other parent. Most of these agreements required child support payments from the noncustodial parent. In 2007, 76.3% of custodial parents due support received at least some payments. (See Figure 2.5.) Almost half (46.8%) of custodial parents received all the payments they were due, up from only 36.9% in 1993. Grall also notes that noncustodial parents who had either joint custody agreements or visitation rights to their children were more likely to pay child support (78.3%) than parents who did not have any visitation rights at all (67.2%).

Differences existed in the child support arrangements for custodial mothers and custodial fathers. In 2007 custodial mothers were much more likely than custodial fathers to be awarded child support (56.9% and 40.4%,

respectively). (See Table 2.9.) On average, custodial mothers were due $5,366 in child support in 2007, and received $3,355. Custodial fathers were due, on average, $5,239 and actually received $3,343. As noted earlier, fewer than half of all custodial parents actually received the full child support due them; only 47.1% of custodial mothers and 45% of custodial fathers received the total amount due.

Grall explains that receipt of child support payments made a significant difference in the household incomes of single-parent families. In 2007 the average family income of custodial parents who received at least some of the child support due them was $34,100, and the child support represented 12.9% of the total household income. Child support represented 15.4% of the total household income for those parents who received all of the child support due them. In contrast, custodial parents who had child support agreements but received none of the child support due had an average income of only $29,300.

TABLE 2.7

Income, monthly food stamp benefits, and household size by household composition, fiscal year 2009

Households with:	Gross monthly countable income (Dollars)	Net monthly countable income (Dollars)[a]	Monthly SNAP benefit (Dollars)	Household size (Persons)	Monthly SNAP benefit per person (Dollars)
Total	711	329	272	2.2	129
Children	865	423	398	3.3	127
Single-adult household	763	356	382	3.0	130
Male adult	705	322	352	2.7	132
Female adult	767	359	384	3.0	130
Multiple-adult household	1,200	663	472	4.3	112
Married head household	1,257	698	479	4.4	110
Other multiple-adult household	1,107	607	461	4.1	113
Children only	572	180	304	2.1	151
Elderly individuals	790	383	128	1.3	101
Living alone	721	319	103	1.0	103
Not living alone	1,071	608	229	2.4	94
Disabled nonelderly individuals[b]	918	467	197	1.9	104
Living alone	750	299	108	1.0	108
Not living alone	1,157	688	322	3.3	99
Other households[c]	250	82	185	1.1	170
Single-person household	206	61	174	1.0	174
Multi-person household	646	271	292	2.2	136
Single-person households	507	191	136	1.0	136

SNAP = Supplemental Nutrition Assistance Program. SSI-CAP = SSI Combined Application Project. SNAP QC = Supplemental Nutrition Assistance Program Quality Control. MFIP = Minnesota Family Investment Program.
[a]Because net income is not used in their benefit determinations, 31,357 MFIP households and 446,540 SSI-CAP households in States that use standardized SSI-CAP benefits are excluded from this column.
[b]Due to changes in the SNAP QC data, the definition of disabled changed in 2003. Beginning with the 2003 report, we are only able to identify households that contain a disabled person. In previous reports, we had additional information that helped to identify which household member was disabled.
[c]Households not containing children, elderly individuals, or disabled individuals.

SOURCE: Joshua Leftin, Andrew Gothro, and Esa Eslami, "Table 3.4. Average Values of Selected Characteristics by Household Composition, Fiscal Year 2009," in *Characteristics of Supplemental Nutrition Assistance Program Households: Fiscal Year 2009*, U.S. Department of Agriculture, Food and Nutrition Service, October 2010, http://www.fns.usda.gov/ora/MENU/Published/snap/FILES/Participation/2009Characteristics.pdf (accessed October 22, 2010)

Government Assistance in Obtaining Child Support

As demonstrated earlier, inadequate financial support from noncustodial parents contributes to the high incidence of poverty among children living in single-parent families. When custodial parents are not paid the child support due them, their families suffer financially and often must turn to public welfare. Therefore, government agencies have an interest in recovering child support from delinquent parents.

In 1975 Congress established the Child Support Enforcement (CSE) Program, a collaborative effort among local, state, and federal agencies, to ensure that children received financial support from both parents. Under the Child Support Recovery Act of 1992, noncustodial parents delinquent on child support due in another state can be prosecuted. CSE services are automatically provided to families receiving assistance under TANF; any support collected usually reimburses the state and federal governments for TANF payments made to the family. Child support services are also available for a small application fee to families not receiving TANF.

Provisions in the Personal Responsibility and Work Opportunity Reconciliation Act of 1996 strengthened and improved child support collection activities. The law established a National Directory of New Hires to track parents across state lines, made the process for establishing paternity faster and easier, and enacted tough new penalties for delinquent parents, including expanded wage garnishment and suspension or revocation of driver's licenses. The law also required single-mother TANF applicants to disclose the paternity of their children and to assign any child support payments to the state. According to the ACF, in *Child Support Enforcement FY 2009 Preliminary Report* (May 2010, http://www.acf.hhs.gov/programs/cse/pubs/2010/reports/preliminary_report_fy 2009/), these efforts have paid off; in FY 2009 CSE handled 15.8 million cases and collected nearly $24.3 billion.

TEENS AND MONEY
Teen Employment

The Bureau of Labor Statistics (BLS) reports in the press release "The Employment Situation: November 2010" (December 3, 2010, http://www.bls.gov/news.release/pdf/empsit.pdf) that in November 2010, 5.8 million (34.6%) out of 16.8 million people aged 16 to 19 years were employed or looking for work. The unemployment rate for this age group was 24.6%, down from 27.1% the month before. Even though the economic recession had

TABLE 2.8

National School Lunch Program, total participation, fiscal years 2005–09

Data as of October 4, 2010

State/Territory	Fiscal year 2005	Fiscal year 2006	Fiscal year 2007	Fiscal year 2008	Fiscal year 2009
					Preliminary
Alabama	565,932	574,060	577,930	586,837	579,890
Alaska	52,091	53,363	53,233	51,911	53,554
Arizona	579,435	607,905	633,312	647,650	655,500
Arkansas	335,891	345,925	347,596	348,858	353,436
California	2,866,246	2,896,191	2,987,912	3,121,420	3,175,074
Colorado	336,565	347,945	364,749	376,744	390,868
Connecticut	301,773	307,389	316,382	316,596	303,002
Delaware	81,032	83,648	85,672	88,351	90,073
District of Columbia	46,976	45,229	41,501	42,746	44,579
Florida	1,523,765	1,523,315	1,536,860	1,557,738	1,560,445
Georgia	1,205,372	1,252,790	1,272,122	1,283,958	1,291,711
Guam	17,055	20,190	19,052	17,938	18,449
Hawaii	121,189	112,822	101,584	101,270	103,807
Idaho	155,700	161,257	165,308	168,458	170,003
Illinois	1,104,595	1,104,900	1,121,006	1,137,683	1,148,891
Indiana	700,890	723,568	744,055	763,328	788,167
Iowa	385,011	390,385	392,976	392,175	394,412
Kansas	326,805	336,461	344,187	350,683	356,495
Kentucky	534,807	542,971	548,586	548,904	570,758
Louisiana	615,879	571,269	583,224	585,533	586,936
Maine	107,685	109,152	108,738	108,496	107,748
Maryland	438,302	444,058	439,590	440,953	432,597
Massachusetts	558,107	559,612	561,853	557,824	547,582
Michigan	869,217	884,793	896,882	901,387	911,528
Minnesota	590,260	597,114	607,537	612,159	614,863
Mississippi	398,951	404,503	405,056	404,694	405,716
Missouri	624,385	634,351	639,003	639,155	645,262
Montana	79,664	83,073	83,844	86,482	86,652
Nebraska	228,691	232,823	237,410	239,956	243,466
Nevada	172,292	181,940	193,461	195,747	183,808
New Hampshire	113,074	112,654	113,628	112,861	110,811
New Jersey	629,815	638,688	654,779	669,759	705,558
New Mexico	211,792	213,111	221,055	217,092	221,822
New York	1,823,454	1,820,880	1,821,026	1,817,651	1,812,488
North Carolina	915,560	945,601	962,774	965,552	961,619
North Dakota	78,418	78,388	78,909	80,038	80,924
Ohio	1,060,938	1,085,362	1,100,203	1,105,460	1,119,510
Oklahoma	402,917	412,947	421,601	424,427	437,585
Oregon	291,326	301,199	304,241	308,164	310,817
Pennsylvania	1,121,383	1,136,505	1,143,426	1,147,643	1,149,917
Puerto Rico	369,889	362,119	384,531	370,336	373,353
Rhode Island	84,080	83,806	85,009	83,915	79,017
South Carolina	482,820	491,154	496,542	499,074	500,742
South Dakota	103,986	105,036	106,218	105,631	106,266
Tennessee	660,282	685,621	584,437	695,370	692,008
Texas	2,892,593	3,007,594	3,079,947	3,172,793	3,257,011
Utah	297,669	304,678	312,438	327,591	337,710
Vermont	55,363	55,431	55,451	54,819	54,859
Virginia	730,970	745,038	749,911	751,889	752,709
Virgin Islands	13,474	11,064	10,552	14,003	13,948
Washington	513,488	522,978	526,710	528,689	532,510
West Virginia	202,574	207,594	208,846	211,106	207,758
Wisconsin	583,338	591,230	598,421	597,111	594,850
Wyoming	51,187	52,305	53,564	55,081	56,424
Dept. of Defense	31,237	28,866	28,824	26,337	27,996
Total	**29,646,189**	**30,132,851**	**30,513,665**	**31,018,029**	**31,313,486**

Participation data are nine-month averages; summer months (June-August) are excluded. Participation is based on average daily meals divided by an attendance factor of 0.927. Department of Defense activity represents children of armed forces personnel attending schools overseas. **Data are subject to revision**.

SOURCE: "National School Lunch Program: Total Participation," U.S. Department of Agriculture, Food and Nutrition Service, October 4, 2010, http://www.fns.usda.gov/pd/01slfypart.htm (accessed October 22, 2010)

officially ended in mid-2009, the unemployment rate continued to be high throughout 2010; in November of that year the unemployment rate for all people was 9.8%. Employment rates among young people are highest during the summer months, when many full-time students are out of school. For example, in the press release "Employment and Unemployment among Youth— Summer 2010" (August 27, 2010, http://www.bls.gov/

FIGURE 2.5

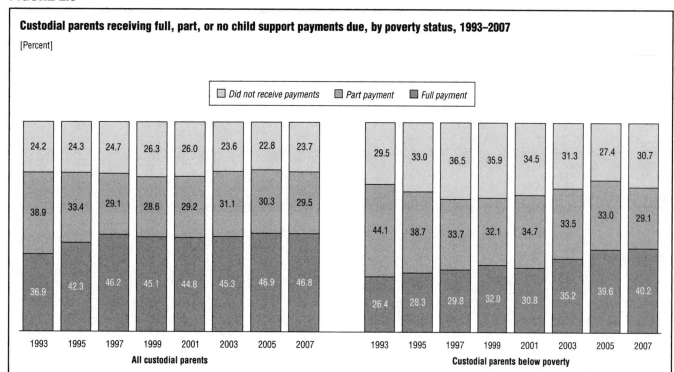

Custodial parents receiving full, part, or no child support payments due, by poverty status, 1993–2007

[Percent]

SOURCE: Timothy S. Grall, "Figure 4. Custodial Parents Receiving Full, Part, or No Child Support Payments Due by Poverty Status: 1993 to 2007," in *Custodial Mothers and Fathers and Their Child Support: 2007*, U.S. Census Bureau, November 2009, http://www.census.gov/prod/2009pubs/p60-237.pdf (accessed October 22, 2010)

news.release/pdf/youth.pdf), the BLS states that the employment of youth between the ages of 16 and 24 years increased by 1.8 million between April and July 2010. Nevertheless, the BLS indicates in "The Employment Situation: November 2010" that the unemployment rate for teens during July, August, and September 2010 remained over 24%.

Stephen Gandel reports in "In a Tough Job Market, Teens Are Suffering Most" (*Time*, January 18, 2010) that the group of workers hit worst by the economic recession that lasted from late 2007 to mid-2009 were 16- to 19-year-olds. He reports that Andrew Sum, the head of the Center for Labor Market Studies at Northeastern University, stated, "Proportionally, more kids have lost jobs in the past few years than the entire country lost in the Great Depression." However, the trend toward fewer teen jobs had actually

begun during the first few years of the first decade of the 21st century, when older workers were beginning to take jobs that once had been held by teens. By 2010 teens made up only 3.2% of the workforce, down from a high of 9% during the mid-1970s. Gandel notes, however, that "there is the silver lining of low teen employment: with fewer work opportunities, more teens are staying in school and striving for higher levels of academic achievement."

Most teens are employed as hourly workers, and they make low wages compared with other age groups. The BLS reports in *Characteristics of Minimum Wage Workers: 2009* (March 1, 2010, http://www.bls.gov/cps/minwage2009tbls.htm) that in 2009, 18.6% of 16- to 19-year-olds earned the federal minimum hourly wage ($6.55 before July 24, 2009, and $7.25 thereafter), compared with only 3.2% of workers aged 25 years and older.

TABLE 2.9

Comparison of custodial parents and those with child support awarded, due, and received, selected years 1993–2007

[Numbers in thousands as of spring of the following year. Parents living with own children under 21 years of age whose other parent is not living in the home. Amounts in 2007 dollars.]

Item	1993 Number	1995 Number	1997 Number	1999 Number	2001 Number	2003 Number	2005 Number	2007 Number
All custodial parents								
Total	**13,690**	**13,715**	**13,949**	**13,529**	**13,383**	**13,951**	**13,605**	**13,743**
Awarded child support	7,800	7,967	7,876	7,945	7,916	8,376	7,802	7,428
Percent	57.0	58.1	56.5	58.7	59.1	60.0	57.3	54.0
Due child support	6,688	6,958	7,018	6,791	6,924	7,256	6,809	6,375
Average child support due (in dollars)	5,060	5,494	5,343	5,917	5,907	5,754	5,931	5,350
Average child support received (in dollars)	3,294	3,620	3,560	3,473	3,701	3,945	3,869	3,354
Received any child support	5,070	5,269	5,282	5,005	5,119	5,548	5,259	4,864
Percent	75.8	75.7	75.3	73.7	73.9	76.5	77.2	76.3
Received full amount of child support	2,466	2,945	3,240	3,066	3,093	3,290	3,192	2,986
Percent	36.9	42.3	46.2	45.1	44.7	45.3	46.9	46.8
Not awarded child support	5,889	5,747	6,074	5,584	5,466	5,576	5,803	6,315
Custodial mothers								
Total	**11,505**	**11,607**	**11,872**	**11,499**	**11,291**	**11,587**	**11,406**	**11,356**
Awarded child support	6,878	7,123	7,080	7,150	7,110	7,436	7,002	6,463
Percent	59.8	61.4	59.6	62.2	63.0	64.2	61.4	56.9
Due child support	5,913	6,224	6,342	6,133	6,212	6,516	6,131	5,551
Average child support due (in dollars)	5,126	5,587	5,367	5,976	6,781	5,835	6,011	5,366
Average child support received (in dollars)	3,363	3,665	3,582	3,570	3,937	4,035	3,887	3,355
Received any child support	4,501	4,742	4,802	4,578	4,639	5,018	4,754	4,253
Percent	76.1	76.2	75.7	74.6	74.7	77.0	77.5	76.6
Received full amount of child support	2,178	2,674	2,945	2,818	2,815	2,948	2,900	2,615
Percent	36.8	43.0	46.4	45.9	45.3	45.2	47.3	47.1
Not awarded child support	4,627	4,484	4,792	4,349	4,181	4,151	4,404	4,893
Custodial fathers								
Total	**2,184**	**2,108**	**2,077**	**2,030**	**2,092**	**2,364**	**2,199**	**2,387**
Awarded child support	922	844	796	795	807	940	800	965
Percent	42.2	40.0	38.3	39.2	38.6	39.8	36.4	40.4
Due child support	775	733	676	658	712	740	678	825
Average child support due (in dollars)	4,557	4,697	5,106	5,370	4,943	5,040	5,199	5,239
Average child support received (in dollars)	2,856	3,249	3,366	2,566	3,374	3,153	3,708	3,343
Received any child support	569	527	479	427	480	530	505	611
Percent	73.4	71.9	70.9	64.9	67.4	71.6	74.5	74.1
Received full amount of child support	288	270	295	248	278	342	292	371
Percent	37.2	36.8	43.6	37.7	39.0	46.2	43.1	45.0
Not awarded child support	1,262	1,263	1,281	1,235	1,285	1,424	1,399	1,422

Note: All child support income amounts are adjusted to reflect 2007 dollars using the Consumer Price Index Research Series Using Current Methods (CPI-U-RS).

SOURCE: Timothy S. Grall, "Table 1. Comparison of Custodial Parent Population and Those with Child Support Awarded, Due, and Received: 1993–2007," in *Custodial Mothers and Fathers and Their Child Support: 2007*, U.S. Census Bureau, November 2009, http://www.census.gov/prod/2009pubs/p60–237.pdf (accessed October 22, 2010)

CHAPTER 3
CARING FOR CHILDREN

SOCIETAL CHANGES AND WORKING MOTHERS

During the first decade of the 21st century women with young children were much more likely to work outside the home than they had been three decades previously. Jane Lawler Dye of the U.S. Census Bureau reports in *Fertility of American Women: June 2004* (December 2005, http://www.census.gov/prod/2005pubs/p20-555.pdf) that in 1976, 31% of women aged 15 to 44 years with a child under 12 months old worked. The Bureau of Labor Statistics (BLS) indicates in the press release "Employment Characteristics of Families—2009" (May 27, 2010, http://www.bls.gov/news.release/pdf/famee.pdf) that by 2009 this percentage had increased to 56.6%. In 2009, 64.2% of mothers with children under the age of six years and 77.3% of mothers with school-age children were in the labor force. (See Table 3.1.)

Many factors contributed to the greater proportion of mothers in the workforce. Legislation passed during the late 1970s made it more possible for women to return to work after the birth of a child. In 1976 tax code changes allowed families a tax credit on child care costs, making it more financially feasible for women to return to work. In 1978 the Pregnancy Discrimination Act was passed, making it illegal for employers to discriminate in hiring, firing, promoting, or determining pay levels based on pregnancy or childbirth. In 1993 the Family and Medical Leave Act was passed, requiring employers to give eligible employees up to 12 weeks of unpaid leave for childbearing or family care each year.

Societal changes also contributed to the greater number of women with young children participating in the labor force. In *Maternity Leave and Employment Patterns, 1961–1995* (November 2001, http://www.census.gov/prod/2001pubs/p70-79.pdf), the most recent study of this kind as of January 2011, Kirsten Smith, Barbara Downs, and Martin O'Connell of the Census Bureau review the changing demographic profile of first-time mothers between the 1960s and the 1990s to explain, in part, this increase. The researchers emphasize that during this period the incidence of first-time motherhood at age 30 and older tripled and that first-time mothers during the 1990s tended to be better educated than first-time mothers during the 1960s. These older, well-educated mothers often viewed their jobs as long-term careers and believed time lost could adversely affect their ability to hold a position and earn promotions and could decrease contributions to retirement funds. This trend continued into the 21st century. Joyce A. Martin et al. of the Centers for Disease Control and Prevention (CDC) note in "Births: Final Data for 2005" (*National Vital Statistics Reports*, vol. 56, no. 6, December 5, 2007) that the mean (average) age of first-time mothers reached 25.2 years in 2003, up from 22.7 years in 1980 and an all-time high for American women; this age remained unchanged through 2005. However, by the end of 2006 Martin et al. indicate in "Births: Final Data for 2006" (*National Vital Statistics Reports*, vol. 57, no. 7, January 7, 2009) that the age had dropped to 25—the first decline in some 40 years. According to Martin et al. in "Births: Final Data for 2007" (*National Vital Statistics Reports*, vol. 58, no. 24, August 9, 2010), the mean age at first birth remained unchanged in 2007.

Furthermore, the increasing number of single mothers meant that more women had to work to support their family. In 1970, 3.4 million women maintained single-parent households; by 2009 this number had nearly tripled to 9.9 million. (See Table 1.7 in Chapter 1.) Changes in government programs that provided assistance to poor families also resulted in increasing numbers of single mothers entering the workforce. In 1996 the federal government placed a two-year time limit on receiving public assistance benefits while not working, requiring poor parents to work even if they had to place young children in day care. In 2009, 67.8% of mothers in single-parent households worked. (See Table 3.2.) Nearly two-thirds (64.6%) of single mothers with children under three years old were in the labor force, with an 18.9% unemployment rate. (See Table 3.3.)

TABLE 3.1

Employment status of population, by sex, marital status, and presence and age of own children under age 18, 2009

[Numbers in thousands]

Characteristic	2009 Total	Men	Women
With own children under 18 years			
Civilian noninstitutional population	64,854	28,778	36,076
Civilian labor force	52,748	26,985	25,763
Participation rate	81.3	93.8	71.4
Employed	48,621	24,989	23,632
Employment-population ratio	75.0	86.8	65.5
Full-time workers[a]	41,003	23,583	17,419
Part-time workers[b]	7,618	1,406	6,212
Unemployed	4,128	1,996	2,132
Unemployment rate	7.8	7.4	8.3
Married, spouse present			
Civilian noninstitutional population	51,634	26,249	25,385
Civilian labor force	42,424	24,763	17,661
Participation rate	82.2	94.3	69.6
Employed	39,732	23,100	16,632
Employment-population ratio	76.9	88.0	65.5
Full-time workers[a]	33,846	21,871	11,975
Part-time workers[b]	5,886	1,229	4,657
Unemployed	2,692	1,663	1,029
Unemployment rate	6.3	6.7	5.8
Other marital status[c]			
Civilian noninstitutional population	13,221	2,529	10,691
Civilian labor force	10,325	2,223	8,102
Participation rate	78.1	87.9	75.8
Employed	8,889	1,889	7,000
Employment-population ratio	67.2	74.7	65.5
Full-time workers[a]	7,157	1,712	5,445
Part-time workers[b]	1,732	177	1,555
Unemployed	1,436	334	1,103
Unemployment rate	13.9	15.0	13.6
With own children 6 to 17 years, none younger			
Civilian noninstitutional population	35,885	15,982	19,903
Civilian labor force	30,200	14,821	15,379
Participation rate	84.2	92.7	77.3
Employed	28,059	13,775	14,284
Employment-population ratio	78.2	86.2	71.8
Full-time workers[a]	23,864	13,067	10,798
Part-time workers[b]	4,194	708	3,486
Unemployed	2,141	1,046	1,095
Unemployment rate	7.1	7.1	7.1
With own children under 6 years			
Civilian noninstitutional population	28,969	12,796	16,173
Civilian labor force	22,549	12,164	10,384
Participation rate	77.8	95.1	64.2
Employed	20,562	11,214	9,348
Employment-population ratio	71.0	87.6	57.8
Full-time workers[a]	17,138	10,517	6,622
Part-time workers[b]	3,424	697	2,726
Unemployed	1,987	950	1,036
Unemployment rate	8.8	7.8	10.0

TABLE 3.1

Employment status of population, by sex, marital status, and presence and age of own children under age 18, 2009 [CONTINUED]

[Numbers in thousands]

Characteristic	2009 Total	Men	Women
With no own children under 18 years			
Civilian noninstitutional population	170,947	85,358	85,589
Civilian labor force	101,394	55,138	46,256
Participation rate	59.3	64.6	54.0
Employed	91,257	48,681	42,576
Employment-population ratio	53.4	57.0	49.7
Full-time workers[a]	71,631	40,368	31,263
Part-time workers[b]	19,626	8,313	11,313
Unemployed	10,137	6,457	3,680
Unemployment rate	10.0	11.7	8.0

[a]Usually work 35 hours or more a week at all jobs.
[b]Usually work less than 35 hours a week at all jobs.
[c]Includes never married; married, spouse absent; divorced; separated; and widowed persons.
Notes: Own children include sons, daughters, step-children, and adopted children. Not included are nieces, nephews, grandchildren, and other related and unrelated children. Detail may not sum to totals due to rounding. Updated population controls are introduced annually with the release of January data.

SOURCE: Adapted from "Table 5. Employment Status of the Population by Sex, Marital Status, and Presence and Age of Own Children under 18, 2008–09 Annual Averages," in *Employment Characteristics of Families—2009*, U.S. Department of Labor, Bureau of Labor Statistics, May 27, 2010, http://www.bls.gov/news.release/pdf/famee.pdf (accessed October 22, 2010)

Married women have also entered the workforce in larger numbers. A decline in men's real wages plus a rising cost of living has led some two-parent families to decide to maintain two incomes to meet financial obligations and pay for their children's future college expenses. According to the Census Bureau, in *The 2010 Statistical Abstract* (2008, http://www.census.gov/compendia/statab/), the median income (half of all people earned more and half earned less) in 2007 for married couples with one or more children under the age of 18 years in which both the husband and wife worked was $86,842, which was significantly higher than the $55,638 median income for married-couple families in which the wife was not in the paid labor force. Table 3.1 shows that 69.6% of married women with children under the age of 18 years were in the labor force in 2009, and Table 3.3 shows that 59.7% of married women with children under the age of three years were in the labor force in that year. According to Table 3.2, in 58.9% of married-couple families with children under 18 years old, both parents were employed. Many families have come to depend on women's economic contributions to the household.

WHO CARES FOR CHILDREN IN THE UNITED STATES?
School-Age Children

Married parents who both work and single parents who work need reliable child care. The Federal Interagency Forum on Child and Family Statistics reports in *America's Children in Brief: Key National Indicators of Well-Being, 2010* (July 2010, http://www.childstats.gov/americaschildren/tables.asp) that about half of children in kindergarten through eighth grade were cared for by someone other than their parents in 2005. (See Figure 3.1.) Of those who were cared for by someone other than parents, younger children were more likely to receive home- or center-based care for before- or after-school hours; children in grades four and up were less likely to receive these

TABLE 3.2

Employment status of parents, by age of youngest child and family type, 2009

[Numbers in thousands]

Characteristic	Number 2009	Percent distribution 2009
With own children under 18 years		
Total	34,762	100.0
Parent(s) employed	30,521	87.8
No parent employed	4,241	12.2
Married-couple families	24,223	100.0
Parent(s) employed	23,179	95.7
Mother employed	16,055	66.3
Both parents employed	14,269	58.9
Mother employed, not father	1,786	7.4
Father employed, not mother	7,124	29.4
Neither parent employed	1,044	4.3
Families maintained by women*	8,308	100.0
Mother employed	5,632	67.8
Mother not employed	2,677	32.2
Families maintained by men*	2,231	100.0
Father employed	1,710	76.6
Father not employed	521	23.4
With own children 6 to 17 years, none younger		
Total	19,699	100.0
Parent(s) employed	17,465	88.7
No parent employed	2,234	11.3
Married-couple families	13,449	100.0
Parent(s) employed	12,867	95.7
Mother employed	9,691	72.1
Both parents employed	8,582	63.8
Mother employed, not father	1,109	8.2
Father employed, not mother	3,176	23.6
Neither parent employed	582	4.3
Families maintained by women*	4,928	100.0
Mother employed	3,578	72.6
Mother not employed	1,350	27.4
Families maintained by men*	1,321	100.0
Father employed	1,019	77.1
Father not employed	302	22.9
With own children under 6 years		
Total	15,063	100.0
Parent(s) employed	13,056	86.7
No parent employed	2,007	13.3
Married-couple families	10,774	100.0
Parent(s) employed	10,312	95.7
Mother employed	6,364	59.1
Both parents employed	5,688	52.8
Mother employed, not father	676	6.3
Father employed, not mother	3,948	36.6
Neither parent employed	462	4.3
Families maintained by women*	3,380	100.0
Mother employed	2,053	60.8
Mother not employed	1,327	39.2
Families maintained by men*	910	100.0
Father employed	691	75.9
Father not employed	219	24.1

*No spouse present.
Notes: Own children include sons, daughters, step-children, and adopted children. Not included are nieces, nephews, grandchildren, and other related and unrelated children. Detail may not sum to totals due to rounding. Updated population controls are introduced annually with the release of January data.

SOURCE: Adapted from "Table 4. Families with Own Children: Employment Status of Parents by Age of Youngest Child and Family Type, 2008–09 Annual Averages," in *Employment Characteristics of Families—2009*, U.S. Department of Labor, Bureau of Labor Statistics, May 27, 2010, http://www.bls.gov/news.release/pdf/famee.pdf (accessed October 22, 2010)

types of care and more likely to care for themselves. The report notes that only 2.6% of children in kindergarten through third grade cared for themselves regularly, whereas 22.2% of older children did.

SELF-CARE—LATCHKEY KIDS. The term *latchkey kids* is used to describe children who are left alone or unsupervised either during the day or before or after school. These are children five to 14 years of age whose parents report "child cares for self" as either the primary or secondary child care arrangement. In 2005 approximately 5.6 million school-age children cared for themselves regularly without adult supervision. (See Table 3.4.) Self-care was higher among children who lived with their father without their mother present than it was among children who lived with their mother, with or without their father present, in all age groups. Most of these children were 12 years and older, but 1.5 million children 11 years and younger regularly took care of themselves. In *Who's Minding the Kids? Child Care Arrangements: Spring 2005/Summer 2006* (August 2010, http://www.census.gov/prod/2010pubs/p70-121.pdf), Lynda Laughlin of the Census Bureau finds that the percentage of children in self-care declined between 1997 and 2005.

TWENTY-FIRST-CENTURY COMMUNITY LEARNING CENTERS. More than half of all families use after-school programs, and in many families parents rely on after-school care to provide a safe and nurturing place for their children while they are working. In response to concerns about the availability of quality after-school programs, the U.S. Department of Education initiated Twenty-First-Century Community Learning Centers (21st CCLC), which was authorized under Title X, Part I, of the Elementary and Secondary Education Act and reauthorized under Title IV, Part B, of the No Child Left Behind Act. This initiative gives grants to low-performance elementary and middle schools in rural and urban areas to provide after-school opportunities for their students, both educational and recreational. In 1997 the 21st CCLC had a budget of only $1 million; however, by fiscal year 2010 the program's budget had increased 10-fold, to nearly $1.2 billion. According to the Department of Education, in "21st CCLC Profile and Performance Information Collection System" (2010, http://ppics.learningpt.org/ppics/publicGrantSearch.asp), by December 2010 the 21st CCLC supported 4,418 after-school programs across the country.

Deborah Lowe Vandell, Elizabeth R. Reisner, and Kim M. Pierce note in *Outcomes Linked to High-Quality After-school Programs: Longitudinal Findings from the Study of Promising Afterschool Programs* (October 2007, http://www.newdayforlearning.org/docs/HIllPPReport.pdf) that participation in high-quality after-school programs in 2007 was associated with improved outcomes among disadvantaged students. The study included a group of 3,000 low-income, ethnically diverse elementary and middle school students. These students improved their

TABLE 3.3

Employment status of mothers with own children under three years old, by single year of age of youngest child and marital status, 2009

[Numbers in thousands]

Characteristic	Civilian noninsti-tutional population	Total	Percent of population	Civilian labor force					
				Employed				Unemployed	
				Total	Percent of population	Full-time workers[a]	Part-time workers[b]	Number	Percent of labor force
2009									
Total mothers									
With own children under 3 years old	9,476	5,787	61.1	5,191	54.8	3,626	1,565	595	10.3
2 years	2,848	1,855	65.1	1,693	59.4	1,195	498	162	8.7
1 year	3,398	2,104	61.9	1,880	55.3	1,314	566	224	10.6
Under 1 year	3,231	1,828	56.6	1,619	50.1	1,117	502	209	11.4
Married, spouse present									
With own children under 3 years old	6,784	4,047	59.7	3,780	55.7	2,657	1,123	267	6.6
2 years	2,053	1,288	62.7	1,208	58.8	858	350	80	6.2
1 year	2,425	1,465	60.4	1,369	56.4	963	406	96	6.6
Under 1 year	2,306	1,293	56.1	1,204	52.2	836	368	90	7.0
Other marital status[c]									
With own children under 3 years old	2,693	1,740	64.6	1,411	52.4	969	442	328	18.9
2 years	795	567	71.3	485	61.0	337	148	82	14.4
1 year	973	639	65.6	511	52.5	351	160	127	20.0
Under 1 year	925	534	57.8	415	44.9	281	134	119	22.3

[a]Usually work 35 hours or more a week at all jobs.
[b]Usually work less than 35 hours a week at all jobs.
[c]Includes never married; married, spouse absent; divorced; separated; and widowed persons.
Notes: Own children include sons, daughters, step-children, and adopted children. Not included are nieces, nephews, grandchildren, and other related and unrelated children. Detail may not sum to totals due to rounding. Updated population controls are introduced annually with the release of January data.

SOURCE: Adapted from "Table 6. Employment Status of Mothers with Own Children under 3 Years Old by Single Year of Age of Youngest Child and Marital Status, 2008–09 Annual Averages," in *Employment Characteristics of Families—2009*, U.S. Department of Labor, Bureau of Labor Statistics, May 27, 2010, http://www.bls.gov/news.release/pdf/famee.pdf (accessed October 22, 2010)

FIGURE 3.1

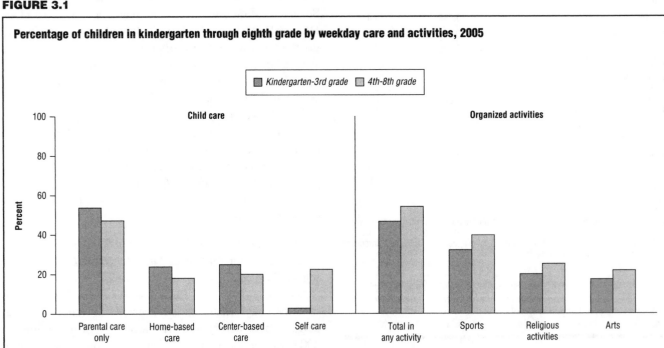

Percentage of children in kindergarten through eighth grade by weekday care and activities, 2005

SOURCE: "Figure FAM3.C. Percentage of Children in Kindergarten through 8th-Grade by Weekday Care and Activities, 2005," in *America's Children in Brief: Key National Indicators of Well-Being, 2010*, Federal Interagency Forum on Child and Family Statistics, July 2010, http://www.childstats.gov/americaschildren/fam_fig.asp#fam3c (accessed October 15, 2010)

TABLE 3.4

Prevalence of self-care among grade school-aged children by selected characteristics for those living with mother, 2005

[Numbers in thousands]

Characteristic	Total	Age of child 5 to 11 years	Age of child 12 to 14 years
Total children 5 to 14 years	**39,570**	**26,986**	**12,584**
Living with father[a]	**1,732**	**1,050**	**683**
Number in self-care	330	76	254
Percent in self-care	19.0	7.2	37.2
Living with mother	**37,837**	**25,937**	**11,901**
Number in self-care	5,285	1,404	3,881
Percent in self-care	14.0	5.4	32.6
Race and Hispanic origin of mother			
White alone	14.6	5.8	33.9
Non-Hispanic	16.0	6.3	36.4
Black alone	11.8	4.3	27.7
Asian alone	8.4	2.8	22.0
Hispanic (any race)	9.7	3.8	24.1
Marital status of mother			
Married[b]	13.2	4.9	32.0
Separated, divorced, widowed	19.5	8.6	37.4
Never married	10.8	4.7	27.6
Poverty status of family[c]			
Below poverty level	10.4	5.1	22.9
At or above poverty level	14.9	5.5	34.7
100–199 percent of poverty level	10.5	4.1	25.7
200 percent of poverty level or higher	16.6	6.1	37.9
Employment schedule of mother			
Not employed	8.5	3.5	21.3
Employed (all)	16.5	6.4	37.2
Self-employed	15.1	6.7	32.2
Not self-employed[d]	16.7	6.3	37.7
Full-time[e]	18.0	6.7	39.9
Part-time	13.2	5.3	31.3
Worked day shift	17.5	6.7	39.1
Worked nonday shift	15.0	5.7	34.9
Enrichment activities of child			
Participated in an activity	21.2	9.3	49.4
Did not participate in an activity	12.8	4.8	30.1
Average hours per week in self-care among children in self-care	**6.0**	**4.9**	**6.4**
Number of hours in self-care per week			
(Percent distribution)			
Total	**100.0**	**100.0**	**100.0**
Less than 2 hours	28.4	37.6	25.1
2 to 4 hours	26.8	24.5	27.6
5 to 9 hours	23.9	22.5	24.4
10 or more hours	20.9	15.4	22.9

[a]Mother not present in the household, so father is the designated parent. Self-care is not shown by father's characteristics due to small sample size.
[b]Includes married spouse present and spouse absent (excluding separated).
[c]Excludes those with missing income data.
[d]Includes mothers with wage and salary jobs and employment arrangements other than self-employed.
[e]Those who work 35 or more hours per week are considered working full-time.

SOURCE: Lynda Laughlin, Table 5. Prevalence of Self-Care among Grade School-Aged Children by Selected Characteristics for Those Living with Mother: Spring 2005," in *Who's Minding the Kids? Child Care Arrangements: Spring 2005/Summer 2006*, U.S. Census Bureau, August 2010, http://www.census.gov/prod/2010pubs/p70–121.pdf (accessed October 22, 2010)

standardized test scores and work habits and reduced problem behaviors. They also posted gains in teacher-reported social skills.

Children Younger Than Five (Preschoolers)

During the summer of 2006, 84.6% of children aged four years and younger whose mothers worked were in nonparental care at least some of the time. (See Table 3.5.) The largest proportion of these children were in center-based care (15.8%), followed by grandparent care (13.4%) and other nonrelative care (9.6%). Fathers watched children whose mothers worked 12.8% of the time.

The Federal Interagency Forum on Child and Family Statistics reports in *America's Children in Brief* that 50.7% of children under the age of two years and 73.7% of children aged three to six years were in nonparental care at least some of the time in 2005. Among the youngest children, home-based care by a relative was the most common (22%), followed by care in a center-based program (19.6%) and home-based care by a nonrelative (15.6%). Among older preschoolers, center-based programs were by far the most common; 57.1% of three- to six-year-olds were enrolled in these programs, whereas 22.7% were cared for in a home by a relative and 11.7% were cared for in a home by a nonrelative. These numbers reflect the fact that as their children grow from infancy to school age, working mothers often change child care arrangements to meet the needs of their children, their families, and their employers. Making child care arrangements for infants and toddlers is often more difficult than for older children because fewer organized child care facilities admit infants and very young children, primarily due to the cost involved in hiring enough workers and adapting facilities to provide adequate care for babies. In addition, many parents prefer, if possible, to keep their infants in a home environment as long as possible. Also, many mothers view center-based programs, which often have an educational focus, as most appropriate for older preschoolers.

FACTORS THAT AFFECT CHILD CARE
Preschool Child Care

RACIAL AND ETHNIC DIFFERENCES. In 2006 Hispanic mothers of preschoolers relied more heavily on relatives to provide child care than did other mothers. More than one out of five (20.3%) Hispanic preschoolers were cared for by grandparents or other relatives in that year, compared with 16.4% of non-Hispanic white preschoolers and 16.1% of non-Hispanic African-American preschoolers. (See Table 3.5.) Non-Hispanic white preschoolers (27.4%) and non-Hispanic African-American preschoolers (24.9%) were more likely to be cared for by nonrelatives or in center-based programs than were Hispanic preschoolers (20.1%).

TABLE 3.5

Percentage of preschool children by type of care arrangement and child and family characteristics, selected years 1985–2006

Type of child care (during mother's work hours)	1985	1988	1990	1991	1993	1995	1997	1999	2002	2005	2006[a]
Percent											
Total											
Mother care[b]	8.1	7.6	6.4	8.7	6.2	5.4	3.2	3.0	3.2	4.4	2.5
Father care[b]	15.7	15.1	16.5	20.0	15.9	16.6	17.7	17.1	17.5	17.3	12.8
Grandparent care	15.9	13.9	14.3	15.8	17.0	15.9	17.5	19.7	18.6	19.6	13.4
Other relative care[c]	8.2	7.2	8.8	7.7	9.0	5.5	7.4	8.0	6.2	6.6	3.8
Center-based care[d]	23.1	25.8	27.5	23.1	29.9	25.1	20.4	21.0	24.3	23.8	15.8
Other nonrelative care[e]	28.2	28.9	25.1	23.3	21.6	28.4	20.2	18.8	17.2	16.0	9.6
Other[f]	0.8	1.6	1.3	1.6	1.1	2.9	13.7	12.4	13.0	12.0	42.0
Poverty status											
Below 100% poverty											
Mother care[b]	—	11.3	—	9.5	8.1	4.5	3.9	2.9	4.1	7.8	1.2
Father care[b]	—	15.0	—	26.7	16.2	20.1	18.7	14.5	19.9	19.8	13.6
Grandparent care	—	19.4	—	16.3	20.0	22.4	20.7	23.8	19.7	19.8	16.2
Other relative care[c]	—	11.3	—	11.4	15.8	7.0	12.3	13.5	10.0	8.8	4.8
Center-based care[d]	—	21.6	—	21.1	21.0	25.8	14.9	18.3	15.9	18.2	12.2
Other nonrelative care[e]	—	21.1	—	15.1	18.8	16.5	14.7	18.0	12.6	11.8	4.6
Other[f]	—	0.8	—	2.7	1.2	3.5	14.6	8.8	17.6	13.7	47.3
100% poverty and above											
Mother care[b]	—	7.3	—	8.5	5.9	5.5	3.1	2.9	3.1	3.8	2.5
Father care[b]	—	15.1	—	19.4	16.0	16.4	17.7	17.6	17.3	17.1	12.7
Grandparent care	—	13.4	—	15.6	16.0	15.1	17.2	19.3	18.7	19.7	13.2
Other relative care[c]	—	6.8	—	7.3	8.0	5.3	6.8	7.3	5.7	6.2	3.7
Center-based care[d]	—	27.8	—	25.1	32.3	24.8	21.2	21.1	25.1	24.8	16.4
Other nonrelative care[e]	—	29.6	—	24.2	21.8	29.9	20.9	19.4	18.4	16.7	10.3
Other[f]	—	1.6	—	1.5	1.1	2.8	12.9	12.2	11.7	11.4	41.2
Race and Hispanic origin of mother[g]											
White											
Mother care[b]	—	—	—	—	—	5.8	3.7	3.2	3.5	4.8	2.8
Father care[b]	—	—	—	—	—	17.8	18.7	18.1	18.4	18.4	13.8
Grandparent care	—	—	—	—	—	15.5	16.5	17.7	17.9	19.2	13.6
Other relative care[c]	—	—	—	—	—	4.5	6.5	7.6	4.9	5.5	3.5
Center-based care[d]	—	—	—	—	—	24.3	19.8	20.1	23.2	22.4	15.5
Other nonrelative care[e]	—	—	—	—	—	29.0	21.2	20.9	18.4	17.1	10.5
Other[f]	—	—	—	—	—	2.9	13.6	12.1	13.5	12.4	40.3
White, non-Hispanic											
Mother care[b]	—	—	—	—	—	6.1	4.0	3.2	3.7	4.9	3.1
Father care[b]	—	—	—	—	—	17.6	18.9	18.1	19.1	19.3	14.0
Grandparent care	—	—	—	—	—	15.4	15.3	17.0	16.5	17.5	13.7
Other relative care[c]	—	—	—	—	—	4.0	5.7	6.2	3.6	3.8	2.7
Center-based care[d]	—	—	—	—	—	24.8	21.0	22.2	24.3	24.5	16.4
Other nonrelative care[e]	—	—	—	—	—	29.4	21.1	21.3	19.6	17.7	11.0
Other[f]	—	—	—	—	—	2.7	13.9	12.0	13.3	12.0	38.9
Black											
Mother care[b]	—	—	—	—	—	2.1	0.7	1.8	1.2	3.1	0.7
Father care[b]	—	—	—	—	—	8.8	11.9	12.9	13.5	12.3	7.2
Grandparent care	—	—	—	—	—	16.0	23.7	25.1	21.6	19.5	10.3
Other relative care[c]	—	—	—	—	—	9.9	13.2	10.6	12.6	10.9	5.8
Center-based care[d]	—	—	—	—	—	32.5	25.8	27.0	27.4	29.6	17.9
Other nonrelative care[e]	—	—	—	—	—	28.3	14.3	13.1	14.3	13.3	6.4
Other[f]	—	—	—	—	—	2.3	10.2	9.4	9.2	11.1	51.4

POVERTY MAKES A DIFFERENCE. According to the Federal Interagency Forum on Child and Family Statistics, in *America's Children in Brief*, 85.3% of preschoolers whose mothers worked full time (35 hours or more each week) and 69.7% of preschoolers whose mothers worked part time were regularly in nonparental care in 2005. However, the type of care varied by the income levels of these families. A substantial number of children from low-income families are cared for in unregulated home-based settings. Gina Adams, Kathryn Tout, and Martha Zaslow note in *Early Care and Education for Children in Low-Income Families: Patterns of Use, Quality, and Potential Policy Implications* (May 2007, http://www.urban.org/Uploaded PDF/411482_early_care.pdf) that "several observational studies have found unregulated home-based care of lower quality than regulated home-based settings in which low-income children participate. Studies question specific aspects of quality, such as prolonged exposure to television, missed opportunities for learning, and health and safety issues." In "Snapshots of America's Families III: Children in Low-Income Families Are Less Likely to Be in Center-Based Child Care" (January 27, 2004, http://www.urban .org/UploadedPDF/310923_snapshots3_no16.pdf), Jeffrey Capizzano and Gina Adams find that preschoolers from lower-income families (families with an income less than 200% of the poverty line) were less likely to be in

TABLE 3.5

Percentage of preschool children by type of care arrangement and child and family characteristics, selected years 1985–2006 [CONTINUED]

Type of child care (during mother's work hours)	1985	1988	1990	1991	1993	1995	1997	1999	2002	2005	2006[a]
Black, non-Hispanic											
Mother care[b]	—	—	—	—	—	2.2	0.8	1.9	1.2	3.3	0.7
Father care[b]	—	—	—	—	—	8.9	11.7	12.4	13.2	11.9	6.9
Grandparent care	—	—	—	—	—	15.7	23.9	24.4	22.9	19.5	10.1
Other relative care[c]	—	—	—	—	—	10.1	13.0	10.9	12.0	11.3	6.0
Center-based care[d]	—	—	—	—	—	33.2	26.4	27.5	27.0	29.5	18.3
Other nonrelative care[e]	—	—	—	—	—	27.9	13.9	13.5	13.7	13.2	6.6
Other[f]	—	—	—	—	—	1.9	10.3	9.3	9.9	11.2	51.0
Hispanic											
Mother care[b]	—	—	—	—	—	3.6	1.3	2.6	2.7	3.4	1.6
Father care[b]	—	—	—	—	—	19.0	17.5	18.6	15.1	14.7	12.6
Grandparent care	—	—	—	—	—	17.0	23.2	21.9	23.9	27.0	14.5
Other relative care[c]	—	—	—	—	—	8.7	12.6	14.0	12.0	12.8	5.8
Center-based care[d]	—	—	—	—	—	20.8	12.4	10.9	19.8	14.2	12.3
Other nonrelative care[e]	—	—	—	—	—	25.0	21.7	18.2	13.9	14.2	7.8
Other[f]	—	—	—	—	—	5.8	11.4	13.6	12.6	13.7	45.4
Educational attainment of mother											
Less than high school											
Mother care[b]	—	—	—	—	—	6.3	3.6	1.7	4.1	5.4	2.1
Father care[b]	—	—	—	—	—	18.2	17.5	14.4	19.2	22.3	10.7
Grandparent care	—	—	—	—	—	21.2	18.4	23.4	15.5	16.7	19.1
Other relative care[c]	—	—	—	—	—	10.8	15.2	20.7	12.0	15.4	9.4
Center-based care[d]	—	—	—	—	—	16.9	12.7	16.3	17.5	12.0	6.0
Other nonrelative care[e]	—	—	—	—	—	20.8	17.3	13.5	17.4	11.7	7.1
Other[f]	—	—	—	—	—	4.8	15.2	9.9	14.2	16.2	45.3
High school diploma or equivalent											
Mother care[b]	—	—	—	—	—	5.6	2.1	3.5	2.5	4.1	2.4
Father care[b]	—	—	—	—	—	16.6	19.0	20.3	19.7	16.6	12.1
Grandparent care	—	—	—	—	—	20.5	20.3	23.5	23.2	25.7	16.2
Other relative care[c]	—	—	—	—	—	5.4	7.8	7.9	6.0	9.4	4.9
Center-based care[d]	—	—	—	—	—	25.7	18.1	18.8	20.0	18.4	11.5
Other nonrelative care[e]	—	—	—	—	—	23.2	19.0	14.2	14.5	13.0	6.9
Other[f]	—	—	—	—	—	2.6	13.6	11.7	13.9	12.7	45.8
Some college, including vocational/ technical/associate's degree											
Mother care[b]	—	—	—	—	—	4.9	3.5	1.9	3.2	4.3	1.6
Father care[b]	—	—	—	—	—	18.4	19.3	16.7	19.3	17.7	12.8
Grandparent care	—	—	—	—	—	14.2	18.5	20.1	20.8	21.9	13.2
Other relative care[c]	—	—	—	—	—	5.8	7.1	7.4	7.5	6.6	4.3
Center-based care[d]	—	—	—	—	—	25.6	22.1	18.6	23.2	23.8	13.7
Other nonrelative care[e]	—	—	—	—	—	27.7	16.6	21.1	15.3	15.5	9.3
Other[f]	—	—	—	—	—	3.1	12.8	14.1	10.6	10.1	44.9
Bachelor's degree or higher											
Mother care[b]	—	—	—	—	—	5.2	3.7	4.0	3.5	4.6	3.4
Father care[b]	—	—	—	—	—	14.4	14.9	15.7	13.7	16.6	13.6
Grandparent care	—	—	—	—	—	11.4	13.5	14.4	13.9	13.1	10.9
Other relative care[c]	—	—	—	—	—	3.4	5.0	4.0	3.4	2.7	1.5
Center-based care[d]	—	—	—	—	—	26.0	23.5	27.5	29.9	30.5	22.4
Other nonrelative care[e]	—	—	—	—	—	36.9	26.6	24.4	22.6	19.9	12.1
Other[f]	—	—	—	—	—	2.3	12.6	9.9	13.0	12.7	35.9
Family structure											
Two married parents											
Mother care[b]	—	—	—	—	—	6.2	3.7	3.4	3.5	4.9	2.9
Father care[b]	—	—	—	—	—	18.7	20.6	19.9	20.6	19.5	13.5
Grandparent care	—	—	—	—	—	14.4	14.7	16.4	17.3	17.6	11.6
Other relative care[c]	—	—	—	—	—	4.8	6.0	6.4	4.7	4.8	2.4
Center-based care[d]	—	—	—	—	—	23.0	19.6	20.7	22.7	24.0	16.8
Other nonrelative care[e]	—	—	—	—	—	29.4	20.9	19.7	17.2	16.3	10.1
Other[f]	—	—	—	—	—	3.1	14.4	13.4	13.8	12.7	42.5

center-based care (24.9%) than children from higher-income families (31.2%). The Federal Interagency Forum on Child and Family Statistics indicates in *America's Children in Brief* that data support this conclusion. In 2005, 42.2% of preschoolers from families whose incomes were above 200% of the poverty line were in center-based care, compared with 29.4% of children from families with incomes 100% to 199% of the poverty line and 28.3% of children from families with incomes below the poverty line.

FORMAL CHILD CARE FACILITIES

Even though no comprehensive data exist on the types or quality of child care facilities in the United States, the National Association for Regulatory Administration

TABLE 3.5

Percentage of preschool children by type of care arrangement and child and family characteristics, selected years 1985–2006 [CONTINUED]

Type of child care (during mother's work hours)	1985	1988	1990	1991	1993	1995	1997	1999	2002	2005	2006[a]
Mother only											
Mother care[b]	—	—	—	—	—	2.8	1.5	1.9	2.5	3.0	1.4
Father care[b]	—	—	—	—	—	10.4	9.1	10.1	9.8	12.1	11.0
Grandparent care	—	—	—	—	—	20.5	26.6	29.1	22.7	24.5	18.1
Other relative care[c]	—	—	—	—	—	7.2	12.3	12.2	10.2	11.0	7.5
Center-based care[d]	—	—	—	—	—	30.3	23.1	21.5	27.0	23.4	13.0
Other nonrelative care[e]	—	—	—	—	—	26.1	17.7	17.6	18.4	15.6	8.4
Other[f]	—	—	—	—	—	2.4	9.5	7.4	9.2	10.2	40.3

—Not available.

[a]SIPP child care data collected in 2006 cannot be compared directly with SIPP child care data from previous years due to seasonality differences such as preschool closings, seasonal variations in school activities, and availability of child care arrangements. The 2006 child care data was collected during summer months, whereas previous survey years typically collected data during spring or fall months.

[b]Mother and father care includes care while the mother worked.

[c]Other relatives include siblings and other relatives.

[d]Center-based care includes day care centers, nursery schools, preschools, and Head Start programs.

[e]Other nonrelative care includes family day care providers, in-home babysitters, and other nonrelatives providing care in either the child's or provider's home.

[f]Other for 1985–1993 includes children in kindergarten or grade school, in a school-based activity, or in self care. In 1995, it also includes children with no regular arrangement. Beginning in 1997, other includes children in kindergarten or grade school, self-care, and with no regular arrangement, but does not include school-based activities, as they were deleted as categorical choices for preschoolers.

[g]For race and Hispanic-origin data in this table: From 1995 to 2002, following the 1977 OMB standards for collecting and presenting data on race, the Survey of Income and Program Participation (SIPP) asked respondents to choose one race from the following: White, Black, American Indian or Alaskan Native, or Asian or Pacific Islander. The Census Bureau also offered an "Other" category. Beginning in 2004, following the 1997 OMB standards for collecting and presenting data on race, the SIPP asked respondents to choose one or more races from the following: White, Black or African American, Asian, American Indian or Alaska Native, or Native Hawaiian or Other Pacific Islander. The Census Bureau also offered an "Other" category. All race groups discussed in this table from 2004 onward refer to people who indicated only one racial identity within the racial categories presented. People who responded to the question on race by indicating only one race are referred to as the race-alone population. The use of the race-alone population in this table does not imply that it is the preferred method of presenting or analyzing data. Data from 2004 onward are not directly comparable with data from earlier years. Data on race and Hispanic origin are collected separately. Persons of Hispanic origin may be of any race.

Notes: Employed mothers are those with wage and salary employment or other employment arrangements including contingent work and self-employment. Data for years 1995 to 2005 were proportionally redistributed to account for tied responses for the primary arrangement so that they total to 100 percent and are comparable to earlier years. Data for 2006 was also proportionally redistributed, but is not comparable to earlier years due to seasonality differences.

estimates in *The 2008 Child Care Licensing Study* (May 2010, http://www.naralicensing.org/associations/4734/files/1005_2008_Child%20Care%20Licensing%20Study_Full_Report.pdf) that in 2008 there were 329,882 licensed child care facilities in the United States, including 107,199 licensed child care centers and 199,216 licensed family child care homes. More than 9.8 million children are taken care of in these licensed facilities, and over 75% of these children are in center-based programs. Many more unlicensed child care facilities exist, but because they are not regulated, no reliable statistics are collected.

The Federal Interagency Forum on Child and Family Statistics reports in *America's Children in Brief* that 50.7% of all children aged two and under and 73.7% of all children aged three to six years spent time in nonparental care each week in 2005. Their care providers are major influences in their lives. Many working parents discover that quality and affordable care is difficult to find. In some communities child care is hard to find at any cost. Shortages of child care for infants, sick children, and children with special needs and for school children before and after school pose problems for many parents.

Regulations and Quality of Care

Federal assistance to low-income families to pay for child care eroded during the late 20th century at the same time that the government imposed requirements that more low-income parents work. The 1996 welfare reform law, the Personal Responsibility and Work Opportunity Reconciliation Act, eliminated the guarantee that families on welfare would receive subsidized child care and replaced it with the Child Care and Development Block Grant to states. Even though the legislation gave states wide discretion in the use of these funds, it also imposed penalties if states failed to meet criteria for getting low-income parents into the workforce.

This legislation pushed the issue of regulation of child care facilities to the forefront. In 1989 the National Institute of Child Health and Human Development (NICHD) initiated the Study of Early Child Care. This comprehensive ongoing longitudinal study was designed to answer many questions about the relationship between child care experiences and children's developmental outcomes. The 1999 phase of the study examined whether the amount of time children spent in child care affected their interactions with their mother. The results showed that the number of hours infants and toddlers spent in child care was modestly linked to the sensitivity of the mother to her child, as well as to the engagement of the child with the mother in play activities. Children in consistent quality day care showed less problem behavior, whereas those who switched day care arrangements showed more problem behaviors. Children in quality care centers had higher cognitive and language development than those in lower-quality centers.

The second phase of the study, *The NICHD Study of Early Child Care and Youth Development: Findings for Children up to Age 4 1/2 Years* (January 2006, http://www.nichd.nih.gov/publications/pubs/upload/seccyd_051206.pdf), found that the quality of child care had an impact on children's social and intellectual development. The study defined a better quality of care as care that met ideal adult-to-child ratios, maintained ideal group sizes, and had well-trained child care providers. It also focused on the quality of children's actual day-to-day experiences in child care by observing children's social interactions and their activities with toys.

The study found that children who were in higher-quality child care had better cognitive function and language development in the first three years of life, as well as greater school readiness by age four and a half. Children in higher-quality care were also more sensitive to other children, more cooperative, and less aggressive and disobedient than were children in lower-quality care. Lastly, the study found that children who were cared for in child care centers rather than in home-based care had better cognitive and language development, but also showed somewhat more behavior problems both in the child care setting and once they began kindergarten.

Child Care during Nonstandard Hours

Many parents choose to have one parent work nonstandard hours to allow both parents to provide child care at different times of the day. According to the BLS, in the press release "Workers on Flexible and Shift Schedules in May 2004" (July 1, 2005, http://www.bls.gov/news.release/pdf/flex.pdf), in 2004, the most recent year for which statistics were available as of January 2011, 27 million workers, or 27.5% of all full-time wage and salary workers, worked flexible hours and were able to vary their work hours to fit their schedules. That number was more than twice as many workers as in May 1985, but down from a high of 28.6% in May 2001. Flexible schedules were most common among managers (44.7%) and professionals (31.5%), and were more common among non-Hispanic white (28.7%) and Asian-American (27.4%) workers than among African-American (19.7%) and Hispanic (18.4%) workers. By contrast, the percentage of those who worked an evening or overnight shift had fallen from 18% in 1991 to 14.8% in 2004. When asked why they worked a non-daytime schedule, 8.2% of shift workers answered they did so for better family or child care arrangements.

THE COST OF CHILD CARE

In August 2010 the National Association of Child Care Resource and Referral Agencies (NACCRRA) published *Parents and the High Cost of Child Care: 2010 Update* (http://www.naccrra.org/docs/Cost_Report_073010-final

.pdf), which surveyed child care costs across the country. The survey shows that the average yearly cost for child care in a child care center for a four-year-old ranged from $4,050 in Mississippi to $13,150 in Massachusetts. For an infant, annual costs jumped to $4,550 in Mississippi and to $18,750 in Massachusetts.

Low-Income Families

The NACCRRA notes in *Parents and the High Cost of Child Care: 2010 Update* that in 2009 an infant in a two-parent family with an income at the poverty level ($18,310) paid an average of 48.7% of their income for center-based care. Families at 150% of the poverty level ($27,465) paid 32.5% of their income on center-based care, and families at 200% of the poverty level ($36,620) paid 24.3% of their income on center-based care. In some states the proportion of income spent for infant care was even higher.

In *Who's Minding the Kids? Child Care Arrangements: Summer 2006 Detailed Tables* (2009, http://www.census.gov/population/www/socdemo/child/tables-2006.html), the Census Bureau estimates that in 2006 the average married-couple family with a working mother with a preschool child spent 8.5% of its income on child care, whereas single mothers spent 11% of their family income on child care. Families living below the poverty level in which the mother was employed paid an average of $73 per week (29.2% of the family income) in child care costs, compared with families not in poverty, who paid an average of $145 per week (8.8% of the family income). Many poor and low-income families were forced to enroll their children in low-cost, and often poor-quality, child care centers. As a result, these children spent much of their day in unstimulating and possibly unsafe environments.

Government Assistance with Child Care

BLOCK GRANTS. In some cases low-income and poor parents can receive government assistance in paying for child care. Recognizing that child care assistance helps contribute to a productive workforce, every state has a child care assistance program that subsidizes some child care using federal block grant money and state funds for those on welfare and for low-income working families. In some states parents receive a voucher that they can use to pay for a portion of child care costs; in other states payments are made directly to the child care provider of the parents' choice. However, according to the U.S. Government Accountability Office, in *Child Care: Multiple Factors Could Have Contributed to the Recent Decline in the Number of Children Whose Families Receive Subsidies* (May 2010, http://www.gao.gov/new.items/d10344.pdf), the number of children who received child care assistance between 2006 and 2008 actually declined by 170,000 children. Only 17% of eligible children received assistance in 2008.

HEAD START. Perhaps the best-known and most successful government-funded child care program is Head Start, a federal program begun in 1965 under the Administration for Children and Families (ACF) of the U.S. Department of Health and Human Services. The free program provides early education, health care, social services, and free meals to preschool children in families whose incomes are below the poverty line or who receive public assistance. In "Head Start Program Fact Sheet" (2010, http://www.acf.hhs.gov/programs/ohs/about/fy2010.html), the ACF states that Head Start operates in every state, and in fiscal year 2009 it served 904,153 children. The Children's Defense Fund reports in "Head Start Basics: 2005" (April 2005, http://cdf.childrensdefense.org/site/Doc Server/headstartbasics2005.pdf?docID=616) that the program provides many benefits, including a greater likelihood that children will do well in school and graduate from high school. Nevertheless, the program came under some criticism for a lack of accountability built into funding policies. The editorial "A New Beginning for Head Start" (*Washington Post*, October 4, 2010) reports on new funding rules that were proposed by the Department of Health and Human Services. If adopted, the rules would require that the bottom 25% of Head Start organizations be required to reapply for their grants.

TAX CREDITS. The Federal Dependent Care Tax Credit helps families by allowing them to claim an income tax credit for part of their child care expenses for children under the age of 13 years. The credit is on a sliding scale, ranging from 20% to 35% of qualified expenses; therefore, lower-income families receive slightly larger credits.

According to the Internal Revenue Service, in "Child and Dependent Care Credit" (2010, http://www.irs.gov/publi cations/p17/ch32.html#d0e71607), in 2010 parents could claim up to $3,000 in qualified expenses for one child or $6,000 for two or more children.

FAMILY LEAVE. In 1993 Congress enacted the Family and Medical Leave Act (FMLA), requiring employers with 50 or more employees to give unpaid time off (12 weeks in any 12-month period) to employees to care for newborn or newly adopted children, sick family members, or for personal illness. The employee must be returned to the same position—or one equivalent in pay, benefits, and other terms of employment—and must receive uninterrupted health benefits. The U.S. Department of Labor reports that before this legislation, fewer than a quarter of all workers received family leave benefits and that most of those who did worked in establishments of more than 100 employees.

As of January 2011, the most recent information on family and medical leave takers came from a government survey that was conducted in 2000. Jane Waldfogel of Columbia University states in "Family and Medical Leave: Evidence from the 2000 Surveys" (*Monthly Labor Review*, September 2001) that in 2000, 17.9% of FMLA leave takers took their leave to care for a newborn, newly adopted, or newly placed foster child; 9.8% used it to care for a sick child; and 7.8% used it as maternity or disability time. Of all employees covered by the FMLA with children 18 months and younger, 45.1% of men and 75.8% of women had taken an FMLA leave in the previous 18 months.

CHAPTER 4
HEALTH AND SAFETY

FACTORS AFFECTING CHILDREN'S HEALTH

A variety of factors affect children's health. These range from prenatal influences; access to and quality of health care; poverty, homelessness, and hunger; childhood diseases; and diet and exercise. This chapter discusses these factors and looks at the leading causes of death among infants, children, and adolescents.

Birth Defects

In "Birth Defects: Frequently Asked Questions (FAQs)" (October 28, 2009, http://www.cdc.gov/ncbddd/bd/faq1.htm), the Centers for Disease Control and Prevention (CDC) indicates that birth defects affect one out of every 33 babies born. Birth defects are the leading cause of infant deaths. In addition, these babies have a greater chance of illness and disability than do babies without birth defects. Two major birth defects, neural tube defects and fetal alcohol syndrome, are in large part preventable.

NEURAL TUBE DEFECTS. Major defects of the brain and spine are called neural tube defects. According to the CDC, in "Birth Defects," each year neural tube defects caused by the incomplete closing of the spine and skull affect one out of every 1,000 pregnancies. The occurrence of these defects can be greatly reduced by adequate folic acid consumption before and during early pregnancy.

FETAL ALCOHOL SYNDROME. The CDC reports in "Fetal Alcohol Spectrum Disorders (FASDs): Facts about FASDs" (October 6, 2010, http://www.cdc.gov/ncbddd/fasd/facts.html) that alcohol consumption by pregnant women can cause fetal alcohol syndrome (FAS), a birth defect that is characterized by low birth weight, facial abnormalities such as small eye openings, growth retardation, and central nervous system deficits, including learning and developmental disabilities. The condition is a lifelong, disabling condition that puts these affected children at risk for secondary conditions, such as mental health problems, criminal behavior, alcohol and drug abuse, and inappropriate sexual behavior. Not all children affected by prenatal alcohol use are born with the full syndrome, but they may have selected abnormalities.

According to the CDC, in "Fetal Alcohol Spectrum Disorders (FASDs): Data and Statistics" (October 6, 2010, http://www.cdc.gov/ncbddd/fasd/data.html), estimates of the prevalence of FAS vary from 0.2 to 1.5 per 1,000 births in different areas of the United States. Other alcohol-related birth defects are thought to occur three times as often as FAS. In "Alcohol Use among Pregnant and Nonpregnant Women of Childbearing Age—United States, 1991–2005" (*Morbidity and Mortality Weekly Report*, vol. 58, no. 19, May 22, 2009), the CDC finds that between 2001 and 2005, 11.2% of pregnant women drank alcohol, putting their babies at risk for FAS. As many as one out of 50 (1.8%) pregnant women reported binge drinking (having five or more drinks on one occasion).

Health Care

IMMUNIZATIONS. In *America's Children in Brief: Key National Indicators of Well-Being, 2010* (July 2010, http://www.childstats.gov/americaschildren/tables.asp), the Federal Interagency Forum on Child and Family Statistics explains that the proportion of preschool-age children immunized against communicable and potentially dangerous childhood diseases—including diphtheria, tetanus, and pertussis (whooping cough), known collectively as DTP, polio, and measles, mumps, and rubella (MMR)—dropped during the 1980s but rose significantly during the 1990s. By 2008, 93.6% of all children had received three doses of the poliovirus vaccine, 93.5% had received three doses of the hepatitis B vaccine, 92.1% had received the MMR vaccine, 90.9% had received the *haemophilus influenzae* type b vaccine, 90.7% had received the varicella (chicken pox) vaccine, and 85% had received four doses of the DTP vaccine. (See Table 4.1.) More than four out of five of these children received the vaccinations in combined

TABLE 4.1

Percentage of children vaccinated for selected diseases, by poverty status, race, and Hispanic origin, 1996 and 2008

Characteristic	Total		Below 100% poverty		100% poverty and above	
	1996	2008	1996	2008	1996	2008
Total						
Combined series (4:3:1:3:3:1)[c]	—	76.1	—	72.4	—	77.7
Combined series (4:3:1:3:3)[d]	67.7	78.2	61.4	74.1	69.9	80.0
Combined series (4:3:1:3)[e]	76.4	79.6	68.9	75.4	79.2	81.4
Combined series (4:3:1)[f]	78.4	—	71.6	—	80.8	—
DTP (4 doses or more)[g]	81.1	85.0	73.9	76.8	83.6	86.5
Polio (3 doses or more)[h]	91.0	93.6	87.7	91.2	92.0	94.0
MMR (1 dose or more)[i]	90.6	92.1	87.2	90.2	91.9	91.5
Hib (3 doses or more)[j]	91.4	90.9	86.9	85.4	93.1	91.9
Hepatitis B (3 doses or more)[k]	81.8	93.5	78.0	90.7	83.2	93.9
Varicella (1 dose or more)[l]	12.2	90.7	5.4	87.5	15.3	90.4
PCV (3 doses or more)[m]	—	92.8	—	88.5	—	93.7
PCV (4 doses or more)[m]	—	80.1	—	72.7	—	83.1
Hepatitis A (2 doses or more)[n]	—	40.4	—	39.7	—	40.8
White, non-Hispanic						
Combined series (4:3:1:3:3:1)[c]	—	75.3	—	67.7	—	76.8
Combined series (4:3:1:3:3)[d]	68.9	77.8	59.3	70.0	70.5	79.3
Combined series (4:3:1:3)[e]	78.5	79.3	68.0	71.9	80.4	80.7
Combined series (4:3:1)[f]	80.1	—	70.3	—	81.9	—
DTP (4 doses or more)[g]	82.7	85.0	72.4	76.4	84.7	83.6
Polio (3 doses or more)[h]	91.9	93.6	88.2	90.2	92.5	91.9
MMR (1 dose or more)[i]	91.4	91.3	85.1	92.3	92.5	91.9
Hib (3 doses or more)[j]	92.8	90.8	87.4	86.0	93.7	91.1
Hepatitis B (3 doses or more)[k]	82.1	93.4	76.4	90.5	83.3	93.4
Varicella (1 dose or more)[l]	14.5	89.8	6.4	89.9	16.3	91.1
PCV (3 doses or more)[m]	—	92.8	—	89.8	—	92.2
PCV (4 doses or more)[m]	—	81.4	—	72.8	—	80.6
Hepatitis A (2 doses or more)[n]	—	37.6	—	31.1	—	39.1
Black, non-Hispanic						
Combined series (4:3:1:3:3:1)[c]	—	72.7	—	70.2	—	74.9
Combined series (4:3:1:3:3)[d]	66.8	74.2	61.3	71.0	71.9	77.3
Combined series (4:3:1:3)[e]	74.2	75.8	69.3	72.7	79.1	78.6
Combined series (4:3:1)[f]	76.6	—	72.5	—	80.9	—
DTP (4 doses or more)[g]	79.0	80.1	74.3	82.2	83.3	87.7
Polio (3 doses or more)[h]	90.1	91.5	86.8	92.5	92.6	96.3
MMR (1 dose or more)[i]	89.7	92.0	88.3	92.8	90.8	92.6
Hib (3 doses or more)[j]	89.4	88.6	85.9	90.1	92.8	93.6
Hepatitis B (3 doses or more)[k]	81.9	92.1	77.8	91.6	85.0	95.8
Varicella (1 dose or more)[l]	8.6	90.4	—	91.1	12.9	92.7
PCV (3 doses or more)[m]	—	90.9	—	92.5	—	95.7
PCV (4 doses or more)[m]	—	76.4	—	74.9	—	82.3
Hepatitis A (2 doses or more)[n]	—	39.7	—	38.7	—	40.7

series. Children living below the poverty line and African-American children were slightly less likely than the general child population to be immunized.

In 1994 the U.S. Department of Health and Human Services (HHS) implemented the Vaccines for Children (VFC) program, which provides free or low-cost vaccines to children at participating private and public health care provider sites. Eligible children, including children on Medicaid, children without insurance or whose insurance does not cover vaccinations, and Native American or Alaskan Native children, can receive the vaccinations through their primary care physician. Children not covered under the program but whose parents cannot afford vaccinations can receive free vaccines at public clinics under local programs. The HHS states in *Advancing the Health, Safety, and Well-Being of Our People: DHHS FY 2011 Budget in Brief* (March 10, 2010, http://dhhs.gov/asfr/ob/docbudget/2011budgetinbrief.pdf) that the VFC program and Section 317 (the supporting vaccine infrastructure) had a budget of $3.4 billion for fiscal year 2009. Vaccines provided through the program represented about 40% of all childhood vaccines purchased in the country.

It should be noted that vaccinations are not without their risks. In 1988 the National Vaccine Injury Compensation Program (VICP) was established to provide compensation to individuals who are injured by certain vaccines. The Health Resources and Services Administration lists the VICP-covered injuries in "Vaccine Injury Table" (2010, http://www.hrsa.gov/vaccinecompensation/table.htm). Covered injuries include anaphylactic shock, which is associated with the tetanus, pertussis, polio, hepatitis B, and MMR vaccines; encephalitis, which is associated with the pertussis and MMR vaccines; and viral infections, which are associated with the MMR and polio vaccines.

TABLE 4.1

Characteristic	Total		Below 100% poverty		100% poverty and above	
	1996	2008	1996	2008	1996	2008
Hispanic						
Combined series (4:3:1:3:3:1)[c]	—	77.7	—	74.9	—	80.5
Combined series (4:3:1:3:3)[d]	63.7	79.4	62.4	76.6	64.1	82.1
Combined series (4:3:1:3)[e]	71.1	80.7	68.2	77.5	72.7	83.9
Combined series (4:3:1)[f]	74.1	—	70.9	—	74.6	—
DTP (4 doses or more)[g]	77.2	84.9	74.0	82.2	77.5	87.7
Polio (3 doses or more)[h]	89.4	94.3	88.0	92.5	89.8	96.3
MMR (1 dose or more)[i]	88.2	92.8	87.4	92.8	89.0	92.6
Hib (3 doses or more)[j]	88.5	91.9	87.1	90.1	90.3	93.6
Hepatitis B (3 doses or more)[k]	80.8	93.7	79.9	91.6	81.1	95.8
Varicella (1 dose or more)[l]	7.6	91.8	6.3	91.1	11.2	92.7
PCV (3 doses or more)[m]	—	94.1	—	92.5	—	95.7
PCV (4 doses or more)[m]	—	78.6	—	74.9	—	82.3
Hepatitis A (2 doses or more)[n]	—	44.7	—	43.9	—	44.6

—Not available.

[a]Based on family income and household size using U.S. Bureau of Census poverty thresholds for the year of data collection.

[b]From 1996 to 2001, the 1977 OMB Standards for Data on Race and Ethnicity were used to classify persons into one of the following racial groups: White, Black, American Indian or Alaskan Native, or Asian or Pacific Islander. Beginning in 2002, the revised 1997 OMB Standards for Data on Race and Ethnicity were used. Persons could select one or more from the following racial groups: White, Black or African American, American Indian or Alaska Native, Asian, or Native Hawaiian or Other Pacific Islander. Persons of Hispanic origin may be of any race. Included in the total but not shown separately are American Indian or Alaska Native, Asian, Native Hawaiian or Other Pacific Islander and "Two or more races" due to the small sample size. Data on race and Hispanic origin are collected separately but combined for reporting.

[c]The 4:3:1:3:3:1 series consists of 4 doses (or more) of diphtheria, tetanus toxoids, and pertussis (DTP) vaccines, diphtheria and tetanus toxoids (DT), or diphtheria, tetanus toxoids, and any acellular pertussis (DTaP) vaccines; 3 doses (or more) of poliovirus vaccines; 1 dose (or more) of any measles-containing vaccine; 3 doses (or more) of *Haemophilus influenzae* type b (Hib) vaccines; 3 doses (or more) of hepatitis B vaccines; and 1 dose (or more) of varicella vaccine. The collection of coverage rate estimates for this series began in 2002.

[d]The 4:3:1:3:3 series consists of 4 doses (or more) of diphtheria, tetanus toxoids, and pertussis (DTP) vaccines, diphtheria and tetanus toxoids (DT), or diphtheria, tetanus toxoids, and any acellular pertussis (DTaP) vaccines; 3 doses (or more) of poliovirus vaccines; 1 dose (or more) of any measles-containing vaccine; 3 doses (or more) of *Haemophilus influenzae* type b (Hib) vaccines; and 3 doses (or more) of hepatitis B vaccines.

[e]The 4:3:1:3 series consists of 4 doses (or more) of diphtheria, tetanus toxoids, and pertussis (DTP) vaccines, diphtheria and tetanus toxoids (DT), or diphtheria, tetanus toxoids, and any acellular pertussis (DTaP) vaccines; 3 doses (or more) of poliovirus vaccines; 1 dose (or more) of any measles-containing vaccine; and 3 doses (or more) of *Haemophilus influenzae* type b (Hib) vaccines.

[f]The 4:3:1 series consists of 4 doses (or more) of diphtheria, tetanus toxoids, and pertussis (DTP) vaccines, diphtheria and tetanus toxoids (DT), or diphtheria, tetanus toxoids, and any acellular pertussis (DTaP) vaccines, 3 doses (or more) of poliovirus vaccines; and 1 dose (or more) of any measles-containing vaccine.

[g]Diphtheria, tetanus toxoids, and pertussis vaccine (4 doses or more of any diphtheria, tetanus toxoids, and pertussis vaccines, including diphtheria and tetanus toxoids, and any acellular pertussis vaccine).

[h]Poliovirus vaccine (3 doses or more).

[i]Measles-mumps-rubella (MMR) vaccine (1 dose or more) was used beginning in 2005. The previous coverage years reported measles-containing vaccines.

[j]*Haemophilus influenzae* type b (Hib) vaccine (3 doses or more).

[k]Hepatitis B vaccine (3 doses or more).

[l]Varicella vaccine (1 dose or more) is recommended at any visit at or after age 12 months for susceptible children (i.e., those who lack a reliable history of chickenpox).

[m]The heptavalent pneumococcal conjugate vaccine (PCV) is recommended for all children aged less than 5 years. The series consists of doses at ages 2, 4, and 6 months, and a booster dose at ages 12–15 months.

[n]Hepatitis A vaccine (2 doses or more) is recommended for all children ages 12–23 months. The ACIP expanded this recommendation in May, 2006. NIS data prior to 2008 for children aged 19–35 months is not available for Hepatitis A vaccine.

SOURCE: Adapted from "Table HC3. Childhood Immunization: Percentage of Children Ages 19–35 Months Vaccinated for Selected Diseases by Poverty Status, and Race and Hispanic Origin, 1996–2008," in *America's Children in Brief: Key National Indicators of Well-Being, 2010*, Federal Interagency Forum on Child and Family Statistics, July 2010, http://www.childstats.gov/americaschildren/tables.asp (accessed October 15, 2010)

In February 1998 Andrew Wakefield et al. published "Ileal-Lymphoid-Nodular Hyperplasia, Non-specific Colitis, and Pervasive Developmental Disorder in Children" (*Lancet*, vol. 351, no. 9103), which linked the MMR vaccine to autism. The paper led to a slew of scientific studies that tried but failed to replicate Wakefield et al.'s findings. Gardiner Harris reports in "Journal Retracts 1998 Paper Linking Autism to Vaccines" (*New York Times*, February 2, 2010) that the *Lancet* retracted the paper in February 2010 after ethical conflicts in Wakefield et al.'s study had been uncovered. In January 2011 the article "Journal: Study Linking Vaccine to Autism Was Fraud" (Associated Press, January 5, 2011) indicated that a new comparison of the study's reported diagnoses to hospital records showed that Wakefield et al. had altered facts about some of the children in their study. The paper reported that the 12 children studied showed no signs of autism until receiving the MMR vaccine, whereas five of the children had previously documented developmental problems. Furthermore, all the children's cases had been misrepresented in some way.

Harris reports that prior to the *Lancet*'s retraction of Wakefield et al.'s paper, parents' groups in the United States had mobilized to oppose certain vaccinations based on various theories about mechanisms for how vaccinations could trigger autism. Beginning in 2001 parents began to file petitions for compensation under the VICP. In "About the Omnibus Autism Proceeding" (December 21, 2010, http://www.hrsa.gov/vaccinecompensation/omnibuspro ceeding.htm), the Health Resources and Services Administration indicates that by August 2010 over 5,600 cases had been filed and collected in the Omnibus Autism Proceeding. In February 2009 the U.S. Court of Federal

Claims ruled that the MMR vaccine did not cause autism; the following year, in March 2010, the court ruled that thimerosal-containing vaccines also did not cause autism, which essentially ended the lawsuit.

PHYSICIAN VISITS. Children's health depends on access to and usage of medical care. Based on household interviews of a sample of the civilian noninstitutionalized population, the National Center for Health Statistics (NCHS) finds that in 2007, 57% of children under the age of 18 years visited the doctor between one and three times, 25.5% saw the doctor between four and nine times, and 7.2% saw the doctor 10 or more times. (See Table 4.2.) However, 10.3% of children did not see a doctor at all. Poor children have less access to health care than nonpoor children.

HEALTH INSURANCE. One reason some children do not have access to medical care is their lack of health insurance. According to Carmen DeNavas-Walt, Bernadette D. Proctor, and Jessica C. Smith of the U.S. Census Bureau, in *Income, Poverty, and Health Insurance Coverage in the United States: 2009* (September 2010, http://www.census.gov/prod/2010pubs/p60-238.pdf), 10% (7.5 million) of American children had no health insurance coverage in 2009. (See Figure 4.1.) Factors affecting children's access to coverage included their age, race, and ethnicity and their family's economic status. Children between the ages of 12 and 17 years were more likely to be uninsured (11.3%) than children under the age of six years (9.2%). Children living in households with an annual income of less than $25,000 were more likely than children in other households to be uninsured. Hispanic children were the least likely racial or

TABLE 4.2

Health care visits to doctor's offices, emergency departments, and home visits over a 12-month period, by selected characteristics, 1997, 2006, and 2007

[Data are based on household interviews of a sample of the civilian noninstitutionalized population]

Characteristic	Number of health care visits[a]											
	None			1–3 visits			4–9 visits			10 or more visits		
	1997	2006	2007	1997	2006	2007	1997	2006	2007	1997	2006	2007
	Percent distribution											
Total, age-adjusted[b, c]	16.5	17.2	16.4	46.2	46.9	47.2	23.6	23.1	23.6	13.7	12.8	12.8
Total, crude[b]	16.5	17.2	16.3	46.5	46.8	47.1	23.5	23.1	23.7	13.5	12.9	12.9
Age												
Under 18 years	11.8	10.9	10.3	54.1	57.2	57.0	25.2	24.6	25.5	8.9	7.3	7.2
Under 6 years	5.0	4.9	6.2	44.9	50.6	48.3	37.0	34.8	35.8	13.0	9.7	9.7
6–17 years	15.3	13.8	12.4	58.7	60.5	61.4	19.3	19.6	20.3	6.8	6.1	6.0
18–44 years	21.7	25.3	24.1	46.7	45.8	46.3	19.0	17.8	18.4	12.6	11.0	11.2
18–24 years	22.0	25.3	24.9	46.8	47.2	46.9	20.0	17.4	18.1	11.2	10.2	10.1
25–44 years	21.6	25.4	23.9	46.7	45.3	46.1	18.7	17.9	18.5	13.0	11.4	11.6
45–64 years	16.9	16.4	14.9	42.9	44.3	45.3	24.7	23.6	23.9	15.5	15.7	15.9
45–54 years	17.9	18.5	16.8	43.9	46.1	47.1	23.4	21.8	21.2	14.8	13.6	14.9
55–64 years	15.3	13.5	12.3	41.3	41.9	43.0	26.7	26.1	27.6	16.7	18.5	17.2
65 years and over	8.9	6.0	7.0	34.7	33.2	33.1	32.5	36.2	36.2	23.8	24.6	23.6
65–74 years	9.8	6.7	8.4	36.9	34.6	35.4	31.6	36.6	36.0	21.6	22.1	20.3
75 years and over	7.7	5.3	5.5	31.8	31.5	30.6	33.8	35.7	36.4	26.6	27.6	27.5
Sex[c]												
Male	21.3	22.8	21.3	47.1	46.8	47.3	20.6	20.0	20.9	11.0	10.4	10.5
Female	11.8	11.8	11.5	45.4	46.8	47.1	26.5	26.2	26.3	16.3	15.2	15.1
Race[c, d]												
White only	16.0	17.2	16.2	46.1	46.2	46.8	23.9	23.4	24.0	14.0	13.2	13.0
Black or African American only	16.8	16.0	15.5	46.1	49.2	48.4	23.2	23.3	23.4	13.9	11.5	12.7
American Indian or Alaska Native only	17.1	13.5	21.5	38.0	44.2	43.1	24.2	27.6	21.5	20.7	14.7	13.9
Asian only	22.8	21.9	22.0	49.1	51.3	48.9	19.7	18.1	19.9	8.3	8.7	9.2
Native Hawaiian or Other Pacific Islander only	—	*	*	—	*	*	—	*	*	—	*	*
2 or more races	—	16.3	13.0	—	44.8	45.4	—	21.3	24.1	—	17.6	17.5
Hispanic origin and race[c, d]												
Hispanic or Latino	24.9	27.1	25.2	42.3	43.0	44.6	20.3	19.6	20.3	12.5	10.3	9.9
Mexican	28.9	31.1	28.0	40.8	40.8	42.9	18.5	18.3	19.5	11.8	9.8	9.6
Not Hispanic or Latino	15.4	15.4	14.7	46.7	47.6	47.7	24.0	23.7	24.2	13.9	13.2	13.4
White only	14.7	15.0	14.1	46.6	46.9	47.4	24.4	24.2	24.8	14.3	13.9	13.7
Black or African American only	16.9	15.7	15.1	46.1	49.5	48.6	23.1	23.4	23.5	13.8	11.4	12.8
Respondent-assessed health status[c]												
Fair or poor	7.8	12.2	9.4	23.3	21.2	25.4	29.0	28.1	29.5	39.9	38.6	35.7
Good to excellent	17.2	17.8	17.1	48.4	49.3	49.6	23.3	22.8	23.2	11.1	10.1	10.1
Percent of poverty level[c, e]												
Below 100%	20.6	21.0	19.3	37.8	39.5	39.5	22.7	22.3	23.3	18.9	17.2	18.0
100%–less than 200%	20.1	21.6	20.5	43.3	43.5	42.1	21.7	21.5	23.3	14.9	13.3	14.0
200% or more	14.5	15.2	14.6	48.7	49.3	50.0	24.2	23.7	23.7	12.6	11.9	11.7

TABLE 4.2

Health care visits to doctor's offices, emergency departments, and home visits over a 12-month period, by selected characteristics, 1997, 2006, and 2007 [CONTINUED]

[Data are based on household interviews of a sample of the civilian noninstitutionalized population]

	Number of health care visits[a]											
	None			1–3 visits			4–9 visits			10 or more visits		
Characteristic	1997	2006	2007	1997	2006	2007	1997	2006	2007	1997	2006	2007
Hispanic origin and race and percent of poverty level[c, d, e]						Percent distribution						
Hispanic or Latino:												
Below 100%	30.2	32.8	30.5	34.8	35.3	36.9	19.9	19.2	19.3	15.0	12.7	13.3
100%–less than 200%	28.7	29.9	30.0	39.7	42.0	39.6	20.4	19.3	21.2	11.2	8.8	9.1
200% or more	18.9	22.2	19.7	48.8	47.4	51.6	20.4	20.4	19.6	11.9	10.1	9.1
Not Hispanic or Latino:												
White only:												
Below 100%	17.0	16.3	15.4	38.3	38.7	38.1	23.9	24.2	25.5	20.9	20.8	21.0
100%–less than 200%	17.3	18.8	16.2	44.1	43.7	42.0	22.2	22.2	25.5	16.3	15.4	16.3
200% or more	13.8	14.0	13.5	48.2	48.6	49.5	24.9	24.6	24.5	13.1	12.7	12.5
Black or African American only:												
Below 100%	17.4	18.1	15.2	38.5	45.0	43.2	23.4	21.9	24.9	20.7	15.0	16.7
100%–less than 200%	18.8	17.9	17.6	43.7	45.5	46.3	22.9	24.2	21.7	14.5	12.5	14.5
200% or more	15.6	13.5	14.4	51.7	53.6	52.0	22.7	23.5	23.5	10.0	9.3	10.2
Health insurance status at the time of interview[f, g]												
Under 65 years:												
Insured	14.3	14.3	13.5	49.0	50.4	50.7	23.6	23.1	23.5	13.1	12.3	12.3
Private	14.7	14.7	13.9	50.6	52.6	52.8	23.1	22.4	22.6	11.6	10.3	10.7
Medicaid	9.8	11.3	11.4	35.5	37.4	38.2	26.5	25.5	26.2	28.2	25.8	24.3
Uninsured	33.7	39.2	37.4	42.8	42.2	42.8	15.3	12.5	13.6	8.2	6.1	6.2
Health insurance status prior to interview[f, g]												
Under 65 years:												
Insured continuously all 12 months	14.1	14.3	13.4	49.2	50.8	51.0	23.6	23.1	23.5	13.0	11.9	12.1
Uninsured for any period up to 12 months	18.9	19.1	19.8	46.0	46.3	46.0	20.8	20.9	21.4	14.4	13.7	12.8
Uninsured more than 12 months	39.0	45.6	42.9	41.4	40.2	40.7	13.2	9.6	11.5	6.4	4.5	4.9
Percent of poverty level and health insurance status prior to interview[e, f, g]												
Under 65 years:												
Below 100%:												
Insured continuously all 12 months	13.8	12.6	12.4	39.7	43.1	41.8	25.2	24.2	26.0	21.4	20.1	19.8
Uninsured for any period up to 12 months	19.7	17.8	20.7	37.6	39.3	38.1	21.9	23.4	22.1	20.9	19.5	19.1
Uninsured more than 12 months	41.2	50.1	44.3	39.9	35.3	39.4	12.2	9.9	11.0	6.6	4.8	5.3
100%–less than 200%:												
Insured continuously all 12 months	16.0	16.3	15.1	46.4	45.9	44.5	21.9	23.0	24.6	15.8	14.8	15.8
Uninsured for any period up to 12 months	18.8	20.6	17.4	45.1	49.8	45.8	21.0	18.7	22.2	15.0	10.9	14.6
Uninsured more than 12 months	38.7	44.3	42.3	41.0	42.1	39.5	14.0	10.2	13.7	6.3	3.4	4.4
200% or more:												
Insured continuously all 12 months	13.7	14.1	13.2	51.0	52.6	53.3	23.6	22.9	22.8	11.7	10.4	10.7
Uninsured for any period up to 12 months	17.8	18.6	20.2	50.3	48.0	49.9	20.4	20.7	20.3	11.5	12.7	9.5
Uninsured more than 12 months	36.6	42.8	41.8	43.8	42.4	43.3	13.2	9.3	9.6	6.4	*5.5	5.3
Geographic region[c]												
Northeast	13.2	12.1	13.0	45.9	47.6	47.7	26.0	25.1	26.2	14.9	15.2	13.2
Midwest	15.9	15.2	15.5	47.7	48.4	48.8	22.8	23.6	22.4	13.6	12.7	13.3
South	17.2	18.3	16.9	46.1	45.6	45.3	23.3	23.5	24.8	13.5	12.6	13.0
West	19.1	21.7	19.1	44.8	46.7	48.2	22.8	20.2	21.1	13.3	11.3	11.7

ethnic group to receive health insurance coverage—16.8% of Hispanic children were uninsured, compared with 11.5% of African-American children, 10% of Asian-American children, and 7% of non-Hispanic white children. One-third of children who were not citizens were uninsured, which was three times the uninsured rate of native-born and naturalized citizens.

During the first decade of the 21st century the percent of children who were covered by health insurance increased to the highest rate in 20 years, reaching 90.1% in 2008. (See Table 4.3.) However, the overall percent of children who were covered by private health insurance declined from 70.2% in 2000 to 63.5% in 2008. In contrast, public health insurance coverage increased from 24.4% in 2000 to 33.2%

TABLE 4.2

Health care visits to doctor's offices, emergency departments, and home visits over a 12-month period, by selected characteristics, 1997, 2006, and 2007 [CONTINUED]

[Data are based on household interviews of a sample of the civilian noninstitutionalized population]

| | Number of health care visits[a] | | | | | | | | | | | |
| | None | | | 1–3 visits | | | 4–9 visits | | | 10 or more visits | | |
Characteristic	1997	2006	2007	1997	2006	2007	1997	2006	2007	1997	2006	2007
Location of residence[e]						Percent distribution						
Within MSA[h]	16.2	16.8	16.5	46.4	47.5	47.7	23.7	23.1	23.5	13.7	12.6	12.4
Outside MSA[h]	17.3	19.2	15.9	45.4	43.7	44.7	23.3	23.3	24.4	13.9	13.8	15.0

*Estimates are considered unreliable. Data preceded by an asterisk have a relative standard error (RSE) of 20%–30%. Data not shown have an RSE greater than 30%.

—Data not available.
[a]This table presents a summary measure of health care visits to doctor offices, emergency departments, and home visits during a 12-month period.
[b]Includes all other races not shown separately and unknown health insurance status.
[c]Estimates are age-adjusted to the year 2000 standard population using six age groups: Under 18 years, 18–44 years, 45–54 years, 55–64 years, 65–74 years, and 75 years and over.
[d]The race groups, white, black, American Indian or Alaska Native, Asian, Native Hawaiian or Other Pacific Islander, and 2 or more races, include persons of Hispanic and non-Hispanic origin. Persons of Hispanic origin may be of any race. Starting with 1999 data, race-specific estimates are tabulated according to the 1997 Revisions to the Standards for the Classification of Federal Data on Race and Ethnicity and are not strictly comparable with estimates for earlier years. The five single-race categories plus multiple-race categories shown in the table conform to the 1997 Standards. Starting with 1999 data, race-specific estimates are for persons who reported only one racial group; the category 2 or more races includes persons who reported more than one racial group. Prior to 1999, data were tabulated according to the 1977 Standards with four racial groups and the Asian only category included Native Hawaiian or Other Pacific Islander. Estimates for single-race categories prior to 1999 included persons who reported one race or, if they reported more than one race, identified one race as best representing their race. Starting with 2003 data, race responses of other race and unspecified multiple race were treated as missing, and then race was imputed if these were the only race responses. Almost all persons with a race response of other race were of Hispanic origin.
[e]Percent of poverty level is based on family income and family size and composition using U.S. Census Bureau poverty thresholds. Missing family income data were imputed for 24%–29% of persons in 1997–1998 and 31%–34% in 1999–2007.
[f]Estimates for persons under 65 years of age are age-adjusted to the year 2000 standard population using four age groups: Under 18 years, 18–44 years, 45–54 years, and 55–64 years of age.
[g]Health insurance categories are mutually exclusive. Persons who reported both Medicaid and private coverage are classified as having private coverage. Starting with 1997 data, state-sponsored health plan coverage is included as Medicaid coverage. Starting with 1999 data, coverage by the Children's Health Insurance Program (CHIP) is included with Medicaid coverage. In addition to private and Medicaid, the insured category also includes military plans, other government-sponsored health plans, and Medicare, not shown separately. Persons not covered by private insurance, Medicaid, CHIP, state-sponsored or other government-sponsored health plans (starting in 1997), Medicare, or military plans are considered to have no health insurance coverage. Persons with only Indian Health Service coverage are considered to have no health insurance coverage.
[h]MSA is metropolitan statistical area. Starting with 2006 data, MSA status is determined using 2000 census data and the 2000 standards for defining MSAs.
Notes: In 1997, the National Health Interview Survey questionnaire was redesigned. Data for additional years are available.

SOURCE: "Table 80. Health Care Visits to Doctor Offices, Emergency Departments, and Home Visits within the Past 12 Months, by Selected Characteristics: United States, 1997, 2006, and 2007," in *Health, United States, 2009: With Special Feature on Medical Technology*, Centers for Disease Control and Prevention, National Center for Health Statistics, February 2010, http://www.cdc.gov/nchs/data/hus/hus09.pdf (accessed October 15, 2010)

in 2008. Even though most children covered by public health insurance are covered under Medicaid, increases in enrollment under the State Children's Health Insurance Program were responsible for most of the increase after 2000.

To remain in the Medicaid program, families must have their eligibility reassessed at least every six months. If the family income increases above a certain level or other circumstances change even slightly, the family can lose its eligibility for the Medicaid program, disrupting health care coverage.

From the late 1980s through the mid-1990s the numbers of uninsured American children rose as coverage rates for employer-sponsored health insurance declined, even though the proportion of children covered by Medicaid also rose. In 1997, as part of the Balanced Budget Act, Congress created the State Children's Health Insurance Program (CHIP) to expand health insurance to children whose families earned too much money to be eligible for Medicaid but not enough money to pay for private insurance. CHIP provides funding to states to insure children, offering three alternatives: states may use CHIP funds to establish separate coverage programs, to expand their Medicaid coverage, or to use a combination of both. By September 1999 all 50 states had CHIP plans in place, and over the next decade the program gradually expanded to enroll even more children at higher income levels.

The Children's Health Insurance Program Reauthorization Act was signed into law by President Barack Obama (1961–) in February 2009. The Centers for Medicare and Medicaid Services notes in "National CHIP Policy Overview" (August 24, 2010, http://www.cms.gov/National CHIPPolicy/) that President Obama called it a "down payment on my commitment to cover every single American." The Henry J. Kaiser Family Foundation reports in "Children's Health Insurance Program Reauthorization Act of 2009 (CHIPRA)" (February 2009, http://www.kff.org/medicaid/upload/7863.pdf) that the act added $33 billion in funds for children's health insurance coverage through 2013 and was expected to cover 4.1 million children who would have otherwise been uninsured. The act also offered new options to cover pregnant women. According to the Centers for Medicare and Medicaid Services, in "CHIP Ever Enrolled in Year" (February 17, 2010, http://www.cms.gov/NationalCHIPPolicy/downloads/CHIPEverEnrolledYearGraph.pdf), 7.8 million children were enrolled in CHIP in fiscal year 2009, up from 7.4 million the previous fiscal year.

FIGURE 4.1

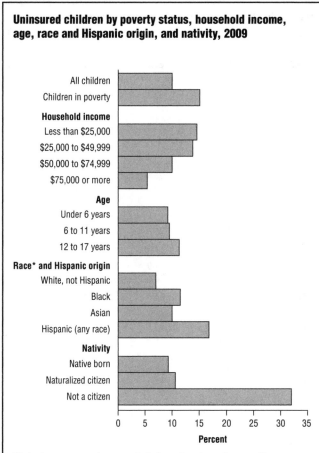

Uninsured children by poverty status, household income, age, race and Hispanic origin, and nativity, 2009

*Federal surveys now give respondents the option of reporting more than one race. This figure shows data using the race-alone concept. For example, Asian refers to people who reported Asian and no other race.

SOURCE: Carmen DeNavas-Walt, Bernadette D. Proctor, and Jessica C. Smith, "Figure 9. Uninsured Children by Poverty Status, Household Income, Age, Race and Hispanic Origin, and Nativity: 2009," in *Income, Poverty, and Health Insurance Coverage in the United States: 2009,* U.S. Census Bureau, September 2010, http://www.census.gov/prod/2010pubs/p60-238.pdf (accessed October 22, 2010)

Homelessness

Under the McKinney-Vento Homeless Assistance Act, the U.S. Department of Education is required to file a report on homeless children who are served by the act. The Department of Education obtains the data from school districts, which use different methods of estimation. In *Report to the President and Congress on the Implementation of the Education for Homeless Children and Youth Program under the McKinney-Vento Homeless Assistance Act* (2006, http://www.ed.gov/programs/homeless/rpt2006 .doc), the most recent report as of January 2011, the Department of Education states that 602,568 children who experienced homelessness at some point during the year were enrolled in school during the 2003–04 school year. Of these children, half (50.3%) lived doubled-up with relatives or friends, 25.3% lived in shelters, 9.9% lived in hotels or motels, and 2.6% were unsheltered—in other words, sleeping outside, in vehicles, or in abandoned buildings. This

number is almost certainly much lower than the number of children who actually experienced homelessness during this period, as the homeless status of children does not always come to the attention of school officials and many homeless children are not enrolled in school.

The U.S. Conference of Mayors finds in *Hunger and Homelessness Survey: A Status Report on Hunger and Homelessness in America's Cities, a 27-City Survey* (December 2010, http://www.usmayors.org/pressreleases/ uploads/2010_Hunger-Homelessness_Report-final%20 Dec%2021%202010.pdf) that on an average night, 30.9% of homeless people were in families with children, 67.8% were single men or women, and 1.3% were unaccompanied youth—usually runaways. According to the Conference of Mayors, for the second straight year the number of sheltered homeless families increased. Between 2009 and 2010 the number of homeless families in the surveyed cities increased by 9%. Three out of four (76%) mayors surveyed said unemployment was a principal cause of homelessness among families with children, and 72% citied the lack of affordable housing and 56% cited poverty. Another major cause of family homelessness was domestic violence: 24% of mayors stated that domestic violence was a principal cause of homelessness among families with children.

The poverty and lack of stability that homelessness brings have a negative impact on children. An example of the poor educational achievement of homeless youths is demonstrated by research by Chapin Hall at the University of Chicago. In "Educational Achievement Is Lower for Homeless Youth at All Grades" (2010, http://www .chapinhall.org/research/inside/educational-achievement- lower-homeless-youth-all-grades), Chapin Hall notes that after analyzing data from the Chicago public school system and a homeless services organization it identified more than 10,000 homeless students during the 2005–06 school year. Chapin Hall finds that homeless students in grades three, five, and eight scored significantly lower on both reading and math as measured by the Illinois Standards Achievement Test. In addition, one-third of homeless students had repeated a grade at least once. Chapin Hall theorizes that homeless children might experience these difficulties because of their need for special education services and their frequent school changes.

Homelessness also has a negative impact on children's health. Catherine Karr of the National Health Care for the Homeless Council argues in *Homeless Children: What Every Health Care Provider Should Know* (May 11, 2010, http://www.nhchc.org/Children/index.htm) that these children suffer from frequent health problems. They are seen in emergency rooms and are hospitalized more often than other poor children. The often crowded and unsanitary conditions they live in lead to a higher rate of infectious diseases, such as upper respiratory infections,

TABLE 4.3

Percentage of children under age 18 covered by health insurance at some time during the year by type of insurance and selected characteristics, 1987–2008

Characteristic	1987	1990	1995	2000	2005	2006	2007	2008
Any health insurance[a]								
Total	**87.1**	**87.0**	**86.2**	**88.4**	**89.1**	**88.3**	**89.0**	**90.1**
Gender								
Male	87.1	86.9	86.3	88.4	88.9	87.9	89.1	90.0
Female	87.1	87.0	86.2	88.4	89.3	88.7	89.0	90.2
Age								
Ages 0–5	87.6	88.5	86.7	88.8	89.6	88.7	89.5	91.3
Ages 6–11	87.3	87.0	86.5	88.7	90.1	88.9	89.7	90.8
Ages 12–17	86.4	85.2	85.5	87.7	87.8	87.4	88.0	88.4
Race and Hispanic origin[b]								
White, non-Hispanic	90.3	90.0	89.5	92.8	—	—	—	—
White-alone, non-Hispanic	—	—	—	—	93.0	92.7	92.7	93.3
Black	83.1	85.4	84.7	86.3	—	—	—	—
Black-alone	—	—	—	—	88.2	85.9	87.8	89.3
Hispanic	71.5	71.6	73.2	75.1	78.5	77.9	80.0	82.8
Private health insurance								
Total	**73.6**	**71.1**	**66.1**	**70.2**	**65.8**	**64.6**	**64.2**	**63.5**
Gender								
Male	73.4	71.1	66.4	70.1	65.7	64.5	64.4	63.7
Female	73.9	71.2	65.8	70.3	66.0	64.8	63.9	63.2
Age								
Ages 0–5	71.7	68.2	60.4	66.5	61.4	60.5	59.3	58.7
Ages 6–11	74.3	72.5	67.2	70.4	66.6	65.4	65.4	64.4
Ages 12–17	75.1	73.0	71.0	73.5	69.2	67.9	67.8	67.4
Race and Hispanic origin[b]								
White, non-Hispanic	83.2	80.8	78.0	81.4	—	—	—	—
White-alone, non-Hispanic	—	—	—	—	78.1	76.9	76.9	76.5
Black	49.2	48.5	43.9	53.9	—	—	—	—
Black-alone	—	—	—	—	48.7	49.0	48.1	46.8
Hispanic	47.9	44.9	38.3	45.2	42.0	40.9	40.4	40.6
Public health insurance[c]								
Total	**19.0**	**21.9**	**26.4**	**24.4**	**29.6**	**29.8**	**31.0**	**33.2**
Gender								
Male	19.2	22.1	26.2	24.7	29.6	29.6	31.0	33.1
Female	18.8	21.7	26.6	24.2	29.7	30.1	31.0	33.4
Age								
Ages 0–5	22.1	27.6	32.6	29.2	34.7	34.7	36.4	39.4
Ages 6–11	18.6	20.0	25.6	24.5	29.8	29.5	30.4	32.9
Ages 12–17	16.1	17.5	20.5	19.8	24.7	25.5	26.2	27.3
Race and Hispanic origin[b]								
White, non-Hispanic	12.1	14.7	17.5	17.2	—	—	—	—
White-alone, non-Hispanic	—	—	—	—	21.2	22.0	22.0	23.1
Black	42.1	45.5	48.8	41.9	—	—	—	—
Black-alone	—	—	—	—	48.0	44.0	47.7	51.0
Hispanic	28.2	31.9	39.0	34.6	41.4	42.3	44.2	47.9

—Not available.

[a]Children are considered to be covered by health insurance if they had public or private coverage at any time during the year. Some children are covered by both types of insurance; hence, the sum of public and private is greater than the total.

[b]For race and Hispanic-origin data in this table: From 1987 to 2002, following the 1977 OMB standards for collecting and presenting data on race, the Current Population Survey (CPS) asked respondents to choose one race from the following: White, Black, American Indian or Alaskan Native, or Asian or Pacific Islander. The Census Bureau also offered an "Other" category. Beginning in 2003, following the 1997 OMB standards for collecting and presenting data on race, the CPS asked respondents to choose one or more races from the following: White, Black or African American, Asian, American Indian or Alaska Native, or Native Hawaiian or Other Pacific Islander. All race groups discussed in this table from 2002 onward refer to people who indicated only one racial identity within the racial categories presented. People who responded to the question on race by indicating only one race are referred to as the race-alone population. The use of the race-alone population in this table does not imply that it is the preferred method of presenting or analyzing data. Data from 2002 onward are not directly comparable with data from earlier years. Data on race and Hispanic origin are collected separately. Persons of Hispanic origin may be of any race.

[c]Public health insurance for children consists mostly of Medicaid, but also includes Medicare, the State Children's Health Insurance Programs (SCHIP), and the Civilian Health and Medical Care Program of the Uniformed Services (CHAMPUS/Tricare).

Note: The data from 1996 to 2004 have been revised since initially published. Estimates beginning in 1999 include follow-up questions to verify health insurance status and use the Census 2000-based weights.

SOURCE: Adapted from "Table HC1. Health Insurance Coverage: Percentage of Children Ages 0–17 Covered by Health Insurance at Some Time during the Year by Type of Health Insurance and Selected Characteristics, 1987–2008," in *America's Children in Brief: Key National Indicators of Well-Being, 2010*, Federal Interagency Forum on Child and Family Statistics, July 2010, http://www.childstats.gov/americaschildren/tables.asp (accessed October 15, 2010)

diarrhea, and scabies. Homeless children live in less structured and often unsafe environments, leaving them more vulnerable to accidents and injury. They tend not to have access to nutritious food and are often malnourished or obese. Homeless children tend to lag behind their housed peers developmentally, and school-age homeless children often have academic problems. The greater likelihood that homeless children come from families plagued by mental illness, drug use, and domestic violence negatively affects their own mental health. In addition, M. Rosa Solorio et al. find in "Predictors of Sexual Risk Behaviors among Newly Homeless Youth: A Longitudinal Study" (*Journal of Adolescent Health*, vol. 42, no. 4, April 2008) that newly homeless youth are likelier to engage in risky sexual behavior if they stay in nonfamily settings because of the lack of supervision and social support. Homelessness results in serious negative consequences for the children's health.

Hunger

Food insecurity is defined as the lack of access to enough food to meet basic needs. Mark Nord et al. of the U.S. Department of Agriculture report in *Household Food Security in the United States, 2009* (November 2010, http://www.ers.usda.gov/Publications/ERR108/ERR108 .pdf) that in 2009, 85.3% of U.S. households were food secure, which remained essentially unchanged from the year before. However, the remaining 14.7% (17.4 million) of U.S. households experienced food insecurity at some time during the year. Most of these households used a variety of coping strategies to obtain adequate food, such as eating less varied diets, participating in food assistance programs, or getting food from community food pantries or soup kitchens. Regardless, 5.7% (6.8 million) of all households experienced very low food security—in other words, some household members reduced or otherwise altered their normal food intake because of a lack of money.

Nord et al. find that a higher percentage of children than adults were food insecure—23.2% of households with children were food insecure. Households experiencing food insecurity tend to go through a sequence of steps as food insecurity increases. First, families begin to worry about having enough food, then they begin to decrease other necessities, then they reduce the quality and quantity of all household members' diets, then they decrease the frequency of meals and the quantity of adult members' food, and finally they decrease the frequency of meals and the quantity of children's food. Even though children are usually protected from being hungry, an estimated one out of every 100 children (1.3%) experienced very low food security on one or more days during 2009. Households with incomes below the poverty line, households with children headed by a single mother, and African-American and Hispanic households were the

most likely to experience food insecurity. Nord et al. note that the prevalence of food insecurity and very low food security were higher in 2008 and 2009 than at any time since the surveys began in 1995, most likely because of the economic recession that began in late 2007 and ended in mid-2009.

EMERGENCY FOOD ASSISTANCE. Feeding America (formerly America's Second Harvest), the nation's largest charitable hunger-relief organization, reports in *Hunger Study, 2010* (February 2010, http://feedingamerica.issuelab .org/research/listing/hunger_in_america_2010_executive _summary) that in 2009, 37 million Americans sought emergency food assistance, which was a substantial increase since 2005, when 25.3 million Americans needed assistance. In *Hunger and Homelessness Survey*, the Conference of Mayors states that all the mayors surveyed reported that requests for emergency food assistance had increased in 2010 and that the total number of emergency food assistance requests increased by 24% during that year. Among those requesting food assistance, more than half (56%) were people in families. The most frequent reasons for hunger cited by city officials were unemployment (88.5% of mayors), high housing costs (50% of mayors), and low wages and poverty (46% of mayors).

Exposure to Toxins

Another threat to children's health is exposure to environmental toxins. Two toxins that children are most frequently exposed to are lead and secondhand smoke.

LEAD POISONING. Because they have smaller bodies and are growing, children suffer the effects of lead exposure more acutely than adults do. Lead poisoning causes nervous system disorders, reduction in intelligence, fatigue, inhibited infant growth, and hearing loss. Toxic levels of lead in a parent can also affect unborn children.

In "Toys" (June 1, 2009, http://www.cdc.gov/nceh/ lead/tips/toys.htm), the CDC indicates that children are primarily exposed to lead in paint and plastics. Leaded paint was banned in the United States in 1978, although children may be exposed to leaded paint in older homes. Even though leaded paint is not used on toys manufactured in the United States, it is still widely used on toys manufactured in other countries. Therefore, children may be exposed to lead when playing with imported toys. In addition, the use of lead in plastics, which makes it more flexible and able to return to its original shape, has not been banned. The CDC explains that "when the plastic is exposed to substances such as sunlight, air, and detergents the chemical bond between the lead and plastics breaks down and forms a dust."

David Barboza reports in "Why Lead in Toy Paint? It's Cheaper" (*New York Times*, September 11, 2007) that in 2007 nearly two dozen toys were recalled because they contained toxic levels of lead paint. Dozens of children's jewelry products, most of them made in China, had also been recalled in 2006 and 2007. In September 2007 Mattel, the world's largest toy maker, announced its third recall in six weeks, asking people to return certain toys made in China that contained high levels of lead paint. Lead paint is sometimes used in manufacturing products for children because it is less expensive than nonleaded paint. Ashland University randomly tested plastic toys and children's jewelry and found high lead levels in many of them, most of which had not been recalled. According to the article "China Bans Lead Paint in Toys Exported to U.S." (Associated Press, September 11, 2007), China signed an agreement in September 2007 to prohibit the use of lead paint on toys for export to the United States. However, Barboza states that "enforcement of the regulations in China is lax."

In "Senate Sends Sweeping Product-Safety Bill on to Bush" (*Washington Post*, August 1, 2008), Annys Shin notes that in response to the lead found in toys in 2007, Congress approved historic legislation that banned lead and other toxic chemicals from toys and provided better policing powers for the Consumer Product Safety Commission. Nevertheless, Lyndsey Layton states in "Lead, Chemicals Found in Toys Despite Stricter Law" (*Washington Post*, November 25, 2009) that the U.S. Public Interest Research Group had tested toys sold in major retail chains in 2009 and found that a number of them still contained illegal amounts of lead and other toxic chemicals.

In "CDC's National Surveillance Data (1997–2007)" (June 1, 2009, http://www.cdc.gov/nceh/lead/data/national .htm), the CDC states that in 2007, 31,524 children in the United States aged five years and younger had confirmed blood lead levels greater than the CDC's recommended level of 10 micrograms per deciliter of blood. This was 1% of all children tested. According to the Commission for Environmental Cooperation, in *Children's Health and the Environment in North America: A First Report on Available Indicators and Measures* (January 2006, http:// www.cec.org/files/PDF/POLLUTANTS/CEH-Indicators-fin_en.pdf), this number had dropped substantially since the early 1970s, due largely to the phasing out of lead in gasoline between 1973 and 1995. Even though children from all social and economic levels can be affected by lead poisoning, children in families with low incomes who live in older, deteriorated housing are at higher risk. Paint produced before 1978 frequently contained lead, so federal legislation now requires owners to disclose any information they may have about lead-based paint before renting or selling a home built earlier than 1978.

SECONDHAND SMOKE AND CHILDREN. Environmental tobacco smoke is a major hazard for children, whose respiratory, immune, and other systems are not as well developed as those of adults. According to the CDC, in "Disparities in Secondhand Smoke Exposure—United States, 1988–1994 and 1999–2004" (*Morbidity and Mortality Weekly Report*, vol. 57, no. 27, July 11, 2008), secondhand or passive smoke

(smoke produced by other people's cigarettes) increases the number of attacks and severity of symptoms in children with asthma and can even cause asthma in preschool-age children. It also causes lower respiratory tract infections, middle-ear disease, and a reduction in lung function in children, and it increases the risk of sudden infant death syndrome. The CDC finds that the percentage of children aged four to 11 years who were regularly exposed to secondhand smoke in their home decreased from 38.2% during the 1988–94 period to 23.8% during the 1999–2004 period, a reduction of 37.7%. The percentage of children aged 12 to 19 years exposed to secondhand smoke decreased from 35.4% during the 1988–94 period to 19.5% during in the 1999–2004 period, for an even larger decline of 44.9%.

In "What Is Third-Hand Smoke? Is It Hazardous?" (*Scientific American*, January 6, 2009), Coco Ballantyne reports on a study of the toxicity of tobacco smoke even after the cigarette has been put out. Jonathan Winickoff of the Dana-Farber/Harvard Cancer Center finds that "the cocktail of toxins that linger in carpets, sofas, clothes and other materials hours or even days after a cigarette is put out" are a health hazard for infants and children. Winickoff explains that "the developing brain is uniquely susceptible to extremely low levels of toxins." This puts infants and children at extremely high risk from the 250 toxins contained in cigarette smoke.

DISEASES OF CHILDHOOD

Overweight and Obese Children

The number of overweight and obese Americans has reached epidemic proportions and has become a national concern. The percentage of obese children and adolescents has grown significantly since the 1970s. Between 1976 and 1980, 6.7% of boys and 6.4% of girls aged six to 11 years were obese, which is defined as having a body mass index at or above the 95th percentile of the sex-specific body mass index growth charts. (See Table 4.4.) For boys this percentage hit a high of 21.2% during the 2007–08 period. Girls also hit a high of 18% in 2007–08.

An upward trend was also seen in the rates of obese adolescents; 4.5% of boys and 5.4% of girls aged 12 to 17 years were obese during the 1976–80 period, whereas 20.8% of adolescent boys and 16.7% of adolescent girls were obese during the 2007–08 period. (See Table 4.4.) The proportion of obese children overall between the ages of six and 17 years more than tripled, from 5.7% during the 1976–80 period to 19.2% during the 2007–08 period.

The percentages of overweight children (in the 85th percentile or above for body mass index) and obese children (in the 95th percentile or above for body mass index) vary by race and ethnicity. In 2009 non-Hispanic African-American adolescents were more likely to be overweight (21%) or obese (15.1%) than non-Hispanic white adolescents (13.6% were overweight and 10.3%

TABLE 4.4

Percentage of children ages 6–17 who are obese[a] by race and Hispanic origin, age, and gender, selected years 1976–2008

Characteristic	1976–1980	1988–1994	1999–2000	2001–2002	2003–2004	2005–2006	2007–2008
Ages 6–17							
Total	5.7	11.2	15.0	16.5	18.0	16.5	19.2
Race and Hispanic origin[b]							
White, non-Hispanic	4.9	10.5	13.2	14.6	17.3	13.8	17.4
Black, non-Hispanic	8.2	14.0	20.7	20.4	21.7	21.3	22.4
Mexican-American	—	15.4	23.1	21.5	19.6	25.6	24.2
Gender							
Male	5.5	11.8	15.7	18.0	19.1	17.2	21.0
Female	5.8	10.6	14.3	15.1	16.8	15.9	17.3
Ages 6–11							
Total	6.5	11.3	15.1	16.3	18.8	15.1	19.6
Gender							
Male	6.7	11.6	15.7	17.5	19.9	16.2	21.2
Female	6.4	11.0	14.3	14.9	17.6	14.1	18.0
Ages 12–17							
Total	5.0	11.1	14.9	16.8	17.2	17.8	18.8
Gender							
Male	4.5	12.0	15.6	18.4	18.3	18.1	20.8
Female	5.4	10.2	14.2	15.2	16.0	17.5	16.7

—Not available.

[a]Previously a body mass index (BMI) at or above the 95th percentile of the sex-specific BMI growth charts was termed overweight (http://www.cdc.gov/growthcharts). Beginning with America's Children, 2010, a BMI at or above the 95th percentile is termed obese to be consistent with other publications of NHANES data. Estimates of obesity are comparable to estimates of overweight in past reports. (Ogden, C.L., and Flegal, K.M. (2010) Defining childhood obesity and overweight using body mass index (BMI). National Health Statistics Report; Hyattsville, MD: National Center for Health Statistics. (forthcoming).)

[b]From 1976 to 1994, the 1977 OMB Standards for Data on Race and Ethnicity were used to classify persons into one of the following four racial groups: White, Black, American Indian or Alaskan Native, or Asian or Pacific Islander. For 1999–2008, the revised 1997 OMB Standards for Data on Race and Ethnicity were used. Persons could select one or more of five racial groups: White, Black or African American, American Indian or Alaska Native, Asian, and Native Hawaiian or Other Pacific Islander. Included in the total but not shown separately are American Indian or Alaska Native, Asian, Native Hawaiian or Other Pacific Islander, and "Two or more races." Beginning in 1999, those in each racial category represent those reporting only one race. Data from 1999 onward are not directly comparable with data from earlier years. Data on race and Hispanic origin are collected separately but combined for reporting. Persons of Mexican origin may be of any race. From 1976 to 2006, the National Health and Nutrition Examination Survey (NHANES) sample was designed to provide estimates specifically for persons of Mexican origin. Beginning in 2007, NHANES allows for reporting of both total Hispanics and Mexican Americans; however, estimates reported here are for Mexican Americans to be consistent with earlier years.

Notes: All estimates have a relative standard error of less than 30 percent and meet agency standards for publication. Observed differences between 2-year estimates for race/ethnic groups are not statistically significant unless noted.

SOURCE: Table Health 7. Obesity: Percentage of Children Ages 6–17 Who Are Obese by Race and Hispanic Origin, Age, and Gender, Selected Years 1976–2008, in *America's Children in Brief: Key National Indicators of Well-Being, 2010*, Federal Interagency Forum on Child and Family Statistics, July 2010, http://www.childstats.gov/americaschildren/tables.asp (accessed October 15, 2010)

were obese). Hispanic adolescents (19.6% were overweight and 15.1% were obese) were also significantly more likely than non-Hispanic white adolescents to be overweight or obese. (See Table 4.5.) Younger students were more likely than older students to be either overweight or obese.

Medical professionals are concerned about this trend because overweight children have an increased risk for premature death in adulthood as well as for many chronic diseases, including coronary heart disease, hypertension, diabetes mellitus (type 2), gallbladder disease, respiratory disease, some cancers, and arthritis. Type 2 diabetes, previously considered an adult disease, has increased dramatically in children and adolescents. Being overweight or obese can also lead to poor self-esteem and depression in children.

Weight problems in children are thought to be caused by a lack of physical activity, unhealthy eating habits, or a combination of these factors, with genetics and lifestyle playing important roles in determining a child's weight. Watching television and playing computer and video games contribute to the inactive lifestyles of some children. According to Danice K. Eaton et al. of the CDC, in "Youth Risk Behavior Surveillance—United States, 2009" (*Morbidity and Mortality Weekly Report*, vol. 59, no. SS-05, June 4, 2010), 24.9% of high school students spent three or more hours per school day on the computer and 32.8% spent three or more hours per school day watching television, often not getting a sufficient amount of physical exercise as a consequence.

Physical activity patterns established during youth may extend into adulthood and may affect the risk of illnesses such as coronary heart disease, diabetes, and cancer. Mental health experts correlate increased physical activity with improved mental health and overall improvement in life satisfaction. Eaton et al. report that only 45.6% of high school boys and 27.7% of high school

TABLE 4.5

Percentage of high school students who were obese and percentage who were overweight, by sex, race and Hispanic origin, and grade, 2009

	Obese			Overweight		
	Female	Male	Total	Female	Male	Total
Category	%	%	%	%	%	%
Race/ethnicity						
White*	6.2	13.8	10.3	13.2	13.9	13.6
Black*	12.6	17.5	15.1	23.3	18.7	21.0
Hispanic	11.1	18.9	15.1	19.5	19.7	19.6
Grade						
9	7.6	15.3	11.8	17.9	16.7	17.2
10	7.7	13.8	11.0	16.9	16.9	16.9
11	8.9	14.5	11.8	13.5	14.4	14.0
12	9.1	17.7	13.5	15.1	14.4	14.7
Total	**8.3**	**15.3**	**12.0**	**15.9**	**15.7**	**15.8**

*Non-Hispanic.
Note: Obese = Students who were ≥95th percentile for body mass index, by age and sex, based on reference data.
Overweight = Students who were ≥85th percentile but ≥95th percentile for body mass index, by age and sex, based on reference data.

SOURCE: Adapted from Danice K. Eaton et al., "Table 90. Percentage of High School Students Who Were Obese and Who Were Overweight, by Sex, Race/Ethnicity, and Grade—United States, Youth Risk Behavior Survey, 2009," in "Youth Risk Behavior Surveillance—United States, 2009," *Morbidity and Mortality Weekly Report*, vol. 59, no. SS-5, June 4, 2010, http://www.cdc.gov/mmwr/pdf/ss/ss5905.pdf (accessed October 22, 2010)

girls had been physically active for at least 60 minutes on five of the seven days preceding the survey in 2009. (See Table 4.6.) Non-Hispanic white students were somewhat more likely to meet recommended levels of physical activity (39.9%) than Hispanic (33.1%) or non-Hispanic African-American (32.6%) students. Fully 29.9% of girls and 17% of boys had not participated in an hour of physical activity on any day in the past seven days preceding the survey. Only 58.3% of high school students played on a sports team, 56.4% attended physical education classes, and 33.3% attended physical education classes daily. (See Table 4.7.) Rigorous activity among high school students also generally declined with age.

Asthma

Another serious disease affecting children is asthma, a chronic respiratory disease that causes attacks of difficulty breathing. In *The State of Childhood Asthma, United States, 1980–2005* (December 12, 2006, http://www.cdc.gov/nchs/data/ad/ad381.pdf), Lara J. Akinbami of the CDC indicates that millions of children in the United States have asthma. In 2005, 8.9% (6.5 million) of children were currently suffering from asthma, and 12.7% (9 million) of children had suffered with it at some point during their lifetime. Childhood asthma caused 27 hospitalizations per 10,000 children in 2004, and caused 12.8 million missed days of school in 2003. The American Lung Association estimates in "Asthma and Children Fact Sheet" (February 2010, http://www.lungusa.org/lung-disease/asthma/resources/facts-and-figures/asthma-children-fact-sheet.html) that up to a million asthmatic children are exposed to secondhand smoke, which worsens their condition.

According to Akinbami, African-American children suffer from asthma at a rate 60% higher than that of non-Hispanic white children, and Puerto Rican children suffer from asthma at a rate 140% higher than non-Hispanic white children. In addition, Akinbami finds that African-American children's asthma is apparently much less well controlled than that of non-Hispanic white children. African-American children have a 250% higher hospitalization rate, a 260% higher emergency department visit rate, and a 500% higher death rate from asthma when compared with non-Hispanic white children. Akinbami speculates that this is due to the lower level and quality of health care that African-American children receive.

HIV/AIDS

The acquired immunodeficiency syndrome (AIDS) was identified as a new disease in 1981, and, according to the CDC, in *HIV Surveillance Report: Diagnoses of HIV Infection and AIDS in the United States and Dependent Areas, 2008* (June 2010, http://www.cdc.gov/hiv/surveillance/resources/reports/2008report/pdf/2008SurveillanceReport.pdf), an estimated 1.1 million cases had been diagnosed in the United States through 2008. AIDS is caused by the human immunodeficiency virus (HIV), which weakens the victim's immune system, making it vulnerable to other opportunistic infections. Young children with AIDS usually have the virus transmitted to them either by an infected parent or through contaminated transfusions of blood or blood products. Adolescents who are sexually active or experimenting with drugs are also vulnerable to HIV infection, which can be spread through sexual intercourse without the use of a condom or through shared hypodermic needles.

TABLE 4.6

Percentage of high school students who were and were not physically active, by sex, race and Hispanic origin, and grade, 2009

Category	Physically active at least 60 minutes/day on all 7 days[a]			Physically active at least 60 minutes/day on 5 or more days[a]			Did not participate in at least 60 minutes of physical activity on any day		
	Female	Male	Total	Female	Male	Total	Female	Male	Total
	%	%	%	%	%	%	%	%	%
Race/ethnicity									
White[b]	12.4	26.2	19.7	31.3	47.3	39.9	25.4	15.9	20.3
Black[b]	10.0	24.4	17.2	21.9	43.3	32.6	43.6	20.6	32.1
Hispanic	10.5	20.7	15.6	24.9	41.3	33.1	30.5	17.4	23.9
Grade									
9	13.6	28.0	21.3	30.8	47.5	39.7	26.9	17.4	21.8
10	12.7	25.3	19.3	30.5	47.4	39.3	30.3	15.7	22.6
11	10.3	23.3	17.0	26.0	46.2	36.4	29.8	16.4	22.9
12	8.6	21.9	15.3	22.4	40.4	31.6	33.0	18.5	25.6
Total	**11.4**	**24.8**	**18.4**	**27.7**	**45.6**	**37.0**	**29.9**	**17.0**	**23.1**

[a]During the 7 days before the survey.
[b]Non-Hispanic.
Note: Activity refers to any physical activity the student was doing that increased their heart rate and made them breathe hard some of the time.

SOURCE: Adapted from Danice K. Eaton et al., "Table 80. Percentage of High School Students Who Were Physically Active, by Sex, Race/Ethnicity, and Grade—United States, Youth Risk Behavior Survey, 2009," and "Table 82. Percentage of High School Students Who Did Not Participate in at Least 60 Minutes of Physical Activity on Any Day, by Sex, Race/Ethnicity, and Grade—United States, Youth Risk Behavior Survey, 2009," in "Youth Risk Behavior Surveillance—United States, 2009," *Morbidity and Mortality Weekly Report*, vol. 59, no. SS-5, June 4, 2010, http://www.cdc.gov/mmwr/pdf/ss/ss5905.pdf (accessed October 22, 2010)

TABLE 4.7

Percentage of high school students who attended physical education classes and percentage who played on at least one sports team, by sex, race and Hispanic origin, and grade, 2009

Category	Attended PE classes[a]			Attended PE classes daily[b]			Played on at least one sports team[c]		
	Female	Male	Total	Female	Male	Total	Female	Male	Total
	%	%	%	%	%	%	%	%	%
Race/ethnicity									
White[d]	56.8	56.1	56.4	29.7	31.4	30.6	57.7	64.0	61.1
Black[d]	49.8	58.9	54.4	34.0	40.1	37.0	46.7	67.6	57.3
Hispanic	57.9	63.1	60.5	39.5	41.5	40.5	44.5	62.0	53.2
Grade									
9	74.3	70.7	72.4	48.2	45.5	46.7	56.6	65.9	61.6
10	56.4	58.6	57.6	32.3	34.9	33.7	56.4	66.8	61.8
11	45.3	50.9	48.2	25.5	29.7	27.6	51.3	63.4	57.6
12	40.7	46.9	43.8	19.6	25.2	22.4	44.1	57.9	51.1
Total	**55.0**	**57.7**	**56.4**	**31.9**	**34.6**	**33.3**	**52.3**	**63.8**	**58.3**

[a]On 1 or more days in an average week when they were in school.
[b]5 days in an average week when they were in school.
[c]Run by their school or community groups during the 12 months before the survey.
[d]Non-Hispanic.

SOURCE: Adapted from Danice K. Eaton et al., "Table 86. Percentage of High School Students Who Attended Physical Education (PE) Classes, by Sex, Race/Ethnicity, and Grade—United States, Youth Risk Behavior Survey, 2009," and "Table 88. Percentage of High School Students Who Played on at Least One Sports Team, by Sex, Race/Ethnicity, and Grade—United States, Youth Risk Behavior Survey, 2009," in "Youth Risk Behavior Surveillance—United States, 2009," *Morbidity and Mortality Weekly Report*, vol. 59, no. SS-5, June 4, 2010, http://www.cdc.gov/mmwr/pdf/ss/ss5905.pdf (accessed October 22, 2010)

In adults the most common opportunistic infections of AIDS are Kaposi's sarcoma (a rare skin cancer) and *pneumocystis carinii* pneumonia. In infants and children a failure to thrive and unusually severe bacterial infections characterize the disease. Except for *pneumocystis carinii* pneumonia, children with symptomatic HIV infection seldom develop opportunistic infections as adults do. More often, they are plagued by recurrent bacterial infections, persistent oral thrush (a common fungal infection of the mouth or throat), and chronic and recurrent

TABLE 4.8

Diagnoses of AIDS in children younger than 13, by year of diagnosis, race and Hispanic origin, 2005–08 and cumulative

| | 2005 | | | 2006 | | | 2007 | | | 2008 | | | Cumulative[b] | |
| | | Estimated[a] | | | Estimated[a] | | | Estimated[a] | | | Estimated[a] | | | |
	No.	No.	Rate	No.	No.	Rate	No.	No.	Rate	No.	No.	Rate	No.	Est. No.[a]
Race/ethnicity														
American Indian/Alaska Native	0	0	0.0	0	0	0.0	0	0	0.0	0	0	0.0	33	33
Asian[c]	1	1	0.1	1	1	0.1	0	0	0.0	1	1	0.1	48	49
Black/African American	38	40	0.5	28	30	0.4	20	22	0.3	19	25	0.3	5,729	5,782
Hispanic/Latino[d]	8	8	0.1	4	4	0.0	3	3	0.0	3	4	0.0	1,785	1,798
Native Hawaiian/Other Pacific Islander	0	0	0.0	0	0	0.0	0	0	0.0	0	0	0.0	7	7
White	4	4	0.0	3	3	0.0	4	4	0.0	5	7	0.0	1,601	1,612
Multiple races	1	1	0.1	1	1	0.1	0	0	0.0	3	3	0.2	65	66
Total[e]	**52**	**55**	**0.1**	**37**	**40**	**0.1**	**27**	**30**	**0.1**	**31**	**41**	**0.1**	**9,270[f]**	**9,349**

[a]Estimated numbers resulted from statistical adjustment that accounted for reporting delays, but not for incomplete reporting. Rates are per 100,000 population.
[b]From the beginning of the epidemic through 2008.
[c]Includes Asian/Pacific Islander legacy cases.
[d]Hispanics/Latinos can be of any race.
[e]Because column totals for estimated numbers were calculated independently of the values for the subpopulations, the values in each column may not sum to the column total.
[f]Includes children of unknown race/ethnicity.

SOURCE: "Table 6a. AIDS Diagnoses Among Children <13 Years of Age, by Race/Ethnicity, 2005–2008 and Cumulative—United States," in *HIV Surveillance Report: Diagnoses of HIV Infection and AIDS in the United States and Dependent Areas, 2008*, vol. 20, Centers for Disease Control and Prevention, June 2010, http://www.cdc.gov/hiv/surveillance/resources/reports/2008report/pdf/table6a-b.pdf (accessed October 22, 2010)

diarrhea. They may also suffer from enlarged lymph nodes, chronic pneumonia, developmental delays, and neurological abnormalities.

HOW MANY ARE INFECTED? According to the CDC, in *HIV Surveillance Report*, at year-end 2008 there were an estimated cumulative total of 9,349 AIDS cases in children under the age of 13 years since record-keeping began in 1981. (See Table 4.8.) African-American children made up the overwhelming majority of these cases (5,782 cases), followed by Hispanic children (1,798 cases), white children (1,612 cases), Asian-American children (49 cases), and Native American or Alaskan Native children (33 cases). At year-end 2008, 4,931 children under the age of 13 years had died from the disease.

MEANS OF TRANSMITTAL. Most babies of HIV-infected mothers do not develop HIV. HIV-positive mothers can reduce the risk of transmission by taking antiretroviral drugs during the last two trimesters of pregnancy and during labor; giving birth by caesarean section; giving the infant a short course of antiretroviral drugs after birth; and not breast-feeding. With these interventions the transmission rate can be reduced to as low as 2%.

The CDC indicates in *HIV Surveillance Report* that even though interventions are effective in preventing HIV transmission from pregnant mothers to babies, the overwhelming majority of children with AIDS contracted it from mothers who were either infected with HIV or at risk for AIDS (8,577 of 9,349 cases, or 91.7%). Another way that HIV/AIDS can be transmitted to children is through blood transfusions that are contaminated with

the virus, although this means of transmission has been all but eliminated during the 21st century.

ADOLESCENTS WITH AIDS. The number of AIDS cases among adolescents is comparatively low. In *HIV Surveillance Report*, the CDC states that by year-end 2008, 7,905 adolescents aged 13 to 19 years had been diagnosed with AIDS since the beginning of the epidemic during the early 1980s. However, because of the long incubation period between the time of infection and the onset of symptoms, it is highly probable that many people who develop AIDS during their early 20s became infected with HIV during their adolescence. By year-end 2008, 40,735 young adults aged 20 to 24 years had been diagnosed since the beginning of the epidemic.

MENTAL HEALTH ISSUES IN YOUNG PEOPLE

Marital Conflict and Divorce

Marital conflict hurts children whether it results in the breakup of marriages or not. Nearly all the studies on children of divorce have focused on the period after the parents separated. However, recent studies suggest that the negative effects children experience may not come so much from divorce itself as from marital discord between parents before divorce. In fact, some research suggests that many problems reported with troubled teens not only began during the marriage but may have contributed to the breakup of the marriage. Amy J. L. Baker reports in "The Long-Term Effects of Parental Alienation on Adult Children: A Qualitative Research Study" (*American Journal of Family Therapy*, vol. 33, no. 4, July–September 2005) that negative effects, such as low self-esteem, depression, drug and/or alcohol abuse, lack of trust, alienation from own children, and an elevated risk of divorce, persist among these children into adulthood. Lester Coleman and Fiona Glenn concur in "The Varied Impact of Couple Relationship Breakdown on Children: Implications for Practice and Policy" (*Children & Society*, vol. 24, no. 3, May 2010). The researchers find that most children caught in their parents' marital breakdown experience short-term distress. This distress can be mediated somewhat by strong family and parent-child relationships and by taking the children's views into account. Some children experience longer-term negative outcomes, including physical and emotional health problems, poor educational achievement, and socioeconomic disadvantage.

Divorce can cause stressful situations for children in several ways. One or both parents may have to move to a new home, removing the children from family and friends who could have given them support. Custody issues can generate hostility between parents. If one or both parents remarry, children are faced with yet another adjustment in their living arrangements.

Eating Disorders

Even though young people who are overweight increase their risk for certain diseases in adulthood, an overemphasis on thinness during childhood may contribute to eating disorders such as anorexia nervosa (a disorder characterized by voluntary starvation) and bulimia nervosa (a disorder in which a person eats large amounts of food then forces vomiting or uses laxatives to prevent weight gain). Girls are both more likely to have a distorted view of their weight and more likely to have eating disorders than boys.

Eaton et al. report that in 2009 students as a whole had a fairly accurate view of their weight: 15.8% of students were overweight (having a body mass index between the 85th and 95th percentile for their age and sex) and 12% were obese (having a body mass index equal to or greater than the 95th percentile for their age and sex). (See Table 4.5.) Approximately 27.7% said they were overweight. (See Table 4.9.) However, girls were much more likely than boys to have a skewed perception of their body size. Even though 31% of male students were overweight or obese, only 22.7% perceived themselves as being overweight and 30.5% were trying to lose weight. Among female students, 24.2% of students were obese or overweight, but 33.1% described themselves as being overweight and fully 59.3% were trying to lose weight.

Most students used healthy ways to lose weight, such as diet and exercise. However, a significant proportion used unhealthy methods such as extended periods of not eating, taking diet pills or laxatives, or inducing vomiting. Over half (51.6%) of female students and a quarter (28.4%) of male students ate less food, fewer calories, or low-fat foods to control their weight. (See Table 4.10.) Another two-thirds (67.9%) of female students and over half (55.7%) of male students exercised to control their weight. However, 14.5% of female students and 6.9% of male students had not eaten for 24 hours or more to lose weight; 6.3% of female students and 3.8% of male students had taken diet pills, powders, or liquids to control their weight; and 5.4% of female students and 2.6% of male students had vomited or taken laxatives to control their weight. (See Table 4.11.) A greater proportion of female students than male students used both healthy and unhealthy behaviors for weight control. In addition, Hispanic and non-Hispanic white students were in general more

TABLE 4.9

Percentage of high school students who thought they had a problem with weight and were trying to lose weight, by sex, race and Hispanic origin, and grade, 2009

	Described themselves as overweight			Were trying to lose weight		
	Female	Male	Total	Female	Male	Total
Category	%	%	%	%	%	%
Race/ethnicity						
White*	32.3	21.3	26.4	61.3	28.4	43.7
Black*	28.7	17.2	22.9	47.3	26.3	36.8
Hispanic	37.6	28.8	33.3	62.4	41.8	52.1
Grade						
9	32.2	22.7	27.1	57.0	31.8	43.5
10	31.1	21.2	25.9	59.4	29.5	43.6
11	33.5	21.8	27.5	60.8	28.0	44.0
12	36.0	25.5	30.6	60.3	32.8	46.4
Total	**33.1**	**22.7**	**27.7**	**59.3**	**30.5**	**44.4**

*Non-Hispanic.

SOURCE: Adapted from Danice K. Eaton et al.,"Table 92. Percentage of High School Students Who Described Themselves As Slightly or Very Overweight and Who Were Trying to Lose Weight, by Sex, Race/Ethnicity, and Grade—United States, Youth Risk Behavior Survey, 2009," in "Youth Risk Behavior Surveillance—United States, 2009," *Morbidity and Mortality Weekly Report*, vol. 59, no. SS-5, June 4, 2010, http://www.cdc.gov/mmwr/pdf/ss/ss5905.pdf (accessed October 22, 2010)

TABLE 4.10

Percentage of high school students who ate less food, fewer calories, or low-fat foods and who exercised, by sex, race and Hispanic origin, and grade, 2009

	Ate less food, fewer calories, or low-fat foods to lose weight or to keep from gaining weight			Exercised to lose weight or to keep from gaining weight		
	Female	Male	Total	Female	Male	Total
Category	%	%	%	%	%	%
Race/ethnicity						
White*	56.5	28.4	41.4	72.2	53.8	62.3
Black*	35.0	23.2	29.2	54.2	51.1	52.6
Hispanic	48.0	32.8	40.4	66.3	64.8	65.6
Grade						
9	49.1	27.5	37.5	67.4	57.6	62.2
10	52.6	26.7	38.9	69.6	53.6	61.1
11	52.7	27.8	39.9	67.5	53.6	60.3
12	52.0	32.4	42.1	66.7	58.0	62.3
Total	**51.6**	**28.4**	**39.5**	**67.9**	**55.7**	**61.5**

Note: Food or exercise taken to lose weight or to keep from gaining weight during the 30 days before the survey.
*Non-Hispanic.

SOURCE: Adapted from Danice K. Eaton et al., "Table 94. Percentage of High School Students Who Ate Less Food, Fewer Calories, or Low-Fat Foods and Who Exercised, by Sex, Race/Ethnicity, and Grade—United States, Youth Risk Behavior Survey, 2009," in "Youth Risk Behavior Surveillance—United States, 2009," *Morbidity and Mortality Weekly Report*, vol. 59, no. SS-5, June 4, 2010, http://www.cdc.gov/mmwr/pdf/ss/ss5905.pdf (accessed October 22, 2010)

TABLE 4.11

Percentage of high school students who engaged in unhealthy behaviors in an effort to lose weight, by sex, race, Hispanic origin, and grade, 2009

	Did not eat for 24 or more hours to lose weight or to keep from gaining weight[a,b]			Took diet pills, powders, or liquids to lose weight or to keep from gaining weight[a]			Vomited or took laxatives to keep from gaining weight[a]		
	Female	Male	Total	Female	Male	Total	Female	Male	Total
Category	%	%	%	%	%	%	%	%	%
Race/ethnicity									
White[c]	14.7	6.1	10.1	7.0	3.6	5.2	5.2	1.8	3.4
Black[c]	12.8	8.0	10.4	3.7	3.8	3.8	3.6	4.6	4.1
Hispanic	15.2	8.8	12.0	6.9	4.6	5.7	6.9	4.0	5.4
Grade									
9	15.7	6.7	10.9	4.7	3.7	4.2	5.6	2.8	4.1
10	14.5	6.5	10.3	6.0	3.0	4.4	5.3	2.2	3.7
11	14.8	7.2	10.9	8.1	4.0	6.0	6.3	2.7	4.5
12	12.6	7.3	9.9	6.6	4.6	5.6	4.2	2.6	3.4
Total	**14.5**	**6.9**	**10.6**	**6.3**	**3.8**	**5.0**	**5.4**	**2.6**	**4.0**

[a]To lose weight or to keep from gaining weight during the 30 days before the survey.
[b]Without a doctor's advice.
[c]Non-Hispanic.

SOURCE: Adapted from Danice K. Eaton et al., "Table 96. Percentage of High School Students Who Did Not Eat for 24 or More Hours and Who Took Diet Pills, Powders, or Liquids, by Sex, Race/Ethnicity, and Grade—United States, Youth Risk Behavior Survey, 2009," and "Table 98. Percentage of High School Students Who Vomited or Took Laxatives, by Sex, Race/Ethnicity, and Grade—United States, Youth Risk Behavior Survey, 2009," in "Youth Risk Behavior Surveillance—United States, 2009," *Morbidity and Mortality Weekly Report*, vol. 59, no. SS-5, June 4, 2010, http://www.cdc.gov/mmwr/pdf/ss/ss5905.pdf (accessed October 22, 2010)

likely than non-Hispanic African-American students to use unhealthy methods of weight control and the use of these methods increased somewhat with age.

Hyperactivity

Attention deficit hyperactivity disorder (ADHD) is one of the most common psychiatric disorders to appear in childhood. No one knows what causes ADHD, although research has focused on biological causes and the role of genetics. Symptoms include restlessness, inability to concentrate, aggressiveness, and impulsivity; and the lack of treatment can lead to problems in school, at work, and in making friends. Methylphenidate, a stimulant, is frequently used to treat hyperactive children. In *Summary Health Statistics for U.S. Children: National Health Interview Survey, 2009* (December 2010, http://www.cdc.gov/nchs/

data/series/sr_10/sr10_247.pdf), Barbara Bloom, Robin A. Cohen, and Gulnur Freeman of the CDC explain that boys are more likely to be diagnosed with ADHD than girls; 11% of boys aged three to 17 years have been diagnosed at some point, compared with 6% of girls.

Drug and Alcohol Use

Few factors negatively influence the health and well-being of young people more than the use of drugs, alcohol, and tobacco. Monitoring the Future, a long-term study on the use of drugs, alcohol, and tobacco conducted by the University of Michigan's Institute for Social Research, annually surveys eighth, 10th, and 12th graders on their use of these substances. According to Lloyd D. Johnston et al. of the Institute for Social Research, in *Monitoring the Future: National Results on Adolescent Drug Use, Overview of Key Findings, 2009* (2010, http://monitoringthe future.org/pubs/monographs/overview2009.pdf), the percentage of high school students who had used an illicit drug during that past year declined between 1997 and 2009, after sharp increases during the early 1990s. Johnston et al. find that in 2009, 36.5% of seniors (who were more likely than eighth or 10th graders to use an illicit drug) had used an illicit drug during the previous 12 months. Concerning the lifetime prevalence rate, 46.7% of 12th graders, 36% of 10th graders, and 19.9% of eighth graders had tried an illicit drug. Alcohol (72.3% of seniors) and marijuana (42% of seniors) were the most commonly used drugs. Eaton et al. find that in 2009, 72.5% of all high school students had tried alcohol and 41.8% had used it during the past month.

(See Table 4.12.) The researchers also note that 36.8% of high school students reported they had tried marijuana, and 20.8% reported they had used it at least once during the 30 days before the survey.

TOBACCO. Most states prohibit the sale of cigarettes to anyone under the age of 18 years, but the laws are often ignored and may carry no penalties for youths who buy cigarettes or smoke in public. In fact, 14.1% of high school students reported in 2009 that they had bought cigarettes in a store or gas station. (See Table 4.13.) The American Lung Association reports in "Children and Teens" (2010, http://www.lungusa.org/stop-smoking/about-smoking/facts-figures/children-teens-and-tobacco .html) that each day 3,900 children smoke their first cigarette—and more than 950 of them will become regular smokers. According to Eaton et al., nearly half (46.3%) of all high school students in 2009 said they had tried cigarettes at some point during their life. (See Table 4.14.) Nearly one out of five (19.5%) high school students had smoked at least one cigarette during the month preceding the survey and 7.3% had smoked at least 20 days during the past month. (See Table 4.15.) Almost twice as many male students smoked heavily than did female students: 11.1% of male adolescents and 4.1% of female adolescents smoked more than 10 cigarettes per day.

It is important to intervene to keep children from smoking. The American Lung Association reports that 85% of smokers started smoking regularly when they were 21 years old and younger and that 68% began when they

TABLE 4.12

Percentage of high school students who drank alcohol and percentage who used marijuana, by sex, race and Hispanic origin, and grade, 2009

	Ever drank alcohol[a]			Current alcohol use[b]			Ever used marijuana[c]			Current marijuana use[d]		
	Female	Male	Total	Female	Male	Total	Female	Male	Total	Female	Male	Total
Category	%	%	%	%	%	%	%	%	%	%	%	%
Race/ethnicity												
White[e]	75.6	72.2	73.8	45.9	43.6	44.7	33.7	37.4	35.7	17.9	23.0	20.7
Black[e]	70.2	64.9	67.6	35.6	31.2	33.4	38.0	44.3	41.2	18.7	25.6	22.2
Hispanic	78.5	74.8	76.6	43.5	42.4	42.9	35.6	44.2	39.9	18.2	25.0	21.6
Grade												
9	66.4	60.8	63.4	35.3	28.4	31.5	25.7	26.9	26.4	15.5	15.5	15.5
10	72.5	69.9	71.1	41.2	40.1	40.6	33.0	37.7	35.5	17.9	23.9	21.1
11	79.0	76.5	77.8	45.6	45.7	45.7	39.5	44.3	42.0	19.5	26.7	23.2
12	80.3	79.0	79.7	50.7	52.6	51.7	40.2	50.9	45.6	19.1	29.9	24.6
Total	**74.2**	**70.8**	**72.5**	**42.9**	**40.8**	**41.8**	**34.3**	**39.0**	**36.8**	**17.9**	**23.4**	**20.8**

[a]Had at least one drink of alcohol on at least 1 day during their life.
[b]Had at least one drink of alcohol on at least 1 day during the 30 days before the survey.
[c]Used marijuana one or more times during their life.
[d]Used marijuana one or more times during the 30 days before the survey.
[e]Non-Hispanic.

SOURCE: Adapted from Danice K. Eaton et al., "Table 36. Percentage of High School Students Who Drank Alcohol, by Sex, Race/Ethnicity, and Grade—United States, Youth Risk Behavior Survey, 2009," and "Table 40. Percentage of High School Students Who Used Marijuana, by Sex, Race/Ethnicity, and Grade—United States, Youth Risk Behavior Survey, 2009," in "Youth Risk Behavior Surveillance—United States, 2009," *Morbidity and Mortality Weekly Report*, vol. 59, no. SS-5, June 4, 2010, http://www.cdc.gov/mmwr/pdf/ss/ss5905.pdf (accessed October 22, 2010)

were 18 years old and younger. Teens say they smoke for a variety of reasons—they "just like it," "it's a social thing," and many young women who are worried about their weight report they smoke because "it burns calories." Many of them note they have seen their parents smoke.

TABLE 4.13

Percentage of high school students who bought cigarettes in a store or gas station, by sex, race and Hispanic origin, and grade, 2009

| | Bought cigarettes in a store or gas station | | |
| | Female | Male | Total |
Category	%	%	%
Race/ethnicity			
White[a]	8.8	19.0	14.1
Black[a]	—[b]	24.8	19.7
Hispanic	11.5	15.0	13.3
Grade			
9	3.5	11.0	7.1
10	9.8	16.8	13.4
11	12.0	18.8	15.8
12	14.9	32.7	23.8
Total	**9.6**	**18.3**	**14.1**

Note: Cigarettes were bought during the 30 days before the survey, among the 15.7% of students nationwide who currently smoked cigarettes and who were aged <18 years.
[a]Non-hispanic.
[b]Not available.

SOURCE: Adapted from Danice K. Eaton et al., "Table 32. Percentage of High School Students Who Usually Obtained Their Own Cigarettes by Buying Them in a Store or Gas Station and Who Currently Used Smokeless Tobacco, by Sex, Race/Ethnicity, and Grade—United States, Youth Risk Behavior Survey, 2009," in "Youth Risk Behavior Surveillance—United States, 2009," *Morbidity and Mortality Weekly Report*, vol. 59, no. SS-5, June 4, 2010, http://www.cdc.gov/mmwr/pdf/ss/ss5905.pdf (accessed October 22, 2010)

CHILDHOOD DEATHS

Infant Mortality

The NCHS defines the infant mortality rate as the number of deaths of babies younger than one year per 1,000 live births. Neonatal deaths occur within 28 days after birth and postneonatal deaths occur 28 to 365 days after birth. The U.S. infant mortality rate declined from 165 deaths per 1,000 live births in 1900 to a low of 6.8 deaths per 1,000 live births between 2003 and 2005. (See Table 4.16.) In *Health, United States, 2009* (February 2010, http://www.cdc.gov/nchs/data/hus/hus09.pdf), the National Center for Health Statistics notes that several factors—including improved access to health care, advances in neonatal medicine, improved public health practices, and improved health of pregnant mothers—contributed to the overall decline in infant mortality during the 20th century.

Not all racial and ethnic groups have reached that record-low infant mortality rate. Between 2003 and 2005 the infant mortality rate for non-Hispanic white infants was 5.7 deaths per 1,000 live births, less than half the rate of 13.6 deaths per 1,000 live births for non-Hispanic African-American infants. (See Table 4.16.) The mortality rates for Native American or Alaskan Native, Hispanic, and Asian or Pacific Islander infants were 8.4, 5.6, and 4.8, respectively.

TABLE 4.14

Percentage of high school students who ever smoked cigarettes, by sex, race and Hispanic origin, and grade, 2009

| | Ever smoked cigarettes[a] | | | Ever smoked cigarettes daily[b] | | |
| | Female | Male | Total | Female | Male | Total |
Category	%	%	%	%	%	%
Race/ethnicity						
White[c]	47.2	45.2	46.1	13.8	13.7	13.7
Black[c]	43.4	43.5	43.5	3.1	5.4	4.3
Hispanic	47.6	54.5	51.0	7.7	9.4	8.6
Grade						
9	37.4	37.9	37.7	7.7	7.8	7.7
10	44.0	44.0	44.0	8.3	9.3	8.9
11	50.0	50.0	50.0	11.7	14.2	13.0
12	54.8	56.1	55.5	15.5	17.1	16.3
Total	**46.1**	**46.3**	**46.3**	**10.6**	**11.7**	**11.2**

[a]Ever tried cigarette smoking, even one or two puffs.
[b]Ever smoked at least one cigarette every day for 30 days.
[c]Non-Hispanic.

SOURCE: Adapted from Danice K. Eaton et al., "Table 26. Percentage of High School Students Who Ever Smoked Cigarettes, by Sex, Race/Ethnicity, and Grade—United States, Youth Risk Behavior Survey, 2009," in "Youth Risk Behavior Surveillance—United States, 2009," *Morbidity and Mortality Weekly Report*, vol. 59, no. SS-5, June 4, 2010, http://www.cdc.gov/mmwr/pdf/ss/ss5905.pdf (accessed October 22, 2010)

Children in smoking households are at risk not only from secondhand smoke but also from this greater likelihood to take up smoking themselves.

TABLE 4.15

Percentage of high school students who currently smoked cigarettes, frequently smoked cigarettes, or smoked more than ten cigarettes per day, by sex, race and Hispanic origin, and grade, 2009

Category	Current cigarette use[a]			Current frequent cigarette use[b]			Smoked more than 10 cigarettes/day[c]		
	Female	Male	Total	Female	Male	Total	Female	Male	Total
	%	%	%	%	%	%	%	%	%
Race/ethnicity									
White[d]	22.8	22.3	22.5	9.0	10.0	9.5	4.3	11.0	7.8
Black[d]	8.4	10.7	9.5	1.4	2.9	2.1	1.3	9.3	5.7
Hispanic	16.7	19.4	18.0	3.2	5.2	4.2	4.4	7.9	6.4
Grade									
9	15.2	12.1	13.5	4.4	4.9	4.7	3.7	12.4	8.0
10	18.7	17.8	18.3	5.6	5.8	5.7	2.7	9.7	6.2
11	20.6	23.9	22.3	7.1	9.5	8.3	3.9	11.7	8.1
12	22.4	28.1	25.2	8.9	13.5	11.2	5.4	10.8	8.5
Total	**19.1**	**19.8**	**19.5**	**6.4**	**8.0**	**7.3**	**4.1**	**11.1**	**7.8**

[a]Smoked cigarettes on at least 1 day during the 30 days before the survey.
[b]Smoked cigarettes on 20 or more days during the 30 days before the survey.
[c]On the days they smoked during the 30 days before the survey, among the 19.5% of students nationwide who currently smoked cigarettes.
[d]Non-Hispanic.

SOURCE: Adapted from Danice K. Eaton et al., "Table 28. Percentage of High School Students Who Currently Smoked Cigarettes, by Sex, Race/Ethnicity, and Grade—United States, Youth Risk Behavior Survey, 2009," and "Table 30. Percentage of High School Students Who Currently Smoked More Than 10 Cigarettes/Day and Who Tried to Quit Smoking Cigarettes, by Sex, Race/Ethnicity, and Grade—United States, Youth Risk Behavior Survey, 2009," in "Youth Risk Behavior Surveillance—United States, 2009," *Morbidity and Mortality Weekly Report*, vol. 59, no. SS-5, June 4, 2010, http://www.cdc.gov/mmwr/pdf/ss/ss5905.pdf (accessed October 22, 2010)

The NCHS lists the 10 leading causes of infant mortality in the United States in 2007. Birth defects (congenital malformations, deformations, and chromosomal abnormalities) were the primary cause of infant mortality (133.6 deaths per 100,000 live births). (See Table 4.17.) Premature delivery or low birth weight was the second-leading cause of infant mortality (108.4 per 100,000 live births). Sudden infant death syndrome (49.1), complications of pregnancy (41), accidents (28.7), complications in the placenta or umbilical cord (26.4), bacterial sepsis (18.3), respiratory distress (17), neonatal hemorrhage (14.2), and diseases of the circulatory system (14.2) complete the list.

SUDDEN INFANT DEATH SYNDROME. Sudden infant death syndrome (SIDS; sometimes called crib death), the unexplained death of a previously healthy infant, was the third-leading cause of infant mortality in the United States in 2006. (See Table 4.18.) Moreover, according to the CDC, in "Safe Sleep for Your Baby: Reduce the Risk of Sudden Infant Death Syndrome" (August 18, 2009, http://www.nichd.nih.gov/publications/pubs/safe_sleep_gen.cfm), SIDS is the leading cause of death among infants aged one to 12 months. In 1992 the American Academy of Pediatrics recommended that babies sleep on their back to reduce the risk of SIDS and launched its "Back to Sleep" campaign to educate parents. It had been a long-held belief that the best position for babies to sleep was on their stomach. Other risk factors for SIDS include maternal use of drugs or tobacco during pregnancy, low birth weight, and poor prenatal care. For reasons not yet under-

stood, even though the overall rate of SIDS has declined since the beginning of the Back to Sleep campaign, it has declined less among African-Americans and Native Americans or Alaskan Natives than among other groups. The National Institute of Child Health and Human Development indicates in "Sudden Infant Death Syndrome" (2010, http://www.nichd.nih.gov/health/topics/Sudden_Infant_Death_Syndrome.cfm) that African-American babies are more than twice as likely to die of SIDS and Native American or Alaskan Native babies are nearly three times as likely to die of SIDS than white babies.

A number of studies have considered the possible causes of and risk factors for SIDS. The article "Serotonin May Be the Key to SIDS" (*Medline Plus*, December 8, 2010) explains that babies who die of SIDS have a significantly lower amount of serotonin than do babies who die of other causes. The lack of serotonin limits the baby's ability to wake up when it is threatened by a lack of oxygen or another health hazard. Belly sleeping, overheating, soft and fluffy bedding or pillows in the crib, and secondhand smoke all pose environmental hazards that can lead to SIDS in the babies whose levels of serotonin are compromised.

Mortality among Older Children

During the second half of the 20th century childhood death rates declined dramatically. Most childhood deaths are from injuries and violence. Even though death rates for all ages decreased, the largest declines were among children.

TABLE 4.16

Infant mortality rates among selected groups by race and Hispanic origin of mother, selected years 1983–2005

[Data are based on linked birth and death certificates for infants]

Race and Hispanic origin of mother	1983–1985[a, g]	1986–1988[a, g]	1989–1991[a, g]	1995–1997[b, g]	1999–2001[b, g]	2003–2005[b, g]
	Infant[c] deaths per 1,000 live births					
All mothers	**10.6**	**9.8**	**9.0**	**7.4**	**6.9**	**6.8**
White	9.0	8.2	7.4	6.1	5.7	5.7
Black or African American	18.7	17.9	17.1	14.1	13.6	13.3
American Indian or Alaska Native	13.9	13.2	12.6	9.2	9.1	8.4
Asian or Pacific Islander[d]	8.3	7.3	6.6	5.1	4.8	4.8
Hispanic or Latina[e, f]	9.2	8.3	7.5	6.1	5.6	5.6
Mexican	8.8	7.9	7.2	5.9	5.4	5.5
Puerto Rican	12.3	11.1	10.4	8.5	8.4	8.1
Cuban	8.0	7.3	6.2	5.3	4.5	4.5
Central and South American	8.2	7.5	6.6	5.3	4.8	4.8
Other and unknown Hispanic or Latina	9.8	9.0	8.2	7.1	6.7	6.6
Not Hispanic or Latina:						
White[f]	8.8	8.1	7.3	6.1	5.7	5.7
Black or African American[f]	18.5	17.9	17.2	14.2	13.7	13.6
	Neonatal[c] deaths per 1,000 live births					
All mothers	**6.9**	**6.3**	**5.7**	**4.8**	**4.6**	**4.6**
White	5.9	5.2	4.7	4.0	3.8	3.8
Black or African American	12.2	11.7	11.1	9.4	9.2	9.0
American Indian or Alaska Native	6.7	5.9	5.9	4.4	4.5	4.3
Asian or Pacific Islander[d]	5.2	4.5	3.9	3.3	3.2	3.3
Hispanic or Latina[e, f]	6.0	5.3	4.8	4.0	3.8	3.9
Mexican	5.7	5.0	4.5	3.8	3.6	3.8
Puerto Rican	8.3	7.2	7.0	5.7	5.9	5.7
Cuban	5.9	5.3	4.6	3.7	3.1	3.1
Central and South American	5.7	4.9	4.4	3.7	3.3	3.4
Other and unknown Hispanic or Latina	6.1	5.8	5.2	4.6	4.4	4.6
Not Hispanic or Latina:						
White[f]	5.7	5.1	4.6	4.0	3.8	3.7
Black or African American[f]	11.8	11.4	11.1	9.4	9.2	9.2

*Estimates are considered unreliable. Rates preceded by an asterisk are based on fewer than 50 deaths in the numerator. Rates not shown are based on fewer than 20 deaths in the numerator.
[a]Rates based on unweighted birth cohort data.
[b]Rates based on a period file using weighted data.
[c]Infant (under 1 year of age) and neonatal (under 28 days).
[d]Starting with 2003 data, estimates are not available for Asian or Pacific Islander subgroups during the transition from single-race to multiple-race reporting.
[e]Persons of Hispanic origin may be of any race.
[f]Prior to 1995, data are shown only for states with an Hispanic-origin item on their birth certificates.
[g]Average annual mortality rate.
Notes: The race groups white, black, American Indian or Alaska Native, and Asian or Pacific Islander include persons of Hispanic and non-Hispanic origin. Starting with 2003 data, some states reported multiple-race data. The multiple-race data for these states were bridged to the single-race categories of the 1977 Office of Management and Budget standards for comparability with other states. National linked files do not exist for 1992–1994. Data for additional years are available.

SOURCE: Adapted from "Table 17. Infant, Neonatal, and Postneonatal Mortality Rates, by Detailed Race and Hispanic Origin of Mother: United States, Selected Years 1983–2005," in *Health, United States, 2009: With Special Feature on Medical Technology,* Centers for Disease Control and Prevention, National Center for Health Statistics, February 2010, http://www.cdc.gov/nchs/data/hus/hus09.pdf (accessed October 15, 2010).

In 2006 three of the leading causes of death of one- to four-year-olds were unintentional injuries, congenital anomalies (birth defects), and malignant neoplasms (cancers). (See Table 4.18.) Homicide was the fourth-leading cause of death in this age group. The remaining deaths were spread across a variety of diseases, including heart disease, influenza and pneumonia, septicemia, and cerebrovascular diseases.

MOTOR VEHICLE INJURIES. The National Highway Traffic Safety Administration notes in *Determine Why There Are Fewer Young Alcohol-Impaired Drivers* (October 2, 2001, http://www.nhtsa.dot.gov/people/injury/research/FewerYoungDrivers/) that even though motor vehicle fatalities decreased by 25% between 1982 and 2000 for 15- to 19-year-olds, traffic accidents were still the leading cause of death for this age group. During the 1980s and early 1990s traffic fatalities linked to teenage drinking fell. This decline was due in large part to stricter enforcement of drinking age laws and driving while intoxicated or driving under the influence laws. Nevertheless, motor vehicle crashes were the leading cause of death among 15- to 20-year-olds in 2003. The U.S. Department of Transportation reports in "Traffic Safety Facts" (May 2007, http://www-nrd.nhtsa.dot.gov/Pubs/810759.pdf) that in 2005, 27.4 of every 100,000 teenagers aged 16 to 20 years were killed in traffic accidents. Many of those killed had been drinking alcohol and were not wearing

TABLE 4.17

Ten leading causes of infant death, by race and Hispanic origin, 2007

[Data are based on a continuous file of records received from the states. Rates are per 100,000 live births.]

Rank[a]	Cause of death (based on the International Classification of Diseases, Tenth Revision, Second Edition, 2004) and race and Hispanic origin	Number	Rate
All races[b]			
...	All causes	29,241	677.3
1	Congenital malformations, deformations and chromosomal abnormalities	5,769	133.6
2	Disorders related to short gestation and low birth weight, not elsewhere classified	4,678	108.4
3	Sudden infant death syndrome	2,118	49.1
4	Newborn affected by maternal complications of pregnancy	1,770	41.0
5	Accidents (unintentional injuries)	1,238	28.7
6	Newborn affected by complications of placenta, cord and membranes	1,139	26.4
7	Bacterial sepsis of newborn	790	18.3
8	Respiratory distress of newborn	735	17.0
9	Neonatal hemorrhage	614	14.2
10	Diseases of the circulatory system	612	14.2
...	All other causes	9,778	226.5
Non-Hispanic white			
...	All causes	13,283	574.4
1	Congenital malformations, deformations and chromosomal abnormalities	2,921	126.3
2	Disorders related to short gestation and low birth weight, not elsewhere classified	1,848	79.9
3	Sudden infant death syndrome	1,145	49.5
4	Newborn affected by maternal complications of pregnancy	784	33.9
5	Accidents (unintentional injuries)	628	27.2
6	Newborn affected by complications of placenta, cord and membranes	503	21.8
7	Respiratory distress of newborn	348	15.0
8	Bacterial sepsis of newborn	342	14.8
9	Neonatal hemorrhage	295	12.8
10	Diseases of the circulatory system	259	11.2
...	All other causes	4,210	182.1
Total black			
...	All causes	8,747	1,285.5
1	Disorders related to short gestation and low birth weight, not elsewhere classified	1,749	257.0
2	Congenital malformations, deformations and chromosomal abnormalities	1,109	163.0
3	Sudden infant death syndrome	630	92.6
4	Newborn affected by maternal complications of pregnancy	611	89.8
5	Accidents (unintentional injuries)	413	60.7
6	Newborn affected by complications of placenta, cord and membranes	364	53.5
7	Bacterial sepsis of newborn	261	38.4
8	Respiratory distress of newborn	240	35.3
9	Necrotizing enterocolitis of newborn	198	29.1
10	Diseases of the circulatory system	192	28.2
...	All other causes	2,980	437.9
Hispanic[c]			
...	All causes	6,056	570.3
1	Congenital malformations, deformations and chromosomal abnormalities	1,474	138.8
2	Disorders related to short gestation and low birth weight, not elsewhere classified	903	85.0
3	Newborn affected by maternal complications of pregnancy	313	29.5
4	Sudden infant death syndrome	275	25.9
5	Newborn affected by complications of placenta, cord and membranes	252	23.7
6	Accidents (unintentional injuries)	149	14.0
7	Bacterial sepsis of newborn	148	13.9
8	Neonatal hemorrhage	141	13.3
9	Diseases of the circulatory system	128	12.1
10	Respiratory distress of newborn	124	11.7
...	All other causes	2,149	202.4

...Category not applicable.
[a]Rank based on number of deaths.
[b]Includes races other than white and black.
[c]Includes all persons of Hispanic origin of any race.
Notes: For certain causes of death such as unintentional injuries, homicides, suicides, and sudden infant death syndrome, preliminary and final data differ because of the truncated nature of the preliminary file. Data are subject to sampling or random variation. Although the infant mortality rate is the preferred indicator of the risk of dying during the first year of life, another measure of infant mortality, the infant death rate, is shown elsewhere in the report. The two measures typically are similar, yet they can differ because the denominators used for these measures are different.
Figures are based on weighted data rounded to the nearest individual, so categories may not add to totals or subtotals. Race and Hispanic origin are reported separately on both the birth and death certificate. Rates for Hispanic origin should be interpreted with caution because of inconsistencies between reporting Hispanic origin on birth and death certificates. Race categories are consistent with the 1977 Office of Management and Budget (OMB) standards. Multiple-race data were reported for deaths by 27 states and the District of Columbia and for births by 25 states. The multiple-race data for these states were bridged to the single-race categories of the 1977 OMB standards for comparability with other states. Data for persons of Hispanic origin are included in the data for each race group, according to the decedent's reported race.

SOURCE: Adapted from Jiaquan Xu, Kenneth D. Kochanek, and Betzaida Tejada-Vera, "Table 8. Infant Deaths and Infant Mortality Rates for the 10 Leading Causes of Infant Death, by Race and Hispanic Origin: United States, Preliminary 2007," in "Deaths: Preliminary Data for 2007," *National Vital Statistics Report*, vol. 58, no. 1, August 19, 2009, http://www.cdc.gov/nchs/data/nvsr/nvsr58/nvsr58_01.pdf (accessed October 22, 2010)

TABLE 4.18

Leading causes of death and numbers of deaths, by age, 1980 and 2006

[Data are based on death certificates]

Age and rank order	1980 Cause of death	Deaths	2006 Cause of death	Deaths
Under 1 year				
. . .	All causes	45,526	All causes	28,527
1	Congenital anomalies	9,220	Congenital malformations, deformations and chromosomal abnormalities	5,819
2	Sudden infant death syndrome	5,510	Disorders related to short gestation and low birth weight, not elsewhere classified	4,841
3	Respiratory distress syndrome	4,989	Sudden infant death syndrome	2,323
4	Disorders relating to short gestation and unspecified low birthweight	3,648	Newborn affected by maternal complications of pregnancy	1,683
5	Newborn affected by maternal complications of pregnancy	1,572	Unintentional injuries	1,147
6	Intrauterine hypoxia and birth asphyxia	1,497	Newborn affected by complications of placenta, cord and membranes	1,140
7	Unintentional injuries	1,166	Respiratory distress of newborn	825
8	Birth trauma	1,058	Bacterial sepsis of newborn	807
9	Pneumonia and influenza	1,012	Neonatal hemorrhage	618
10	Newborn affected by complications of placenta, cord, and membranes	985	Diseases of circulatory system	543
1–4 years				
. . .	All causes	8,187	All causes	4,631
1	Unintentional injuries	3,313	Unintentional injuries	1,610
2	Congenital anomalies	1,026	Congenital malformations, deformations and chromosomal abnormalities	515
3	Malignant neoplasms	573	Malignant neoplasms	377
4	Diseases of heart	338	Homicide	366
5	Homicide	319	Diseases of heart	161
6	Pneumonia and influenza	267	Influenza and pneumonia	125
7	Meningitis	223	Septicemia	88
8	Meningococcal infection	110	Certain conditions originating in the perinatal period	65
9	Certain conditions originating in the perinatal period	84	In situ neoplasms, benign neoplasms and neoplasms of uncertain or unknown behavior	60
10	Septicemia	71	Cerebrovascular diseases	54
5–14 years				
. . .	All causes	10,689	All causes	6,149
1	Unintentional injuries	5,224	Unintentional injuries	2,258
2	Malignant neoplasms	1,497	Malignant neoplasms	907
3	Congenital anomalies	561	Homicide	390
4	Homicide	415	Congenital malformations, deformations and chromosomal abnormalities	344
5	Diseases of heart	330	Diseases of heart	253
6	Pneumonia and influenza	194	Suicide	219
7	Suicide	142	Chronic lower respiratory diseases	115
8	Benign neoplasms	104	Cerebrovascular diseases	95
9	Cerebrovascular diseases	95	Septicemia	84
10	Chronic obstructive pulmonary diseases	85	In situ neoplasms, benign neoplasms and neoplasms of uncertain or unknown behavior	76
15–24 years				
. . .	All causes	49,027	All causes	34,887
1	Unintentional injuries	26,206	Unintentional injuries	16,229
2	Homicide	6,537	Homicide	5,717
3	Suicide	5,239	Suicide	4,189
4	Malignant neoplasms	2,683	Malignant neoplasms	1,644
5	Diseases of heart	1,223	Diseases of heart	1,076
6	Congenital anomalies	600	Congenital malformations, deformations and chromosomal abnormalities	460
7	Cerebrovascular diseases	418	Cerebrovascular diseases	210
8	Pneumonia and influenza	348	Human immunodeficiency virus (HIV) disease	206
9	Chronic obstructive pulmonary diseases	141	Influenza and pneumonia	184
10	Anemias	133	Pregnancy, childbirth and puerperium	179

· · ·Category not applicable.

Note: For cause of death codes based on the International Classification of Diseases, 9th Revision (ICD–9) in 1980 and ICD–10 in 2006.

SOURCE: Adapted from "Table 29. Leading Causes of Death and Numbers of Deaths, by Age: United States, 1980 and 2006," in *Health, United States, 2009: With Special Feature on Medical Technology*, Centers for Disease Control and Prevention, National Center for Health Statistics, February 2010, http://www.cdc.gov/nchs/data/hus/hus09.pdf (accessed October 15, 2010).

TABLE 4.19

Percentage of high school students who rode with a driver who had been drinking alcohol and who drove when they had been drinking alcohol, by sex, race and Hispanic origin, and grade, 2009

	Rode with a driver who had been drinking alcohol[a]			Drove when drinking alcohol[a]		
	Female	Male	Total	Female	Male	Total
Category	%	%	%	%	%	%
Race/ethnicity						
White[b]	26.9	25.5	26.2	8.7	12.7	10.8
Black[b]	28.7	31.2	30.0	4.1	8.7	6.4
Hispanic	34.9	33.5	34.2	7.9	11.0	9.4
Grade						
9	30.0	25.3	27.5	4.8	5.1	5.0
10	27.6	28.3	28.0	5.3	11.0	8.3
11	29.6	29.2	29.4	9.6	13.0	11.4
12	27.9	28.6	28.2	11.4	19.3	15.4
Total	**28.8**	**27.8**	**28.3**	**7.6**	**11.6**	**9.7**

[a]One or more times during the 30 days before the survey.
[b]Non-Hispanic.

SOURCE: Danice K. Eaton et al., "Table 6. Percentage of High School Students Who Rode in a Car or Other Vehicle Driven by Someone Who Had Been Drinking Alcohol and Who Drove a Car or Other Vehicle When They Had Been Drinking Alcohol, by Sex, Race/Ethnicity, and Grade—United States, Youth Risk Behavior Survey, 2009," in "Youth Risk Behavior Surveillance—United States, 2009," *Morbidity and Mortality Weekly Report*, vol. 59, no. SS-5, June 4, 2010, http://www.cdc.gov/mmwr/pdf/ss/ss5905.pdf (accessed October 22, 2010)

their seatbelts. According to the National Highway Traffic Safety Administration, in "Priority Program Areas" (2010, http://www.nhtsa.gov/Driving+Safety/Driver+ Education/Teen+Drivers/ci.Teen+Drivers+-+Additional+ Resources.print), 31% of all young drivers aged 15 to 20 years who were killed in crashes in 2006 had been drinking alcohol.

Eaton et al. find that in 2009, during the month before the survey, 15.4% of high school seniors (those most likely to have their driver's license) reported they had driven a vehicle after drinking alcohol. (See Table 4.19.) Male seniors (19.3%) were more likely than female seniors (11.4%) to drive after drinking. Another 28.3% of all high school students admitted they had ridden with a driver who had been drinking.

SUICIDE. In 2006 suicide was the sixth-leading cause of death among five- to 14-year-olds and the third-leading cause of death in 15- to 24-year-olds. (See Table 4.18.) Debra L. Karch, Linda L. Dahlberg, and Nimesh Patel of the CDC report in "Surveillance for Violent Deaths— National Violent Death Reporting System, 16 States, 2007" (*Morbidity and Mortality Weekly Report*, vol. 59, no. SS-04, May 14, 2010) that the male suicide rate (18.4 deaths per 100,000 population) was more than three and a half times higher than the female suicide rate (5 deaths per 100,000 population). In "Deaths: Leading Causes for 2006" (*National Vital Statistics Reports*, vol. 58, no. 14, March 31, 2010), Melonie Heron of the CDC indicates that in 2006 white males aged 15 to 19 years had nearly twice the suicide rate (12.3 deaths per 100,000 population) of Hispanic males (7.9 per 100,000) or African-American males (7 per 100,000). Among females aged 15 to 19

years the suicide rate for whites (3 deaths per 100,000 population) and Hispanics (2.9 per 100,000) was significantly higher than the rate for African-Americans (1.3 per 100,000).

Eaton et al. questioned high school students regarding their thoughts about suicide. More than one out of seven (13.8%) students surveyed in 2009 claimed that they had seriously thought about attempting suicide during the previous 12 months. (See Table 4.20.) Even though the suicide death rate was much higher among males than females, females (17.4%) were more likely to have considered suicide than males (10.5%). Of all students, 10.9% (13.2% of females and 8.6% of males) had made a specific plan to attempt suicide. Approximately 6.3% of students (8.1% of females and 4.6% of males) said they had attempted suicide during the previous year, and 1.9% of high school students (2.3% of females and 1.6% of males) said they had suffered injuries from the attempt that required medical attention. (See Table 4.21.) These numbers reflect the fact that females of all ages tend to choose less fatal methods of attempting suicide, such as overdosing and cutting veins, than males, who tend to choose more deadly methods, such as shooting or hanging.

These rates reflect the fact that a large proportion of students, particularly female students, feel sad or hopeless. In 2009, 33.9% of female students and 19.1% of male students reported these feelings. (See Table 4.20.) The likelihood that a child will commit suicide increases with the presence of certain risk factors. According to the CDC, in "Homicides and Suicides—National Violent Death Reporting System, United States, 2003–2004"

TABLE 4.20

Percentage of high school students who felt sad or hopeless, who seriously considered attempting suicide, and who made a suicide plan, by sex, race and Hispanic origin, and grade, 2009

	Felt sad or hopeless[a, b]			Seriously considered attempting suicide[c]			Made a suicide plan[c]		
	Female	Male	Total	Female	Male	Total	Female	Male	Total
Category	%	%	%	%	%	%	%	%	%
Race/ethnicity									
White[d]	31.1	17.2	23.7	16.1	10.5	13.1	12.3	8.5	10.3
Black[d]	37.5	17.9	27.7	18.1	7.8	13.0	13.3	6.2	9.8
Hispanic[c]	39.7	23.6	31.6	20.2	10.7	15.4	15.4	9.0	12.2
Grade									
9	35.8	18.6	26.6	20.3	10.0	14.8	14.9	7.3	10.8
10	34.7	18.2	26.1	17.2	10.0	13.4	14.3	9.3	11.7
11	35.5	19.6	27.3	17.8	11.4	14.5	13.4	9.4	11.3
12	28.9	19.8	24.3	13.6	10.5	12.1	9.6	8.8	9.2
Total	**33.9**	**19.1**	**26.1**	**17.4**	**10.5**	**13.8**	**13.2**	**8.6**	**10.9**

[a]Almost every day for 2 or more weeks in a row so that they stopped doing some usual activities.
[b]During the 12 months before the survey.
[c]During the 12 months before the survey.
[d]Non-Hispanic.

SOURCE: Adapted from Danice K. Eaton et al., "Table 20. Percentage of High School Students Who Felt Sad or Hopeless, by Sex, Race/Ethnicity, and Grade—United States, Youth Risk Behavior Survey, 2009," and "Table 22. Percentage of High School Students Who Seriously Considered Attempting Suicide, and Who Made a Plan about How They Would Attempt Suicide, by Sex, Race/Ethnicity, and Grade—United States, Youth Risk Behavior Survey, 2009," in "Youth Risk Behavior Surveillance—United States, 2009," *Morbidity and Mortality Weekly Report*, vol. 59, no. SS-5, June 4, 2010, http://www.cdc.gov/mmwr/pdf/ss/ss5905.pdf (accessed October 22, 2010)

TABLE 4.21

Percentage of high school students who attempted suicide and whose suicide attempt resulted in an injury that required medical treatment, by sex, race and Hispanic origin, and grade, 2009

	Attempted suicide[a, b]			Suicide attempt treated by a doctor or nurse[a]		
	Female	Male	Total	Female	Male	Total
Category	%	%	%	%	%	%
Race/ethnicity						
White[c]	6.5	3.8	5.0	2.0	1.2	1.6
Black[c]	10.4	5.4	7.9	2.5	2.5	2.5
Hispanic	11.1	5.1	8.1	2.7	1.8	2.2
Grade						
9	10.3	4.5	7.3	2.8	1.4	2.1
10	8.8	5.2	6.9	2.3	2.0	2.2
11	7.8	4.7	6.3	2.6	1.7	2.1
12	4.6	3.8	4.2	1.0	1.4	1.2
Total	**8.1**	**4.6**	**6.3**	**2.3**	**1.6**	**1.9**

[a]During the 12 months before the survey.
[b]One or more times.
[c]Non-Hispanic.

SOURCE: Danice K. Eaton et al.,"Table 24. Percentage of High School Students Who Attempted Suicide and Whose Suicide Attempt Resulted in an Injury, Poisoning, or Overdose That Had to Be Treated by a Doctor or Nurse, by Sex, Race/Ethnicity, and Grade—United States, Youth Risk Behavior Survey, 2009," in "Youth Risk Behavior Surveillance—United States, 2009," *Morbidity and Mortality Weekly Report*, vol. 59, no. SS-5, June 4, 2010, http://www.cdc.gov/mmwr/pdf/ss/ss5905.pdf (accessed October 22, 2010)

(*Morbidity and Mortality Weekly Report*, vol. 55, no. 26, July 7, 2006), among the factors whose presence may indicate heightened risk are depression, mental health problems, relationship conflicts, a history of previous suicide attempts, and alcohol dependence.

In addition, the suicide rate among male homosexual teens is believed to be extremely high. Suicidal gay adolescents are not only coping with stressors but also have few coping resources. In "Gay Adolescents and Suicide: Understanding the Association" (*Adolescence*, vol. 40, no. 159, Fall 2005), Robert Li Kitts of Oregon Health and Science University states that "the process of realizing that one is gay and having to accept it is not just an immediate stressor and can actually narrow one's options further by taking away coping resources, such as friends and family.... Gay adolescents who 'come out' (disclose their sexuality) may experience great family discord, rejection, and even failure from the disappointment they elicit.... It would make sense to conclude that homosexuality is an important risk factor for adolescent suicide."

Jeremy Hubbard reports in "Fifth Gay Teen Suicide in Three Weeks Sparks Debate" (ABC News, October 3, 2010) that between September and October 2010 national attention focused on the problem of gay teen suicide when at least five gay teens committed suicide within a period of three weeks. The fifth suicide of Tyler Clementi, a Rutgers University freshman, was directly linked to antigay bullying. Clementi jumped off the George Washington Bridge after his college roommate posted a video on the Internet of him having sex with another man. In "Schools Battle Suicide Surge, Anti-gay Bullying" (CBS News, October 11, 2010), Neil Katz notes that the suicides of Asher Brown and Seth Walsh, both 13-year-olds, were also linked to antigay bullying.

Raymund Flandez reports in "'Glee' Bully Max Adler Becomes Anti-gay Bullying Advocate" (*Wall Street Journal*, November 16, 2010) that the hit television show *Glee* tackled antigay bullying in several of its episodes that aired in November 2010. The show portrayed the bullying that the gay character Kurt Hummel suffered at the hands of the football player Dave Karofsky.

CHAPTER 5
TEEN SEXUALITY AND PREGNANCY

EARLY SEXUAL ACTIVITY

Many teenagers are sexually active. Danice K. Eaton et al. of the Centers for Disease Control and Prevention (CDC) report in "Youth Risk Behavior Surveillance—United States, 2009" (*Morbidity and Mortality Weekly Report*, vol. 59, no. SS-05, June 4, 2010) that 46% of high school students surveyed in grades nine through 12 have had sexual intercourse. (See Table 5.1.) Girls (45.7%) and boys (46.1%) were about equally likely to have had intercourse. Non-Hispanic African-American students (65.2%) were more likely than Hispanic (49.1%) or non-Hispanic white students (42%) to have ever had intercourse.

The proportion of students who had intercourse rose with age; 31.6% of ninth graders, 40.9% of 10th graders, 53% of 11th graders, and 62.3% of 12th graders had ever had intercourse at the time of the survey in 2009. (See Table 5.1.) A number of youth were sexually active before the age of 13 years; 5.9% had had intercourse at age 12 years or younger. This early sexual activity is of concern, especially among young girls. According to studies such as Sonya S. Brady and Bonnie L. Halpern-Felsher's "Adolescents' Reported Consequences of Having Oral Sex versus Vaginal Sex" (*Pediatrics*, vol. 119, no. 2, February 2007), among sexually active young teens, boys tend to feel good about themselves and experience popularity as a result of sexual activity, whereas girls are more likely to feel used and bad about themselves. In addition, Denise D. Hallfors et al. report in "Which Comes First in Adolescence—Sex and Drugs or Depression?" (*American Journal of Preventive Medicine*, vol. 29, no. 3, October 2005) that being sexually active puts adolescents, particularly girls, at risk for depression. Theo G. M. Sandfort et al. find in "Long-Term Health Correlates of Timing of Sexual Debut: Results from a National U.S. Study" (*American Journal of Public Health*, vol. 98, no. 1, January 2008) that early sexual initiation has long-term negative sexual health outcomes for both boys and girls, including a higher likelihood of

engaging in sexually risky behaviors and problems in sexual functioning.

Risk Factors for Early Sexual Activity

The quality of the relationship that children have with their parents is a significant factor in the age of sexual initiation. Maureen M. Black et al. find in "Sexual Intercourse among Adolescents Maltreated before Age 12: A Prospective Investigation" (*Pediatrics*, vol. 124, no. 3, September 2009) that child maltreatment of any type (physical, emotional, or sexual) significantly predicted early sexual intercourse. In fact, youth who reported high levels of emotional distress were particularly likely to become sexually active by the age of 14 years. Cami K. McBride et al. indicate in "Individual and Familial Influences on the Onset of Sexual Intercourse among Urban African American Adolescents" (*Journal of Consulting and Clinical Psychology*, vol. 71, no. 1, February 2003) that family conflict is also linked to early sexual activity among poor urban African-American adolescents. In "Parental Influences on Adolescent Sexual Behavior in High Poverty Settings" (*Archives of Pediatrics and Adolescent Medicine*, vol. 153, no. 10, October 1999), another study of poor African-American children, Daniel Romer et al. find that those who reported high levels of monitoring from parents were less likely to have sex before adolescence (at the age of 10 years or younger) and had lower rates of sexual initiation during their teen years as well.

John Santelli et al. report in "Initiation of Sexual Intercourse among Middle School Adolescents: The Influence of Psychosocial Factors" (*Journal of Adolescent Health*, vol. 34, no. 3, March 2004), a study of inner-city seventh graders, that peer norms about refraining from sex were strongly correlated with seventh and eighth graders abstaining; on the contrary, drug or alcohol use increased the risk of early sexual activity. Other studies, such as S. Liliana Escobar-Chaves et al.'s "Impact of the Media

TABLE 5.1

Percentage of high school students who ever had sexual intercourse and who had sexual intercourse for the first time before age 13 years, by sex, race and Hispanic origin, and grade, 2009

	Ever had sexual intercourse			Had first sexual intercourse before age 13 years		
	Female	Male	Total	Female	Male	Total
Category	%	%	%	%	%	%
Race/ethnicity						
White*	44.7	39.6	42.0	2.2	4.4	3.4
Black*	58.3	72.1	65.2	5.6	24.9	15.2
Hispanic	45.4	52.8	49.1	3.7	9.8	6.7
Grade						
9	29.3	33.6	31.6	3.6	11.3	7.7
10	39.6	41.9	40.9	3.6	9.0	6.5
11	52.5	53.4	53.0	2.7	5.9	4.3
12	65.0	59.6	62.3	2.2	6.4	4.4
Total	**45.7**	**46.1**	**46.0**	**3.1**	**8.4**	**5.9**

*Non-Hispanic.

SOURCE: Adapted from Danice K. Eaton et al., "Table 61. Percentage of High School Students Who Ever Had Sexual Intercourse and Who Had Sexual Intercourse for the First Time before Age 13 Years, by Sex, Race/Ethnicity, and Grade—United States, Youth Risk Behavior Survey, 2009," in "Youth Risk Behavior Surveillance—United States, 2009," *Morbidity and Mortality Weekly Report*, vol. 59, no. SS-5, June 4, 2010, http://www.cdc.gov/mmwr/pdf/ss/ss5905.pdf (accessed October 22, 2010).

on Adolescent Sexual Attitudes and Behaviors" (*Pediatrics*, vol. 116, no. 1, July 2005), find a correlation between exposure to sexual themes in mass media and adolescent sexual activity.

Regret

A number of studies report that both sexes consider social pressure a major factor in engaging in early sexual activity. Peer pressure and a belief that "everyone is doing it" have often been cited as explanations. However, in "Adolescent Girls' Perceptions of the Timing of Their Sexual Initiation: 'Too Young' or 'Just Right'?" (*Journal of Adolescent Health*, vol. 34, no. 5, May 2004), Sian Cotton et al. indicate that most female adolescents (78% of the studied group) felt that they had been "too young" at their first sexual experience.

Steven C. Martino et al. of the RAND Corporation explore in "It's Better on TV: Does Television Set Teenagers up for Regret Following Sexual Initiation" (*Perspectives on Sexual and Reproductive Health*, vol. 41, no. 2, June 2009) one possible reason why nearly two-thirds of adolescents regret their first sexual experience. The researchers conducted a telephone survey of youth aged 12 to 17 years during the spring of 2001, and reinterviewed the same group during the spring of 2002 and the spring of 2004. Martino et al. find that 61% of females and 39% of males who had their first sexual experience during the study period reported that they wished they had waited to have sex. The researchers theorize that "adolescents may infer that they have made a poor decision about when or with whom to initiate intercourse—and thus may regret the decision—if the experience fell short of their expectations." The researchers argue that portrayals of sexuality

in the media, particularly on television, are unrealistic and may contribute to teens' subsequent regret. Martino et al. find that males who were heavy television watchers were more likely to regret the circumstances of their first sexual intercourse than were other males. By contrast, at least in part because female television characters are more often shown to have negative sexual experiences than are male characters, there was no association between heavy television watching and regret among females.

The Media and Teen Concepts of Sexuality

In *Sex on TV 4* (November 2005, http://www.kff.org/entmedia/upload/Sex-on-TV-4-Full-Report.pdf), the most recent report on this topic as of January 2011, the Kaiser Family Foundation and Dale Kunkel et al. of the University of Arizona discuss the results of a study of sexual messages on television. The report finds that the percent of shows with sexual content had increased from 56% in 1998 to 70% in 2005. In addition, in those shows that included sexual content, the number of sexual scenes per hour had risen from 3.2 in 1998 to 5 in 2005—and in the top teen programs, there were on average 6.7 sexual scenes per hour. Of the 20 shows most popular with teenagers, 70% included some sexual content and 45% included sexual behavior. More than one out of 10 (11%) episodes included scenes in which sexual intercourse was depicted or strongly implied. Only 10% of shows most popular with teens that contained sexual content included a reference to sexual risk or responsibility.

The report notes that the portrayal of sex on television does not have wholly negative consequences. In fact, even though references to sexual risk or responsibility are still low, they have increased in recent years. Furthermore, these references can have a big impact. The report states that studies show "consistent evidence that incorporating risk or responsibility messages into television programs with sexual themes and topics can significantly increase viewer sensitivity to critical sexual health concerns."

In September 2010 the American Academy of Pediatrics (AAP) released the policy statement "Sexuality, Contraception, and the Media" (*Pediatrics*, vol. 126, no. 3). The AAP stresses that adolescent exposure to the portrayal of "casual sex and sexuality with no consequences" on television, in music, movies, magazines, and on the Internet are "important factors in the initiation of sexual intercourse." The AAP urges pediatricians to give adolescents straightforward information about human sexuality and contraception rather than promoting abstinence-only, which the AAP argues is ineffective in the face of overwhelming media messages about nonabstinence.

Sexual Activity and Substance Use

Over the years a number of studies have suggested a link between substance use and sexual activity. Researchers find that both sexual activity and a history of multiple partners correlate with some use of drugs, alcohol, and cigarettes. However, Eaton et al. indicate that among sexually active students, only 21.6% reported in 2009 that they had used alcohol or drugs at the time of their last sexual intercourse. (See Table 5.2.) Males (25.9%) were more likely than females (17.1%) to report this behavior. Non-Hispanic African-Americans (18.2%) were less likely than Hispanics (18.9%) or non-Hispanic whites (22.9%) to report using alcohol or drugs during sexual activity.

Brent E. Mancha, Vanessa C. Rojas-Neese, and William W. Latimer find in "Alcohol Use Problem Severity and Problem Behavior Engagement among School-Based Youths in Minnesota" (*Journal of Child and Adolescent Substance Abuse*, vol. 19, no. 3, July 2010) that the frequency and problem severity of alcohol use were associated with higher odds of having engaged in sexual intercourse. In "Adolescent Sexual Behaviors at Varying Levels of Substance Use Frequency" (*Journal of Child and Adolescent Substance Abuse*, vol. 19, no. 1, January 2010), Leah J. Floyd and William Latimer of the Johns Hopkins Bloomberg School of Public Health find in their study of 1,432 middle school and high school students in Minnesota that even though alcohol use and marijuana use were both associated with sexual activity, only marijuana use was associated with having multiple partners. John E. Anderson and Trisha E. Mueller of the CDC find in "Trends in Sexual Risk Behavior and Unprotected Sex among High School Students, 1991–2006: The Role of Substance Use" (*Journal of School Health*, vol. 78, no. 11, November 2008) that adolescents who use drugs or alcohol are more likely to engage in risky sexual behaviors. The researchers report that "in spite of favorable trends in recent years for both sexual risk and drug use among adolescents, the [Youth Risk Behavior Survey] data show that a high percentage of youth are at risk and that many youth remain at dual risk from substance abuse and sexual behaviors."

Voluntary and Nonvoluntary Experiences

The 1995 and 2002 National Survey of Family Growth asked women whether their first sexual experience was voluntary. In "A Demographic Portrait of Statutory Rape"

TABLE 5.2

Percentage of high school students who drank alcohol or used drugs before last sexual intercourse[a] and who were ever taught in school about AIDS or HIV, by sex, race and Hispanic origin, and grade, 2009

	Drank alcohol or used drugs before last sexual intercourse			Were taught in school about AIDS or HIV infection		
	Female	Male	Total	Female	Male	Total
Category	%	%	%	%	%	%
Race/ethnicity						
White[b]	18.2	28.0	22.9	89.6	87.8	88.6
Black[b]	15.2	20.8	18.2	86.9	85.2	86.1
Hispanic	15.0	22.6	18.9	83.2	83.2	83.2
Grade						
9	23.5	25.9	24.7	84.6	81.8	83.1
10	18.1	26.5	22.4	87.7	86.9	87.3
11	14.7	25.9	20.3	89.9	88.8	89.3
12	15.2	25.8	20.2	89.4	89.1	89.3
Total	**17.1**	**25.9**	**21.6**	**87.8**	**86.3**	**87.0**

[a]Among the 34.2% of students nationwide who were currently sexually active.
[b]Non-Hispanic.

SOURCE: Adapted from Danice K. Eaton et al.,"Table 71. Percentage of High School Students Who Drank Alcohol or Used Drugs before Last Sexual Intercourse and Who Were Ever Taught in School about Acquired Immunodeficiency Syndrome (AIDS) or Human Immunodeficiency Virus (HIV) Infection, by Sex, Race/Ethnicity, and Grade—United States, Youth Risk Behavior Survey, 2009," in "Youth Risk Behavior Surveillance—United States, 2009," *Morbidity and Mortality Weekly Report*, vol. 59, no. SS-5, June 4, 2010, http://www.cdc.gov/mmwr/pdf/ss/ss5905.pdf (accessed October 22, 2010)

(2005, http://www.childtrends.org/Files/ConferenceonSex ualExploitationofTeensPresentation.pdf), Kristin Moore and Jennifer Manlove find that 18% of girls whose first sexual experience occurred at the age of 13 years or younger said it was nonvoluntary, compared with 10% of 15- and 16-year-olds and 5% of 17- and 19-year-olds. In addition, Elizabeth Terry-Humen, Jennifer Manlove, and Sarah Cottingham report in "Trends and Recent Estimates: Sexual Activity among U.S. Teens" (June 2006, http://www.childtrends.org/Files//Child_Trends-2006 _06_01_RB_SexualActivity.pdf) that survey respondents were asked to state which of three statements most closely described how much they wanted their first sexual intercourse experience: "I really didn't want it to happen at the time," "I had mixed feelings—part of me wanted it to happen at the time and part of me didn't," and "I really wanted it to happen at the time." Only 34% of adolescent females said they really wanted it to happen at the time, compared with 62% of adolescent males who felt that way. More than one out of 10 (13%) females, compared with 6% of males, reported that they really did not want their first sexual intercourse to happen at that time.

Additionally, Anita Raj, Jay G. Silverman, and Hortensia Amaro find in "The Relationship between Sexual Abuse and Sexual Risk among High School Students: Findings from the 1997 Massachusetts Youth Risk Behavior Survey" (*Maternal and Child Health Journal*, vol. 4, no. 2, June 2000) that almost one-third (30.2%) of the girls and one-tenth (9.3%) of the boys reported having been sexually abused. Sexually abused females were twice as likely to engage in early sexual intercourse and other risky sexual behaviors than girls who had not been abused. Several studies corroborate evidence of the increased sexual risks taken by sexually abused youth, such as Elizabeth M. Saewyc, Lara Leanne Magee, and Sandra E. Pettingell's "Teenage Pregnancy and Associated Risk Behaviors among Sexually Abused Adolescents" (*Perspectives on Sexual and Reproductive Health*, vol. 36, no. 3, May–June 2004); Regina Jones Johnson, Lynn Rew, and R. Weylin Sternglanz's "The Relationship between Childhood Sexual Abuse and Sexual Health Practices of Homeless Adolescents" (*Adolescence*, vol. 41, no. 162, 2006); and Jonathan G. Tubman et al.'s "Abuse Experiences in a Community Sample of Young Adults: Relations with Psychiatric Disorders, Sexual Risk Behaviors, and Sexually Transmitted Diseases" (*American Journal of Community Psychology*, vol. 34, nos. 1–2, September 2004). Christopher D. Houck et al. find in "Sexual Abuse and Sexual Risk Behavior: Beyond the Impact of Psychiatric Problems" (*Journal of Pediatric Psychology*, vol. 35, no. 5, June 1, 2010) that youth who had been sexually abused were significantly more likely to have engaged in sex during their lifetime and within the past 90 days and to have had unprotected sex.

Moreover, early sexual initiation for teenage girls has been linked to several adverse outcomes. In "Associations of Dating Violence Victimization with Lifetime Participation, Co-occurrence, and Early Initiation of Risk Behaviors among U.S. High School Students" (*Journal of Interpersonal Violence*, vol. 22, no. 5, May 2007), Danice K. Eaton et al. of the CDC link early sexual intercourse with dating violence victimization among female students. Erin Schelar, Suzanne Ryan, and Jennifer Manlove argue in "Long-Term Consequences for Teens with Older Sexual Partners" (April 2008, http://www.childtrends.org/Files//Child _Trends-2008_05_06_FS_OlderPartners.pdf) that many girls with an early sexual initiation have partners three or more years older. The combination of early sexual initiation with older sexual partners puts girls at a higher risk for contracting sexually transmitted diseases (STDs). In "Long-Term Health Correlates of Timing of Sexual Debut: Results from a National U.S. Study" (*American Journal of Public Health*, vol. 98, no. 1, January 2008), Theo G. M. Sandfort et al. link early sexual initiation to increased sexual risk behaviors and problems and sexual functioning for both males and females.

CONTRACEPTIVE USE

Too Few Use Contraceptives

Eaton et al. find that 61.1% of sexually active teenagers reported in 2009 that they or their partners had used condoms during their last sexual intercourse. (See Table 5.3.) Non-Hispanic white students reported the highest condom use (63.3%) among sexually active youth, non-Hispanic African-American students reported a rate of 62.4%, whereas Hispanic students reported a rate of just 54.9%. Males (68.6%) were significantly more likely than females (53.9%) to report condom use. However, the use of condoms decreased from the 10th grade (67.8%) to the 12th grade (55%), a period during which the frequency of sexual intercourse increased, probably because older adolescents turned to alternative methods of birth control, such as oral contraception.

Among sexually active students nationwide in 2009, 19.8% reported that they or their partners used oral contraceptives, or "the pill." (See Table 5.3.) Even though this form of contraception protects against pregnancy, it does not protect against STDs. Two and a half times as many non-Hispanic white students (26.8%) reported using birth control pills than did Hispanic (10.8%) or non-Hispanic African-American students (8.1%). This disparity may be due to the need for a prescription for birth control pills; non-Hispanic white students tend to have greater access to medical care than minority students do. Birth control pill use increased between ninth (10.2%) and 12th grade (27.6%).

REASONS FOR USE OR NONUSE OF CONDOMS. Research indicates that adolescents' attitudes and beliefs about their

TABLE 5.3

Percentage of high school students who used a condom during last sexual intercourse and who used birth control pills before last sexual intercourse, by sex, race and Hispanic origin, and grade, 2009

	Condom use[a]			Birth control pill use[a, b]		
	Female	Male	Total	Female	Male	Total
Category	%	%	%	%	%	%
Race/ethnicity						
White[c]	56.1	71.0	63.3	31.4	21.6	26.8
Black[c]	51.8	72.5	62.4	9.8	6.6	8.1
Hispanic	48.0	61.7	54.9	9.9	11.5	10.8
Grade						
9	57.7	69.9	64.0	9.7	10.7	10.2
10	63.5	71.9	67.8	15.6	14.0	14.7
11	54.0	68.9	61.4	22.5	18.9	20.7
12	46.3	65.0	55.0	34.4	19.6	27.6
Total	**53.9**	**68.6**	**61.1**	**23.0**	**16.5**	**19.8**

[a]Among the 34.2% of students nationwide who were currently sexually active.
[b]To prevent pregnancy.
[c]Non-Hispanic.

SOURCE: Adapted from Danice K. Eaton et al.,"Table 65. Percentage of High School Students Who Used a Condom during Last Sexual Intercourse and Who Used Birth Control Pills before Last Sexual Intercourse, by Sex, Race/Ethnicity, and Grade—United States, Youth Risk Behavior Survey, 2009," in "Youth Risk Behavior Surveillance—United States, 2009," *Morbidity and Mortality Weekly Report*, vol. 59, no. SS-5, June 4, 2010, http://www.cdc.gov/mmwr/pdf/ss/ss5905.pdf (accessed October 22, 2010)

relationships with their partners influence whether or not they will use condoms. Drawing on a national survey of male adolescents, Erum Ikramullah and Jennifer Manlove find in "Condom Use and Consistency among Teen Males" (October 2008, http://www.childtrends.org/Files/Child_Trends-2008_10_30_FS_CondomUse.pdf) that even though 71% of male teens reported using a condom the first and most recent time they had sexual intercourse, only half of male teens reported consistent condom use with their most recent sexual partner. Celia M. Lescano et al. find in "Condom Use with 'Casual' and 'Main' Partners: What's in a Name?" (*Journal of Adolescent Health*, vol. 39, no. 3, September 2006) that adolescents were more likely to use a condom with a partner that they perceived as a casual one. However, even when partners were casual ones, teens reported using condoms only about half the time. Therefore, teens were not adequately protecting themselves against STDs even with partners they perceived as more risky. Condom use with partners perceived as main partners was even lower. Lescano et al. state, "Perhaps adolescents overestimate the safety of using condoms 'most of the time' with a casual partner and underestimate the risk of unprotected sex with a 'serious' partner."

Cynthia Grossman et al. find in "Adolescent Sexual Risk: Factors Predicting Condom Use across the Stages of Change" (*AIDS and Behavior*, vol. 12, no. 6, November 2008) that teens who consistently used condoms reported a greater understanding of the importance of using condoms, had better communication about condom use with their partners, and were less likely to perceive themselves as immune to the human immunodeficiency virus (HIV) than their peers who reported inconsistent

condom use. In "Parental Communication as a Protective Factor in Increasing Condom Use among Minority Adolescents" (*International Journal of Adolescent Medicine and Health*, vol. 21, no. 1, January–March 2009), Ruth S. Buzi, Peggy B. Smith, and Maxine L. Weinman find that consistent condom use among adolescents was positively related to the degree of parental communication about sexual topics, particularly among African-American adolescents.

According to Tricia Hall et al., in "Attitudes toward Using Condoms and Condom Use: Differences between Sexually Abused and Nonabused African American Female Adolescents" (*Behavioral Medicine*, vol. 34, no. 2, Summer 2008), there is some evidence that teens who have been sexually abused are less likely to use condoms and more likely to have unprotected sex than their nonabused peers.

SEXUALLY TRANSMITTED DISEASES

Adolescents and young adults have a higher risk of acquiring STDs than older adults. Female adolescents may have an increased susceptibility to chlamydia, a bacterial infection that can cause pelvic inflammatory disease and is a contributing factor in the transmission of HIV. In *Child Health USA 2010* (October 2010, http://www.mchb.hrsa.gov/chusa10/index.html), the Health Resources and Services Administration's Maternal and Child Health Bureau states that chlamydia was the most common reportable STD among adolescents in 2008. It was also more common in adolescents and young adults than in any other age group, with 1,956 cases among every 100,000 teens aged 15 to 19 years. This group also had the highest rates of gonorrhea infection. As Figure 5.1 shows, non-Hispanic African-American teens had much higher rates of both chlamydia and gonorrhea than non-Hispanic white, Hispanic, and Native American or Alaskan Native teens.

The Maternal and Child Health Bureau finds that in 2007 an estimated 6,524 people aged 13 to 24 years were diagnosed with HIV. These cases are on the rise, especially among teenagers. Between 2005 and 2007 the number of diagnoses among 15- to 19-year-olds increased by 35%, and the number of diagnoses among 20- to 24-year-olds increased by 18%.

In "Does Parental Involvement Predict New Sexually Transmitted Diseases in Female Adolescents?" (*Archives of Pediatrics and Adolescent Medicine*, vol. 158, no. 7, July 2004), Julie A. Bettinger et al. test whether parental involvement had any impact on the rates of STDs among low-income African-American adolescent girls. The researchers find that when these high-risk teens perceived their parents as exercising a high degree of supervision over their activities, they had lower rates of both gonorrhea and chlamydia infection. Anne M. Teitelman, Sarah J. Ratcliffe, and Julie A. Cederbaum find in "Parent-Adolescent Communication about Sexual Pressure, Maternal Norms about Relationship Power, and STI/HIV Protective Behaviors of Minority Urban Girls"

FIGURE 5.1

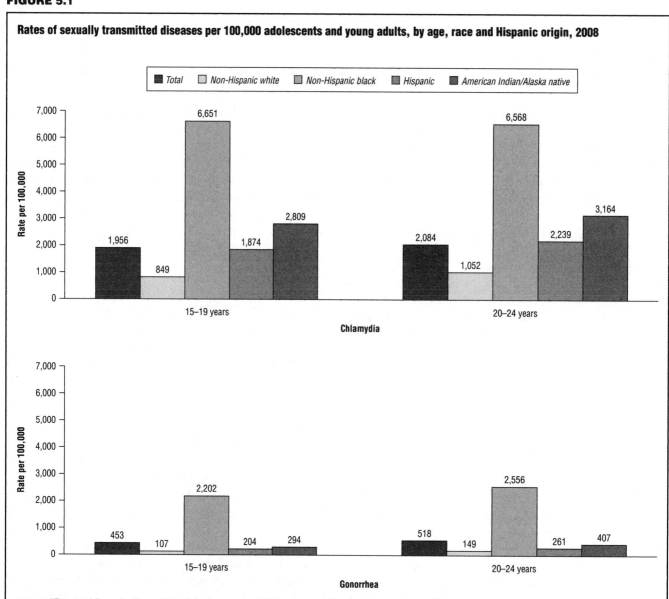

Rates of sexually transmitted diseases per 100,000 adolescents and young adults, by age, race and Hispanic origin, 2008

SOURCE: "Reported Sexually Transmitted Infections among Adolescents and Young Adults, by Age and Race/Ethnicity, 2008," in *Child Health USA 2010*, U.S. Department of Health and Human Services, Maternal and Child Health Bureau, October 2010, http://www.mchb.hrsa.gov/chusa10/hstat/hsa/pages/217sti.html (accessed October 25, 2010)

(*American Psychiatric Nurses Association Journal*, vol. 14, no. 1, February–March 2008) that racial and ethnic minority adolescent females who communicated with their parents about sex were better able to be consistent in condom use.

Human Papillomavirus Vaccine

One STD, the human papillomavirus (HPV), can cause genital warts and cervical cancer in women. Cases of HPV are not required to be reported to the CDC, but the Maternal and Child Health Bureau indicates in *Child Health USA 2010* that HPV is the most common STD in the United States. Approximately 25% of females aged 14 to 19 years and almost 45% of young women aged 20 to 24 years are infected. At least half of sexually active people will get HPV; most of the time, it resolves on its own. However, sometimes it lingers and causes cell changes that can lead to cervical cancer. In "What Are the Key Statistics about Cervical Cancer?" (December 23, 2010, http://www.cancer.org/Cancer/CervicalCancer/DetailedGuide/cervical-cancer-key-statistics), the American Cancer Society estimates that in 2010 about 12,200 women were diagnosed with cervical cancer and 4,210 women died from it. A large proportion of cervical cancer cases are caused by HPV, perhaps in combination with other factors. Clinical trials for a new vaccine against certain strains of HPV, which are given in three doses over a six-month period, show that the vaccine is nearly 100% effective. The CDC notes in "Human Papillomavirus (HPV)" (October 13, 2010, http://www.cdc.gov/std/hpv/default.htm) that it began recommending in 2006 that the new vaccine be given to girls aged 11 to 12 years, before they become sexually active, to prevent the transmission of HPV.

However, such recommendations stirred up controversy, which heated up in February 2007, when Rick Perry (1950–), the governor of Texas, issued an executive order making the state the first to require that girls entering the sixth grade be vaccinated as a condition for enrolling in public school. Liz Austin Peterson reports in "Texas Gov. Orders Anti-cancer Vaccine" (Associated Press, February 3, 2007) that conservative groups feared that such a requirement undermined abstinence education and would condone premarital sex. In "Virginity or Death!" (*Nation*, May 30, 2005), Katha Pollitt explains that others argued for mandatory vaccination because young girls will not abstain from sexual activity due to fear of cervical cancer, HPV cannot be prevented by condom use, and 70% of cases of cervical cancer can be prevented by this vaccine.

James Colgrove, Sara Abiola, and Michelle M. Mello indicate in "HPV Vaccination Mandates—Lawmaking amid Political and Scientific Controversy" (*New England Journal of Medicine*, vol. 363, no. 8, August 19, 2010) that by February 2010 bills to make HPV vaccination mandatory had been introduced in 24 states. However,

only Virginia and the District of Columbia enacted these laws, and Virginia's law included extremely broad opt-out provisions. The researchers propose that the bills in the other states failed because of two factors: a lack of long-term safety data on the vaccine and the sexually transmitted nature of HPV. Colgrove, Abiola, and Mello note that "some social conservatives objected to a compulsory policy because they believed that protecting teenagers against a sexually transmitted disease might undermine prevention messages that emphasize abstinence."

TEEN CHILDBEARING TRENDS

Brady E. Hamilton, Joyce A. Martin, and Stephanie J. Ventura of the CDC report in "Births: Preliminary Data for 2008" (*National Vital Statistics Reports*, vol. 58, no. 16, April 6, 2010) that the birthrate for women aged 15 to 19 years dropped in 2008 after a two-year increase in 2006 and 2007. (See Figure 5.2.) Among girls aged 15 to 17 years the birthrate dropped from 38.6 births per 1,000 women in 1991 to 21.7 births per 1,000 women in 2008. Among young women aged 18 to 19 years the birthrate dropped from 94 births per 1,000 women in 1991 to 70.7 births per 1,000 women in 2008. Most births to teens are to unmarried women. (See Table 5.4.) Childbearing by unmarried women jumped to record high levels in 2008, to 1.7 million births.

According to Hamilton, Martin, and Ventura, every race and ethnic group saw a decrease in teen births in 2008. Hispanic teens aged 15 to 19 years had the highest

FIGURE 5.2

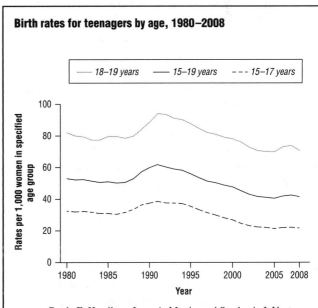

Birth rates for teenagers by age, 1980–2008

SOURCE: Brady E. Hamilton, Joyce A. Martin, and Stephanie J. Ventura, "Figure 1. Birth Rates for Teenagers by Age: United States, Final 1980–2006 and Preliminary 2007 and 2008," in "Births: Preliminary Data for 2008," *National Vital Statistics Reports*, vol. 58, no. 16, April 6, 2010, http://www.cdc.gov/nchs/data/nvsr/nvsr58/nvsr58_16.pdf (accessed October 25, 2010)

TABLE 5.4

Births to unmarried women, by age, 2007 and 2008

[Data are based on continuous file of records received from the states. Figures are based on weighted data rounded to the nearest individual, so categories may not add to total]

Age of mother	Number		Percent	
	2008	2007	2008	2007
All ages	1,727,950	1,714,643	40.6	39.7
Under 20 years	382,779	386,702	86.8	85.7
Under 15 years	5,721	6,142	99.1	98.8
15–19 years	377,058	380,560	86.7	85.5
15–17 years	127,181	130,519	93.7	92.8
18–19 years	249,878	250,041	83.5	82.1
20–24 years	641,245	644,591	60.9	59.5
25–29 years	397,679	389,169	33.2	32.2
30–34 years	193,618	185,425	20.2	19.3
35–39 years	88,953	86,343	18.2	17.3
40–54 years	23,676	22,411	20.8	19.9

SOURCE: Brady E. Hamilton, Joyce A. Martin, and Stephanie J. Ventura, "Table 7. Number and Percentage of Births to Unmarried Women, by Age: United States, Preliminary 2007 and Preliminary 2008," in "Births: Preliminary Data for 2008," *National Vital Statistics Reports*, vol. 58, no. 16, April 6, 2010, http://www.cdc.gov/nchs/data/nvsr/nvsr58/nvsr58_16.pdf (accessed October 25, 2010)

birthrate, at 77.4 births per 1,000 women, followed by non-Hispanic African-American teens, at 62.9 births per 1,000 women, and Native American or Alaskan Native teens, at 58.4 births per 1,000 women. Asian or Pacific Islander teens had the lowest birthrate, at 16.2 births per 1,000 women, and non-Hispanic white teens also had a fairly low birthrate, at 26.7 births per 1,000 women.

Consequences for Teen Mothers and Their Children

Teenage mothers and their babies face more health risks than older women and their babies. Teenagers who become pregnant are more likely than older women to suffer from pregnancy-induced hypertension and eclampsia (a life-threatening condition that sometimes results in convulsions and/or coma). Teenagers are more likely to have their labor induced, and an immature pelvis can cause prolonged or difficult labor, possibly resulting in bladder or bowel damage to the mother, infant brain damage, or even death of the mother and/or the child.

Even though most health risks are similar for children born to teenage and older mothers, teenage mothers may have a higher prevalence of certain risk factors. For example, the National Center for Health Statistics notes in *Health, United States, 2009* (February 2010, http://www.cdc.gov/nchs/data/hus/hus09.pdf) that in 2006 teenagers had high rates of smoking during pregnancy (10.3% for 15- to 17-year-olds and 15.1% for 18- to 19-year-olds) and that smokers (12%) were much more likely to have low birth weight babies than nonsmokers (7.7%). In the fact sheet "Preventing Infant Mortality" (January 13, 2006, http://www.hhs.gov/news/factsheet/infant.html), the U.S. Department of Health and Human Services indicates that teenagers in general are at a higher risk of having low birth weight babies. Michael Klitsch finds in "Youngest Mothers' Infants Have Greatly Elevated

Risk of Dying by Age One" (*Perspectives on Sexual and Reproductive Health*, vol. 35, no. 1, January–February 2003) that babies born to adolescents have a greater risk of dying between one and 12 months after birth.

Few teenage mothers are ready for the emotional, financial, and psychological responsibilities and challenges of parenthood. Becoming a parent at a young age usually cuts short a teenage mother's education, limiting her ability to support herself and her child. David M. Fergusson, Joseph M. Boden, and L. John Horwood of the Christchurch Health and Development Study in New Zealand report in "Abortion among Young Women and Subsequent Life Outcomes" (*Perspectives on Sexual and Reproductive Health*, vol. 39, no. 1, March 2007) that educational attainment is lower among teen mothers than among teens who had an abortion. Additionally, Susheela Singh et al. note in "Socioeconomic Disadvantage and Adolescent Women's Sexual and Reproductive Behavior: The Case of Five Developed Countries" (*Family Planning Perspectives*, vol. 33, no. 6, November–December 2001) that 40% of American women aged 20 to 24 years who gave birth before the age of 20 years had an income of less than 149% of the federal poverty guideline.

The children of teen mothers also face several consequences. In *Playing Catch-Up: How Children Born to Teen Mothers Fare* (January 2005, http://www.thenational campaign.org/resources/pdf/pubs/PlayingCatchUp.pdf), Elizabeth Terry-Humen, Jennifer Manlove, and Kristin A. Moore examine data on kindergarteners to determine the relationship between the age a woman has a child and how her child does in several key areas: cognition and knowledge, language and communication skills, approaches to learning, emotional well-being and social skills, and physical well-being and motor development. The researchers find that children born to mothers aged 17 years and younger had lower general knowledge scores and language and communication skills, compared with children born to mothers aged 20 years and older. Children's approaches to learning, physical well-being, and emotional development, as well as their social skills and emotional well-being, were relatively unaffected by maternal age. In sum, Terry-Humen, Manlove, and Moore state, "Children born to mothers aged 17 and younger began kindergarten with lower levels of school readiness.... The children born to mothers in their 20s clearly outperformed those whose mothers were still teenagers at time of birth, and the most consistent and pronounced differences were observed when comparing children born to mothers aged 17 and younger to those children born to mothers aged 22-29."

Greg Pogarsky, Terence P. Thornberry, and Alan J. Lizotte come to similar conclusions in "Developmental Outcomes for Children of Young Mothers" (*Journal of Marriage and Family*, vol. 68, no. 2, May 2006). The researchers note that boys born to young mothers had elevated risks of drug use, gang membership, unemployment, and early parenthood, whereas girls had elevated risks of becoming young mothers themselves.

In "The Ripples of Adolescent Motherhood: Social, Educational, and Medical Outcomes for Children of Teen and Prior Teen Mothers" (*Academic Pediatrics*, vol. 10, no. 5, September–October 2010), Douglas P. Jutte et al. highlight that all the children of mothers who first gave birth during their teens faced a similar degree of risk, even if the higher-birth-order children were born when their mothers had reached their 20s or 30s. Negative outcomes included risks for poor health and educational and socioeconomic disadvantages. In addition, these negative consequences for children of adolescent mothers extended into later childhood, adolescence, and young adulthood.

Adolescent Fathers

According to the Child Trends Databank, in *Teen Births* (December 10, 2007, http://www.childtrendsdata bank.org/pdf/13_PDF.pdf), 15- to 19-year-old males had a birthrate of 16.8 births per 1,000 males in 2005, down from a high of 24.7 births per 1,000 males in 1991. This rate was substantially lower than the 2005 rate for teenage girls of 40.5 births per 1,000 females. The rate was higher for African-American male teens (32.2 births per 1,000 males) than for white male teens (14.2 births per 1,000 males); data for Hispanic male teens were unavailable. The difference between the male adolescent and female adolescent birthrates is due in part to the fact that many teen mothers have older partners, as well as to the underreporting of information about fathers on birth certificates. In *Facts at a Glance* (November 2003, http://www.child trends.org/Files/FAAG2003.pdf), the most recent Child Trends publication that addressed this topic as of January

2011, the databank reports that 38% of births to mothers aged 18 years and younger were to fathers four or more years older than the mother. In some cases teen mothers have been sexually abused by their older partners.

These studies alert officials who design programs for the prevention of pregnancy and STDs to pay attention not only to preadolescent and adolescent males but also to older males who are partners of teenage girls. Because these men are typically out of the public school system, officials agree that programs must be broader in scope.

TEEN ABORTION

The CDC reports that 820,000 abortions were performed in 2005. (See Table 5.5.) The Guttmacher Institute conducted a survey and estimated that a much higher number of abortions had been performed in 2005: over 1.2 million. The rate of abortions per 100 live births had decreased from a high of 35.9 in 1980 to 23.3 in 2005. Girls under the age of 15 years had the highest rate of abortions (76.4 per 100 live births) in 2005, followed by girls aged 15 to 19 years (35.8 per 100 live births). All other age groups had lower rates of abortion. For all age groups, African-Americans had the highest abortion rate of any race or ethnic group (46.7 per 100 live births), followed by Hispanics (20.5 per 100 live births) and non-Hispanic whites (15.8 per 100 live births). As Table 5.5 shows, the abortion rates for teens have declined dramatically since the late 1980s, as have the pregnancy and birthrates.

States have varying laws on parental involvement in minors' abortion decisions. In "An Overview of Abortion Laws" (December 1, 2010, http://www.guttmacher.org/statecenter/spibs/spib_OAL.pdf), the Guttmacher Institute reports that 15 states and the District of Columbia required no parental involvement in minors' abortions. Thirty-five states required some parental involvement, 22 required one or both parents to consent to the procedure, and 11 required that one or both parents be notified.

HOMOSEXUALITY

In *Just the Facts about Sexual Orientation and Youth: A Primer for Principals, Educators, and School Personnel* (2008, http://www.apa.org/pi/lgbt/resources/just-the-facts.pdf), the American Psychological Association (APA) stresses that sexual orientation is one aspect of the identity of adolescents—not a mental disorder. According to the APA, sexual orientation is developed across a lifetime and along a continuum; in other words, teens are not necessarily simply homosexual or heterosexual, but may feel varying degrees of attraction to people of both genders. The APA explains that gay, lesbian, and bisexual adolescents face prejudice and discrimination that negatively affect their educational experiences and emotional and physical health. Their legitimate fear of being hurt as a

TABLE 5.5

Legal abortions and legal abortion ratios, by selected patient characteristics, selected years 1973–2005

[Data are based on reporting by state health departments and by hospitals and other medical facilities]

Characteristic	1973	1975	1980	1985	1990	1995	1999[a]	2000[b]	2003[c]	2004[c]	2005[d]
						Number of legal abortions reported in thousands					
Centers for Disease Control and Prevention (CDC)	616	855	1,298	1,329	1,429	1,211	862	857	848	839	820
Guttmacher Institute[e]	745	1,034	1,554	1,589	1,609	1,359	1,315	1,313	1,287	1,222	1,206
						Abortions per 100 live births[f]					
Total CDC	**19.6**	**27.2**	**35.9**	**35.4**	**34.4**	**31.1**	**25.6**	**24.5**	**24.1**	**23.8**	**23.3**
Age											
Under 15 years	123.7	119.3	139.7	137.6	81.8	66.4	70.9	70.8	83.0	76.2	76.4
15–19 years	53.9	54.2	71.4	68.8	51.1	39.9	37.5	36.1	37.4	36.2	35.8
20–24 years	29.4	28.9	39.5	38.6	37.8	34.8	31.6	30.0	30.0	29.1	28.3
25–29 years	20.7	19.2	23.7	21.7	21.8	22.0	20.8	19.8	19.5	19.1	18.7
30–34 years	28.0	25.0	23.7	19.9	19.0	16.4	15.2	14.5	14.4	14.3	14.0
35–39 years	45.1	42.2	41.0	33.6	27.3	22.3	19.3	18.1	17.3	17.0	16.8
40 years and over	68.4	66.8	80.7	62.3	50.6	38.5	32.9	30.1	29.3	28.6	27.8
Race											
White[g]	32.6	27.7	33.2	27.7	25.8	20.3	17.7	16.7	16.5	16.1	15.8
Black or African American[h]	42.0	47.6	54.3	47.2	53.7	53.1	52.9	50.3	49.1	47.2	46.7
Hispanic origin[i]											
Hispanic or Latina	—	—	—	—	—	27.1	26.1	22.5	22.8	21.1	20.5
Not Hispanic or Latina	—	—	—	—	—	27.9	25.2	23.3	23.4	23.6	22.3
Marital status											
Married	7.6	9.6	10.5	8.0	8.7	7.6	7.0	6.5	6.3	6.1	5.8
Unmarried	139.8	161.0	147.6	117.4	86.3	64.5	60.4	57.0	53.8	51.0	48.5
Previous live births[j]											
0	43.7	38.4	45.7	45.1	36.0	28.6	24.3	22.6	22.7	23.0	22.6
1	23.5	22.0	20.2	21.6	22.7	22.0	20.6	19.4	19.0	19.0	18.2
2	36.8	36.8	29.5	29.9	31.5	30.6	29.0	27.4	27.1	26.4	25.4
3	46.9	47.7	29.8	18.2	30.1	30.7	29.8	28.5	28.3	27.4	26.4
4 or more[k]	44.7	43.5	24.3	21.5	26.6	23.7	24.2	23.7	23.4	22.9	21.9
						Percent distribution[l]					
Total	**100.0**	**100.0**	**100.0**	**100.0**	**100.0**	**100.0**	**100.0**	**100.0**	**100.0**	**100.0**	**100.0**
Period of gestation											
Under 9 weeks	36.1	44.6	51.7	50.3	51.6	54.0	57.6	58.1	60.5	61.4	62.1
9–10 weeks	29.4	28.4	26.2	26.6	25.3	23.1	20.2	19.8	18.0	17.6	17.1
11–12 weeks	17.9	14.9	12.2	12.5	11.7	10.9	10.2	10.2	9.7	9.3	9.3
13–15 weeks	6.9	5.0	5.1	5.9	6.4	6.3	6.2	6.2	6.2	6.3	6.3
16–20 weeks	8.0	6.1	3.9	3.9	4.0	4.3	4.3	4.3	4.2	4.0	3.8
21 weeks and over	1.7	1.0	0.9	0.8	1.0	1.4	1.5	1.4	1.4	1.4	1.4
Previous induced abortions											
0	—	81.9	67.6	60.1	57.1	55.1	53.7	54.7	55.3	55.0	54.9
1	—	14.9	23.5	25.7	26.9	26.9	27.1	26.4	25.7	25.8	25.8
2	—	2.5	6.6	9.8	10.1	10.9	11.5	11.3	11.2	11.3	11.4
3 or more	—	0.7	2.3	4.4	5.9	7.1	7.7	7.6	7.8	7.9	7.9

—Data not available.

[a]In 1998 and 1999, Alaska, California, New Hampshire, and Oklahoma did not report abortion data to CDC. For comparison, in 1997, the 48 corresponding reporting areas reported about 900,000 legal abortions.

[b]In 2000, 2001, and 2002, Alaska, California, and New Hampshire did not report abortion data to CDC.

[c]In 2003 and 2004, California, New Hampshire, and West Virginia did not report abortion data to CDC.

[d]In 2005 California, Louisiana, and New Hampshire did not report abortion data to CDC.

[e]No surveys were conducted in 1983, 1986, 1989, 1990, 1993, 1994, 1997, 1998, 2001, 2002, or 2003. Data for these years were estimated by interpolation.

[f]For calculation of ratios by each characteristic, abortions with characteristic unknown were distributed in proportion to abortions with characteristic known.

[g]For 1989 and later years, white race includes women of Hispanic ethnicity.

[h]Before 1989, black race includes races other than white.

[i]Data from 20–22 states, the District of Columbia (DC), and New York City (NYC) were included in 1991–1993. The number of reporting areas increased to 25 states, DC, and NYC in 1994–2004. States were excluded either because they did not collect data on Hispanic origin or due to incomplete reporting of Hispanic data (greater than 15% unknown Hispanic origin).

[j]For 1973–1975, data indicate number of living children.

[k]For 1975, data refer to four previous live births, not four or more. For five or more previous live births, the ratio is 47.3.

[l]For calculation of percent distribution by each characteristic, abortions with characteristic unknown were excluded.

Notes: The number of areas reporting adequate data (less than or equal to 15% missing) for each characteristic varies from year to year. Data for additional years are available.

SOURCE: "Table 14. Legal Abortions and Legal Abortion Ratios, by Selected Patient Characteristics: United States, Selected Years 1973–2005," in *Health, United States, 2009: With Special Feature on Medical Technology*, Centers for Disease Control and Prevention, National Center for Health Statistics, February 2010, http://www.cdc.gov/nchs/data/hus/hus09.pdf (accessed October 15, 2010). Non-government data from the Guttmacher Institute.

result of disclosing their sexuality often leads to a feeling of isolation. All these factors account for lesbian, gay, and bisexual adolescents' higher rates of emotional distress, suicide attempts, risky sexual behavior, and substance use. The APA underscores the need for school personnel to be as open and accepting as possible to support these adolescents.

STD AND PREGNANCY PREVENTION PROGRAMS FOR TEENS

Abstinence

In response to the growing concern about out-of-wedlock births and the threat of acquired immunodeficiency syndrome (AIDS), several national youth organizations and religious groups began campaigns during the early and mid-1990s to encourage teens to sign an abstinence pledge—a promise to abstain from sexual activity until marriage. Debra Hauser of Advocates for Youth indicates in *Five Years of Abstinence-Only-until-Marriage Education: Assessing the Impact* (2004, http://www.advocates foryouth .org/component/content/article/623-five-years-of-abstinence-only-until-marriage-education-assessing-the-impact) that in 1996 the federal government committed $250 million over the following five years to fund state initiatives to promote abstinence as Title V of the Social Security Act. Even though only 11 states made the results of their evaluations of the effectiveness of these programs public, Hauser indicates that Advocates for Youth examined these evaluations and found that the programs "showed few short-term benefits and no lasting, positive impact.... No program was able to demonstrate a positive impact on sexual behavior over time."

In fact, some studies of abstinence-only education programs find that they have a negative impact on teens' sexual health. In "Sexuality Education Policies and Sexually Transmitted Disease Rates in the United States" (*International Journal of STD & AIDS*, vol. 21, no. 4, April 2010), Matthew Hogben, Harrell Chesson, and Sevgi O. Aral compare rates of STDs among teenagers aged 15 to 19 years in states with mandates to emphasize abstinence, with mandates to cover abstinence, or with no mandates to address abstinence. The researchers find that states that emphasized abstinence in their sex education programs had the highest mean (average) rates of infection, whereas the states with no mandate to cover abstinence had the lowest rates of infection. States with mandates to cover, but not to emphasize, abstinence had STD rates in the middle. Hogben, Chesson, and Aral conclude that "for states with elevated rates, policies mandating coverage [of abstinence] may be useful, although policies emphasizing abstinence show no benefit."

Even though the administration of George W. Bush (1946–) had placed a new emphasis on abstinence among teens, the Obama administration signaled its intent to provide funding for other types of sex education for youth that focused on pregnancy and disease prevention. The White House explains in *A New Era of Responsibility: Renewing America's Promise* (2009, http://www.whi tehouse.gov/omb/assets/fy2010_new_era/A_New_Era_of _Responsibility2.pdf) that President Barack Obama's (1961–) 2010 budget proposal provided funding for "medically-accurate and age-appropriate information to youth who have already become sexually active," signaling a potential change of direction for the new administration. The Department of Health and Human Services states in *Advancing the Health, Safety, and Well-Being of Our People: DHHS FY 2011 Budget in Brief* (March 10, 2010, http://dhhs.gov/asfr/ob/docbudget/2011budgetin brief.pdf) that funding for abstinence-only programs was eliminated in the 2009, 2010, and 2011 budgets.

Evidence does suggest that many teens are sexually active and as such need education on how to reduce risk. Eaton et al. find that in 2009, 46% of high school students had had sexual intercourse—45.7% of females and 46.1% of males. (See Table 5.1.) Younger students were less likely to be currently sexually active than were older students. Even though 46% of all students had ever had sexual intercourse, 62.3% of high school seniors had.

In this context, abstinence-only education will do little to prevent teen pregnancy or the spread of STDs. As John Santelli et al. state in "Abstinence and Abstinence-Only Education: A Review of U.S. Policies and Programs" (*Journal of Adolescent Health*, vol. 38, no. 1, January 2006), "Although abstinence is a healthy behavioral option for teens, abstinence as a sole option for adolescents is scientifically and ethically problematic.... We believe that abstinence-only education programs ... are morally problematic, by withholding information and promoting questionable and inaccurate opinions. Abstinence-only programs threaten fundamental human rights to health, information, and life."

Sex and STD/HIV Education in Schools

The Kaiser Family Foundation reports in "State Sex and STD/HIV Education Policy, as of August 1, 2010" (http://www.statehealthfacts.org/comparetable.jsp?ind= 567&cat=11) that as of August 2010, 35 states and the District of Columbia required schools to provide education on HIV/AIDS and other STDs, although in all cases parents were allowed to remove their children from sex education classes. Twenty-five states required schools to stress the importance of abstinence in STD and HIV/ AIDS education, and 12 states required abstinence to be covered. Eighteen states required schools to teach students about contraception, but none required that it be stressed.

According to Gladys Martinez, Joyce Abma, and Casey Copen of the National Center for Health Statistics, in "Educating Teenagers about Sex in the United States" (September

2010, http://www.cdc.gov/nchs/data/databriefs/db44.pdf), teenagers receive formal sex education not only at school but also at churches and community centers. Using data from the 2006–08 survey of National Survey of Family Growth, the researchers find that almost all teenagers received some formal sex education. (See Figure 5.3.) However, only about two-thirds of all teenagers received information on methods of birth control (62% of males and 70% of females). Only nine out of 10 teens received information about how to prevent HIV infection (89% of males and 88% of females) or STDs (92% of males and 93% of females). The largest number of teens reported first receiving information on how to say no to sex, birth control, STDs, and HIV prevention in middle school. (See Figure 5.4.)

FIGURE 5.3

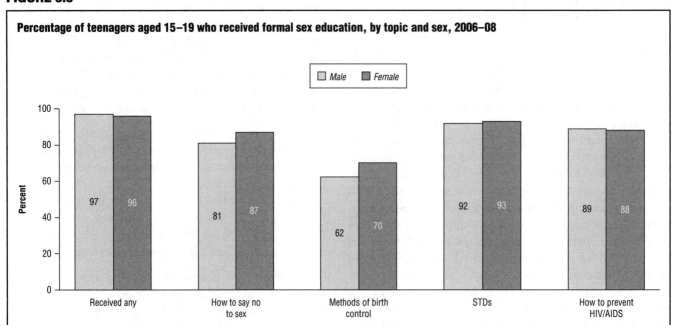

Percentage of teenagers aged 15–19 who received formal sex education, by topic and sex, 2006–08

SOURCE: Gladys Martinez, Joyce Abma, and Casey Copen, "Figure 1. Teenagers 15–19 Who Received Formal Sex Education by Topic and Sex: United States, 2006–2008," in "Educating Teenagers about Sex in the United States," *NCHS Data Brief*, no. 44, September 2010, http://www.cdc.gov/nchs/data/databriefs/db44.pdf (accessed October 25, 2010)

FIGURE 5.4

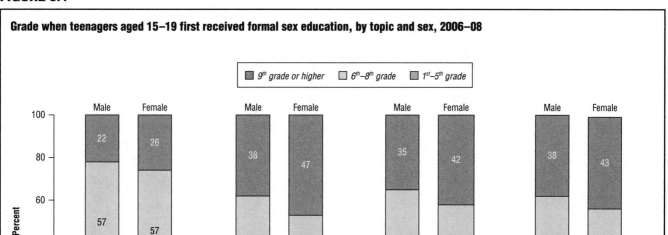

Grade when teenagers aged 15–19 first received formal sex education, by topic and sex, 2006–08

Legend: 9th grade or higher · 6th–8th grade · 1st–5th grade

How to say no to sex:
- Male: 22 / 57 / 21
- Female: 26 / 57 / 17

Methods of birth control:
- Male: 38 / 52 / 10
- Female: 47 / 46 / 7

STDs:
- Male: 35 / 55 / 10
- Female: 42 / 53 / 5

How to prevent HIV/AIDS:
- Male: 38 / 54 / 8
- Female: 43 / 50 / 6

Note: Formal instruction refers to instruction in school, church, community center, or some other place.

SOURCE: Gladys Martinez, Joyce Abma, and Casey Copen, "Figure 2. Grade When Teenagers 15–19 First Received Formal Sex Education by Topic and Sex: United States, 2006–2008," in "Educating Teenagers about Sex in the United States," *NCHS Data Brief*, no. 44, September 2010, http://www.cdc.gov/nchs/data/databriefs/db44.pdf (accessed October 25, 2010)

CHAPTER 6
GETTING AN EDUCATION

Despite the controversies surrounding the quality and direction of American education, the United States remains one of the most highly educated nations in the world. According to Thomas D. Snyder and Sally A. Dillow, in *Digest of Education Statistics, 2009* (April 2010, http://nces.ed.gov/pubs2010/2010013.pdf), in the fall of 2009, 75.2 million Americans were enrolled students in elementary and secondary schools and colleges. (See Table 6.1.) An additional 4.7 million were teachers and faculty at these institutions and 5.4 million were employed as administrative and support staff.

THE NO CHILD LEFT BEHIND ACT

However, during the 1980s there was growing concern that American youth were falling behind young people in other industrialized countries in educational achievement. In response, the National Education Goals Panel was created in 1989 to further the achievement of several national goals, including increasing the high school graduation rate and student competency in English, mathematics, science, history, and geography. Even though a task force recommended the panel's reauthorization in 1999, the passage of the No Child Left Behind (NCLB) Act shut down the panel in 2002.

The NCLB made huge changes to the laws defining and regulating the federal government's role in kindergarten through 12th-grade education. The law is based on four basic education reform principles. According to the U.S. Department of Education, in "Four Pillars of NCLB" (July 1, 2004, http://www.ed.gov/nclb/overview/intro/4pillars.html), the four principles are:

- Stronger accountability for results

- Increased flexibility and local control

- Expanded options for parents

- An emphasis on teaching methods that have been proven to work

Accountability

Under the NCLB, schools are required to demonstrate "adequate yearly progress" toward statewide proficiency goals, including closing the achievement gap between advantaged and disadvantaged students. Those schools that do not demonstrate progress face corrective action and restructuring measures. Progress reports are public, so parents can stay informed about their school and school district. Schools that are making or exceeding adequate yearly progress are eligible for awards.

The accountability outlined under the NCLB is measured through standards testing, and federal financing of schools depends on the results of these mandated tests. The testing provisions of the NCLB are the subject of much debate. Martin R. West of the Brookings Institution explains in "No Child Left Behind: How to Give It a Passing Grade" (December 2005, http://www.brookings.edu/papers/2005/12education_west.aspx) that advocates see testing as a means of raising expectations and helping guarantee that all children are held to the same high standards. They argue that many young people have passed through school without acquiring the basic reading and math skills needed in society and especially in an information-oriented economy. By contrast, Amanda Paulson indicates in "Next Round Begins for No Child Left Behind" (*Christian Science Monitor*, January 8, 2007) that critics of testing say classroom experiences become limited to the need to teach students with the test in mind—and what is tested is only a sample of what children should know. Furthermore, critics claim that standards exams tend to test for those things most easily measured and not the critical thinking skills students need to develop. In addition, the tests measure only how students perform on the tests at one point in time, not their progress over time.

President Barack Obama (1961–) entered office in 2009 as a critic of the NCLB. In "Obama: Revise No Child

TABLE 6.1

Estimated number of participants in elementary and secondary education and in higher education, fall 2009

[In millions]

Participants	All levels (elementary, secondary, and postsecondary degree-granting)	Elementary and secondary schools			Postsecondary degree-granting institutions		
		Total	Public	Private	Total	Public	Private
1	2	3	4	5	6	7	8
Total	**85.3**	**62.8**	**56.1**	**6.7**	**22.4**	**16.4**	**6.0**
Enrollment	75.2	55.6	49.8	5.8	19.6	14.5	5.0
Teachers and faculty	4.7	3.7	3.2	0.5	1.0	0.6	0.3
Other professional, administrative, and support staff	5.4	3.5	3.1	0.4	1.9	1.3	0.6

Notes: Includes enrollments in local public school systems and in most private schools (religiously affiliated and nonsectarian). Excludes federal schools. Excludes private preprimary enrollment in schools that do not offer kindergarten or above. Degree-granting institutions grant associate's or higher degrees and participate in Title IV federal financial aid programs. Data for teachers and other staff in public and private elementary and secondary schools and colleges and universities are reported in terms of full-time equivalents. Detail may not sum to totals because of rounding.

SOURCE: Thomas D. Snyder and Sally A. Dillow, "Table 1. Projected Number of Participants in Educational Institutions, by Level and Control of Institution: Fall 2009," in *Digest of Education Statistics, 2009*, U.S. Department of Education, National Center for Education Statistics, April 2010, http://nces.ed.gov/pubs2010/2010013_1.pdf (accessed October 25, 2010)

Left Behind Law" (*Washington Post*, March 14, 2010), Nick Anderson reports on Obama's proposal to overhaul the law. Proficiency testing would continue and be expanded to include history and science. The new law would put more emphasis on the progress of students toward proficiency goals, rather than on continuing the pass-fail approach of the NCLB in its current form. Under Obama's plan, the lowest-achieving 5% of schools would be required to take aggressive actions, such as replacing 50% of the staff, replacing the principal, or even closing their doors. The Department of Education states in "ESEA Reauthorization: A Blueprint for Reform" (December 15, 2010, http://www.ed.gov/policy/elsec/leg/blueprint/index.html) that Obama's proposal "challenges the nation to embrace education standards that would put America on a path to global leadership."

Proficiency Testing

Obama's plan also called for continuing testing of students to measure educational progress. A look at the changes in proficiency test scores over time is one way to gauge the performance of the educational system.

In *Condition of Education 2010* (May 2010, http://nces.ed.gov/pubs2010/2010028.pdf), the National Center for Education Statistics (NCES) lists test results for a series of years. The percentage of both fourth and eighth graders who tested at or above proficient (indicating solid academic achievement) in reading rose from 29% of both groups in 1992 to 33% of fourth graders and 32% of eighth graders in 2009. The percentage of fourth graders at or above proficiency in mathematics rose from 18% in 1992 to 39% in 2009; the percentage of eighth graders at or above proficiency rose from 21% in 1992 to 34% in 2009. Despite improvements, especially in mathematics, fewer than one out of three eighth graders had achieved

proficiency in each area by 2009, and proficiency levels had not changed appreciably in the previous two years, except for math proficiency among eighth graders, which had risen two percentage points.

The public's opinion of school performance is low. Snyder and Dillow present data on the "grades" that the public gives to schools nationally. Based on a scale of A=4, B=3, C=2, D=1, and F=0, the average grade given by adults to the nation's schools hit a high of 2.18—slightly better than a C—in 1987. By 2009 the average grade had dropped to 1.89, lower than it had been in 2002, when the NCLB was passed. Adults rated their local schools higher than the nation's schools as a whole, giving their local schools a 2.45. Nevertheless, the high rating of local schools was still only about a C+.

Another way to evaluate the U.S. educational system is to compare it to the systems of other industrialized countries. In *Comparative Indicators of Education in the United States and Other G-8 Countries: 2009* (March 2009, http://nces.ed.gov/pubs2009/2009039.pdf), David C. Miller et al. compare the U.S. educational system with the systems in eight other highly industrialized nations: Canada, France, Germany, Italy, Japan, the Russian Federation, Scotland, and the United Kingdom. U.S. students compared poorly to other countries measured in reading and mathematics proficiency. Fourth graders in the United States scored a 540 on the combined reading literacy scale, fourth behind Germany (548), Italy (551), and Russia (565). Miller et al. also describe the international achievement benchmarks in mathematics: low (a score of 400), intermediate (a score of 475), high (a score of 550), and advanced (625). Seventy-seven percent of U.S. fourth graders reached the intermediate benchmark, whereas 78% of German fourth graders, 79% of English fourth graders, 81% of Russian fourth graders, and 89% of Japanese fourth graders did. Only 40% of U.S. fourth graders reached the high international benchmark, whereas 48% of both English and Russian fourth graders and 61% of Japanese fourth graders did.

The Voucher Controversy

Many people believe that problems such as large class sizes, poor teacher training, and lack of computers and supplies in public schools are unsolvable within the current public school system. One solution proposed during the early 1990s was the school voucher system: The government would provide a certain amount of money each year to parents in the form of a voucher to enroll their children at the school of their choice, either public or private. School vouchers became a highly polarized issue, with strong opinions both for and against the idea.

The National Education Association (NEA), a union of teachers and one of the larger unions in the country, immediately objected to school vouchers, arguing that voucher programs would divert money from the public education system and make the current problems worse. The union also argued that giving money to parents who choose to send their child to a religious or parochial school is unconstitutional. Furthermore, there was little evidence that supported the idea that voucher programs lead to better educational outcomes. For example, in *An Evaluation of the Effect of D.C.'s Voucher Program on Public School Achievement and Racial Integration after One Year* (January 2006, http://www.manhattan-institute .org/pdf/ewp_10.pdf), Jay P. Greene and Marcus A. Winters indicate that the District of Columbia voucher program had no effect on student performance in public schools. Furthermore, Kim K. Metcalf of the Center for Evaluation and Education Policy finds in *Evaluation of the Cleveland Scholarship and Tutoring Program: Exploring Families' Educational Choices* (December 2003, http:// ceep.indiana.edu/projects/PDF/200312d_clev_6_phon_rep .pdf) no difference in the academic achievement of voucher-eligible students who used them to attend private school and those who chose to remain in public school.

Supporters of vouchers claim that parents should be able to choose the best educational environment for their children. They also argue that vouchers would give all people, not just the wealthy or middle class, the opportunity for a better education for their children in private schools. Most important, supporters believe that making the educational system a free-market enterprise, in which parents could choose which school their children would attend, would force the public educational system to provide a higher standard of education to compete.

During the legislative process of getting the NCLB through Congress, President George W. Bush (1946–) agreed to drop the vouchers provision from the legislation, recognizing that debate on the vouchers issue could prevent the bill from being passed. Frustrated at the national level, supporters of vouchers turned to state and local governments. Programs launched in Wisconsin, Florida, and Ohio provided students in some overcrowded or poorly performing schools with vouchers that could be used for private tuition. All these programs were met with court challenges. In June 2002 the U.S. Supreme Court upheld in *Zelman v. Simmons-Harris* (536 U.S. 639) the use of public money for religious school tuition in Cleveland, Ohio, calling the city's voucher plan "a program of true private choice." David Harrison reports in "Private-School Vouchers Return to Education Agenda" (*Stateline*, December 21, 2010) that by December 2010 there were 18 voucher programs operating in 12 states.

President Obama did not support voucher programs. The administration decided to let the federally funded voucher program expire in the District of Columbia. Nevertheless, Harrison reports that Mitchell E. Daniels Jr. (1949–), the governor of Indiana, and the newly elected Republican governors in Florida, Nevada, and Wisconsin were pushing voucher plans that stood a good chance of being passed in 2011 in the Republican-controlled legislatures of three of those states (Florida, Indiana, and Wisconsin).

Public School Choice: No Child Left Behind and Charter Schools

In lieu of a voucher program, the NCLB offered a public school choice program. Parents of students enrolled in "failing" public schools were allowed to move their children to a better-performing public or charter school. Local school districts were required to provide this choice and provide students with transportation to the alternative school. However, Anderson reports that President Obama's proposal to overhaul the NCLB was criticized because it would no longer allow parents to transfer their children out of "failing" schools.

The NCLB also expanded the creation and use of charter schools. Public charter schools are funded by government money and run by a group under an agreement, or charter, with the state that exempts it from many state or local regulations that govern most public schools. In return for these exemptions and funding, the school must meet certain standards. The Department of Education notes in *A Commitment to Quality: National Charter School Policy Forum Report* (October 2008, http://www .ed.gov/admins/comm/choice/csforum/report.pdf) that by 2008, 40 states and the District of Columbia had 4,300 charter schools, in which more than 1.2 million students were enrolled. President Obama expanded funding for charter schools. The Department of Education reports in "Funding Highlights" (January 2010, http://www.gpoac cess.gov/usbudget/fy11/pdf/budget/education.pdf) that funding for new and ongoing charter schools increased from $409 million in fiscal year (FY) 2010 to $490 million in FY 2011.

RACE TO THE TOP

The American Recovery and Reinvestment Act (ARRA), which was signed into law by President Obama in February 2009, included $4.4 billion for a new program called the Race to the Top Fund. According to the Department of Education, in "Race to the Top Program: Executive Summary" (November 2009, http://www2.ed.gov/programs/racetothetop/executive-summary.pdf), the program was "designed to encourage and reward States that are creating the conditions for education innovation and reform." Grants would be awarded to states on a competitive basis to reward states that had developed educational reform that could accomplish four key objectives:

- Prepare students to succeed in college and the workplace

- Measure student growth and success to help teachers improve instruction

- Recruit and retain the best teachers

- Help the lowest-achieving schools succeed

Forty-six states and the District of Columbia applied to the program. The ARRA Race to the Top Fund awarded grants in two phases. For the first phase, the Department of Education announced in the press release "Delaware and Tennessee Win First Race to the Top Grants" (March 29, 2010, http://www2.ed.gov/news/pressreleases/2010/03/03292010.html) that Delaware would receive $100 million and Tennessee would receive $500 million to implement school reform. For the second phase, the Department of Education stated in the press release "Nine States and the District of Columbia Win Second Round Race to the Top Grants" (http://www.ed.gov/news/press-releases/nine-states-and-district-columbia-win-second-round-race-top-grants) that there were 10 more winners: the District of Columbia, Florida, Georgia, Hawaii, Maryland, Massachusetts, New York, North Carolina, Ohio, and Rhode Island. The grants ranged from $700 million each to New York and Florida to $75 million each to Hawaii, Rhode Island, and the District of Columbia.

THE COST OF PUBLIC EDUCATION

The average annual expenditure per student in the public school system in constant 2007–08 dollars more than doubled between 1970 and 2007, from $4,489 per pupil in 1970–71 to $10,041 per pupil during the 2006–07 school year. (See Figure 6.1.) Each year, when the federal budget is determined by Congress, the debate over funding for the public education system turns into a fierce battle. Public school officials and teachers stress the importance of investing in the public education system by arguing that more money will provide more teachers, educational mate-

FIGURE 6.1

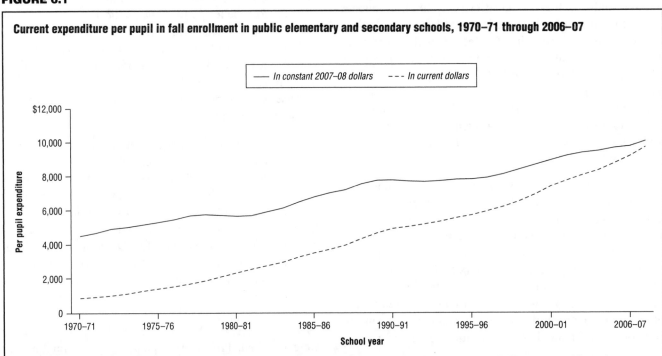

Current expenditure per pupil in fall enrollment in public elementary and secondary schools, 1970–71 through 2006–07

SOURCE: Thomas D. Snyder and Sally A. Dillow, "Figure 10. Current Expenditure per Pupil in Fall Enrollment in Public Elementary and Secondary Schools: 1970–71 through 2006–07," in *Digest of Education Statistics, 2009*, U.S. Department of Education, National Center for Education Statistics, April 2010, http://nces.ed.gov/pubs2010/2010013_2a.pdf (accessed October 25, 2010)

rials, and (eventually) a better education to students. They point to school buildings in need of repair and classes that meet in hallways and other cramped areas because of a lack of space. Opponents of increasing public school funding suggest that more money does not create a better education—better teachers do. To support their argument, they point to the increase in spending per pupil while some measurements of academic achievement remain low.

PREPRIMARY SCHOOL

Preprimary Growth

Participating in early childhood programs such as nursery school, Head Start, prekindergarten, and kindergarten helps prepare children for the academic challenges of first grade. In contrast to the declining elementary and secondary school enrollment between 1970 and 1980, preprimary enrollment showed substantial growth, increasing from 4.1 million in 1970 to 4.9 million in 1980. (See Table 6.2 and Figure 6.2.) By 2008 enrollment had grown to 7.9 million.

Not only did the numbers of children enrolled in early childhood programs increase but also the percentage of all three- to five-year-olds enrolled increased substantially between 1965 and 2008. In 1965, 27.1% of three- to five-year-olds were enrolled in nursery school or kindergarten; by 2008, 63% were enrolled. (See Table 6.2.) Nevertheless,

the percentage of children enrolled in preprimary programs declined in 2008 to its lowest level since 1995.

Even though programs such as Head Start and other locally funded preschool programs are available to children in low-income families, preprimary school attendance is still generally linked to parental income and educational achievement levels. In fact, the economic recession that began in late 2007 and ended in mid-2009 probably accounted for the decline in preprimary enrollment in 2008. According to the NCES, in *Condition of Education 2010*, 51% of four-year-olds from households with an income below the poverty level in 2005–06 and 59.6% of four-year-olds from households with an income at or above the poverty level were enrolled in preprimary programs. (See Table 6.3.) Over a quarter (26.3%) of four-year-olds from households with incomes below the poverty threshold were in Head Start programs, compared with just 8.2% of children from households with higher incomes.

Preschool enrollment rates are even more strongly correlated with their parents' educational level. In 2005–06 the enrollment rate of children in center-based care whose parents had not earned a high school diploma was only 43.4%. (See Table 6.3.) The enrollment rate of children whose parents had a high school diploma or equivalent was 51.7%, for those whose parents had some college it was 55.5%, for those whose parents had a bachelor's degree

TABLE 6.2

Enrollment of 3- to 5-year-old children in preprimary programs, by level and control of program and by attendance, selected years 1965–2008

[Numbers in thousands]

Year and age	Total population, 3 to 5 years old	Enrollment by level and control						Enrollment by attendance		
		Total	Percent enrolled	Nursery school		Kindergarten		Full-day	Part-day	Percent full-day
				Public	Private	Public	Private			
1	2	3	4	5	6	7	8	9*	10	11
Total, 3 to 5 years old										
1965	12,549	3,407	27.1	127	393	2,291	596	—	—	—
1970	10,949	4,104	37.5	332	762	2,498	511	698	3,405	17.0
1975	10,185	4,955	48.7	570	1,174	2,682	528	1,295	3,659	26.1
1980	9,284	4,878	52.5	628	1,353	2,438	459	1,551	3,327	31.8
1985	10,733	5,865	54.6	846	1,631	2,847	541	2,144	3,722	36.6
1990	11,207	6,659	59.4	1,199	2,180	2,772	509	2,577	4,082	38.7
1995*	12,518	7,739	61.8	1,950	2,381	2,800	608	3,689	4,051	47.7
2000*	11,858	7,592	64.0	2,146	2,180	2,701	565	4,008	3,584	52.8
2004*	12,362	7,969	64.5	2,428	2,243	2,812	484	4,507	3,461	56.6
2005*	12,134	7,801	64.3	2,409	2,120	2,804	468	4,548	3,253	58.3
2006*	12,186	8,010	65.7	2,481	2,156	2,960	413	4,723	3,286	59.0
2007*	12,326	8,056	65.4	2,532	2,037	3,088	400	4,578	3,478	56.8
2008*	12,583	7,928	63.0	2,609	1,961	2,982	376	4,615	3,313	58.2

—Not available.

*Data collected using new procedures. Data may not be comparable with figures prior to 1994.

Notes: Data are based on sample surveys of the civilian noninstitutional population. Although cells with fewer than 75,000 children are subject to wide sampling variation, they are included in the table to permit various types of aggregations. Detail may not sum to totals because of rounding.

SOURCE: Adapted from Thomas D. Snyder and Sally A. Dillow, "Table 43. Enrollment of 3-, 4-, and 5-Year-Old Children in Preprimary Programs, by Level of Program, Control of Program, and Attendance Status: Selected Years, 1965 through 2008," in *Digest of Education Statistics, 2009*, U.S. Department of Education, National Center for Education Statistics, April 2010, http://nces.ed.gov/pubs2010/2010013_2a.pdf (accessed October 25, 2010)

FIGURE 6.2

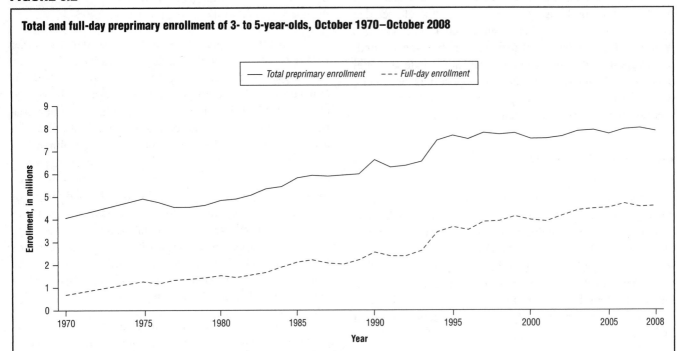

Total and full-day preprimary enrollment of 3- to 5-year-olds, October 1970–October 2008

SOURCE: Thomas D. Snyder and Sally A. Dillow, "Figure 7. Total and Full-Day Preprimary Enrollment of 3- to 5-year-olds: October 1970 through October 2008," in *Digest of Education Statistics, 2009*, U.S. Department of Education, National Center for Education Statistics, April 2010, http://nces.ed.gov/pubs2010/2010013_2a.pdf (accessed October 25, 2010)

it was 65.7%, and for those whose parents had any graduate or professional school it was 70.8%. These percentages likely reflect three things: parents with higher educational levels are more likely to continue working after becoming parents, they are better able to pay for these programs, and they value the educational benefits of preprimary programs for their children.

HEAD START. The Head Start program, which was established as part of the Economic Opportunity Act of 1964, is one of the most durable and successful federal programs for low-income and at-risk children. Directed by the Administration for Children and Families (ACF), Head Start is designed to help improve the social competence, learning skills, health, and nutrition of children from low-income households so they can begin school on a more level footing with children from higher-income households. Regulations require that 90% of children enrolled in Head Start be from low-income households.

The ACF notes in "Head Start Program Fact Sheet Fiscal Year 2010" (2010, http://eclkc.ohs.acf.hhs.gov/hslc/About%20Head%20Start/fHeadStartProgr.htm) that in FY 2009, 904,153 children were served by Head Start programs. Of these children, 39.9% were white, 35.9% were Hispanic, 30% were African-American, 4% were Native American or Alaskan Native, and 2.3% were Asian-American or Pacific Islander. Most participating children were three and four years old (36% and 51%, respectively). A significant

portion (11.5%) of enrolled children had disabilities, including developmental disabilities, health impairments, visual handicaps, hearing impairments, emotional disturbances, speech and language impairments, orthopedic handicaps, and learning disabilities.

According to the ACF, the average cost per child for Head Start in FY 2009 was $7,600. Between its inception in 1965 and 2009, Head Start provided services to more than 27 million children and their families. The budget for Head Start in FY 2009 was $7.1 billion; $7.2 billion had been appropriated for FY 2010. In FY 2009 the ARRA appropriated an additional $2.1 billion for the Head Start and Early Head Start programs to expand enrollment by 64,000 children.

ELEMENTARY AND SECONDARY SCHOOL

Enrollment

All U.S. states require students to attend school through at least the age of 16 years; therefore, preprimary, elementary, and secondary school enrollments reflect the number of births over a specified period. Because of the baby boom following World War II (1939–1945), school enrollment grew rapidly during the 1950s and 1960s, when those children reached school age. Elementary enrollment reached a then-record high in 1969, as did high school enrollment in 1971.

TABLE 6.3

Percentage distribution of the early education and child care arrangements of the 2001 birth cohort at about 4 years old, by type of arrangement and selected child and family characteristics, 2005–06

Child or family characteristic	Percentage distribution of population[a]	No regular nonparental arrangement	Percentage distribution by primary type of care arrangement[b]					Multiple arrangements[d]
			Home-based care		Center-based care[c]			
			Relative care	Nonrelative care	Total	Head Start	Other than Head Start	
Total	100.0	20.0	13.1	7.6	57.5	12.7	44.8	1.9
Sex of child								
Male	51.2	19.3	13.1	7.5	58.0	12.9	45.1	2.1
Female	48.8	20.7	13.1	7.6	56.9	12.4	44.5	1.7
Race/ethnicity of child								
White	53.8	17.9	11.0	9.2	60.1	6.8	53.3	1.9
Black	13.8	16.0	13.9	4.3	62.4	25.4	37.1	3.3
Hispanic	25.1	27.2	15.9	6.2	49.4	18.6	30.9	1.2
Asian	2.6	17.5	16.0	3.4	60.7	5.5	55.3	2.3!
Pacific Islander	0.2	22.3!	45.0!	‡	19.9!	5.0!	14.9!	‡
American Indian/Alaska Native	0.5	20.0	14.0	5.3	59.6	31.1	28.5	1.1!
More than one race	4.0	17.8	17.5	8.9	53.9	12.2	41.7	1.8!
Age of child								
Less than 48 months	16.4	27.3	13.9	8.7	48.0	10.6	37.4	2.2
48.0 to 52.9 months	38.1	19.9	13.0	8.3	56.8	12.0	44.8	2.0
53.0 to 57.9 months	36.5	16.5	13.1	6.7	62.2	14.4	47.8	1.5
58.0 or more months	9.0	20.9	12.0	6.3	58.1	12.0	46.1	2.7
Mother's employment status								
Full-time (35 hours or more)	39.4	8.5	18.5	13.4	57.4	11.4	46.1	2.1
Part-time (less than 35 hours)	19.7	13.4	15.9	8.5	59.3	10.1	49.2	2.9
Looking for work	5.8	28.5	12.6	2.1!	54.7	24.3	30.4	2.0!
Not in labor force	34.3	35.6	4.6	1.5	57.3	13.7	43.7	1.0!
No mother in household	0.8	9.6!	36.0	9.5!	41.1	14.4!	26.7	3.8!
Parents' highest level of education								
Less than high school	10.4	34.0	16.5	4.0	43.4	22.2	21.2	2.1!
High school completion	25.0	22.6	17.1	6.7	51.7	21.4	30.3	2.0
Some college/vocational	31.6	20.6	14.9	7.3	55.5	13.0	42.5	1.7
Bachelor's degree	16.8	16.0	8.4	8.1	65.7	3.3	62.4	1.8
Any graduate/professional school	16.2	9.7	6.2	11.2	70.8	2.0	68.8	2.0
Poverty status[e]								
Below poverty threshold	24.8	27.6	15.0	4.4	51.0	26.3	24.7	2.0
At or above poverty threshold	75.2	17.4	12.5	8.6	59.6	8.2	51.4	1.9
Socioeconomic status[f]								
Lowest 20 percent	20.0	30.5	15.0	5.0	47.1	24.7	22.4	2.3
Middle 60 percent	60.0	19.6	15.0	7.4	56.2	12.5	43.7	1.8
Highest 20 percent	20.0	10.3	5.5	10.7	71.6	1.0	70.6	1.9

!Interpret data with caution (estimates are unstable).
‡ Reporting standards not met (too few cases).
[a]Distribution of weighted Early Childhood Longitudinal Study, Birth Cohort (ECLS-B) survey population between 44 and 65 months of age with data on primary care arrangements.
[b]Primary type of care arrangement is the type of nonparental care in which the child spent the most hours.
[c]Care provided in places such as early learning centers, nursery schools, and preschools, including Head Start.
[d]Children who spent an equal amount of time in each of two or more arrangements.
[e]Poverty status based on Census Bureau guidelines from 2002, which identify a dollar amount determined to meet a household's needs, given its size and composition. In 2002, a family was considered to live below the poverty threshold if its income was less than or equal to $18,392.
[f]Socioeconomic status (SES) was measured by a composite score on parental education and occupations and on family income.
Notes: Estimates weighted by W3R0. Estimates for children at about 4 years old pertain to children assessed between 44 and 65 months.
Race categories exclude persons of Hispanic ethnicity. Detail may not sum to totals because of rounding and suppression of cells that do not meet standards.

SOURCE: Michael Planty et al., "Table 2-1. Percentage Distribution of the Early Education and Child Care Arrangements of the 2001 Birth Cohort at about 4 Years Old, by Type of Arrangement and Selected Child and Family Characteristics: School Year 2005–06," in *The Condition of Education 2008*, U.S. Department of Education, National Center for Education Statistics, June 2008, http://nces.ed.gov/pubs2008/2008031_App1.pdf (accessed October 25, 2010)

During the late 1960s the birthrate began to decline, resulting in steadily falling school enrollment. An echo effect occurred during the late 1970s and early 1980s, when those born during the baby boom began their own families. This echo effect triggered an increase in school enrollment starting in the mid-1980s. In 1985 public elementary and secondary school enrollment increased for the first time since 1971 and continued to increase, reaching 55.3 million in 2006. (See Figure 6.3.) It is projected to reach 59.8 million by 2018. In 2006, 38.9 million students were enrolled in prekindergarten to eighth grade and 16.4 million were enrolled in high school.

FIGURE 6.3

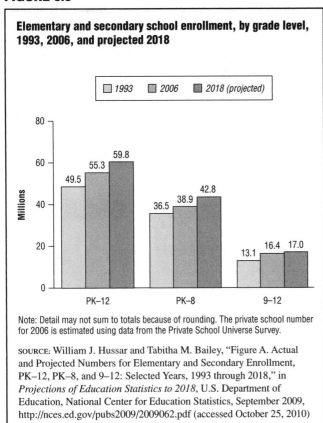

Elementary and secondary school enrollment, by grade level, 1993, 2006, and projected 2018

Note: Detail may not sum to totals because of rounding. The private school number for 2006 is estimated using data from the Private School Universe Survey.

SOURCE: William J. Hussar and Tabitha M. Bailey, "Figure A. Actual and Projected Numbers for Elementary and Secondary Enrollment, PK–12, PK–8, and 9–12: Selected Years, 1993 through 2018," in *Projections of Education Statistics to 2018*, U.S. Department of Education, National Center for Education Statistics, September 2009, http://nces.ed.gov/pubs2009/2009062.pdf (accessed October 25, 2010)

Private Schools

Enrollment in public schools far surpasses enrollment in private schools. Snyder and Dillow indicate that in the fall of 2009 only 10.5% of all primary and secondary school students were enrolled in private schools. Private school enrollment has risen more slowly than school enrollment overall, and as a result the proportion of students enrolled in private schools declined slightly between 1980 and 2009. In 2009, 5.8 million students were enrolled in private schools—4.5 million were in prekindergarten to eighth grade and 1.4 million were in ninth to 12th grades.

CATHOLIC SCHOOLS. According to Stephen P. Broughman, Nancy L. Swaim, and Patrick W. Keaton, in *Characteristics of Private Schools in the United States: Results from the 2007–08 Private School Universe Survey* (March 2009, http://nces.ed.gov/pubs2009/2009313.pdf), 22.2% of all private schools were Catholic and 42.5% of private school students attended Catholic schools in 2007–08. Economic and social changes have caused a decline in both Catholic school enrollment and in the number of Catholic schools. In *United States Catholic Elementary and Secondary Schools, 2009–2010: The Annual Statistical Report on Schools, Enrollment, and Staffing* (2010, http://www.ncea.org/news/AnnualDataReport.asp#full), Dale McDonald and Margaret M. Schultz find that in 1997–98 there were 8,223 Catholic schools in the United States; by 2009–10 there were only 7,094.

OTHER RELIGIOUS AND NONSECTARIAN PRIVATE SCHOOLS. The other types of private schools are non-Catholic religious schools and nonsectarian (nonreligious) schools. According to Broughman, Swaim, and Keaton, non-Catholic religious schools made up 45.7% of all private schools and enrolled 38.1% of all private school students in 2007–08. Nonsectarian schools enrolled only 19.4% of private school students in 32.1% of private schools.

Dropping Out

DROPOUT RATES. Status dropouts are 16- to 24-year-olds who have not finished high school and are not enrolled in school. Snyder and Dillow report that status dropout rates decreased from 1970, when 15% of young people were status dropouts, to 2008, when 8% of young people were status dropouts. (See Table 6.4.) In 2008 the Hispanic status dropout rate was considerably higher, at 18.3%, than that of African-Americans (9.9%) or whites (4.8%). (See Table 6.5.)

Dropout rates also fluctuate greatly according to family income. In 2008, 16.4% of people aged 16 to 24 years from families who had the lowest incomes (bottom 25%) had dropped out of school, which was more than seven times the dropout rate of 16- to 24-year-olds whose families had the highest incomes (2.2%). (See Table 6.4.)

Status dropout rates are consistently lower for women than for men regardless of race or ethnicity. This has been the case since 1980. (See Table 6.5.) In 2008 the status dropout rate for young women aged 16 to 24 years was 7.5%, whereas males of the same age had a status dropout rate of 8.5%.

RETURNING TO SCHOOL OR GETTING AN ALTERNATIVE DIPLOMA. The decision to drop out of high school does not necessarily mean the end of a young person's education. Many former students return to school to get their diploma or to take the test necessary to obtain an alternative credential or degree, such as a general equivalency diploma (GED). Snyder and Dillow note that in 2008, 469,000 GEDs were issued. Many young people who earn their GED continue their education by earning associate's, bachelor's, or advanced degrees.

Special Populations

STUDENTS WITH DISABILITIES. In 1976 Congress passed the Education of the Handicapped Act, which required schools to develop programs for disabled children. Formerly, parents of many disabled students had few options other than institutionalization or nursing care. The Education of the Handicapped Act required that disabled children be put in the "least restrictive environment," which led to increased efforts to educate them in regular classrooms (known as mainstreaming).

TABLE 6.4

Percent of high school dropouts among persons 16–24 years old (status dropout rate), by income level, and percentage distribution of status dropouts, by labor force status and educational attainment, 1970–2008

Year	Status dropout rate	Status dropout rate, by family income quartile				Percentage distribution of status dropouts, by labor force status					Percentage distribution of status dropouts, by years of school completed			
		Lowest quartile	Middle low quartile	Middle high quartile	Highest quartile	Total	Employed[a]	Unemployed	Not in labor force	Total	Less than 9 years	9 years	10 years	11 or 12 years
1	2	3	4	5	6	7	8	9	10	11	12	13	14	15
1970	15.0	28.0	21.2	11.7	5.2	100.0	49.8	10.3	39.9	100.0	28.5	20.6	26.8	24.0
1971	14.7	28.8	20.7	10.9	5.1	100.0	49.5	10.9	39.6	100.0	27.9	21.7	27.8	22.7
1972	14.6	27.6	20.8	10.2	5.4	100.0	51.2	10.2	38.6	100.0	27.5	20.8	29.0	22.7
1973	14.1	28.0	19.6	9.9	4.9	100.0	53.2	9.2	37.5	100.0	26.5	20.9	27.4	25.3
1974	14.3	—	—	—	—	100.0	51.8	12.3	35.9	100.0	25.4	20.1	28.7	25.8
1975	13.9	28.8	18.0	10.2	5.0	100.0	46.0	15.6	38.4	100.0	23.5	21.1	27.5	27.9
1976	14.1	28.1	19.2	10.1	4.9	100.0	48.8	16.0	35.2	100.0	24.3	20.1	27.8	27.8
1977	14.1	28.5	19.0	10.4	4.5	100.0	52.9	13.6	33.6	100.0	24.3	21.7	27.3	26.6
1978	14.2	28.2	18.9	10.5	5.5	100.0	54.3	12.4	33.3	100.0	22.9	20.2	28.2	28.8
1979	14.6	28.1	18.5	11.5	5.6	100.0	54.0	12.7	33.3	100.0	22.6	21.0	28.6	27.8
1980	14.1	27.0	18.1	10.7	5.7	100.0	50.4	17.0	32.6	100.0	23.6	19.7	29.8	27.0
1981	13.9	26.4	17.8	11.1	5.2	100.0	49.8	18.3	31.9	100.0	24.3	18.6	30.2	26.9
1982	13.9	27.2	18.3	10.2	4.4	100.0	45.2	21.1	33.7	100.0	22.9	20.8	28.8	27.6
1983	13.7	26.5	17.8	10.5	4.1	100.0	48.4	18.2	33.4	100.0	23.0	19.3	28.8	28.8
1984	13.1	25.9	16.5	9.9	3.8	100.0	49.7	17.3	32.9	100.0	23.6	21.4	27.5	27.5
1985	12.6	27.1	14.7	8.3	4.0	100.0	50.1	17.5	32.4	100.0	23.9	21.0	27.9	27.2
1986	12.2	25.4	14.8	8.0	3.4	100.0	51.1	16.4	32.5	100.0	25.4	21.5	25.7	27.4
1987	12.6	25.5	16.6	8.0	3.6	100.0	52.4	13.6	34.0	100.0	25.9	20.7	26.0	27.5
1988	12.9	27.2	15.4	8.2	3.4	100.0	52.9	‡	‡	100.0	28.9	19.3	25.1	26.8
1989	12.6	25.0	16.2	8.7	3.3	100.0	53.2	13.8	33.0	100.0	29.4	20.8	24.9	25.0
1990	12.1	24.3	15.1	8.7	2.9	100.0	52.5	13.3	34.2	100.0	28.6	20.9	24.4	26.1
1991	12.5	25.9	15.5	7.7	3.0	100.0	47.5	15.8	36.7	100.0	28.6	20.5	26.1	24.9
1992[b]	11.0	23.4	12.9	7.3	2.4	100.0	47.6	15.0	37.4	100.0	21.6	17.5	24.4	36.5
1993[b]	11.0	22.9	12.7	6.6	2.9	100.0	48.7	12.8	38.5	100.0	20.5	16.6	24.1	38.8
1994[b]	11.4	20.7	13.7	8.7	4.9	100.0	49.5	13.0	37.5	100.0	23.9	16.2	20.3	39.6
1995[b]	12.0	23.2	13.8	8.3	3.6	100.0	48.9	14.2	37.0	100.0	22.2	17.0	22.5	38.3
1996[b]	11.1	22.0	13.6	7.0	3.2	100.0	47.3	15.0	37.7	100.0	20.3	17.7	22.6	39.4
1997[b]	11.0	21.8	13.5	6.2	3.4	100.0	53.3	13.2	33.5	100.0	19.9	15.7	22.3	42.1
1998[b]	11.8	22.3	14.9	7.7	3.5	100.0	55.1	10.3	34.6	100.0	21.0	14.9	21.4	42.6
1999[b]	11.2	21.0	14.3	7.4	3.9	100.0	55.6	10.0	34.4	100.0	22.2	16.3	22.5	39.0

TABLE 6.4

Percent of high school dropouts among persons 16–24 years old (status dropout rate), by income level, and percentage distribution of status dropouts, by labor force status and educational attainment, 1970–2008 [CONTINUED]

		Status dropout rate, by family income quartile				Percentage distribution of status dropouts, by labor force status				Percentage distribution of status dropouts, by years of school completed				
Year	Status dropout rate	Lowest quartile	Middle low quartile	Middle high quartile	Highest quartile	Total	Employed[a]	Unemployed	Not in labor force	Total	Less than 9 years	9 years	10 years	11 or 12 years
1	2	3	4	5	6	7	8	9	10	11	12	13	14	15
2000[b]	10.9	20.7	12.8	8.3	3.5	100.0	56.9	12.3	30.8	100.0	21.5	15.3	23.1	40.0
2001[b]	10.7	19.3	13.4	9.0	3.2	100.0	58.3	14.8	26.9	100.0	18.4	16.8	23.8	40.9
2002[b]	10.5	18.8	12.3	8.4	3.8	100.0	57.4	13.3	29.2	100.0	22.8	17.1	21.3	38.9
2003[b]	9.9	19.5	10.8	7.3	3.4	100.0	53.5	13.7	32.9	100.0	21.2	18.2	20.7	40.0
2004[b]	10.3	18.0	12.7	8.2	3.7	100.0	53.0	14.3	32.7	100.0	21.4	15.9	22.5	40.3
2005[b]	9.4	17.9	11.5	7.1	2.7	100.0	56.9	11.9	31.2	100.0	18.9	16.8	21.4	42.9
2006[b]	9.3	16.5	12.1	6.3	3.8	100.0	56.4	11.7	32.0	100.0	22.1	13.4	20.7	43.9
2007[b]	8.7	16.7	10.5	6.4	3.2	100.0	55.5	11.2	33.3	100.0	21.2	16.9	22.9	39.0
2008[b]	8.0	16.4	9.4	5.4	2.2	100.0	46.8	16.3	36.9	100.0	18.4	15.2	23.8	42.6

—Not available.

‡Reporting standards not met.

[a]Includes persons employed, but not currently working.

[b]Because of changes in data collection procedures, data may not be comparable with figures for years prior to 1992.

Notes: "Status" dropouts are 16- to 24-year-olds who are not enrolled in school and who have not completed a high school program, regardless of when they left school. People who have received GED (General Education Diploma) credentials are counted as high school completers.

Data are based on sample surveys of the civilian noninstitutionalized population, which excludes persons in prisons, persons in the military, and other persons not living in households. Some data have been revised from previously published figures. Detail may not sum to totals because of rounding.

SOURCE: Thomas D. Snyder and Sally A. Dillow, "Table 109. Percentage of High School Dropouts among Persons 16 to 24 Years Old (Status Dropout Rate), by Income Level, and Percentage Distribution of Status Dropouts, by Labor Force Status and Educational Attainment: 1970 through 2008," in *Digest of Education Statistics, 2009*, U.S. Department of Education, National Center for Education Statistics, April 2010, http://nces.ed.gov/pubs2010/20100013_2b.pdf (accessed October 25, 2010)

TABLE 6.5

Percentage of high school dropouts among persons 16–24 years old (status dropout rate), by sex, race and Hispanic origin, selected years 1960–2008

Year	Total status dropout rate				Male status dropout rate				Female status dropout rate			
	All races[a]	White	Black	Hispanic	All races[a]	White	Black	Hispanic	All races[a]	White	Black	Hispanic
1	2	3	4	5	6	7	8	9	10	11	12	13
1960[b]	27.2	—	—	—	27.8	—	—	—	26.7	—	—	—
1970[c]	15.0	13.2	27.9	—	14.2	12.2	29.4	—	15.7	14.1	26.6	—
1975	13.9	11.4	22.9	29.2	13.3	11.0	23.0	26.7	14.5	11.8	22.9	31.6
1980	14.1	11.4	19.1	35.2	15.1	12.3	20.8	37.2	13.1	10.5	17.7	33.2
1985	12.6	10.4	15.2	27.6	13.4	11.1	16.1	29.9	11.8	9.8	14.3	25.2
1990	12.1	9.0	13.2	32.4	12.3	9.3	11.9	34.3	11.8	8.7	14.4	30.3
1995[d]	12.0	8.6	12.1	30.0	12.2	9.0	11.1	30.0	11.7	8.2	12.9	30.0
2000[d]	10.9	6.9	13.1	27.8	12.0	7.0	15.3	31.8	9.9	6.9	11.1	23.5
2005[d, e]	9.4	6.0	10.4	22.4	10.8	6.6	12.0	26.4	8.0	5.3	9.0	18.1
2006[d, e]	9.3	5.8	10.7	22.1	10.3	6.4	9.7	25.7	8.3	5.3	11.7	18.1
2007[d, e]	8.7	5.3	8.4	21.4	9.8	6.0	8.0	24.7	7.7	4.5	8.8	18.0
2008[d, e]	8.0	4.8	9.9	18.3	8.5	5.4	8.7	19.9	7.5	4.2	11.1	16.7

—Not available.
[a]Includes other racial/ethnic categories not separately shown.
[b]Based on the April 1960 decennial census.
[c]White and Black include persons of Hispanic ethnicity.
[d]Because of changes in data collection procedures, data may not be comparable with figures for years prior to 1992.
[e]White and Black exclude persons identifying themselves as two or more races.
Notes: "Status" dropouts are 16- to 24-year-olds who are not enrolled in school and who have not completed a high school program, regardless of when they left school. People who have received GED (General Education Diplomacy) credentials are counted as high school completers. All data except for 1960 are based on October counts. Data are based on sample surveys of the civilian noninstitutionalized population, which excludes persons in the military, and other persons not living in households. Race categories exclude persons of Hispanic ethnicity except where otherwise noted.

SOURCE: Adapted from Thomas D. Snyder and Sally A. Dillow, "Table 108. Percentage of High School Dropouts among Persons 16 to 24 Years Old (Status Dropout Rate), by Sex and Race/Ethnicity: Selected Years, 1960 through 2008," in *Digest of Education Statistics, 2009*, U.S. Department of Education, National Center for Education Statistics, April 2010, http://nces.ed.gov/pubs2010/2010013_2b.pdf (accessed October 25, 2010).

The law defined *handicapped children* as those who were mentally retarded, hard of hearing or deaf, orthopedically impaired, speech-and language-impaired, visually impaired, seriously emotionally disturbed, or otherwise health-impaired. It also included children with specific learning disabilities who require special education and related services.

In 1990 the Individuals with Disabilities Education Act was passed. This was a reauthorization and expansion of the earlier Education of the Handicapped Act. It added autism and traumatic brain injury to the list of disabilities covered by the law, and amendments added in 1992 and 1997 increased coverage for infants and toddlers and for children with attention deficit disorder and attention deficit hyperactivity disorder. The law required public school systems to develop an Individualized Education Program for each disabled child, reflecting the needs of individual students. In December 2004 the Individuals with Disabilities Education Improvement Act was signed into law by President Bush, which reauthorized the Individuals with Disabilities Education Act and brought it in line with the provisions of the NCLB.

As a result of legislation that enforces their rights, increased numbers of disabled children have been served in public schools. Between 1976–77 and 2007–08 the proportion of all students who participated in federal education programs for children with disabilities increased from 8.3% to 13.4%. (See Table 6.6.) In the 2007–08 school year the highest proportion of students needed services for specific learning disabilities (5.2%), followed by students who needed help with speech or language impairments (3%) and students who were mentally retarded (1%). According to the Office of Special Education Programs, in *29th Annual Report to Congress on the Implementation of the Individuals with Disabilities Education Act, 2007* (December 2010, http://www2.ed.gov/about/reports/annual/osep/2007/parts-b-c/29th-vol-1.pdf), 298,150 children from birth through age two and 704,087 children aged three to five years received early intervention services in 2005. Another 6.1 million children aged six to 21 years received special education and related services.

HOMELESS CHILDREN. Homelessness harms children in many ways, including hindering their ability to attend and succeed in school. Homeless children have difficulty with transportation to school, maintaining necessary documents, and attaining privacy needed for homework, sleep, and interaction with parents in a shelter. Experts report that when compared with children who are poor but housed, homeless children miss more days of school, more often repeat a grade, and are more often put into special education classes.

The McKinney-Vento Homeless Assistance Act of 1987 required in Title VII, subtitle B, that each state provide "free, appropriate, public education" to homeless youth. The law

TABLE 6.6

Number of children with disabilities who were served under Individuals with Disabilities Education Act, Part B, as a percentage of total public K–12 enrollment, by type of disability, 1976–77 to 2007–08

Type of disability	1976–77	1980–81	1990–91	1995–96	1997–98	1998–99	1999–2000	2000–01	2001–02	2002–03	2003–04	2004–05	2005–06	2006–07	2007–08[a]
1	2	3	4	5	6	7	8	9	10	11	12	13	14	15	16
							Number served as a percent of total enrollment[d]								
All disabilities	**8.3**	**10.1**	**11.4**	**12.4**	**12.8**	**13.0**	**13.2**	**13.3**	**13.4**	**13.5**	**13.7**	**13.8**	**13.7**	**13.6**	**13.4**
Specific learning disabilities	1.8	3.6	5.2	5.8	5.9	6.0	6.0	6.1	6.0	5.9	5.8	5.7	5.6	5.4	5.2
Speech or language impairments	2.9	2.9	2.4	2.3	2.3	2.3	2.3	3.0	2.9	2.9	3.0	3.0	3.0	3.0	3.0
Mental retardation	2.2	2.0	1.3	1.3	1.3	1.3	1.3	1.3	1.3	1.2	1.2	1.2	1.1	1.1	1.0
Emotional disturbance	0.6	0.8	0.9	1.0	1.0	1.0	1.0	1.0	1.0	1.0	1.0	1.0	1.0	0.9	0.9
Hearing impairments	0.2	0.2	0.1	0.1	0.1	0.2	0.2	0.2	0.2	0.2	0.2	0.2	0.2	0.2	0.2
Orthopedic impairments	0.2	0.1	0.1	0.1	0.1	0.1	0.2	0.2	0.2	0.2	0.2	0.2	0.1	0.1	0.1
Other health impairments[b]	0.3	0.2	0.1	0.3	0.4	0.5	0.5	0.6	0.7	0.8	1.0	1.1	1.2	1.2	1.3
Visual impairments	0.1	0.1	0.1	0.1	0.1	0.1	0.1	0.1	0.1	0.1	0.1	0.1	0.1	0.1	0.1
Multiple disabilities	—	0.2	0.2	0.2	0.2	0.2	0.2	0.3	0.3	0.3	0.3	0.3	0.3	0.3	0.3
Deaf-blindness	—	#	#	#	#	#	#	#	#	#	#	#	#	#	#
Autism	—	—	—	0.1	0.1	0.1	0.1	0.2	0.2	0.3	0.3	0.4	0.5	0.5	0.6
Traumatic brain injury	—	—	—	#	#	#	#	#	#	#	#	#	#	#	0.1
Developmental delay[c]	—	—	—	—	#	#	#	0.4	0.5	0.6	0.6	0.7	0.7	0.7	0.7
Preschool disabled[c]	†	†	0.9	1.2	1.2	1.2	1.2	†	†	†	†	†	†	†	†

—Not available. †Not applicable. #Rounds to zero.

[a]Data do not include Vermont, for which 2007–08 data were not available. In 2006–07, the total number of 3- to 21-year-olds served in Vermont was 14,010.

[b]Other health impairments include having limited strength, vitality, or alertness due to chronic or acute health problems such as a heart condition, tuberculosis, rheumatic fever, nephritis, asthma, sickle cell anemia, hemophilia, epilepsy, lead poisoning, leukemia, or diabetes.

[c]Prior to 1990–91 and after 1999–2000, preschool children are included in the counts by disability condition. For other years, preschool children are not included in the counts by disability condition, but are separately reported.

[d]Based on the total enrollment in public schools, prekindergarten through 12th grade.

Notes: Prior to October 1994, children and youth with disabilities were served under Chapter 1 of the Elementary and Secondary Education Act as well as under the Individuals with Disabilities Education Act (IDEA), Part B. Data reported in this table for years prior to 1994–95 include children ages 0–21 served under Chapter 1. Data are for the 50 states and the District of Columbia. Increases since 1987–88 are due in part to new legislation enacted in fall 1986, which added a mandate for public school special education services for 3- to 5-year-old disabled children. Some data have been revised from previously published figures. Detail may not sum to totals because of rounding.

SOURCE: Adapted from Thomas D. Snyder and Sally A. Dillow, "Table 50. Children 3 to 21 Years Old Served under Individuals with Disabilities Education Act, Part B, by Type of Disability: Selected Years, 1976–77 through 2007–08," in Digest of Education Statistics, 2009, U.S. Department of Education, National Center for Education Statistics, April 2010, http://nces.ed.gov/pubs2010/20100013_2a.pdf (accessed October 25, 2010).

further required that all states develop a plan to address the denial of access to education to homeless children.

The McKinney-Vento Homeless Education Assistance Improvements Act of 2001 went further to address inequities that affect homeless children in the public school system. New guidance for states and school systems released by the Department of Education in April 2003 noted the main differences between the old and new programs:

- Homeless children may no longer be segregated in a separate program on the basis of their homeless status.

- Schools must immediately enroll homeless students even if they are missing some of the documentation normally required.

- Upon parental request, states and school districts must provide transportation for homeless children to the school they attended before they became homeless.

- School districts must designate a local liaison for homeless children and youths.

HOMESCHOOLED CHILDREN. A number of parents who are unhappy with public schools teach their children at home. The NCES indicates in "1.5 Million Homeschooled Students in the United States in 2007" (December 2008, http://nces.ed.gov/pubs2009/2009030.pdf) that approximately 1.5 million, or 2.9% of school-age children, were being homeschooled in the spring of 2007. Both the number and percentage of homeschooled children had increased since 2003.

Parents choose to homeschool their children for a variety of reasons. The NCES reports that more than one-third (36%) of the homeschooling parents surveyed in the National Household Education Survey said the most important reason they chose to homeschool was to provide religious or moral instruction. Another 21% said their most important reason was concern about the school environment, and 17% said their primary concern was dissatisfaction with the academic instruction available at other schools.

States have differing requirements for parents who teach their children at home. According to the Home School Legal Defense Association, some states, such as Idaho and New Jersey, give parents the right to educate their children as they see fit, and impose only minor controls or none at all. Other states have more strict regulations. Highly regulated states, such as New York, Vermont, and Pennsylvania, require parents to get curriculum approved, send achievement test scores, or meet qualification requirements. Opponents of homeschooling argue that parents may not be qualified to be teachers, but proponents believe that parents can gain teaching skills through experience, just as other teachers do.

HIGHER EDUCATION: OFF TO COLLEGE

Formal schooling beyond high school is increasingly being viewed as a necessity, not only to young people's development but also to their economic success. Many parents consider helping their children attend college to be an important financial responsibility.

College Entrance Examinations

Most students who want to enter a college or university in the United States must take either the American College Test (ACT) or the SAT (once known as the Scholastic Aptitude Test, then the Scholastic Assessment Test, now simply the SAT I) as part of their admission requirements. The ACT is a curriculum-based achievement test, measuring proficiency in reading, math, English, and science, whereas the SAT is the primary admissions test to measure a student's mathematical and verbal reasoning ability in a way intended to assess readiness for college. Students who take these tests usually plan to continue their education beyond high school; therefore, these tests do not profile all high school students.

MORE STUDENTS ARE TAKING SAT AND ACT EXAMS, WITH MIXED RESULTS. The College Board notes in "2010 College-Bound Seniors Results Underscore Importance of Academic Rigor" (September 13, 2010, http://www.collegeboard.com/press/releases/213182.html) that the number of students who take the SAT has grown steadily; in 2010 nearly 1.6 million students took the SAT, an all-time high. The article "ACT Scores Dip, but More Students Meet College Benchmarks" (Associated Press, August 18, 2010) explains that the number of students taking the ACT increased as well; nearly 1.6 million students took the ACT in 2010, up 30% from 2005. The increased numbers taking the SAT and ACT suggest that more high school graduates are pursuing a college education.

Performance on the SAT is measured on a scale of 200 to 800 for each of three sections, with the established average score being around 500 for each. According to the College Board, in *2010 College-Bound Seniors* (September 2010, http://professionals.collegeboard.com/prof download/2010-total-group-profile-report-cbs.pdf), between 1972 and 2010 the average critical reading scores on the SAT declined from 530 to 501. By contrast, the results for the math section of the SAT dropped and then rebounded during this same period, from 509 in 1972 to 516 in 2010. Writing was tested for the first time in 2006; test takers received an average score of 497 in that year and 492 in 2010. The ACT is scored on a scale of 1 to 36, with 36 being the highest possible score. The ACT notes in *ACT Profile Report—National* (June 30, 2010, http://www.act.org/news/data/10/pdf/profile/National2010 .pdf?utm_campaign=cccr10&utm_source=benchmark& utm_medium=web) that the average ACT scores, after improving for several years, dropped slightly in 2010. In 1970 the average composite ACT score was 19.9, and in 2010 the average composite score was 21, down from 21.1 the year before.

CHARACTERISTICS OF TEST TAKERS. The College Board reports in *2010 College-Bound Seniors* that more women than men took the SAT in 2010—53.4% of those who took the SAT were women. More women than men have taken the SAT since the 1970s as well. Men scored higher on both the critical reading and math sections of the SAT test in 2010 (average scores of 503 and 534, respectively), compared with women (498 and 500, respectively). Women, however, scored higher on the writing section than did men (498 and 486, respectively).

The College Board explains that despite improvements in the SAT scores of minority students, most lagged behind those of white students. In 2010 white students scored a mean of 528 on critical reading, 536 on math, and 516 on writing. African-Americans scored an average of 429 on critical reading, 428 on math, and 420 on writing, the lowest average scores of any racial or ethnic group. Mexican-Americans scored an average of 454 on critical reading, 467 on math, and 448 on writing; and Puerto Ricans scored 454 on critical reading, 452 on math, and 443 on writing. Native Americans or Alaskan Natives scored 485 on critical reading, 492 on math, and 467 on writing. Asian-Americans or Pacific Islanders scored an average of 519 on critical reading, 591 on math, and 526 on writing.

According to the ACT, in *ACT Profile Report—National*, the 2010 test results show that Asian-Americans scored an average of 23.4, whites scored an average of 22.3, Native Americans or Alaskan Natives scored an average of 19, Hispanics scored an average of 18.6, and African-Americans scored an average of 16.9. Scores for all groups except African-Americans were up since 2006. ACT data for 2010 show that fewer minority test takers had taken the core college-preparatory coursework and that groups that had taken more core coursework, such as whites and Asian-Americans, tended to score higher on the ACT. Lack of preparation often translated into poor educational outcomes for African-Americans and Hispanics. In *Mind the Gaps: How College Readiness Narrows Achievement Gaps in College Success* (2010, http://www.act.org/research/policymakers/pdf/MindTheGaps.pdf), the ACT notes, "We need to ensure that all students, including underrepresented racial/ethnic minority students and students from lower-income families, have access to high school coursework that is of sufficient depth and intensity to adequately prepare them for college and career." ACT data demonstrate that gaps in college success rates narrow substantially if students are adequately prepared for college.

Projected Enrollment

Enrollment in institutions of higher education is expected to rise through 2018, due not only to large numbers of children of baby boomers approaching college age but also to the increasing numbers of people of all ages seeking advanced learning. Enrollment in degree-granting postsecondary institutions stood at 18.2 million

FIGURE 6.4

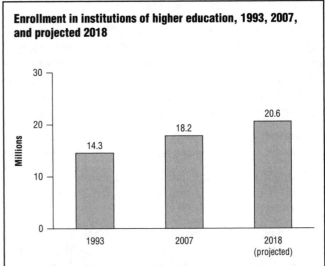

Enrollment in institutions of higher education, 1993, 2007, and projected 2018

SOURCE: William J. Hussar and Tabitha M. Bailey, "Figure C. Actual and Middle Alternative Projected Numbers for Total Enrollment in Degree-Granting Institutions: Selected Years 1993 through 2018," in *Projections of Education Statistics to 2018*, U.S. Department of Education, National Center for Education Statistics, September 2009, http://nces.ed.gov/pubs2009/2009062.pdf (accessed October 25, 2010)

in 2007 and is expected to reach 20.6 million by 2018. (See Figure 6.4.)

Community College Enrollment during the Economic Downturn

During times of economic distress, in general, more people return to community colleges for job retraining or to learn different skills to pursue new careers. This trend was observed during the economic recession that lasted from late 2007 to mid-2009. As described by Caitlin McDevitt, in "Junior College Squeeze: Community Colleges across the Country Are Seeing Enrollment Climb Just as Local Governments Scale Back Funding" (*Newsweek*, December 15, 2008), "the American Association of Community Colleges [AACC] reports that community-college enrollment rose 8 to 10 percent." According to Rachel Streitfeld, in "Unemployed Workers Heading Back to School" (CNN.com, February 14, 2009), the AACC president George Boggs "has heard from 75 college presidents reporting double-digit enrollment increases [during the winter 2009] semester." Boggs suggested that "community colleges are a big part of the solution to this economic downturn." However, Boggs explained that even though the community colleges have assisted unemployed workers by decreasing or freezing their tuition, setting up scholarship programs, or using financial assistance to cover the costs of books and transportation, the spike in applications has imposed a heavy financial burden on some schools that have already been struggling to keep tuition costs low. Boggs stated, "Many [community colleges] are reporting that it is the highest-ever enrollment that they have had. ... And several are reporting a waiting list of students that they can not accommodate. ... It wouldn't surprise me to hear that about a half-million students are being turned away from our community colleges today." In fact, the article "Demand Tests Two-Year Colleges" (*Wall Street Journal*, September 30, 2010) reports that community colleges in New York City stopped accepting applications on August 1 for both 2009–10 and 2010–11 academic years.

College Costs

Paying for a college education, even at public four-year institutions, now ranks as one of the most costly investments for American families. Snyder and Dillow indicate that in 2008–09 the average annual in-state cost at a four-year public college, including tuition and room and board, was $14,256. For one year at a private four-year college, the average cost for tuition and room and board was $31,704. Public college tuition varied widely among states, from $3,057 in the Wyoming to $11,316 in Vermont. Most states with the highest tuition were in the Northeast and most with the lowest tuition were in the South and West.

FINANCIAL ASSISTANCE FOR STUDENTS. According to Snyder and Dillow, during the 2007–08 academic year two-thirds (65.6%) of about 20.9 million undergraduates enrolled in postsecondary institutions received some type of financial aid from federal, state, institutional, or other sources to meet their educational expenses. More than a quarter (27.6%) of undergraduates received some form of federal grant, 38.5% received some type of nonfederal grant, and 34.9% took out federal student loans. Federal assistance that goes directly to students includes Pell Grants (the annual maximum was increased to $5,500 for the 2010–11 academic year), the Stafford Student Loan Program (a maximum loan of $12,500 per year for dependent undergraduate students), and Supplemental Education Opportunity Grants (which range from $100 to $4,000 per year).

Snyder and Dillow note that during the 2007–08 academic year, 80.7% of dependent undergraduate students whose families earned less than $20,000 per year and 78.5% of students whose families earned between $20,000 and $39,999 per year received financial aid. However, due to the high cost of college, students even in high-income brackets received financial aid to help pay for college; 56.4% of dependent undergraduate students whose families earned $100,000 or more received some form of financial aid in 2007–08.

AMERICAN OPPORTUNITY TAX CREDIT. The Obama administration included the American Opportunity Tax Credit in the ARRA. This credit refunded up to $2,500 per year in college costs for the tax years 2009 and 2010. The full amount was available to all Americans whose adjusted gross income was $80,000 or less. Katelyn Sabochik notes in "What the American Opportunity Tax Credit Means for College Students" (October 13, 2010, http://www.whitehouse.gov/blog/2010/10/13/what-american-opportunity-tax-credit-means-college-students) that the White House called on Congress to make the tax credit permanent.

EDUCATIONAL ATTAINMENT AND EARNINGS

The educational attainment of the U.S. population has risen steadily since the 1940s. In *Educational Attainment in the United States: 2009, Detailed Tables* (September 22, 2010, http://www.census.gov/hhes/socdemo/education/data/cps/2009/tables.html), the U.S. Census Bureau states that in 2009, 86.7% of adults older than the age of 25 years had graduated from high school—the highest number ever. Nearly three out of 10 (29.3%) had earned a bachelor's degree or higher.

The level of educational attainment has traditionally been higher for men than for women. In 2009, however, for the eighth year in a row, the Census Bureau indicates that the high school graduation rate for women aged 25 years and older (87.7%) exceeded that of men (86.2%). In 2009, 30.1% of men and 29.1% of women had obtained bachelor's degrees or higher. Even though college attainment has increased since 1990 for both men and women, women are narrowing the gap and making faster gains then men. In fact, the Census Bureau notes in the press release "Census Bureau Reports Nearly 6 in 10 Advanced Degree Holders Age 25–29 Are Women" (April 20, 2010, http://www.census.gov/newsroom/releases/archives/education/cb10-55.html) that among 25- to 29-year-olds, 58% of those who held an advanced degree in 2009 were women.

Educational attainment of the over-25 population also varied by race and ethnic origin. According to the Census Bureau, Asian-Americans were by far the most likely to hold a bachelor's degree or higher (53%), followed by non-Hispanic whites (33%), African-Americans (19%), and Hispanics (13%).

Education is a good investment because earning levels rise with increased education. According to the Census Bureau (2010, http://www.census.gov/hhes/www/cpstables/032010/perinc/new03_001.htm), for people aged 25 years and older who had not finished high school, the average annual income in 2009 was $24,289. High school graduates earned an average income of $32,812 in 2009, and people with an associate's degree earned an average income of $41,529. The incomes of college graduates increased with the level of the degree earned. People with a bachelor's degree had average earnings of $58,762, whereas holders of professional degrees earned an average of $128,578 in 2009.

CHAPTER 7
JUVENILE CRIME AND VICTIMIZATION

THE UNIFORM CRIME REPORTS AND THE NATIONAL CRIME VICTIMIZATION SURVEY

Two main government sources collect crime statistics. The Federal Bureau of Investigation (FBI) compiles the annual Uniform Crime Reports (UCR). The FBI notes in *Crime in the United States, 2009* (September 2010, http://www2.fbi.gov/ucr/cius2009/) that the UCR, which was begun in 1930, now collects data from 17,985 city, county, and state law enforcement agencies.

The second set of crime statistics is the National Crime Victimization Survey (NCVS), which is prepared by the Bureau of Justice Statistics (BJS). Established in 1972, the survey is an annual federal statistical study that measures the levels of victimization resulting from criminal activity in the United States. According to the BJS, in "National Crime Victimization Survey (NCVS)" (December 20, 2010, http://bjs.ojp.usdoj.gov/index.cfm?ty=dcdetail&iid=245), the survey collects data from a nationally representative sample of approximately 76,000 households each year, containing about 135,300 people, on the "frequency, characteristics and consequences of criminal victimization in the United States." The survey was previously known as the National Crime Survey, but it was redesigned and renamed in 1992 to emphasize the measurement of victimization that is experienced by citizens. The survey was created because there was concern that the UCR did not fully portray the true volume of crime. The UCR provides data on crimes reported to law enforcement authorities, but it does not estimate how many crimes go unreported.

The NCVS is designed to complement the UCR. It measures the levels of criminal victimization of people and households for the crimes of rape, robbery, assault, burglary, motor vehicle theft, and larceny. Murder is not included because the NCVS data are gathered through interviews with victims. Definitions for these crimes are the same as those established by the UCR.

Some observers believe the NCVS is a better indicator of the volume of crime in the United States than the UCR. Nonetheless, like all surveys, it is subject to error. The survey depends on people's memories of incidents that happened up to six months earlier. Many times, a victim is not certain what happened, even moments after the crime occurred. In addition, the NCVS limits the data to victims aged 12 years and older, an admittedly arbitrary age selection.

CRIME TRENDS
Violent and Property Crimes

Jennifer L. Truman and Michael R. Rand of the BJS report in *Criminal Victimization, 2009* (October 2010, http://bjs.ojp.usdoj.gov/content/pub/pdf/cv09.pdf) that in 2009 U.S. residents experienced 20.1 million violent and property victimizations. Of these crimes, 15.6 million were property crimes (burglary, motor vehicle theft, and theft), 4.3 million were violent crimes (rape or sexual assault, robbery, aggravated assault, and simple assault), and 133,000 were personal thefts (pocket-picking and purse-snatching). Rates for all types of crime had decreased from 2008.

According to Truman and Rand, between 2000 and 2009 the average yearly rate of violent crimes per 1,000 people aged 12 years and older declined by 39%. In 2009 the violent crime rate was 17.1 per 1,000 people, a decrease of 11.2% from 2008. Property crime rates decreased by 29% between 2000 and 2009. In 2009 the property crime rate was 127.4 per 1,000 people, a decline of 5.5% since 2008. The personal theft rate stayed the same between 2008 and 2009 at 0.5%.

The UCR reports that most violent crimes—including murder, nonnegligent manslaughter, forcible rape, robbery, and aggravated assault—declined by 5.3% between 2008 and 2009, from a rate of 457.5 per 100,000 inhabitants in 2008 to 429.4 per 100,000 inhabitants in 2009. The UCR also records decreasing violent crime rates over time.

Between 2005 and 2009 the violent crime rate decreased by 5.2%, and between 2000 and 2009 the violent crime rate decreased by 7.5%.

According to the UCR, there were an estimated 9.3 million property crimes, including burglary, larceny-theft, and motor vehicle theft, in 2009, down from 9.8 million in 2008. The property crime rate had decreased from 3,211.5 per 100,000 inhabitants in 2008 to 3,036.1 per 100,000 inhabitants in 2009. This decline continued a long-term trend. The property crime rate had decreased 11.5% since 2005 and 16.1% since 2000.

Trends in Juvenile Crime

According to the FBI, from the mid-1980s through the mid-1990s youth violence and crime grew at rapid rates. In *Juvenile Victims and Offenders: 2006 National Report* (March 2006, http://www.ojjdp.ncjrs.gov/ojstatbb/nr2006/downloads/NR2006.pdf), the most recent report on this topic as of January 2011, Howard N. Snyder and Melissa Sickmund of the National Center for Juvenile Justice look at juvenile homicide trends. They find that between 1980 and 2002 murders by juveniles were highest in 1993 and 1994. During this 22-year span the murders involving juvenile offenders acting alone decreased 68% and murders involving two or more juvenile offenders fell 60%.

Nevertheless, the earlier surge in youth crime and violence caused much concern in society. Various groups, both public and private, undertook the mission of trying to uncover the reasons juvenile crime was on the rise. Lawmakers responded by toughening existing laws and finding ways to try more juveniles as adults. Courts levied stricter sentences, and parents and educators looked into various programs and methods that were geared to help their children and students deal with the situation. (See Chapter 10.)

However, the rise in juvenile crime did not last. Snyder and Sickmund note that in the 10-year period between 1994 and 2003, juvenile arrests decreased by 18%, compared with a 1% increase in arrests of adults during the same period. The arrest rate of juveniles for murder in 2003 was the lowest since at least 1980. According to Snyder and Sickmund, "The juvenile violent crime wave predicted by some in the mid-1990s has not occurred."

JUVENILE OFFENDERS

For some young people, their teenage and young adult years are difficult and challenging times. Even though their peers are playing sports, going to proms, participating in school activities, heading to college, and making plans for the future, some juveniles and youths are, for whatever reason, committing crimes and having brushes with the law. A juvenile delinquent is a person who has committed a crime but is below the age at which an individual carries adult responsibilities and can be sentenced as an adult. When dealing with young offenders, each state has its own definition of the term *juvenile*: Most states put the upper age limit at 17 years old, although some states set it as low as 14 years old.

When reporting its national crime statistics, the FBI considers those under the age of 18 years to be juveniles. The FBI often divides its juvenile crime statistics into age-based subcategories, such as aged 16 years and older and aged 15 years and younger, to demonstrate how juvenile offenses vary by age. The FBI does the same with youth, who are often defined as aged 18 to 24 years. However, some organizations and studies classify youth age ranges differently, citing youths as those aged 18 to 21 years or aged 18 to 25 years.

The U.S. Department of Justice defines crime as all behaviors and acts for which society provides formally approved punishments. Written law, both federal and state, defines which behaviors are criminal and which are not. Some behaviors, such as murder, robbery, and burglary, have always been considered criminal. Other actions, such as domestic violence or driving under the influence of drugs or alcohol, became classified as criminal actions more recently. Other changes in society have also influenced crime. For example, the widespread use of computers provides new opportunities for white-collar cybercrime, including identity theft and the malicious spread of computer viruses and worms.

Crime can range from actions as simple as taking a candy bar from a store without paying for it, to those as severe and violent as murder. Most people have broken some law, wittingly or unwittingly, at some time during their life. Therefore, the true extent of criminality is impossible to measure. Researchers can only keep records of what is reported by victims or known to law enforcement authorities.

Risk Factors for Youth Violence

Various government entities, schools, student and parent organizations, and research groups have devoted countless hours to the issue of youth violence. One of their goals is to find ways to recognize the potential for violent behavior in youth before it becomes a serious problem. They work individually and sometimes collectively to outline trends in youth violence and to determine what factors lead to violent behavior.

The Centers for Disease Control and Prevention (CDC) outlines in "Understanding Youth Violence: Fact Sheet" (2008, http://www.cdc.gov/ncipc/pub-res/YVFactSheet.pdf) the risk factors that increase the likelihood that a young person will become violent. These factors include a history of violent victimization or prior violence; drug, alcohol, or tobacco use; association with delinquent peers; a dysfunctional family life; poor grades; and poverty in the family or community. The CDC recommends several approaches to stopping youth violence, including programs to improve family relationships, school-based programs to treat nonviolent social development, role modeling through mentoring programs, and changes to physical and social environments to address the social and economic causes of violence.

In "Fact Sheet: Juvenile Delinquency" (2008, http://aspe.hhs.gov/hsp/08/boys/FactSheets/jd/report.pdf), the U.S. Department of Health and Human Services outlines individual, familial, and community risk factors for juvenile delinquency among boys. Individual risk factors include early aggressive behavior, concentration problems, drug or alcohol abuse, association with antisocial peers, and too much unstructured leisure time. Familial risk factors include childhood maltreatment, dysfunctional parenting, lack of supervision, and parental criminality. Community risk factors include exposure to community violence and poverty.

Margaret A. Zahn et al. examine the risk factors for girls' delinquency in *Girls Study Group: Understanding and Responding to Girls' Delinquency* (April 2010, http://www.ncjrs.gov/pdffiles1/ojjdp/226358.pdf). The researchers point out that certain types of trauma—particularly sexual abuse—occur more often among delinquent girls. Mental disorders diagnosed among girls that result from trauma, such as depression, anxiety, and posttraumatic stress disorder, have a strong relationship to female delinquency. Other risk factors include physical abuse, early onset of puberty, inconsistent or lax parental supervision, parental criminality, family instability, and poverty.

Homicide

The UCR defines murder and nonnegligent manslaughter as "the willful (nonnegligent) killing of one human being by another." However, it also stipulates that "deaths caused by negligence, suicide, or accident; justifiable homicides; and attempts to murder or assaults to murder ... are scored as aggravated assaults." Approximately 15,241 murders and nonnegligent manslaughters occurred in 2009, down 7.3% from 2008.

In 2009, 15,760 people were identified as murder offenders, including 850 males and 73 females under the age of 18 years, and 3,258 males and 280 females under the age of 22 years. (See Table 7.1.) Because the identity of all murder offenders is not known, such figures are lower than they would be if all offenders had been identified. Those under the age of 18 years represented 5.9% of all known murder offenders in that year, whereas those under the age of 22 years represented 22.5% of all known murder offenders. Only 7.6% of all known murderers were female; 92.1% of all murder offenders under the age of 18 years and 92% of all murder offenders under the age 22 years were male.

In 2009, 5,286 (33.5%) of all known murderers were white, 5,890 (37.4%) were African-American, and 4,339

(27.5%) were of unknown race. (See Table 7.1.) These proportions were similar for juvenile murderers. Among 923 youths under the age of 18 years, 539 (58.4%) murder offenders were African-American, 353 (38.2%) were white, 27 (2.9%) were "other," and 4 (0.4%) were unknown. Among 3,541 youths under the age of 22 years, 2,098 (59.2%) were African-American, 1,348 (38.1%) were white, 68 (1.9%) were "other," and 27 (0.8%) were unknown.

Rape

The UCR reports that even though there were an estimated 88,097 forcible rapes reported in 2009 (a 2.6% decrease from the previous year), only 16,442 people were arrested for rape in that year. Rape is one of the most underreported crimes, and the low arrest rate demonstrates how few perpetrators are caught. Of those actually arrested, 766 (4.7%) were under the age of 15 years and 2,385 (14.5%) were under the age of 18 years.

Aggravated and Simple Assault

The UCR defines aggravated assault as "an unlawful attack by one person upon another for the purpose of inflicting severe or aggravated bodily injury. ... This type of assault is usually accompanied by the use of a weapon or by other means likely to produce death or great bodily harm. Attempted aggravated assault that involves the display of—or threat to use—a gun, knife, or other weapon is included in this crime category because serious personal injury would likely result if the assault were completed." In 2009 an estimated 806,843 aggravated assaults were reported. In its arrest reports, the UCR notes that 331,372 people were arrested for aggravated assault in that year. Of that number, 11,946 (3.6%) were under the age of 15 years and 39,467 (11.9%) were under the age of 18 years.

By contrast, simple assaults are assaults or attempted assaults not involving a weapon and not resulting in serious injury to the victim. These include acts such as assault and battery, resisting or obstructing the police, and hazing. In its arrest reports, the UCR lists a category called "other assaults" (to differentiate between these types of assaults and aggravated assaults). The UCR notes that 1,036,754 people were arrested for other assaults in 2009. Of that number, 63,405 (6.1%) were under the age of 15 years and 172,984 (16.7%) were under the age of 18 years.

Robbery, Burglary, and Larceny-Theft

Robbery, burglary, and larceny-theft are different crimes under the UCR. Robbery is "the taking or attempting to take anything of value from the care, custody, or control of a person or persons by force or threat of force or violence and/or by putting the victim in fear" and is categorized as a violent crime. Burglary involves "the unlawful entry of a structure to commit a felony or theft" and is classified as a property crime. Larceny-theft, which

TABLE 7.1

Murder offenders by age, sex, and race, 2009

Age	Total	Sex			Race			
		Male	Female	Unknown	White	Black	Other	Unknown
Total	15,760	10,391	1,197	4,172	5,286	5,890	245	4,339
Percent distribution[a]	100.0	65.9	7.6	26.5	33.5	37.4	1.6	27.5
Under 18[b]	923	850	73	0	353	539	27	4
Under 22[b]	3,541	3,258	280	3	1,348	2,098	68	27
18 and over[b]	9,846	8,728	1,097	21	4,794	4,731	215	106
Infant (under 1)	0	0	0	0	0	0	0	0
1 to 4	0	0	0	0	0	0	0	0
5 to 8	1	1	0	0	0	1	0	0
9 to 12	10	9	1	0	5	5	0	0
13 to 16	465	422	43	0	186	264	13	2
17 to 19	1,765	1,642	123	0	638	1,077	36	14
20 to 24	2,682	2,425	253	4	1,119	1,484	54	25
25 to 29	1,794	1,592	195	7	781	957	38	18
30 to 34	1,123	971	152	0	577	517	18	11
35 to 39	800	685	113	2	481	287	20	12
40 to 44	602	496	105	1	341	234	21	6
45 to 49	562	480	78	4	365	176	11	10
50 to 54	402	351	51	0	256	130	10	6
55 to 59	215	185	29	1	142	60	11	2
60 to 64	145	130	14	1	99	40	4	2
65 to 69	72	66	6	0	54	16	2	0
70 to 74	42	37	5	0	34	7	1	0
75 and over	89	86	2	1	69	15	3	2
Unknown	4,991	813	27	4,151	139	620	3	4,229

[a]Because of rounding, the percentages may not add to 100.0.
[b]Does not include unknown ages.

SOURCE: Expanded Homicide Data Table 3. Murder Offenders by Age, Sex, and Race, 2009, in *Crime in the United States, 2009*, U.S. Department of Justice, Federal Bureau of Investigation, September 2010, http://www2.fbi.gov/ucr/cius2009/offenses/expanded_information/data/shrtable_03.html (accessed October 26, 2010)

is also a property crime, is "the unlawful taking, carrying, leading, or riding away of property from the possession or constructive possession of another" and includes crimes such as shoplifting, pocket-picking, purse-snatching, thefts from motor vehicles, thefts of motor vehicle parts and accessories, bicycle thefts, and so on. These offenses, taken together, are disproportionately committed by young people.

The UCR estimates that 408,217 robbery offenses were committed in 2009, which was an 8% decrease from the previous year and the lowest number of robberies since 2000. In 2009, 100,702 people were arrested for robbery; those arrested were disproportionately young people. Of that number, 4,601 (4.6%) were under the age of 15 years and 25,280 (25.1%) were under the age of 18 years.

In 2009 the UCR recorded 2,199,125 burglary offenses, a decrease of 1.3% from the previous year. Burglary has a particularly low arrest rate. The UCR notes that 235,226 people were arrested for burglary in 2009. Of that number, 16,173 (6.9%) perpetrators were under the age of 15 years and 59,432 (25.3%) were under the age of 18 years.

The UCR recorded 6,327,230 larceny-theft offenses in 2009, a decrease of 4% from 2008 and a 9% decrease from 1999. In its arrest reports, the UCR notes that 1,060,754 people were arrested for larceny-theft in 2009. Of that number, 70,216 (6.6%) perpetrators were under the age of 15 years and 254,865 (24%) were under the age of 18 years.

Motor vehicle theft is also disproportionately perpetrated by young people, usually in urban areas. In 2009 there were 794,616 motor vehicle thefts nationwide, a substantial decrease (17.1%) from the year before. Nearly nine out of 10 (88.7%) motor vehicle thefts occurred in metropolitan areas. In its arrest reports, the UCR notes that 64,169 people were arrested for motor vehicle theft in 2009. Of those arrested, 3,094 (4.8%) were under the age of 15 years and 15,724 (24.5%) were under the age of 18 years.

Computer Crime

Illegally accessing a computer, known as hacking, is a crime committed frequently by juveniles. When it is followed by manipulation of the information in private, corporate, or government databases and networks, it can be quite costly. Another means of computer hacking involves the creation of what is known as a virus program. A virus program is one that resides inside another program and is activated by some predetermined code to create havoc in the host computer. Virus programs can be spread through the sharing of disks and programs, by downloading executable files on the Internet, or, most commonly, through e-mail attachments.

Cases of juvenile hacking have been reported since the 1980s. In 1998 the U.S. Secret Service filed the first criminal case against a juvenile for a computer crime. The unnamed hacker shut down the Worcester, Massachusetts, airport in 1997 for six hours. The airport was integrated into the Federal Aviation Administration traffic system by telephone lines. The accused gained access to the communications system and disabled it by sending a series of computer commands that changed the data carried on the system. As a result, the airport could not function. (No accidents occurred during that time, however.) According to the Department of Justice, the juvenile pleaded guilty in return for two years' probation, a fine, and community service.

Juveniles are sometimes caught hacking into school computer systems in an effort to change their grades and the grades of other students. Michael Birnbaum and Jenna Johnson report in "Students at Potomac School Hack into Computers; Grades Feared Changed" (*Washington Post*, January 29, 2010) on an incident in Maryland. Johnson explains in "Officials Can't Prove Who Changed Md. High-Schoolers' Grades" (*Washington Post*, March 9, 2010) that the culprits—at least eight students—had stolen teachers' computer passwords using USB key loggers, then used those passwords to change grades for several months before being detected. Even though eight students were accused in the scheme, there was no way to prove who changed the grades. At times, as in the case of 23 Fort Bend, Texas, students charged with hacking into the local high school's system during the 2007–08 school year, the monetary loss to the school system can be so large as to trigger felony charges. The hackers could have faced second-degree felony charges, carrying a penalty of up to 20 years in prison. However, the students were eventually punished by sending them to an alternative education class within the high school.

Other types of computer crime typically perpetrated by juveniles include trading stolen credit card and Social Security numbers and pirating computer software that will be sold. Because of computer networks, juveniles and other perpetrators can commit these types of crimes on a large scale. In "It's Not Just Fun and 'War Games'—Juveniles and Computer Crime" (April 26, 2005, http://www.cybercrime.gov/usamay2001_7.htm), Joseph V. DeMarco, the former assistant U.S. attorney in the Southern District of New York, states that "the enormous computing power of today's PCs make it possible for minors to commit offenses which are disproportionately serious to their age." Teens can commit property offenses on a large scale using computers, can portray themselves as adults in an online world, and "appear to have an ethical

'deficit' when it comes to computer crimes." He points out that children and teens who would never commit robbery, burglary, or assault may in fact commit online crimes. For example, in May 2008 a 15-year-old boy was arrested in Downington, Pennsylvania, for hacking into a school computer system and copying files that contained personal information and Social Security numbers of school employees. Such information could be used to perpetrate identity theft.

Juveniles convicted of computer crimes sometimes face imprisonment in juvenile detention centers. The article "Teen Hacker Sentenced to 11 Months" (Associated Press, April 20, 2009) reports that in April 2009 a 17-year-old hacker known by his online moniker "Dschocker" had been sentenced to 11 months in detention after taking control of thousands of computers and using them for distributed denial-of-service attacks aimed at preventing Internet sites or services from functioning. He also stole Internet Service Provider subscriber numbers and used them to make fake 911 calls prompting SWAT team responses.

In October 2008, 20-year-old David Kernell, a college student at the University of Tennessee, was indicted for hacking into vice presidential candidate Sarah Palin's (1964–) Yahoo e-mail account the previous month. The article "Details Emerge in Palin E-mail Hacking" (Associated Press, September 18, 2008) notes that the break-in to the personal e-mail account could have ramifications for the government because Palin's "administration embraced Yahoo accounts as an alternative to government e-mail, which could possibly be released to the public under Alaska's Open Records Act." In March 2009 Kernell pleaded not guilty to fraud, unlawful electronic transmission of material outside of Tennessee, and attempts to conceal records to impede an FBI investigation. In April 2010 Kernell was convicted of unauthorized access to a protected computer and destroying records to impede a federal investigation. The following November he was sentenced to 366 days of prison followed by three years of probation.

Illegal Drug Use

Various studies show that many violent offenders are substance abusers. For some people, drugs and alcohol may cause violent tendencies to surface. Lloyd D. Johnston et al. of the Institute for Social Research find in *Monitoring the Future: National Results on Adolescent Drug Use, Overview of Key Findings, 2009* (2010, http://monitoringthefuture.org/pubs/monographs/overview2009.pdf) that in 2009, 36.5% of 12th graders, 29.4% of 10th graders, and 14.5% of eighth graders had used an illicit drug in the past year. Among 12th graders, marijuana/hashish use was highest (32.8%), followed by Vicodin (9.7%), narcotics (9.2%), amphetamines (6.6%), tranquilizers (6.3%), and barbiturates (5.2%). Two-thirds (66.2%) had used alcohol in the past 12 months.

Other drugs gaining popularity in recent years include so-called club drugs, such as ecstasy (MDMA), Rohypnol, GHB, and ketamine. These drugs are popular among teenagers at dance clubs and raves. Because each of these club drugs is scheduled under the Controlled Substances Act (Title II of the Comprehensive Drug Abuse Prevention and Control Act of 1970), they are illegal and their use constitutes a criminal offense. Johnston et al. note that in 2009, 4.3% of high school seniors had used MDMA, 1.7% had used ketamine, 1.1% had used GHB, and 1% had used Rohypnol in the previous 12 months.

In its arrest reports, the UCR notes that 1,305,191 people were arrested on drug abuse violations in 2009. Of that number, 21,093 (1.6%) were under the age of 15 years and 134,610 (10.3%) were under the age of 18 years.

JUVENILE VICTIMS OF CRIME

Between 1994 and 2009 the rate of violent victimizations dropped in all age categories, but especially among young people. In *Criminal Victimization in the United States, 1994* (May 1997, http://bjs.ojp.usdoj.gov/content/pub/pdf/Cvius942.pdf), the BJS indicates that in 1994 the violent victimization rate for those aged 12 to 15 years was 114.8 per 1,000 people. The violent victimization rate in that age group then dropped steadily to 36.8 per 1,000 people in 2009. (See Table 7.2.) For those aged 16 to 19 years, the violent victimization rate in 1994 was 121.7 per 1,000 people. It then decreased steadily to 30.3 per 1,000 people in 2009. (See Table 7.2.)

Violent crime rates are highest for young people aged 24 years and younger; after the age of 25 years the violent victimization rate declines steadily. In 2009, 16- to 19-year-olds were nearly two times as likely as 35- to 49-year-olds to be victimized by violent crime. (See Table 7.2.)

Becoming a victim of crime can have serious consequences—outcomes that the victim neither asks for nor deserves. Victims rarely expect to be victimized and seldom know where to turn for help. Victims may end up in the hospital to be treated and released, or they may be confined to bed for days, weeks, or longer. Injuries may be temporary, or they may be permanent and forever change the way the victims live their life. Victims may lose money or property, or in the case of homicide their life. In many cases they lose their confidence, self-esteem, and feelings of security.

Scott Menard of the University of Colorado, Boulder, notes in *Short- and Long-Term Consequences of Adolescent Victimization* (February 2002, http://www.ncjrs.gov/pdffiles1/ojjdp/191210.pdf) that adolescent victimization leads to long-term consequences. When compared with adults who were not victimized as adolescents, adults who were victimized as adolescents are more likely to have drug problems and to perpetrate violence. They are also more likely to commit acts of domestic violence and become victims of domestic violence than are adults who were not victimized as adolescents. In addition, they are nearly twice as likely to become victims of violent crime and nearly three times as likely to commit property offenses. Their risk of developing posttraumatic stress disorder is also twice as great.

In "Considerations for the Definition, Measurement, Consequences, and Prevention of Dating Violence Victimization among Adolescent Girls" (*Journal of Women's Health*, vol. 18, no. 7, July 2009), Andra L. Teten et al. specifically look at consequences that result from physical or sexual assault by a dating partner. This is particularly important because estimates suggest that between 3% to 10% of adolescent girls experience this type of violence. The researchers suggest that depression, substance use, eating disorders, suicidal ideation or attempts, sexual risk behaviors, and future revictimization are outcomes related to dating violence. Adult survivors of adolescent dating violence sometimes present with increased risk of medical disorders. In addition, adolescent victims of dating violence are more likely than adult victims to develop posttraumatic stress disorder.

In the aftermath of crime, when victims most need support and comfort, there is often no one available who understands. Parents or spouses may be dealing with their own feelings of guilt and anger for not being able to protect their loved ones. Friends may withdraw, not knowing what to say or do. As a result, victims may lose their sense of self-esteem and no longer trust other people. These effects of violent victimization can be particularly devastating when the victim is a young person.

Child Abuse and Neglect

It is impossible to determine how many children suffer abuse. All observers can do is count the number of reported cases—which include only those known to public authorities—or they can survey families, in which case parents may deny or downplay abuse. As a result, estimates of child abuse are generally considered low. The Administration for Children, Youth, and Families (ACYF) is the primary source of national information on abused and neglected children that has been reported to state child protective services agencies.

According to the ACYF, in *Child Maltreatment 2008* (2010, http://www.acf.hhs.gov/programs/cb/pubs/cm08/cm08.pdf), in 2008 an estimated 3.3 million children were alleged to have been abused or neglected and approximately 772,000 children were found to be victims of child maltreatment. Reports most often came from professional sources, such as educators (16.9%), the legal system (16.3%), social service employees (10.6%),

TABLE 7.2

Rates of violent crime, by gender, race, Hispanic origin, and age of victim, 2009

Demographic characteristics of victim	Population	Total	Violent victimizations per 1,000 persons age 12 or older				
			Rape/sexual assault	Robbery	Total assault	Aggravated assault	Simple assault
Gender							
Male	124,041,190	18.4	0.2[a]	2.7	15.6	4.3	11.3
Female	130,064,420	15.8	0.8	1.6	13.5	2.3	11.2
Race							
White	206,331,920	15.8	0.4	1.6	13.7	2.7	11.0
Black	31,046,560	26.8	1.2	5.6	19.9	6.8	13.0
Other race[b]	13,982,530	9.8	—[a]	0.5[a]	9.3	1.9[a]	7.4
Two or more races	2,744,600	42.1	—[a]	5.2[a]	36.9	9.3[a]	27.5
Hispanic origin							
Hispanic	35,375,280	18.1	0.5[a]	3.4	14.2	3.2	11.0
Non-Hispanic	218,238,010	17.0	0.5	1.9	14.6	3.3	11.3
Age							
12–15	16,230,740	36.8	0.9[a]	3.1	32.8	6.9	25.9
16–19	17,203,070	30.3	0.6[a]	5.2	24.6	5.3	19.3
20–24	20,620,150	28.1	0.8[a]	3.5	23.8	7.5	16.3
25–34	41,073,240	21.5	0.8[a]	2.8	17.9	4.5	13.4
35–49	64,323,190	16.1	0.4[a]	2.0	13.7	2.6	11.1
50–64	56,651,170	10.7	0.3[a]	1.1	9.3	1.9	7.5
65 or older	38,004,060	3.2	0.2[a]	0.4[a]	2.5	0.3[a]	2.2

Note: Violent crimes measured by the National Crime Victimization Survey include rape, sexual assault, robbery, aggravated assault, and simple assault. Because the NCVS interviews persons about their victimizations, murder and manslaughter cannot be included.
—Rounds to less than 0.05 violent victimizations per 1,000 persons age 12 or older.
[a]Based on 10 or fewer sample cases.
[b]Includes American Indians, Alaska Natives, Asians, Native Hawaiians, and other Pacific Islanders.

SOURCE: Jennifer L. Truman and Michael R. Rand, "Table 5. Rates of Violent Crime, by Gender, Race, Hispanic Origin, and Age of Victim, 2009," in *Criminal Victimization, 2009*, U.S. Department of Justice, Office of Justice Programs, Bureau of Justice Statistics, October 2010, http://bjs.ojp.usdoj.gov/content/pub/pdf/cv09.pdf (accessed October 26, 2010)

medical professionals (8.3%), and mental health professionals (4.3%). (See Figure 7.1.) Less often reports were made by nonprofessionals, such as relatives (7.3%), parents (6.7%), friends and neighbors (5.1%), and a small percentage of the victims themselves (0.5%) and perpetrators (0.1%).

In 2008, 71.6% of reported victims suffered neglect, 16.2% were physically abused, 9.1% were sexually abused, and 7.3% were emotionally or psychologically abused. (See Table 7.3.) The highest rate of victimization was among infants (21.8 per 1,000 males and 21.3 per 1,000 females). (See Figure 7.2.) The rate of occurrence generally decreased as the child's age increased.

The most tragic result of child maltreatment is death. The ACYF indicates that in 2008 an estimated 1,740 children died as a result of abuse or neglect. Children in the youngest age groups were the most likely to die of maltreatment; 79.8% of the children who died were three years old or younger.

The largest group of abusers were mothers acting alone (38.3%), followed by fathers acting alone (18.1%). (See Figure 7.3.) In 17.9% of cases both parents abused their children. Abuse of children was overwhelmingly perpetrated by parents (81.2%); only 9.8% of perpetrators

were not parents (9% were unknown or missing). Parental abuse is probably the most devastating of all abuse because child victims have absolutely no place to turn for help or support.

Missing Children

During the 1980s, as a result of several high-profile abductions and tragedies, the media focused public attention on the problem of missing children. Citizens became concerned and demanded action to address what appeared to be a national crisis. Attempting to discover the nature and dimension of the problem, Congress passed the Missing Children's Assistance Act of 1984. The legislation mandated the Office of Juvenile Justice and Delinquency Prevention (OJJDP) to conduct national incidence studies to determine the number of juveniles who were "victims of abduction by strangers" and the number of children who were victims of "parental kidnapping." The result was the National Incidence Studies of Missing, Abducted, Runaway, and Thrownaway Children (NISMART), the first of which was conducted in 1988, with the results published in 1990. The second and more recent NISMART was conducted mainly in 1999, with many of the data published in a series of reports in October 2002.

The Missing Children's Assistance Act also called for the creation of a national resource center for missing

FIGURE 7.1

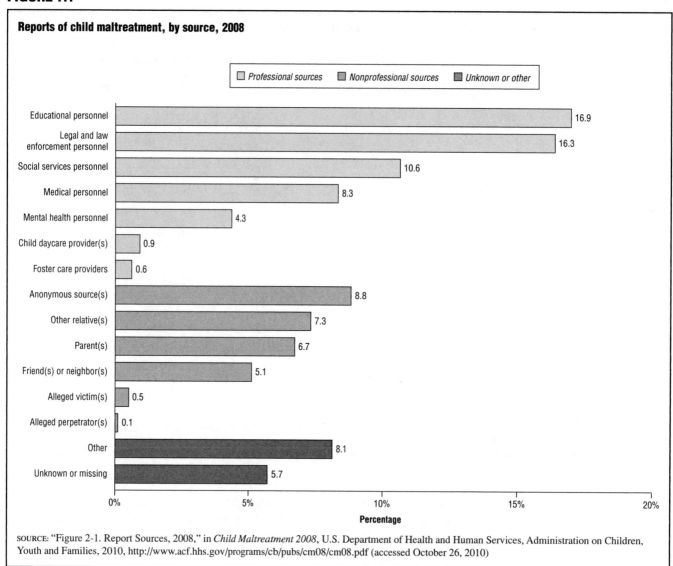

Reports of child maltreatment, by source, 2008

Source	
Educational personnel	16.9
Legal and law enforcement personnel	16.3
Social services personnel	10.6
Medical personnel	8.3
Mental health personnel	4.3
Child daycare provider(s)	0.9
Foster care providers	0.6
Anonymous source(s)	8.8
Other relative(s)	7.3
Parent(s)	6.7
Friend(s) or neighbor(s)	5.1
Alleged victim(s)	0.5
Alleged perpetrator(s)	0.1
Other	8.1
Unknown or missing	5.7

Legend: Professional sources, Nonprofessional sources, Unknown or other

SOURCE: "Figure 2-1. Report Sources, 2008," in *Child Maltreatment 2008*, U.S. Department of Health and Human Services, Administration on Children, Youth and Families, 2010, http://www.acf.hhs.gov/programs/cb/pubs/cm08/cm08.pdf (accessed October 26, 2010).

and exploited children. The result was the founding of the National Center for Missing and Exploited Children, a private, nonprofit organization founded that same year. The center operates a 24-hour hotline, provides state and local governments and private agencies information, reports data on missing and exploited children to the Department of Justice annually, helps train and provides assistance to law enforcement agencies, tracks patterns of attempted child abductions, operates a cyber tipline for reports of Internet-related child sexual exploitation, and disseminates information on the prevention of child abduction and sexual exploitation and Internet safety.

FAMILY ABDUCTIONS. According to Heather Hammer, David Finkelhor, and Andrea J. Sedlak of the OJJDP, in *Children Abducted by Family Members: National Estimates and Characteristics* (October 2002, http://www.ncjrs.gov/html/ojjdp/nismart/02/index.html), a family abduction is "the taking or keeping of a child by a family member in violation of a custody order, a decree, or other legitimate custodial rights, where the taking or keeping involved some element of concealment, flight, or intent to deprive a lawful custodian indefinitely of custodial privileges." In 1999, 203,900 children were victims of a family abduction. About half (53%) of these were abducted by biological fathers and 25% by biological mothers. Most family abducted children were not missing for long—46% were gone less than a week, and only 21% were gone for a month or more. Nearly four out of 10 (42%) were abducted from a single-parent family. At the time the survey was done, 91% of the children had been returned, 6% had been located but not returned, and less than 1% had not been located or returned (there was no information on outcomes for 2% of the cases).

In *The Crime of Family Abduction* (May 2010, http://www.ncjrs.gov/pdffiles1/ojjdp/229933.pdf), the OJJDP highlights the harm that is done to the 200,000 children who are the victims of family abduction annually. Even though the OJJDP emphasizes the physical dangers of family abduction to children, it states that "most often,

TABLE 7.3

Child abuse victims by age group and maltreatment type, 2008

Age group	Victims Number	Medical neglect Number	Medical neglect Percent	Neglect Number	Neglect Percent	Other abuse Number	Other abuse Percent	Physical abuse Number	Physical abuse Percent
<1	91,652	3,083	3.4	71,968	78.5	9,348	10.2	15,658	17.1
1	54,008	1,557	2.9	44,166	81.8	5,307	9.8	5,917	11.0
2	50,816	1,049	2.1	41,431	81.5	4,609	9.1	5,780	11.4
3	47,263	876	1.9	37,011	78.3	4,203	8.9	5,678	12.0
4–7	175,773	3,191	1.8	126,918	72.2	13,980	8.0	27,510	15.7
8–11	141,185	2,868	2.0	96,755	68.5	11,185	7.9	23,480	16.6
12–15	135,306	2,894	2.1	84,627	62.5	9,919	7.3	26,644	19.7
16–17	46,795	1,023	2.2	29,270	62.5	3,469	7.4	9,819	21.0
Unknown or missing	3,164	49	1.5	1,920	60.7	195	6.2	651	20.6
Total	**745,962**	**16,590**		**534,066**		**62,215**		**121,137**	
Percent			2.2		71.6		8.3		16.2

Age group	Psychological abuse Number	Psychological abuse Percent	Sexual abuse Number	Sexual abuse Percent	Unknown maltreatment Number	Unknown maltreatment Percent	Total victims Number	Total victims Percent
<1	4,171	4.6	470	0.5	153	0.2	104,851	114.4
1	3,634	6.7	558	1.0	136	0.3	61,275	113.5
2	3,327	6.5	968	1.9	143	0.3	57,307	112.8
3	3,221	6.8	2,394	5.1	119	0.3	53,502	113.2
4–7	13,373	7.6	15,232	8.7	542	0.3	200,746	114.2
8–11	12,233	8.7	16,122	11.4	558	0.4	163,201	115.6
12–15	10,584	7.8	23,959	17.7	591	0.4	159,218	117.7
16–17	3,419	7.3	7,946	17.0	240	0.5	55,186	117.9
Unknown or missing	296	9.4	353	11.2	64	2.0	3,528	111.5
Total	**54,258**		**68,002**		**2,546**		**858,814**	
Percent		7.3		9.1		0.3		115.1

Note: Based on data from 49 States.

SOURCE: "Table 3-12. Age and Maltreatment Types of Victims, 2008," in *Child Maltreatment 2008*, U.S. Department of Health and Human Services, Administration on Children, Youth and Families, 2010, http://www.acf.hhs.gov/programs/cb/pubs/cm08/cm08.pdf (accessed October 26, 2010)

FIGURE 7.2

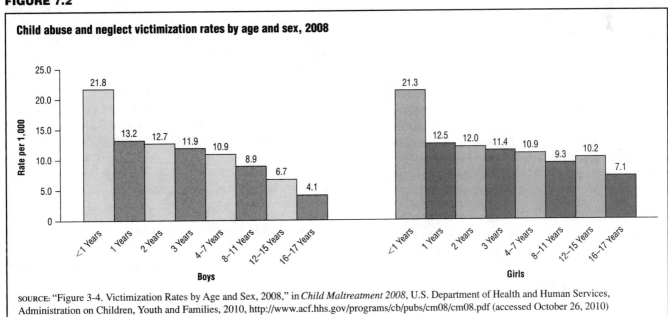

Child abuse and neglect victimization rates by age and sex, 2008

SOURCE: "Figure 3-4. Victimization Rates by Age and Sex, 2008," in *Child Maltreatment 2008*, U.S. Department of Health and Human Services, Administration on Children, Youth and Families, 2010, http://www.acf.hhs.gov/programs/cb/pubs/cm08/cm08.pdf (accessed October 26, 2010)

however, the worst damage is imperceptible to the eye, occurring deep within the child, leaving traces that may last a lifetime." The concealment of the child, the depri- vation of contact with other family members, and the physical flight are all traumatic and leave a lasting impact. Other damaging aspects of family abduction include being

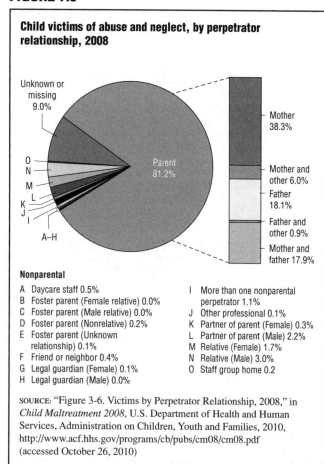

FIGURE 7.3

Child victims of abuse and neglect, by perpetrator relationship, 2008

Unknown or missing 9.0%

Parent 81.2%

Mother 38.3%

Mother and other 6.0%

Father 18.1%

Father and other 0.9%

Mother and father 17.9%

Nonparental

A Daycare staff 0.5%
B Foster parent (Female relative) 0.0%
C Foster parent (Male relative) 0.0%
D Foster parent (Nonrelative) 0.2%
E Foster parent (Unknown relationship) 0.1%
F Friend or neighbor 0.4%
G Legal guardian (Female) 0.1%
H Legal guardian (Male) 0.0%

I More than one nonparental perpetrator 1.1%
J Other professional 0.1%
K Partner of parent (Female) 0.3%
L Partner of parent (Male) 2.2%
M Relative (Female) 1.7%
N Relative (Male) 3.0%
O Staff group home 0.2

SOURCE: "Figure 3-6. Victims by Perpetrator Relationship, 2008," in *Child Maltreatment 2008*, U.S. Department of Health and Human Services, Administration on Children, Youth and Families, 2010, http://www.acf.hhs.gov/programs/cb/pubs/cm08/cm08.pdf (accessed October 26, 2010)

made to fear discovery, being given a new name and identity, not being allowed to grieve the loss of those left behind, being told to lie about the past, coercion and emotional abuse by the abductor, being kept out of school, and being told lies about the searching parent.

According to the FBI, in "Parental Kidnappings" (http://www.fbi.gov/wanted/parent), as of January 2011 there were 24 individuals "most wanted" for parental kidnappings. In the most recent case, Reiko Nakata Greenberg-Collins left Santa Ana, California, with her six-year-old son. At the time, she was involved in a custody dispute with the child's father. Greenberg-Collins was charged with child abduction and unlawful flight to avoid prosecution. The FBI believes that she has fled to Japan.

Mirela Iverac reports in "Protecting Kids: Rethinking the Hague Convention" (*Time*, December 10, 2010) on new research on child abduction cases that shows that at times mothers abduct their children to protect them from abusive fathers. Researchers Jeffrey Edleson and Taryn Lindhorst emphasize that even though child abduction is in most cases wrong, judges should have discretion in implementing laws to make it easier for battered women to prevent their children from being returned to abusive fathers. For example, Elizabeth Ann Stratton is on the FBI most wanted list for abducting her nine-year-

old son and six-year-old daughter in December 1997. She sent a letter to the county district attorney's office stating that she had taken the children and left the state. She was believed to have been in contact with a group that helps domestic violence victims. She was charged with parental kidnapping and unlawful flight to avoid prosecution.

NONFAMILY ABDUCTIONS. Even though far fewer children are abducted by strangers than by family members, the consequences are often far worse. Violence, the use of force or weapons, sexual assault, and murder are more prevalent in nonfamily abductions. David Finkelhor, Heather Hammer, and Andrea J. Sedlak of the OJJDP state in *Nonfamily Abducted Children: National Estimates and Characteristics* (October 2002, http://www.ncjrs.gov/pdffiles1/ojjdp/196467.pdf) that 58,200 children were abducted by nonfamily members in 1999. Nearly half (46%) of these were sexually assaulted by their abductors. Only 115 of the abductions were "stereotypical kidnappings," in which a child was abducted by a slight acquaintance or stranger, detained overnight, transported 50 miles (80 km) or more, held for ransom or with intention to keep permanently, or killed. Most nonfamily abducted children (59%) were 15 to 17 years old and 65% were female. The perpetrators were strangers 37% of the time and were three times as likely to be male as female. Most perpetrators (67%) were aged 13 to 29 years. Most nonfamily abducted children (91%) were away for 24 hours or less, and 99% returned alive. The remaining 1% were either killed or had not been located at the time of the survey.

In a widely publicized case, 14-year-old Elizabeth Smart was taken from her bedroom in Salt Lake City, Utah, in June 2002 by Brian David Mitchell (1953–). Mitchell succeeded in keeping Smart concealed for nine months. In March 2003 Smart was spotted with Mitchell and Mitchell's wife, Wanda Barzee (1945–), on a Salt Lake City street. Mitchell and Barzee were arrested. During the five-week trial, Smart described daily sexual assaults and other abuses. Barzee pleaded guilty to kidnapping and unlawful transportation of a minor across state lines in 2009 and was sentenced to 15 years in prison. In December 2010 Mitchell was found guilty of the same charges. He faced a maximum penalty of life in prison. As of January 2011, Mitchell was awaiting his sentencing.

RUNAWAYS AND THROWNAWAYS. In *Runaway/Thrownaway Children: National Estimates and Characteristics* (October 2002, http://www.missingkids.com/en_US/documents/nismart2_runaway.pdf), Hammer, Finkelhor, and Sedlak note that runaways are children who meet at least one of the following criteria:

• A child leaves home without permission and stays away overnight.

• A child 14 years old or younger (or older and mentally incompetent) who is away from home chooses not to come home when expected to and stays away overnight.

- A child 15 years old or older who is away from home chooses not to come home and stays away two nights.

During the 1970s the term *throwaways* or *thrownaways* was given by researchers to juveniles who were made to leave home or were abandoned. A thrownaway child meets one of the following criteria:

- A child is asked or told to leave home by a parent or other household adult, no adequate alternative care is arranged for the child by a household adult, and the child is out of the household overnight.
- A child who is away from home is prevented from returning home by a parent or other household adult, no adequate alternative care is arranged for the child by a household adult, and the child is out of the household overnight.

The number of runaways and thrownaways is difficult to estimate because the children's status is oftentimes concealed by either the runaways themselves or the families of thrownaways. As a result, the OJJDP now combines its estimates of runaways and thrownaways. According to Hammer, Finkelhor, and Sedlak, 1.7 million youths had a runaway/thrownaway episode in 1999. The runaway episode was thought to indicate that these children were endangered in the following ways:

- The child had been physically or sexually abused at home in the year before the episode or was afraid of abuse upon return (21%)
- The child was substance dependent (19%)
- The child was 13 years old or younger (18%)
- The child was in the company of someone known to be abusing drugs (18%)
- The child was using hard drugs (17%)

Most runaway/thrownaway youth (68%) were 15 years old or older, and half were females. Most runaways (77%) were gone for less than one week, and more than 99% returned. An estimated 38,600 of the runaways were at risk of sexual endangerment (assault, attempted assault, or prostitution) while away from home.

Murder Victims

According to the BJS, homicide rates for all age groups have been declining since the mid-1990s. Even though violent crime has diminished, it still plays a significant role as a cause of death for youth. However, Arialdi M. Miniño, Jiaquan Xu, and Kenneth D. Kochanek of the CDC indicate in "Deaths: Preliminary Data for 2008" (*National Vital Statistics Report*, vol. 59, no. 2, December 9, 2010) that in 2008 the leading cause of death among both males and females under the age of 24 years was accidents. Of the leading causes of death in 2008, homicides accounted for many abbreviated lives as well, and these deaths increased in number among older youth.

The homicide death rate for infants under the age of one was quite high at 7.9 per 100,000 live births in 2008. After that age the homicide death rate declined to 2.5 per 100,000 population among one- to four-year-olds and 0.8 per 100,000 population among five- to 14-year-olds. Nevertheless, homicide was the third-leading cause of death among one- to four-year-olds and the fourth-leading cause of death among five- to 14-year-olds. The homicide death rate rose again after the age 14 years.

UCR data confirm that murder victims are disproportionately young people. Out of 13,636 murder victims in 2009, 1,348 victims were under the age of 18 years, including 913 males and 435 females. (See Table 7.4.) The number of young murder victims more than doubled when looking at all victims under the age of 22 years. Of the 3,304 murder victims in this age range, 2,603 were male and 701 were female. One out of 10 (9.9%) murder victims was under the age of 18 years and one-quarter (24.2%) was under the age of 22 years.

African-Americans are also disproportionately victims of homicide. Nearly equal numbers of whites (6,568) and African-Americans (6,556) were murdered in 2009 (see Table 7.4), even though whites far outnumber African-Americans in the general population, according to the U.S. Census Bureau (June 2010, http://www.census.gov/popest/national/asrh/NC-EST2009-srh.html). Of victims under the age of 18 years, 654 (4.8%) were white and 639 (4.7%) were African-American. Of victims under the age of 22 years, 1,381 (10.1%) were white and 1,813 (13.3%) were African-American. Homicide has been and is still the leading cause of death for African-American teenagers, both male and female, although victimization rates for African-American teens declined dramatically between the early 1990s and 2000.

VICTIM-OFFENDER RELATIONSHIP. Snyder and Sickmund report that the most frequent killers of children under the age of six years were their parents, whereas parents were less likely to be involved in the murder of teens aged 15 to 17 years, although this varied by the gender of the child. Almost two-thirds (61%) of all female juveniles killed were murdered by a parent or stepparent, compared with only one-quarter (26%) of all male juveniles. Fifty percent of all male juveniles killed were murdered by an acquaintance, compared with only 29% of all female juveniles. Females were also less likely than males to be murdered by a stranger (3% and 18%, respectively).

The risk of being killed by a parent decreased with age: 62% of murder victims aged five years and younger were killed by a parent or stepparent, compared with 40% of children aged six to 11 years, 11% of children aged 12 to 14 years, and 3% of children aged 15 to 17 years. In

TABLE 7.4

Murder victims, by age, sex, and race, 2009

Age	Total	Sex			Race			
		Male	Female	Unknown	White	Black	Other	Unknown
Total	13,636	10,496	3,122	18	6,568	6,556	360	152
Percent distribution[a]	100.0	77.0	22.9	0.1	48.2	48.1	2.6	1.1
Under 18[b]	1,348	913	435	0	654	639	44	11
Under 22[b]	3,304	2,603	701	0	1,381	1,813	79	31
18 and over[b]	12,095	9,459	2,632	4	5,821	5,847	313	114
Infant (under 1)	193	102	91	0	106	72	9	6
1 to 4	298	158	140	0	159	129	9	1
5 to 8	72	34	38	0	40	27	4	1
9 to 12	71	36	35	0	43	23	5	0
13 to 16	400	319	81	0	190	199	9	2
17 to 19	1,246	1,068	178	0	476	738	22	10
20 to 24	2,426	2,081	344	1	931	1,407	64	24
25 to 29	1,941	1,605	335	1	789	1,097	39	16
30 to 34	1,534	1,216	318	0	645	845	25	19
35 to 39	1,205	950	255	0	573	583	40	9
40 to 44	1,006	734	271	1	543	419	34	10
45 to 49	926	642	284	0	559	337	23	7
50 to 54	701	519	181	1	423	242	27	9
55 to 59	455	309	146	0	286	144	21	4
60 to 64	312	216	96	0	210	88	11	3
65 to 69	227	152	75	0	165	57	4	1
70 to 74	134	85	49	0	104	26	1	3
75 and over	296	146	150	0	233	53	10	0
Unknown	193	124	55	14	93	70	3	27

[a]Because of rounding, the percentages may not add to 100.0.
[b]Does not include unknown ages.

SOURCE: Expanded Homicide Data Table 2. Murder Victims by Age, Sex, and Race, 2009, in *Crime in the United States, 2009*, U.S. Department of Justice, Federal Bureau of Investigation, September 2010, http://www2.fbi.gov/ucr/cius2009/offenses/expanded_information/data/shrtable_02.html (accessed October 26, 2010)

contrast, the risk of being killed by an acquaintance or a stranger increased with age. Twenty-eight percent of children under the age of six years were killed by an acquaintance, compared with 66% of 15- to 17-year-olds; only 3% of the youngest children were killed by strangers, compared with 25% of 15- to 17-year-olds.

WEAPONS USED IN MURDERS OF JUVENILES. According to Snyder and Sickmund, the number of youths dying as a result of firearms increased 152% between 1985 and 1993 before declining. Even though the number of homicides involving no firearm declined very little between 1993 and 2002, a huge drop in the number of homicides involving a firearm resulted in the overall number of juvenile homicides falling to their lowest level since 1984 in 2002.

The FBI reports that these trends continued in 2009; firearms were used in most murders of juveniles and young adults in that year. Of 1,348 murder victims under the age of 18 years, 684 (50.7%) were killed with firearms. (See Table 7.5.) Of 3,304 murder victims under the age of 22 years, 2,311 (69.9%) were killed with firearms. A lower proportion of the youngest murder victims were killed by firearms, but that proportion rose with age. The most firearms-related murders were in the 20- to 24-year-old age group (1,934 deaths). However, the greatest percentage of

firearms-related murders was among those aged 17 to 19 years (1,051 out of 1,246 murders, or 84.3%). Other weapons most frequently used to kill juveniles included personal weapons (hands, feet, fists, and so on), especially among the youngest children, and knives.

Rape

For several reasons, the statistics on rape are incomplete. The crime often goes unreported. The BJS estimates that only about one-third of the cases of completed or attempted rape are ever reported to police; other organizations estimate that the percentage of reported rapes is even lower. Because its data are collected through interviews, the BJS recognizes an underreporting in its statistics as well. Acquaintance rape is far more common than stranger rape. Most experts conclude that in 80% to 85% of all rape cases, the victim knows the rapist.

The UCR defines forcible rape as "the carnal knowledge of a female forcibly and against her will. Attempts or assaults to commit rape by force or threat of force are also included; however, statutory rape (without force) and other sex offenses are excluded." Rape is a crime of violence in which the victim may suffer serious physical injury and long-term psychological pain. In 2009 the UCR recorded 88,097 reported cases of rape, a decrease of 2.6% from the

TABLE 7.5

Murder victims by age and weapon, 2009

Age	Total murder victims	Firearms	Knives or cutting instruments	Blunt objects (clubs, hammers, etc.)	Personal weapons (hands, fists, feet, etc.)[a]	Poison	Explosives	Fire	Narcotics	Strangulation	Asphyxiation	Other weapon or weapon not stated[b]
Total	13,636	9,146	1,825	611	801	6	2	99	45	121	77	903
Percent distribution[c]	100.0	67.1	13.4	4.5	5.9	*	*	0.7	0.3	0.9	0.6	6.6
Under 18[d]	1,348	684	101	80	271	2	0	19	10	13	26	142
Under 22[d]	3,304	2,311	277	109	301	2	0	23	14	19	35	213
18 and over[d]	12,095	8,378	1,713	525	502	4	2	75	35	108	46	707
Infant (under 1)	193	8	2	24	104	0	0	2	3	2	13	35
1 to 4	298	47	8	33	130	1	0	4	6	4	5	60
5 to 8	72	30	8	6	9	0	0	2	0	4	2	11
9 to 12	71	29	13	1	8	1	0	5	1	1	3	10
13 to 16	400	308	40	12	16	0	0	3	0	1	2	17
17 to 19	1,246	1,051	113	17	17	1	0	3	4	2	5	34
20 to 24	2,426	1,934	257	42	46	0	0	9	3	8	10	117
25 to 29	1,941	1,518	237	34	38	0	0	3	3	22	4	82
30 to 34	1,534	1,118	212	43	42	0	0	4	6	17	6	86
35 to 39	1,205	844	167	46	48	0	2	10	1	14	0	73
40 to 44	1,006	626	180	54	54	0	0	7	5	10	2	68
45 to 49	926	522	165	61	71	1	0	14	1	14	1	76
50 to 54	701	379	130	68	54	1	0	10	2	7	6	44
55 to 59	455	230	94	41	35	0	0	6	0	4	4	41
60 to 64	312	149	63	35	27	0	0	3	3	1	2	29
65 to 69	227	98	40	37	21	1	0	1	1	2	4	22
70 to 74	134	56	29	16	13	0	0	1	2	5	1	11
75 and over	296	115	56	35	40	1	0	7	4	3	2	33
Unknown	193	84	11	6	28	0	0	5	0	0	5	54

[a]Pushed is included in personal weapons.
[b]Includes drowning.
[c]Because of rounding, the percentages may not add to 100.0.
[d]Does not include unknown ages.
*Less than one-tenth of 1 percent.

SOURCE: Expanded Homicide Data Table 9. Murder Victims by Age, by Weapon, 2009, in *Crime in the United States, 2009*, U.S. Department of Justice, Federal Bureau of Investigation, September 2010, http://www2.fbi.gov/ucr/cius2009/offenses/expanded_information/data/shrtable_09.html (accessed October 26, 2010)

year before. The rate of forcible rapes was reported at a rate of 56.6 offenses per 100,000 females.

Rape victims are disproportionately young. According to the BJS, in 2007 females aged 20 to 24 years experienced the highest rates (5.9 per 1,000 people), followed by females aged 16 to 19 years (4.9 per 1,000 people). (See Table 7.6.) Furthermore, the BJS finds that in 2007 only 44.7% of those aged 12 to 19 years who acknowledged being victims of rape/sexual assault reported the incident to police. (See Table 7.7.)

Aggravated and Simple Assault

In *Criminal Victimization in the United States, 2007 Statistical Tables* (February 2010, http://bjs.ojp.usdoj .gov/content/pub/pdf/cvus07.pdf), the BJS reports that in 2007 aggravated assault was most common among young people. It occurred at a rate of 2.8 per 1,000 people aged 12 to 15 years, 7.2 per 1,000 people aged 16 to 19 years, and 7.5 per 1,000 people aged 20 to 24 years. After that age the rate began to decline. Among white males, those aged 16 to 19 years experienced the highest rate of aggravated assault (12.9 per 1,000 people), whereas among African-American males, the rates of aggravated assault tended to rise with age, from 3.7 per 1,000 people aged 16 to 19 years to 7.6 per 1,000 people aged 50 to 64 years. (See Table 7.8.) African-American women in the 25 to 34

age group experienced the highest rate of aggravated assault (8.8 per 1,000 people), whereas white women in the 20 to 24 age group experienced the highest rate (4.3 per 1,000 people).

The BJS notes that in 2007 simple assault occurred at a rate of 35.5 per 1,000 people aged 12 to 15 years, 34.2 per 1,000 people aged 16 to 19 years, and 21.2 per 1,000 people aged 20 to 24 years, after which the rate began to decline. Younger African-American males had a slightly higher simple assault victimization rate than did white males in the same age group. African-American males aged 16 to 19 years had a simple assault rate of 33.9 per 1,000 people, compared with a rate of 28.9 per 1,000 people among white males of that age. (See Table 7.8.) However, rates among white and African-American males aged 12 to 15 years were essentially the same.

Robbery and Theft

The BJS reports in *Criminal Victimization in the United States, 2007 Statistical Tables* that in 2007 robbery occurred at a rate of 4.2 per 1,000 people aged 12 to 15 years and 6.4 per 1,000 people aged 16 to 19 years, after which the rate began to decline. Young males, both white and African-American, had high rates of robbery victimization; however, the rate among young African-American males was higher. (See Table 7.8.)

TABLE 7.6

Victimization rates for persons age 12 and over, by gender and age of victims and type of crime, 2007

Gender and age	Total population	Rate per 1,000 persons in each age group							Rate per 1,000 persons in each age group			
		Crimes of violence	Completed violence	Attempted/ threatened violence	Rape/ sexual assault[a]	Robbery			Assault			Purse snatching/ pocket picking
						Total	With injury	Without injury	Total	Aggravated	Simple	
Male												
12–15	8,588,740	48.3	15.6	32.8	0.0*	7.2	3.6*	3.6*	41.1	4.1	37.0	1.1*
16–19	8,641,090	55.8	16.1	39.7	0.0*	11.1	3.2*	7.9	44.7	12.5	32.3	1.9*
20–24	10,583,760	35.6	11.1	24.5	0.0*	3.9	0.3*	3.6	31.7	10.5	21.2	1.9*
25–34	20,300,040	26.4	6.9	19.4	0.0*	4.4	1.4*	3.0	22.0	5.4	16.6	1.4*
35–49	32,473,980	17.0	3.0	14.0	0.1*	1.5	0.3*	1.2	15.4	3.1	12.3	0.5*
50–64	26,058,340	13.7	3.4	10.3	0.3*	2.6	0.9*	1.7	10.8	3.3	7.5	0.1*
65 and over	15,476,740	2.1*	0.2*	2.0*	0.0*	0.5*	0.2*	0.3*	1.7*	0.3*	1.3*	1.0*
Female												
12–15	8,166,690	38.2	15.0	23.3	2.0*	1.1*	0.0*	1.1*	35.2	1.4*	33.8	0.4*
16–19	8,340,660	44.2	15.8	28.4	4.9	1.5*	1.0*	0.5*	37.8	1.7*	36.2	1.2*
20–24	10,168,270	34.7	12.3	22.4	5.9	3.2*	1.5*	1.7*	25.7	4.4	21.2	0.3*
25–34	20,049,690	23.0	9.5	13.5	2.3	2.4	1.2*	1.2*	18.2	4.1	14.1	0.9*
35–49	33,162,430	18.3	5.9	12.5	1.8	1.3	0.8*	0.6*	15.2	3.2	12.0	0.7*
50–64	27,619,120	9.5	2.4	7.1	0.3*	1.0*	0.4*	0.6*	8.3	1.4	6.9	0.5*
65 and over	20,715,300	2.8	1.3*	1.5*	0.2*	0.6*	0.3*	0.3*	2.0	0.3*	1.7	0.6*

Note: The 2007 rates are comparable to 2005 and previous years, but not to 2006 because of changes in methodology.
Detail may not add to total shown because of rounding.
* Estimate is based on 10 or fewer sample cases.
[a]Includes verbal threats of rape and threats of sexual assault.

SOURCE: "Table 4. Personal Crimes, 2007: Victimization Rates for Persons Age 12 and over, by Gender and Age of Victims and Type of Crime," in *Criminal Victimization in the United States, 2007—Statistical Tables,* U.S. Department of Justice, Office of Justice Programs, Bureau of Justice Statistics, February 2010, http://bjs.ojp.usdoj.gov/content/pub/pdf/cvus07.pdf (accessed October 26, 2010)

TABLE 7.7

Percent of victimizations reported to police by type of crime and age of victims, 2007

	Percent of victimizations reported to the police				
Type of crime	12–19	20–34	35–49	50–64	65 and over
All personal crimes	**33.4%**	**51.9%**	**55.5%**	**49.1%**	**61.1%**
Crimes of violence	32.8	51.4	54.9	48.8	56.1
Completed violence	51.2	57.9	71.3	59.3	66.1*
Attempted/threatened violence	23.6	48.1	49.4	45.3	51.1*
Rape/sexual assault[a]	44.7*	40.2	33.7*	65.1*	59.3*
Robbery	68.0	59.4	71.9	65.1	81.4*
Completed/property taken	68.3	59.9	89.0	69.2	86.2*
With injury	80.1	80.6	100.0*	82.9*	100.0*
Without injury	61.6	48.3	79.1*	61.8*	60.6*
Attempted to take property	66.9*	57.9*	39.8*	55.4*	73.0*
With injury	73.3*	100.0*	64.0*	100.0*	0.0*
Without injury	62.5*	44.5*	33.5*	32.2*	73.0*
Assault	27.6	51.0	54.7	45.3	48.2*
Aggravated	39.1	63.6	58.5	59.7	76.0*
With injury	60.5*	73.6	90.8*	72.0*	0.0*
Threatened with weapon	31.3	58.3	52.0	57.0	76.0*
Simple	26.0	46.9	53.7	40.7	42.6*
With minor injury	43.5	54.6	73.5	44.2*	57.9*
Without injury	20.0	44.7	48.8	40.1	36.6*
Purse snatching/pocket picking	54.5*	64.0	71.2*	61.1*	77.5*

*Estimate is based on 10 or fewer sample cases.
[a]Includes verbal threats of rape and threats of sexual assault.

SOURCE: "Table 96. Personal Crimes, 2007: Percent of Victimizations Reported to the Police, by Type of Crime and Age of Victims," in *Criminal Victimization in the United States, 2007—Statistical Tables*, U.S. Department of Justice, Office of Justice Programs, Bureau of Justice Statistics, February 2010, http://bjs.ojp.usdoj.gov/content/pub/pdf/cvus07.pdf (accessed October 26, 2010)

TABLE 7.8

Violent victimization rates for persons age 12 and over, by race, gender, and age of victims and type of crime, 2007

Race, gender, and age	Total population	Rate per 1,000 persons in each age group							
		Crimes of violence[a]		Robbery		Aggravated assault		Simple assault	
		Number	Rate	Number	Rate	Number	Rate	Number	Rate
White only									
Male									
12–15	6,470,500	309,850	47.9	34,750	5.4	35,070	5.4	240,030	37.1
16–19	6,691,760	345,240	51.6	65,550	9.8	86,230	12.9	193,470	28.9
20–24	8,335,730	340,840	40.9	29,220*	3.5*	103,900	12.5	207,710	24.9
25–34	16,227,230	425,470	26.2	48,680	3.0	86,690	5.3	290,090	17.9
35–49	26,784,190	462,020	17.2	29,680*	1.1*	78,340	2.9	350,520	13.1
50–64	22,072,790	282,240	12.8	47,230	2.1	60,010	2.7	170,310	7.7
65 and over	13,694,390	31,050*	2.3*	5,240*	0.4*	5,320*	0.4*	20,490*	1.5*
Female									
12–15	6,218,220	224,560	36.1	5,620*	0.9*	0*	0.0*	202,680	32.6
16–19	6,340,770	282,860	44.6	8,220*	1.3*	8,890*	1.4*	241,160	38.0
20–24	7,812,100	295,130	37.8	28,970*	3.7*	33,780*	4.3*	172,590	22.1
25–34	15,452,290	302,660	19.6	29,550*	1.9*	47,540	3.1	181,260	11.7
35–49	26,443,090	476,950	18.0	27,550*	1.0*	75,660	2.9	338,650	12.8
50–64	22,973,230	220,940	9.6	19,270*	0.8*	19,560*	0.9*	176,200	7.7
65 and over	17,954,090	56,070	3.1	10,420*	0.6*	5,820*	0.3*	35,040	2.0
Black only									
Male									
12–15	1,413,490	65,110	46.1	12,880*	9.1*	0*	0.0*	52,230	37.0
16–19	1,295,030	64,780	50.0	16,100*	12.4*	4,730*	3.7*	43,950	33.9
20–24	1,399,960	28,090*	20.1*	11,710*	8.4*	3,550*	2.5*	12,840*	9.2*
25–34	2,382,740	68,450	28.7	26,270*	11.0*	15,620*	6.6*	26,560*	11.1*
35–49	3,648,780	69,820	19.1	18,960*	5.2*	21,710*	6.0*	29,140*	8.0*
50–64	2,591,240	52,910	20.4	17,410*	6.7*	19,790*	7.6*	15,720*	6.1*
65 and over	1,137,080	2,010*	1.8*	2,010*	1.8*	0*	0.0*	0*	0.0*
Female									
12–15	1,339,870	61,910	46.2	0*	0.0*	7,390*	5.5*	54,520	40.7
16–19	1,301,030	41,180	31.7	4,200*	3.2*	5,080*	3.9*	31,910*	24.5*
20–24	1,494,740	45,320	30.3	3,550*	2.4*	7,410*	5.0*	34,350	23.0
25–34	2,918,020	129,910	44.5	12,420*	4.3*	25,720*	8.8*	88,990	30.5
35–49	4,430,020	70,230	15.9	13,850*	3.1*	9,860*	2.2*	36,520	8.2
50–64	3,127,560	34,860	11.1	6,970*	2.2*	13,890*	4.4*	11,110*	3.6*
65 and over	1,905,910	2,470*	1.3*	2,470*	1.3*	0*	0.0*	0*	0.0*

Note: The 2007 rates are comparable to 2005 and previous years, but not to 2006 because of changes in methodology.
Excludes data on persons of "Other" races and persons indicating two or more races.
*Estimate is based on 10 or fewer sample cases.
[a]Includes data on rape and sexual assault, not shown separately.

SOURCE: "Table 10. Violent Crimes, 2007: Number of Victimizations and Victimization Rates for Persons Age 12 and over, by Race, Gender, and Age of Victims and Type of Crime," in *Criminal Victimization in the United States, 2007—Statistical Tables*, U.S. Department of Justice, Office of Justice Programs, Bureau of Justice Statistics, February 2010, http://bjs.ojp.usdoj.gov/content/pub/pdf/cvus07.pdf (accessed October 26, 2010)

CHAPTER 8

VIOLENCE AND GANGS

THE SCOPE OF THE GANG PROBLEM

Gangs have a long history in the United States, dating back to the 1800s. The United States became a so-called melting pot during the 19th century as people of diverse ethnicities and religions entered the country. Some immigrants joined gangs to help them gain a group identity, defend themselves against other groups, and establish a unified presence. Even though people feared street gangs of the 19th century, the gangs of the 21st century pose a greater threat to public safety than in years past.

Most criminal activities of the street gangs of the early 20th century involved delinquent acts or petty crimes, such as brawls with rival gangs. As the 20th century progressed, however, gangs became involved in more serious crimes. By the late 20th century law enforcement officials had come to regard gang members in general as serious criminals who engaged in the illegal trafficking of drugs or weapons and used intimidation tactics and violence to pursue their goals. Respondents to the National Youth Gang Survey (NYGS) emphasized that a gang was defined by involvement in group criminal activity along with some degree of definition of a group as a separate entity, such as having a name, displaying distinct colors or symbols, or engaging in activities to protect the group's so-called territory. Law enforcement officers note that during the 1980s and 1990s more and more gang members began to support themselves through dealing drugs, such as crack cocaine and heroin. Many were said to have easy access to high-powered weapons. In addition, the proliferation of gangs during the late 20th century meant that groups moved beyond city boundaries into suburban and rural areas as well. This movement into new territories occurred about the same time that youth violence surged during the 1980s and early 1990s.

Researchers noted various reasons for the growth of gangs during the end of the 20th century. According to Finn-Aage Esbensen of the University of Nebraska,

Omaha, in *Preventing Adolescent Gang Involvement* (September 2000, http://www.ncjrs.gov/pdffiles1/ojjdp/182210.pdf), "American society witnessed a reemergence of youth gang activity and media interest in this phenomenon in the 1980's and 1990's. 'Colors,' 'Boyz n the Hood,' other Hollywood productions, and MTV brought Los Angeles gang life to suburban and rural America." These media portrayals might have further enticed youth to become involved in gangs.

In an effort to track the growth and activities of gangs, the Office of Juvenile Justice and Delinquency Prevention's (OJJDP) National Youth Gang Center (now the National Gang Center [NGC]) began conducting the NYGS in 1996. The National Gang Center reports in "National Youth Gang Survey Analysis" (2009, http://www.national gangcenter.gov/Survey-Analysis/Methodology) that for purposes of the survey, researchers annually query all police and sheriff departments serving cities and counties with populations of 50,000 or more (25,000 or more before 2002), as well as all suburban county police and sheriff's departments. Because gang membership has moved beyond large metropolitan areas, the NYGS also queries a random sample of law enforcement agencies in cities with populations between 2,500 and 25,000 and in rural counties. Not all jurisdictions that receive the survey respond, but a majority of jurisdictions do. Survey participants are instructed to provide information on youth gangs within their jurisdictions. Motorcycle gangs, prison gangs, adult gangs, and hate or ideology-based groups are not included in the sample.

Statistics about gang membership show that the increased concern about gangs had its basis in the growth of gangs during the 1990s. According to Walter B. Miller of the OJJDP, in *The Growth of Youth Gang Problems in the United States: 1970–98* (April 2001, http://www.ncjrs.gov/pdffiles1/ojjdp/181868-1.pdf), during the 1970s about 1% of U.S. cities and about 40% of the states reported having problems with youth gangs. By the late 1990s the percentage of U.S. cities with gang problems grew to 7%, and youth gangs were reported in all 50 states and the District of Columbia. Gang growth in cities soared during the 1980s and 1990s, with the number of gangs reportedly increasing by 281%. Between 1995 and 1998 gang activity was recorded in 1,100 cities and in 450 counties where it had not been previously reported.

At first, gangs tended to be big-city problems—the NYGS indicated that most cities with populations over 100,000 reported that the proliferation of gangs became a problem between 1985 and the early 1990s. After that time, however, gangs spread to smaller areas. It is true that the larger the population, the greater the likelihood of the existence of gangs in that area. Arlen Egley Jr. and Christina E. O'Donnell of the NGC find in "Highlights of the 2007 Youth Gang Survey" (April 2009, http://www.ncjrs.gov/pdffiles1/ojjdp/225185.pdf) that 86% of law enforcement agencies in larger cities reported gang problems in 2007. Half (50%) of all suburban counties, 35% of all cities with a population of 2,500 to 49,999, and 15% of rural counties reported gang problems in their jurisdictions that year.

The huge growth in gangs and gang membership slowed during the late 1990s. When comparing statistics between the 1996 and 2000 surveys, Arlen Egley Jr. of the NGC finds in the fact sheet "National Youth Gang Survey Trends from 1996 to 2000" (February 2002, http://www.ncjrs.gov/pdffiles1/ojjdp/fs200203.pdf) that "the proportion of respondents that reported youth gangs in their jurisdiction decreased over the survey years, from 53 percent in 1996 to 40 percent in 2000." In *National Youth Gang Survey, 1999–2001* (July 2006, http://www.ncjrs.gov/pdffiles1/ojjdp/209392.pdf), Arlen Egley Jr., James C. Howell, and Aline K. Major of the NGC estimate that there were approximately 21,500 gangs present in the United States in 2002.

However, by 2008 these numbers had increased. Arlen Egley Jr., James C. Howell, and John P. Moore of the NGC estimate in "Highlights of the 2008 National

Youth Gang Survey" (March 2010, http://www.ncjrs.gov/pdffiles1/ojjdp/229249.pdf) that 27,900 gangs with 774,000 gang members were active in the United States in 2008. Even though small cities and rural counties saw a decrease in gangs between 2007 and 2008, all jurisdictions saw an increase in gangs and gang members between 2002 and 2008. (See Table 8.1.) Overall, the number of gangs increased by 28.4% during this period, and the estimated number of gang members increased by 5.8%.

According to the National Gang Intelligence Center, in *National Gang Threat Assessment 2009* (January 2009, http://www.justice.gov/ndic/pubs32/32146/32146p.pdf), the modern street gang takes many forms. Individual members, gang cliques, or entire gang organizations engage in trafficking in drugs; operating car theft rings; committing homicides, assaults, robberies, and other felonies; and terrorizing neighborhoods. Some of the most ambitious gangs spread out from their home jurisdictions to other cities and states to expand their drug distribution territories, recruit new members, escape other gangs, or hide from law enforcement. The most dangerous gangs are regional and national gangs. In 2009, 11 national-level street gangs had been identified in the United States.

Whereas during the 1970s gangs tended to be tightly organized groups made up of African-American or Hispanic inner-city males, gangs in the 21st century can vary widely regarding membership, power structure, and ages and ethnicities of members. The National Gang Intelligence Center identifies three major types of gangs: street gangs, motorcycle gangs, and prison gangs. Most youth gang members belong to street gangs.

YOUTH GANG ACTIVITIES

Researchers, law enforcement agencies, and community groups devote time to learning more about gangs and the types of characteristics they share. Much study has gone into gang slang, graffiti, hand signs, colors, and initiations, among other characteristics. The goal is to learn more about how gangs communicate and interact, both internally and externally, as well as test themselves

TABLE 8.1

Percentage of law enforcement agencies reporting gang problems, 2002–08

	Percentage change, 2002–2008			Percentage change, 2007–2008		
	Gang-problem jurisdictions	Gangs	Gang members	Gang-problem jurisdictions	Gangs	Gang members
Rural counties	+16.4	+26.3	+7.8	−6.2	−23.2	−20.9
Smaller cities	+15.0	+35.0	+14.6	−9.7	−4.2	−14.5
Suburban counties	+21.8	+30.1	+9.6	−8.6	+11.2	−2.2
Larger cities	+12.5	+23.3	+2.2	+0.4	+7.0	+3.0
Overall estimate in study population	+15.4	+28.4	+5.8	−7.7	+2.3	−1.8

SOURCE: "Table 1. Percentage Change in Gang Estimates from 2002 to 2008," in *Highlights of the 2008 National Youth Gang Survey*, U.S. Department of Justice, Office of Justice Programs, Office of Juvenile Justice and Delinquency Prevention, March 2010, http://www.ncjrs.gov/pdffiles1/ojjdp/229249.pdf (accessed October 28, 2010)

and each other. If educators, law enforcement officials, and other concerned adults can recognize the signs that young people may be involved in gangs, they will be better able to intervene.

James C. Howell of the NGC points out in "Menacing or Mimicking? Realities of Youth Gangs" (*Juvenile and Family Court Journal*, vol. 58, no. 2, Spring 2007) that many youth gangs, particularly in rural areas and small cities, create a myth that they are more powerful and dangerous than they really are to provide members with maximum protection. They do this by imitating the clothing, graffiti, symbols, slang, and other signals of much more dangerous big-city gangs. Some of these signals are described in this chapter.

Various gangs have created their own slang language. Even though some terms are used in gangs throughout the country, others are only used regionally and within certain gangs. Several terms originated with the infamous Bloods and Crips gangs of Los Angeles, California, who have been adversaries for many years. Examples include "banging" (involved in gang activities), "colors" (clothing of a particular color, such as jackets, shoes, or bandanas, worn by gang members to identify themselves as part of the gang), "O.G." ("original gangster," meaning a gang member who has killed someone, or a founding member or leader of a gang), "tagging" (marking a territory with graffiti), and "turf" (territory).

Graffiti

The most common type of graffiti is that of personal musings—thoughts written down quickly in public places, such as restrooms and phone booths. Sometimes humorous, this type of graffiti might be of a sexual context or might include memorable quotes. Tagging is another type of graffiti. A tag is a signature, or moniker, that may incorporate the artist's physical features or symbolize his or her personality. Tags are usually found on exterior building walls in urban areas. They may also appear on mass transit systems (buses and trains), freeway overpasses, and other areas for all to see and wonder how it got there. Mural-type graffiti is known as piecing or bombing. The piece usually contains elaborate depictions or a montage of images. Often, slogans appear within the piece. Whereas tags can be done quickly, piecing may take several hours to complete and require many cans of spray paint in a variety colors.

Gang graffiti employs all the aforementioned types. Gangs use graffiti for many purposes. In some instances it may be a way of communicating messages to other gang members by functioning like a newsletter. Tags or monikers may be used to show a gang's hierarchy. Pieces may memorialize a dead gang member or pay tribute to the crimes committed by gang members. Some pieces may enumerate rules in the gang's society, whereas others may advertise a gang's presence in the neighborhood. Gang graffiti may also serve as a threatening message to rival gangs—as if to say, "Stay away from our turf." In the 21st century all types of graffiti are perceived as vandalism and a public nuisance and are punishable by law in the United States.

Hand Signs

Hand signs are a way of communicating concepts or ideas without using words. However, only those individuals who are familiar with the gesture's meaning are able to understand the message being conveyed. The rise of gang hand signs began in the Los Angeles area during the 1950s. Since that time many gangs have developed hand signs for use between members of the group. Gang members "throw" or "flash" hand signs as a way of communicating among themselves, such as to send secret messages to other members within the group. For example, placing a clenched fist over the heart means "I'll die for you."

According to *Recognize the Signs* (May 2006, http://www.nj.gov/oag/gang-signs-bro.pdf), by the New Jersey Office of the Attorney General and the Juvenile Justice Commission, each gang usually has a hand sign that symbolizes affiliation with the gang. For example, the Los Angeles Bloods use the sign B (creating a circle with the thumb and index finger, with the other fingers raised) to signify membership in the gang. Crips use a sign that represents the letter C. Even though this is a good way for gang members to recognize other members or affiliates, it can be used against them as well. A gang might use gestures created by a rival gang in an act called false flagging. When this occurs, a gang member will flash a rival gang's hand sign as a way to infiltrate the opposing gang or to lure an unsuspecting adversary into a bad situation.

Flying the Colors

The idea of wearing different colors to identify opposing sides is not new. For example, during wartime opposing armies use different colors to symbolize their cause or to protect their territory. Flags, uniforms, and the like were made in the color chosen to represent the nation or army at war. By donning the color of the army, soldiers were identified as being on one side or the other, and the enemy could be spotted more easily. During the American Revolution (1775–1783) most of the British forces wore red uniforms; thus, they were called the Redcoats. To distinguish themselves from the British, the American colonists chose uniforms of blue.

This is also true of gangs. *Recognize the Signs* notes that for many years gangs have used color to distinguish themselves from rival gangs and to protect their territory. Gang members often show support for the gang by wearing so-called uniforms. Sporting clothes in the gang's colors, such as bandanas, shoes, jackets, jewelry, and other articles of clothing, shows a person's membership in one gang over another. For example, the two largest gangs in the Los Angeles area are the Bloods and the Crips. The Bloods use red, and the Crips use blue. Harold O. Levy notes in "The Great Truancy Cover-Up" (*Yale Review*, vol. 96, no. 3, July 2008) that during the high school lunch period members of rival gangs play poker with red and blue playing cards to signify their gang affiliations. These colors are a way to symbolize the gang's unity, power, and pride.

However, "flying the colors" can be a disadvantage to gangs. The *2005 National Gang Threat Assessment* (2005, http://www.ojp.usdoj.gov/BJA/what/2005_threat_assesment.pdf), by the U.S. Department of Justice, the Bureau of Justice Assistance, and the National Alliance of Gang Investigators Associations, indicates that colors make it easier to recognize gang members not only by rival gangs but also by law enforcement and school officials. Law enforcement officials have been able to crack down on gang-related criminal activities by rounding up juveniles and youths wearing gang colors. In response to this new threat, many gangs have opted to forego their traditional colors and are developing new methods of identification. Like the modern-day army, gang members are beginning to camouflage themselves from their rivals by making their "uniforms" less conspicuous. Wearing a hat tilted to the left may show membership in a gang whose rivals are those who wear their pant legs rolled up.

Technology

The National Gang Intelligence Center reports in *National Gang Threat Assessment 2009* that technology is playing an increasing role in both gang communication and the recruitment of gang members. Street gangs use disposable cell phones to arrange drug transactions. They also use social networking sites such as MySpace and instant messaging to arrange transactions. Websites are used to intimidate other gangs as well as to recruit new members. Self-produced songs and videos are posted on YouTube and other sites for the same purposes.

CHARACTERISTICS OF GANG MEMBERS

Based on reports by law enforcement agencies, most gang members are male; however, female involvement in gangs is on the rise in the 21st century. In fact, the National Gang Intelligence Center indicates in *National Gang Threat Assessment 2009* that law enforcement officials are having trouble identifying female gang members, which may lead to some underreporting of female gang involvement. For example, in high-crime neighborhoods similar proportions of girls (29.4%) and boys (32.4%) claimed to be gang members in 2008. In addition, the center notes that among mixed-sex gangs, girls are assuming greater positions of power. However, all-female gangs continue to be rare.

In "Preventing Female Gang Involvement: Development of the Joint-Interest Core and Balance Model of Mother/Daughter Leisure Functioning" (*Aggression and Violent Behavior*, vol. 15, no. 1, January–February 2010), Gretchen Snethen of Indiana University explains that the risk factors for girls' involvement in gangs include being the victim of violent crimes or sexual abuse and living in a chaotic home environment. Female gang members were more likely than male gang members to compare the gang to a family. Some girls join gangs to maintain a relationship with a boyfriend who is in the gang. Snethen notes that initiation rites for female gang members often involve sexual abuse, including having consensual or nonconsensual sex with multiple male gang members. Female gang members often have to perform sexual favors for males on request.

Gang members are not always juveniles; in fact, over time law enforcement agencies have reported that a larger percentage of gang members are adults. Regardless, in "Menacing or Mimicking," Howell reports that gangs have a particular appeal to some youth. Gangs sometimes serve as families for children whose own families may be dysfunctional. Gang members have said there is often little need to intimidate youngsters to recruit them because they know what youth need and are willing to provide it in return for the child's commitment. Gangs provide emotional support, shelter, and clothing—in essence, just what the child's family may not be providing.

According to Howell, the racial and ethnic composition of gangs generally reflects the local population. Among school-aged gang members, 25% are white, 25% are Hispanic, 31% are African-American, and 20% are of other racial and ethnic groups. Minorities are overrepresented among gang members because gangs arise and persist in economically disadvantaged and socially disorganized areas, and minority communities are overrepresented in these communities. The Bureau of Justice Assistance notes in *Addressing Community Gang Problems: A Practical Guide* (May 1998, http://www.ncjrs.gov/pdffiles/164273.pdf) that "it is not necessarily race that explains gang life, for gang members usually come from socially and economically disadvantaged communities."

The *2005 National Gang Threat Assessment* also notes the connection between recent immigrant communities and gangs. New immigrant communities are often isolated by language barriers and difficulties in finding employment. Gangs are attractive to many in Hispanic immigrant communities because they provide support and protection. By contrast, Asian communities are less likely than other communities to report criminal activity to law enforcement agencies. As a result, gangs often victimize these communities.

Reasons for Joining a Gang

Why juveniles, youths, and even adults participate in gangs is the subject of much study in the United States.

Studies include those by Howell, in *Youth Gangs: An Overview* (August 1998, http://www.ncjrs.gov/pdffiles/167249 .pdf) and in *Youth Gang Programs and Strategies* (August 2000, http://www.ncjrs.gov/pdffiles1/ojjdp/171154.pdf); and Phelan A. Wyrick and James C. Howell, in "Strategic Risk-Based Response to Youth Gangs" (*Juvenile Justice*, vol. 9, no. 1, September 2004). The reasons vary greatly among gang members, but there are a few basic motives. It is important to note, however, that even though these factors may cause some people to join gangs, they do not prompt most people to do so. Some of the most common reasons to join a gang are:

- Feeling marginalized by society and seeking a commonality with others in similar situations

- Wanting power and respect

- Having friends involved in gangs and wanting to be a part of that

- Desiring a sense of belonging when that is not available through a traditional family setting

- Seeking safety and/or protection from bullies, rival gangs, family members, or others

- Having power in numbers

- Ending poverty and joblessness by turning to criminal activities, such as stealing and drug trafficking

- Needing to feel a sense of purpose

- Having trouble or a disinterest in school

- Living in neighborhoods or communities where other troubled youth roam the streets

- Adding organization and structure to one's life

- Having feelings of low self-esteem that are diminished through encouragement from other gang members

In *Early Precursors of Gang Membership: A Study of Seattle Youth* (December 2001, http://www.ncjrs.gov/ pdffiles1/ojjdp/190106.pdf), Karl G. Hill, Christina Lui, and J. David Hawkins note that they tracked juveniles in Seattle, Washington, over the course of several years to learn more about their involvement in gang-related activities. During the multiyear study the researchers tracked a group of 808 fifth-graders through the age of 18 years. They learned that 15.3% (124 students) of study participants joined a gang between the ages of 13 and 18 years. Of those joining gangs, 69% stayed in a gang for less than one year, whereas 0.8% of study participants who joined a gang at the age of 13 years were still in a gang when they were 18 years old.

According to Hill, Lui, and Hawkins, those children who stayed in a gang for several years "were the most behaviorally and socially maladjusted," often exhibiting "early signs of violent and externalizing behavior (e.g., aggression, oppositional behavior, and inattentive and hyperactive behaviors)." Children who associated with antisocial peers were more than twice as likely to remain in a gang for more than one year.

Hill, Lui, and Hawkins identify the various risk factors that potentially lead to gang involvement. These factors include having a learning disability, having access to marijuana, experiencing low academic achievement, living near other troubled youth in the neighborhood, and having a living arrangement that includes one parent along with other unrelated adults.

Recruitment and Initiation

Gang recruiters offer prospective members a chance to be a part of something—to gain a sense of belonging that might be lacking in their life. Through the use of graffiti, the wearing of colors or tattoos, or intimidation tactics, the gang recruits new members to increase its power. In turn, some juveniles see this power in the schools or on the sides of buildings and may feel pressured into joining a gang. In some instances gang members threaten juveniles into joining by offering protection from bullies or rival gangs. Other juveniles might be eager to join a gang, thinking it is cool and exciting to be part of a clique that engages in criminal activity.

In response to gang recruitment activities, some states and localities have changed their laws to make any kind of gang recruitment, even if it does not involve criminal behavior, illegal. For example, in 2007 Illinois proposed to amend its criminal code by making street gang recruitment on school grounds or public property a felony, even if it did not involve the use or threat of physical force; the law went into effect on January 1, 2010. Gang recruitment of any kind is illegal in Virginia, and recruitment of minors is a felony in New York.

As is common in some social clubs, many prospective gang inductees must undergo an initiation to show the gang that they are worthy enough to be accepted into the group. However, Howell points out in "Menacing or Mimicking" that reports of prospective gang members victimizing innocent people are extremely overblown urban legends. Instead, initiates generally have to endure an initiation rite that is similar to severe hazing. In rare instances a new member may be "blessed in" (not having to prove his or her worth) because a brother or a sister is already a member of the gang.

Studies show that in many cases adolescents may refuse to join a gang or leave it without fear of reprisal, even though gangs try to maintain the illusion that leaving is impossible. Terence P. Thornberry, David Huizinga, and Rolf Loeber report in "The Causes and Correlates Studies: Findings and Policy Implications" (*Juvenile Justice*, vol. 9, no. 1, September 2004) that this was borne out by OJJDP-supported longitudinal studies in Denver, Colorado

(1988–1999), in Rochester, New York (1986–1997), and in the Seattle Social Development Project in Washington (1985–2001), all of which showed that more than half (54% to 69%) of youths who joined gangs in those cities remained for one year or less, whereas only 9% to 21% stayed for three or more years. Howell explains that "youths can dissolve their gang membership by reversing the process by which they joined, by gradually disassociating with other members."

Indicators of Gang Involvement

Many groups—such as the Crime and Violence Prevention Center of the California Attorney General's Office, in *Gangs: A Community Response* (June 2003, http://www.worldwidelawenforcement.com/docs/Gangs_Commresp.pdf); Wyrick and Howell's "Strategic Risk-Based Response to Youth Gangs"; and the Department of Justice, in "A Parent's Quick Reference Card" (May 2007, http://www.usdoj.gov/usao/wie/justice_for_all/publications/GangCardforParentsEnglish.pdf)—have compiled lists to aid parents, siblings, educators, and others in looking for signs that a juvenile has joined a gang. Even though a youth may present several warning signs that might indicate he or she is in a gang, these signs are not foolproof—that is, the youth may actually not be in a gang or even be a so-called wannabe or gonnabe (at-risk youth). However, the more signs that a juvenile exhibits increases the likelihood that he or she is headed for gang involvement. The following are some potential warning signs:

- Experiences a sudden drop in school grades

- Lacks interest in school and other activities that were once important

- Becomes truant (skips school)

- Comes home late

- Acts more outwardly aggressive or outright defiant

- Develops a new circle of friends who seem more rough and tough

- Behaves more secretively and is less forthcoming

- Changes clothing style; begins wearing some colors exclusively or wears clothes in a unique way consistently (such as rolling up pant legs)

- Exhibits more antisocial tendencies and becomes withdrawn or uninterested in family activities

- Suddenly acquires costly material possessions (such as CDs, DVDs, or electronics equipment) or large amounts of cash, and the source of the funds cannot be explained

- Starts using a new nickname (or street name)

- Becomes fascinated with weapons, particularly guns

- Has new cuts and bruises indicating evidence of being in a fight, and is unable to provide a reasonable explanation

- Sports new unusual tattoos

- Writes gang graffiti on notebooks, schoolbooks, and posters

- Develops an increased interest in gangsta rap music

- Hides a stash of spray paint, permanent markers, and other graffiti supplies

- Has encounters with law enforcement

- Shows dependency on drugs and/or alcohol

THE SPREAD OF GANGS

Several Hispanic gangs originated in California but have since spread throughout the nation. According to the National Gang Intelligence Center, in *National Gang Threat Assessment 2009*, Southern California gang members who moved out of the state united under the name Sureño (or Sur 13). Norteños are gang members who originated in Northern California; they are believed to have an alliance with an outlaw motorcycle gang that helps them acquire drugs and aids them in defending against Hispanic gangs from Southern California. Mara Salvatrucha (MS 13) is an El Salvadoran street gang that originated in Los Angeles but spread to New York; Atlanta, Georgia; Dallas, Texas; and the District of Columbia. In 2008 MS 13 was estimated to have between 8,000 and 10,000 members in the United States. Vice Lord Nation is a collection of structured gangs based in Chicago but in 2008 was present in 74 cities, primarily in the Great Lakes region, with an estimated 30,000 to 35,000 members nationwide. Tiny Rascal Gangsters is a large and violent Asian street gang association that had at least 60 gangs with an estimated 5,000 to 10,000 members in 2008. All national-level gangs are believed to engage in drug trafficking as well as in other crimes, such as burglary, identity theft, money laundering, assault, and homicide.

A gang subculture has also emerged on Native American reservations. These gangs are primarily composed of youth and engage in less criminal behavior than other gangs. According to the *2005 National Gang Threat Assessment*, "gang behavior [on reservations] is more about group cohesiveness, predatory activities, and a party atmosphere than it is about organized criminal behavior with a profit motive." Gangs on reservations tend to be small and unaligned with large, national gang networks. However, the National Gang Intelligence Center indicates that a notable exception is the Native Mob, which is the largest and most violent Native American gang in the United States and has expanded beyond the reservations. Whereas gang-related violent crime is on an increase nationwide, most gang activity on reservations is associated with graffiti, vandalism, and drug sales.

In an effort to learn more about Native American gangs, the NGC conducted a survey and Aline K. Major et al. reported the findings in *Youth Gangs in Indian Country*

(March 2004, http://www.ncjrs.gov/pdffiles1/ojjdp/202714.pdf). The researchers note that the survey included "persons of American Indian, Alaska Native, or Aleut heritage who reside within the limits of Indian reservations, pueblos, rancherias, villages, dependent Indian communities, or Indian allotments, and who together comprise a federally recognized tribe or community." Major et al. report that in 2000 youth gangs were active in 23% of Native American communities. Fifty-nine percent of communities reporting active gangs estimated the number of gangs between one and five, 19% estimated the number to be between six and 10, and 6% estimated the number to be more than 10. Thirty-two percent of the communities with gangs believed the gangs consisted of 25 or fewer people, 12% estimated 26 to 50 people, and 16% estimated more than 50 people. According to the researchers, about 75% of gang members were juveniles. Females made up 20% of Native American gang members. According to Major et al., a mix of both males and females existed in 82% of the Native American gangs and 10% of gangs on reservations were thought to be female-dominated. The researchers also note that 78% of gangs on reservations were of Native American, Alaskan Native, or Aleut descent and the remaining 22% were of other ethnic or racial backgrounds, most notably Hispanic and non-Hispanic white.

Some researchers classify gangs not according to their racial and ethnic makeup, but to what purposes they serve and their organizational structure. In *National Victim Assistance Academy Textbook* (June 2002, http://www.valor-national.org/ovc/toc.html), the Department of Justice's Office for Victims of Crime outlines gang research that was conducted by the sociologist Carl S. Taylor. Taylor categorized gangs into three types:

- Scavenger gangs: these types of gangs act spontaneously and lack organization, have frequent changes in leadership, tend to have members who are low achievers, and are regarded unfavorably by other types of gangs.

- Territorial gangs: these types of gangs are highly organized, prone to fighting to establish territories, use formal initiations, and are formed mainly for social reasons.

- Corporate gangs: these types of gangs are highly structured, engage in drug trafficking, require members to live by a strict set of rules with harsh punishments for those who break them, and have members who can be considered actual "gangsters." Members of corporate gangs tend to be more intelligent than members of scavenger and territorial gangs, but they may lack formal schooling.

GANGS IN SCHOOLS

The presence of street gangs is a growing concern in U.S. schools. Various educators and students acknowledge the presence of gangs in their school. These gangs are often involved in illegal activities, such as violence, drugs, and weapons trafficking. Gang presence in schools often leads to fear among students who are not affiliated with gangs and may encourage nongang members to join a gang for protection. In schools with significant gang presence, the level of violence is frequently higher than in schools with less gang presence.

In *Indicators of School Crime and Safety: 2009* (December 2009, http://nces.ed.gov/pubs2010/2010012.pdf), Rachel Dinkes, Jana Kemp, and Katrina Baum address the issue of student reports of street gangs in schools. Between 2001 and 2005 urban students were the most likely to acknowledge the presence of street gangs at their school during the previous six months. (See Table 8.2.) By 2005 more than one-third (36.2%) of urban students said these gangs were present at their school. Suburban students (20.8%) and rural students (16.4%) followed. Even though law enforcement officials surveyed in the 2009 NYGS stated that gang membership held steady during the first decade of the 21st century, an increasing number of students reported gang activity at their school. In 2001, 20.1% of students reported gangs at their school, and in 2007, 23.2% of students reported gangs at their school.

According to Dinkes, Kemp, and Baum, the percentage of public school students reporting gangs at their school far eclipsed the percentage of private school students reporting gangs at their school. In 2007, 24.9% of students in public schools reported gang activity at their school, whereas only 5.2% of students in private schools reported similar gang activity. (See Table 8.2.)

African-American and Hispanic students were more likely than white or Asian-American students to report that gangs were present at their school in 2007. Over one-third of African-American students (37.6%) and Hispanic students (36.1%) reported gangs at their school. (See Table 8.2.) In contrast, 17.4% of Asian-American students and 16% of white students reported the presence of gangs at their school.

Indicators of Gang Presence at School

In *Youth Gangs in Schools* (August 2000, http://www.ncjrs.gov/pdffiles1/ojjdp/183015.pdf), James C. Howell and James P. Lynch note that even in elementary and secondary schools youth gangs can present serious crime problems. They describe various studies that asked surveyed students to explain why they believed gangs were present in their school. The students' responses included:

- The gang has a recognized name (80%)

- The surveyed student has spent time with gang members (80%)

TABLE 8.2

Percentage of students ages 12–18 who reported that gangs were present at school, by urbanicity and selected student and school characteristics, selected years 2001–07

Student or school characteristic	2001				2003				2005				2007[a]			
	Total	Urban	Suburban	Rural	Total	Urban	Suburban	Rural	Total	Urban	Suburban	Rural	Total	Urban	Suburban	Rural
Total	20.1	28.9	18.3	13.3	20.9	30.9	18.4	12.3	24.2	36.2	20.8	16.4	23.2	‡	‡	‡
Sex																
Male	21.4	31.9	18.9	14.0	22.3	32.1	20.5	12.2	25.3	37.4	22.4	16.1	25.1	‡	‡	‡
Female	18.8	25.9	17.5	12.5	19.5	29.7	16.3	12.4	22.9	35.0	19.1	16.7	21.3	‡	‡	‡
Race/ethnicity[b]																
White	15.5	20.5	15.4	12.1	14.2	19.8	13.8	10.7	16.8	23.7	16.0	14.1	16.0	‡	‡	‡
Black	28.6	32.4	25.4	22.5	29.5	32.8	28.3	21.8!	37.6	41.8	36.2	24.4	37.6	‡	‡	‡
Hispanic	32.0	40.3	27.1	16.8!	37.2	42.6	34.6	12.7!	38.9	48.9	32.1	26.2	36.1	‡	‡	‡
Asian	—	—	—	—	—	—	—	—	20.2	25.0	18.1	19.0!	17.4	‡	‡	‡
Other	21.4	27.0	20.0	‡	22.0	30.6	18.2	‡	27.7	33.9	29.0	‡	26.4	‡	‡	‡
Grade																
6th	11.2	14.9	9.0	11.0	10.9	21.6	7.5	‡	12.1	19.9	8.9	8.3!	15.3	‡	‡	‡
7th	15.7	23.7	13.7	8.9	16.3	25.5	13.2	9.4	17.3	24.2	14.9	15.2	17.4	‡	‡	‡
8th	17.3	24.0	16.6	10.1	17.9	25.2	16.2	10.9	19.1	30.5	14.6	14.7	20.6	‡	‡	‡
9th	24.3	35.3	20.8	18.9	26.1	38.2	24.3	13.8	28.3	40.3	24.8	21.0	28.0	‡	‡	‡
10th	23.6	33.1	22.3	14.4	26.3	35.3	24.1	18.0	32.6	50.6	27.9	22.0	28.1	‡	‡	‡
11th	24.2	34.2	22.7	15.8	23.4	34.6	20.4	15.0	28.0	44.3	25.5	13.3!	25.9	‡	‡	‡
12th	21.1	34.1	18.6	11.5!	22.2	34.8	19.3	13.3	27.9	39.5	25.1	15.8!	24.4	‡	‡	‡
Sector																
Public	21.6	31.9	19.5	13.7	22.5	33.7	19.9	12.8	25.8	39.1	22.3	17.2	24.9	‡	‡	‡
Private	4.9	5.0	4.3!	‡	3.9	6.0	2.4!	‡	4.2	7.7	3.0!	‡	5.2	‡	‡	‡

—Not available.

!Interpret data with caution.

‡Reporting standards not met.

[a]In 2007, the reference period was the school year, whereas in prior survey years the reference period was the previous 6 months. Cognitive testing showed that estimates from 2007 are comparable to previous years.

[b]Race categories exclude persons of Hispanic ethnicity. Other includes American Indian, Alaska Native, Asian (prior to 2005), Pacific Islander, and, from 2003 onward, more than one race. Due to changes in racial/ethnic categories, comparisons of race/ethnicity across years should be made with caution.

Notes: Data for 2005 have been revised from previously published figures. All gangs, whether or not they are involved in violent or illegal activity, are included. "At school" includes the school building, on school property, on a school bus, or going to and from school. In 2005 and 2007, the unit response rate for this survey did not meet NCES statistical standards; therefore, interpret the data with caution. Due to a redesign of the methods used to measure urbanicity, estimates for 2007 locales are not shown.

SOURCE: Rachel Dinkes, Jana Kemp, and Katrina Baum, "Table 8.1. Percentage of Students Ages 12–18 Who Reported That Gangs Were Present at School, by Urbanicity and Selected Student and School Characteristics: Various Years: 2001–2007," in Indicators of School Crime and Safety: 2009, U.S. Department of Education, National Center for Education Statistics, and U.S. Department of Justice, Bureau of Justice Statistics, December 2009, http://nces.ed.gov/programs/crimeindicators2009/tables/table_08_1.asp (accessed October 28, 2010)

- The gang members wear clothing or other items identifying their group (71%)
- The gang marks or tags its territory with graffiti (56%)
- The gang commits acts of violence (50%)
- The gang has a recognized territory (47%)
- The gang members have tattoos (37%)
- The gang members have a recognized leader (33%)

Gangs and Drugs at School

Howell and Lynch comment on the connection between drug availability and gang presence at school. They note, "Where none of the drugs was easy to get, only 25 percent of surveyed students said gangs were present. This percentage increased from 42 percent when only one drug was readily available to 69 percent when seven drugs were readily available, and then dropped slightly when eight or nine drugs were readily available." When eight and nine drugs were available at school, the percentage of students reporting gangs decreased to 63% and 62%, respectively. It is unclear whether the availability of drugs was because of the gang activity, or if the presence of gangs was part of an underlying problem that contributed to the availability of drugs. Dinkes, Kemp, and Baum note that "the availability of drugs on school property has a disruptive and corrupting influence on the school environment." They also indicate that 22.3% of

high school students reported that drugs were available to them on school property in 2007, down from about 32.1% in 1995. (See Figure 8.1.)

Gang Criminality at School

Howell and Lynch include survey respondents' impressions about the presence of gangs in school and the gangs' relationship to crime. According to the researchers, "The students reported that most of the gangs they see at school are actively involved in criminal activities. About two-thirds of the students reported that gangs are involved in none or only one of three types of criminal acts: violence, drug sales, or carrying guns. Nevertheless, students said that a small proportion of gangs in schools (8 percent) are involved in all three types of crimes, and these gangs are probably responsible for the most disruption and violent victimization in and around schools." Howell and Lynch indicate that other studies include a variety of other criminal activities known to be perpetrated by gang members.

Howell and Lynch also state that gangs contribute substantially to victimizations at school. It is believed that some students join gangs to avoid persecution by gang members. For them, gang membership serves as a form of protection from other students who may threaten them or wish them harm.

GANG CRIME AND VIOLENCE

In "The Impact of Gang Formation on Local Patterns of Crime" (*Journal of Research in Crime and Delinquency*,

FIGURE 8.1

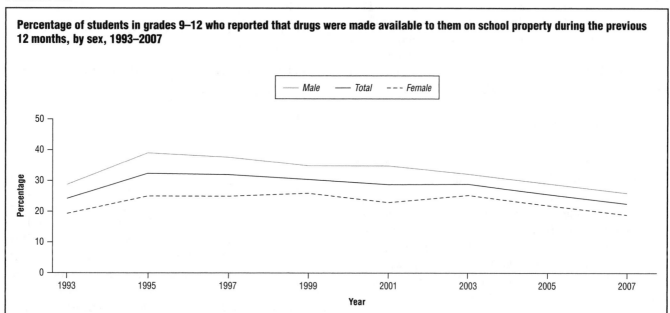

Percentage of students in grades 9–12 who reported that drugs were made available to them on school property during the previous 12 months, by sex, 1993–2007

Note: "On school property" was not defined for survey respondents.

SOURCE: Rachel Dinkes, Jana Kemp, and Katrina Baum, "Figure 9.1. Percentage of Students in Grades 9–12 Who Reported That Drugs Were Made Available to Them on School Property during the Previous 12 Months, by Sex: Various Years, 1993–2007," in *Indicators of School Crime and Safety: 2009*, U.S. Department of Education, National Center for Education Statistics, and U.S. Department of Justice, Bureau of Justice Statistics, December 2009, http://nces.ed.gov/pubs2010/2010012.pdf (accessed October 28, 2010)

vol. 44, no. 2, May 2007), George Tita and Greg Ridgeway acknowledge that gang members commit more crimes and more serious crimes than do nongang members, but they also examine whether the emergence of gangs have an impact on the crime rate. They argue that gangs typically form in areas that have higher crime than other areas, but once gangs form, they attract or generate even higher levels of crime. Tita and Ridgeway state, "The formation of gang set space facilitates drug and shots-fired activity at the neighborhood level, just as gang membership facilitates drug-market activities and gun carrying or usage among active gang members." The following is a discussion of gang involvement in specific criminal activities.

Homicides

The impact and severity of gang activity in an area is often measured by the numbers of gang-related homicides. The term *gang-motivated homicides* refers to those murders that further the interests of a gang, whereas *gang-related homicides* generally refers to murders where a gang member is either a perpetrator or the victim. Most localities use the broader gang member–based definition, rather than the motive-based definition, when classifying a homicide as gang related.

Some evidence suggests that even though the number of active gangs and gang membership is holding steady, gang violence is getting worse. According to Egley, Howell, and Moore, there is a clear relationship between population size and gang-related homicides. Nearly 20% of larger cities reported that gang-related homicides increased in 2008. In the largest cities with populations greater than 250,000, gang-related homicides increased by 10% between 2002 and 2008. In addition, the National Gang Intelligence Center reports in *National Gang Threat Assessment 2009* that gang members are increasingly carrying and using firearms. Between 2002 and 2007, 94.3% of gang-related homicides involved the use of a firearm.

Drug Trafficking and Other Crime

Gangs use drug trafficking as a major source of financial gain. In *National Gang Threat Assessment 2009*, the National Gang Intelligence Center indicates that in 2008, 58% of all law enforcement respondents to the NYGS reported that gangs in their communities were involved in selling drugs, up from 45% in 2004. Law enforcement agencies believed this was especially true in the distribution of marijuana, followed by cocaine (powder and crack), MDMA, methamphetamine, illegal pharmaceutical drugs, and heroin. (See Figure 8.2.)

Egley, Howell, and Moore find that gang-related crime increased in a significant portion of locales across the United States between 2007 and 2008. Specifically, 44% of law enforcement agencies surveyed reported an increase in gang-related aggravated assault, 41% reported

an increase in drug sales, and 41% reported an increase in the use of firearms.

The National Gang Intelligence Center also reports that gangs are thought to be increasingly associating themselves with organized crime groups, such as Mexican drug organizations and Asian and Russian organized crime. Imprisoning gang members is thought to do little to curb their activities, and the return of previously imprisoned gang members to communities is believed to intensify criminal activity, drug trafficking, and violence in those communities. In addition, California-style gangs have been found throughout the United States.

CONSEQUENCES OF BEING IN A GANG

Being in a gang can be dangerous. Former members can tell many stories about the difficulties one encounters in gang life. Besides living a life with the potential for more violence and crime than the average youth would experience, many other consequences exist. Even though such consequences might vary considerably among individuals, Dana Peterson, Terrance J. Taylor, and Finn-Aage Esbensen, in "Gang Membership and Violent Victimization" (*Justice Quarterly*, vol. 21, no. 4, December 2004), and Thornberry, Huizinga, and Leober address some of the most commonly encountered consequences:

- Becoming a school dropout
- Having little opportunity to secure a good, legal job
- Being unable to hold a steady job
- Becoming antisocial and having difficulty socializing outside the gang
- Having an increased likelihood of being a victim of violent crime
- Entering motherhood or fatherhood at an early age
- Ending up in prison or jail for gang crimes
- Developing a dependency on drugs and/or alcohol
- Experiencing a higher risk of premature death

GANG PREVENTION STRATEGIES

The OJJDP runs a Gang Reduction Program in certain high-risk neighborhoods. Four pilot sites have been funded: East Los Angeles, California; Milwaukee, Wisconsin; North Miami Beach, Florida; and Richmond, Virginia. These programs use the OJJDP's Comprehensive Gang Model, which is described in *Best Practices to Address Community Gang Problems: OJJDP's Comprehensive Gang Model* (October 2010, http://www.ncjrs.gov/pdffiles1/ojjdp/231200.pdf). This model has been extensively researched and refined in the pilot sites to provide information to other communities searching for ways to combat gang problems in their locales.

FIGURE 8.2

Percentage of law enforcement agencies reporting gang involvement in drug distribution, by drug type, 2004–08

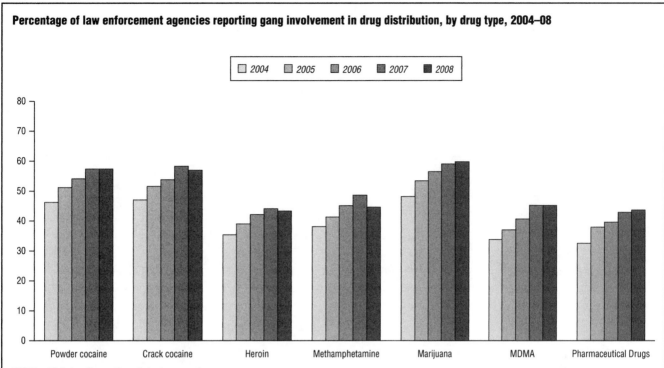

MDMA = Methylenedioxymethamphetamine, or ecstasy

SOURCE: "Figure 4. Percentage of Law Enforcement Agencies Reporting Gang Involvement in Drug Distribution, by Drug Type, 2004–2008," in *National Gang Threat Assessment, 2009*, National Gang Intelligence Center, January 2009, http://www.justice.gov/ndic/pubs32/32146/32146p.pdf (accessed October 28, 2010)

Five key strategies are included in the Comprehensive Gang Model:

- Community mobilization: involvement of local citizens, including former gang-involved youth, community groups, agencies, and coordination of programs and staff functions within and across agencies.

- Opportunities provision: development of a variety of specific education, training, and employment programs targeting gang-involved youth.

- Social intervention: involving youth-serving agencies, schools, grassroots groups, faith-based organizations, police, and other juvenile/criminal justice organizations in "reach-ing out" to gang-involved youth and their families, and linking them with the conventional world and needed services.

- Suppression: formal and informal social control procedures, including close supervision and monitoring of gang-involved youth by agencies of the juvenile/criminal justice system and also by community-based agencies, schools, and grassroots groups.

- Organizational change and development: development and implementation of policies and procedures that result in the most effective use of available and potential resources, within and across agencies, to better address the gang problem.

CHAPTER 9
CRIME AND VIOLENCE IN THE SCHOOLS

School is supposed to be a safe haven where young people can go to learn the basics of mathematics, literature, science, and other subjects without fearing for their safety, feeling intimidated, or being harassed. Even though school administrators and teachers work toward making the environment safe and secure, crime and violence do find their way into the hallways and classrooms and onto the school grounds. Despite media emphasis on topics such as school shootings, fatal violence at schools is relatively low. Nonfatal crime, however, occurs in far greater numbers, sometimes even more frequently at school than away from school.

Safety is and will continue to be a concern at schools. A rash of school shootings and bomb threats that occurred during the 1990s, and that continue to occur in the 21st century, brought increasing attention to school safety issues and what must be done to protect students. Two particularly troubling incidences were the shootings at Colorado's Columbine High School in 1999 and the more recent tragedy at the Virginia Polytechnic Institute and State University in the spring of 2007, in which a student killed 32 people and then himself. Various studies about school violence and crime were issued during the late 1990s and the first decade of the 21st century as researchers examined past trends and tried to predict patterns for the future. The studies ranged from how many children bring weapons to school to how many children are injured in fights, are afraid to go to school, or are subjected to disciplinary actions. Educators, school administrators, parents, and students themselves remain vigilant in striving to make schools safe places where youth are able to learn and prepare for the future.

Exactly how much crime and violence exist in U.S. schools in the 21st century? Has it increased or decreased in recent years? What effect did the Columbine High School shootings have on students and public opinion in general? Is there a danger that students, educators, and school officials will underreport school crime and violence to police?

VIOLENT DEATHS AT SCHOOL

During the 2007–08 school year there were 43 school-associated violent deaths in elementary and secondary schools, including 21 homicides and five suicides of school-aged youth. (See Table 9.1.) This number was down from the previous school year, when 58 violent deaths occurred—including 30 homicides and eight suicides of school-age youth. That number represented the highest number of school-associated deaths (including staff, students, and nonstudents) in any year of the study.

Rachel Dinkes, Jana Kemp, and Katrina Baum state in *Indicators of School Crime and Safety: 2009* (December 2009, http://nces.ed.gov/pubs2010/2010012.pdf) that between July 1, 1992, and June 30, 2008, 742 school-associated violent deaths occurred across the United States, including 396 homicides of school-age children. (See Table 9.1.) Despite the understandable fear that is generated by the media coverage of events, the possibility of being killed at school is very minimal. The percentage of youth homicides occurring at school was less than 2% from 1992 to 2008; the percentage of youth suicides occurring at school was less than 1% during this period. However, Americans were shocked by the rash of school shootings during the 1990s and some were afraid to send their children to school. The shootings at Columbine High School, in particular, weighed heavily on many students' and parents' minds.

Columbine High School

The tragedy began around 11:10 a.m. on April 20, 1999, as senior Eric Harris (1981–1999) arrived at the student parking lot at Columbine High School in Littleton, a suburb of Denver, Colorado. A short time later, Harris's friend and classmate Dylan Klebold (1982–1999) arrived. Carrying two large duffel bags, they walked together to the school cafeteria. Each of the bags contained a 20-pound (9.1-kg) propane bomb, which was

TABLE 9.1

Number of school-associated violent deaths by location, 1992–2008

Year	Total student, staff, and nonstudent school-associated violent deaths[a]	Homicides of youth ages 5–18		Suicides of youth ages 5–18	
		Homicides at school[b]	Total homicides[c]	Suicides at school[b]	Total suicides[d]
1992–93	57	34	2,689	6	1,680
1993–94	48	29	2,879	7	1,723
1994–95	48	28	2,654	7	1,767
1995–96	53	32	2,512	6	1,725
1996–97	48	28	2,189	1	1,633
1997–98	57	34	2,056	6	1,626
1998–99	47	33	1,762	4	1,597
1999–2000	38[e]	14[e]	1,537	8[e]	1,415
2000–01	33[e]	14[e]	1,466	5[e]	1,493
2001–02	38[e]	16[e]	1,468	6[e]	1,400
2002–03	35[e]	18[e]	1,515	9[e]	1,331
2003–04	45[e]	23[e]	1,437	4[e]	1,285
2004–05	51[e]	22[e]	1,535	7[e]	1,471
2005–06	43[e]	20[e]	1,646	3[e]	1,408
2006–07	58[e]	30[e]	1,748	8[e]	1,296
2007–08	43[e]	21[e]	—	5[e]	—

—Not available.

[a]A school-associated violent death is defined as "a homicide, suicide, legal intervention (involving a law enforcement officer), or unintentional firearm-related death in which the fatal injury occurred on the campus of a functioning elementary or secondary school in the United States" while the victim was on the way to or from regular sessions at school or while the victim was attending or traveling to or from an official school-sponsored event. Victims include students, staff members, and others who are not students, from July 1, 1992, through June 20, 2008.
[b]Youth ages 5–18 from July 1, 1992, through June 30, 2008.
[c]Youth ages 5–18 from July 1, 1992, through June 30, 2007.
[d]Youth ages 5–18 in the calendar year from 1992 to 2006.
[e]The data from 1999–2000 onwards are considered preliminary until interviews with school and law enforcement officials have been completed. The details learned during the interviews can occasionally change the classification of a case.
Note: "At school" includes on school property, on the way to or from regular sessions at school, and while attending or traveling to or from a school-sponsored event. Estimates were revised and may differ from previously published data.

SOURCE: Rachel Dinkes, Jana Kemp, and Katrina Baum, "Table 1.1. Number of School-Associated Violent Deaths, Homicides, and Suicides of Youth Ages 5–18, by Location and Year: 1992–2008," in *Indicators of School Crime and Safety: 2009*, U.S. Department of Education, National Center for Education Statistics, and U.S. Department of Justice, Bureau of Justice Statistics, December 2009, http://nces.ed.gov/programs/crimeindicators/crimeindicators2009/tables/table_01_1.asp (accessed October 28, 2010)

set to detonate at exactly 11:17 a.m. Harris and Klebold looked for an inconspicuous place to leave their bomb-concealing bags among the hundreds of other backpacks and bags there. After choosing a spot, Harris and Klebold returned to the parking lot to wait for the bombs to detonate.

Part of their plan was aimed at diverting the Littleton Fire Department, the Jefferson County Sheriff's Office, and other emergency personnel away from the high school as the pair stormed the school. To achieve this, they had planted pipe bombs 3 miles (4.8 km) southwest of the high school that were set to explode and start grass fires. As the explosions began, Harris and Klebold prepared to reenter the school, this time via the west exterior steps. That location is the highest point on campus and allows a view of the student parking lots and the cafeteria's entrances and exits. Both Harris and Klebold, dressed in black trench coats, concealed 9mm semiautomatic weapons from view. As they approached, the pair pulled out shotguns from a duffel bag and opened fire toward the west doors of the school, killing 17-year-old Rachel Scott.

After entering the school, they roamed the halls, library, and cafeteria, among other areas, killing 12 other victims, including a teacher, before finally killing themselves. In the process they also injured 23 other students physically and many others emotionally. The details of the event are outlined in *The Columbine High School Shootings: Jefferson County Sheriff Department's Investigation Report* (May 15, 2000) by the Jefferson County Sheriff's Department. Since that time, more documents and videotapes have been made available to the victims' families, the media, and others as well.

Investigations after the Columbine shootings focused on incidents in the boys' past that might have indicated the potential for such violent behavior. Among the people most surprised by the shootings were Klebold's family. Tom Klebold, Dylan's father, told investigators that his son had never showed any interest in guns. The Klebolds told authorities that Dylan had been accepted at the University of Arizona and had planned to study computer science. Klebold's friends and teachers described him as a nice, normal teenager. However, authorities also learned that Klebold and Harris were often subjected to harassment and bullying from other students. Much discussion of this fact was reported by the media, which prompted various research organizations to look into the effects of bullying on juveniles. Some wondered if the ridicule from other students had prompted Harris and Klebold to seek revenge.

The Federal Bureau of Investigation Examines School Shooters

Previous school shooting incidents prompted the Federal Bureau of Investigation (FBI) to spend two years researching this phenomenon. In *The School Shooter: A Threat Assessment Perspective* (September 2000, http://www.fbi.gov/stats-services/publications/school-shooter), Mary Ellen O'Toole of the FBI asserts that the profile of a school shooter cannot be determined, nor is it possible to create a checklist of the warning signs that indicate the next juvenile who will bring lethal violence to school. O'Toole's intent, however, is to assist school personnel and others in assessing threats and to keep any planned violence from occurring.

O'Toole uses a four-pronged approach in assessing "the totality of the circumstances" known about a student in four major areas: the student's personality, family dynamics, school dynamics, and social dynamics. O'Toole states, "If an act of violence occurs at a school, the school becomes the scene of the crime. As in any violent crime, it is necessary to understand what it is about the school which might have influenced the student's decision to offend there rather than someplace else."

According to O'Toole, the FBI has established the following factors in making this determination:

- The student's attachment to school—the student appears to be detached from school, including other students, teachers, and school activities.

- Tolerance for disrespectful behavior—the school does little to prevent or punish disrespectful behavior between individual students or groups of students.

- Inequitable discipline—discipline is inequitably (unfairly) applied (or has the perception of being inequitably applied) by students and/or staff.

- Inflexible culture—the school's culture is static, unyielding, and insensitive to the changes in society and the changing needs of newer students and staff.

- Pecking order among students—certain groups of students are officially or unofficially given more prestige and respect than others.

- Code of silence—few students feel they can safely tell teachers or administrators if they are concerned about another student's behavior or attitudes. Little trust exists between students and staff.

- Unsupervised computer access—access to computers and the Internet is unsupervised and unmonitored.

Students are able to use the school's computers to play violent computer games or to explore inappropriate websites, such as those that promote violent hate groups or give instructions for making a bomb.

Despite the factors that might indicate a school will be more likely to be the site of a deadly incident, O'Toole reemphasizes in "School Shootings: What You Should Know" (October 6, 2006, http://www.fbi.gov/news/stories/2006/october/school_shoot100606) that there might be nothing that can be done to prevent a violent incident from occurring. However, she states that school personnel should be vigilant by paying attention to students' moods and behaviors and taking all threats seriously.

SECURITY AND DISCIPLINE

After Columbine, as students, teachers, and parents became more worried about school safety, U.S. schools began implementing security measures to try to prevent future violent incidents. According to Dinkes, Kemp, and Baum, during the 2007–08 school year, 90% of public schools controlled access to school buildings during school hours, 58% required faculty and staff to wear identification, 55% used security cameras to monitor the school, 5% used random metal detector checks, and 1% used daily metal detector checks. Nearly all schools (99%) required visitors to sign in.

Security measures differed by school level. Dinkes, Kemp, and Baum state that during the 2007–08 school year buildings or grounds were more likely to be monitored in primary schools than in middle or high schools. Elementary school students were more likely to be required to wear uniforms than older students. Drug tests, security cameras, random sweeps for contraband, metal detector checks, and drug-sniffing dogs were much more likely to be used in high schools than in earlier grades. Critics of increased surveillance in schools contend that bullying, stalking, and harassment present the real risk to students and believe that stronger counseling and early intervention programs are urgently needed.

In fact, efforts to decrease violence in schools have had mixed results. Dinkes, Kemp, and Baum find that victimizations declined from 9.5% in 1995 to 4.3% in 2005. However, there was no measurable change in the decline of victimizations between 2005 and 2007. The rate of violent crimes, including rape and attempted rape, sexual assault, physical attack or threat of physical attack with or without a weapon, and robbery, rose from 1.2% to 1.6% between 2005 and 2007. For the first time, the rates of violent crime victimization among young people at school (26 per 1,000 students) were higher than the rates of these crimes away from school (20 per 1,000 students). During the 2007–08 school year 75% of schools experienced at least one violent crime during the year and 17% experienced at least one serious violent crime.

Kylee Crews, Jack Crews, and Freda Turner detail in "School Violence Is Not Going away So Proactive Steps Are Needed" (*College Teaching Methods and Styles Journal*, vol. 4, no. 1, January 2008) 19 steps that schools should take to reduce school violence. The recommendations include teaching students about the progression of violence-related problems (e.g., name-calling, harassment, and violence), creating student-led antiviolence programs, notifying law enforcement officials when activities are suspicious, maintaining an anonymous reporting system, training teachers and students about hate crimes, keeping accurate records, and educating parents about the hazards of violent video games.

Disciplinary Problems and Actions

Schools contend with a wide range of disciplinary problems that can affect the safety and positive educational experience of students and staff alike. These include bullying, gang activities, verbal abuse of teachers, disrespectful acts against teachers, widespread disorder in the classroom, cult or extremist group activities, and racial tension. According to Dinkes, Kemp, and Baum, 25% of public schools experienced problems with student bullying during the 2007–08 school year. (See Figure 9.1.) Bullying was a particular problem in middle schools; 44% of middle school students, 22% of high school students, and 21% of primary school students reported that they had been bullied at school.

Other discipline problems at public schools in 2007–08 included gang activities, student acts of disrespect for teachers, and student verbal abuse of teachers. Whereas 14% of schools overall reported gang activities, over half (52%) of large schools with more than 1,000 students reported gang activities at school. Widespread disorder in the classroom was a problem in 8% of city schools but in only 2% or 3% of suburban, town, or rural schools.

One of the ways that schools attempt to deal with safety issues is to take serious disciplinary action (suspensions of five days or more, expulsions, and transfers to specialized schools) against students who commit crimes and violent acts. Dinkes, Kemp, and Baum note that almost half (46%) of public schools took at least one serious disciplinary action against a student during the 2007–08 school year. Three-quarters (76%) of these actions involved out-of-school suspensions lasting five days or more, 19% involved transfers to specialized schools, and 5% were removals with no services for the remainder of the school year.

These serious disciplinary actions were taken for a variety of offenses. Nearly three out of 10 (31%) public schools took serious disciplinary actions in response to physical attacks or fights. (See Figure 9.2.) Twenty-one percent of schools took these actions in response to insubordination; 19% took these actions in response to the distribution, possession, or use of illegal drugs; and 10%

of schools took these actions in response to the distribution, possession, or use of alcohol. Fifteen percent of public schools took a serious disciplinary action in response to the use or possession of a weapon other than a firearm, and 3% of public schools took these actions in response to the use or possession of a firearm or explosive device.

NONFATAL CRIMES

Between 1992 and 2007 the rate of nonfatal crimes against students between the ages of 12 and 18 years at school (in the building, on school property, and en route to and from school) generally declined. (See Figure 9.3.) National Crime Victimization Survey (NCVS) data show that even though thefts often occur more frequently at school than they do away from school, the reverse is true of serious violent crimes such as sexual assault, rape, aggravated assault, and robbery. In 2007 over 1.5 million crimes were committed against students at school, including 118,300 serious violent crimes. (See Table 9.2.)

Some students are more likely to be victimized at school than are others. Males (58 per 1,000 students) experienced a higher rate of crime than females (56 per 1,000 students) did in general, although females experienced a higher rate of theft (33 per 1,000 students) than did males (30 per 1,000 students). (See Table 9.2.) In general, younger students had a higher rate of victimization than did older students. In 2007, 67 out of every 1,000 students aged 12 to 14 years experienced nonfatal crimes at school, compared with 49 out of every 1,000 students aged 15 to 18 years. White students (62 per 1,000) were more likely to experience nonfatal crimes at school than were Hispanic students (52 per 1,000) or African-American students (42 per 1,000).

Physical Fights, Injuries, and Forcible Rape

According to Danice K. Eaton et al. of the Centers for Disease Control and Prevention, in "Youth Risk Behavior Surveillance—United States, 2009" (*Morbidity and Mortality Weekly Report*, vol. 59, no. SS-05, June 4, 2010), in 2009, 31.5% of students nationwide reported being in one or more physical fights anywhere (not necessarily at school) during the last 12 months. (See Table 9.3.) Male students (39.3%) were more likely to report this behavior than female students (22.9%). A higher proportion of non-Hispanic African-American students (41.1%) and Hispanic students (36.2%) acknowledged fighting than did non-Hispanic white students (27.8%). However, the proportion of students fighting decreased as students got older. Ninth graders (37%) fought the most, followed by 10th graders (33.5%), 11th graders (28.6%), and 12th graders (24.9%).

Even though Eaton et al. report that 31.5% of students acknowledged physically fighting in the past year, only 11.1% of students fought on school property in 2009. More male students (15.1%) than female students (6.7%)

FIGURE 9.1

Percentage of public schools reporting selected discipline problems that occurred at school, by school level, 2007–08

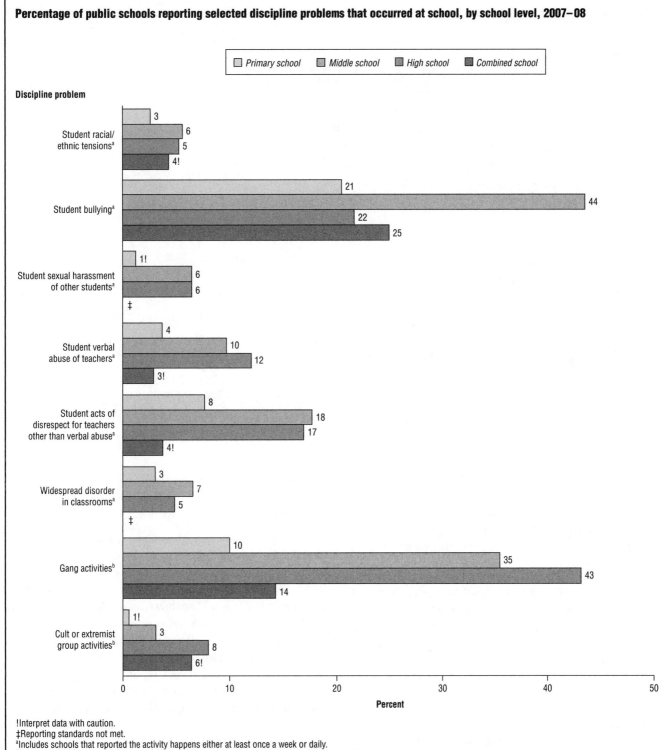

☐ Primary school ☐ Middle school ☐ High school ■ Combined school

!Interpret data with caution.
‡Reporting standards not met.
[a]Includes schools that reported the activity happens either at least once a week or daily.
[b]Includes schools that reported the activity has happened at all at their school during the school year.
Note: Primary schools are defined as schools in which the lowest grade is not higher than grade 3 and the highest grade is not higher than grade 8. Middle schools are defined as schools in which the lowest grade is not lower than grade 4 and the highest grade is not higher than grade 9. High schools are defined as schools in which the lowest grade is not lower than grade 9. Combined schools include all other combinations of grades, including K–12 schools. Responses were provided by the principal or the person most knowledgeable about crime and safety issues at the school. "At school" was defined for respondents to include activities that happen in school buildings, on school grounds, on school buses, and at places that hold school-sponsored events or activities. Respondents were instructed to respond only for those times that were during normal school hours or when school activities or events were in session, unless the survey specified otherwise.

SOURCE: Rachel Dinkes, Jana Kemp, and Katrina Baum, "Figure 7.1. Percentage of Public Schools Reporting Selected Discipline Problems That Occurred at School, by School Level: School Year 2007–08," in *Indicators of School Crime and Safety: 2009*, U.S. Department of Education, National Center for Education Statistics, and U.S. Department of Justice, Bureau of Justice Statistics, December 2009, http://nces.ed.gov/pubs2010/2010012.pdf (accessed October 28, 2010)

FIGURE 9.2

Percentage of public schools that took a serious disciplinary action for selected offenses, by type of offense, 2007–08

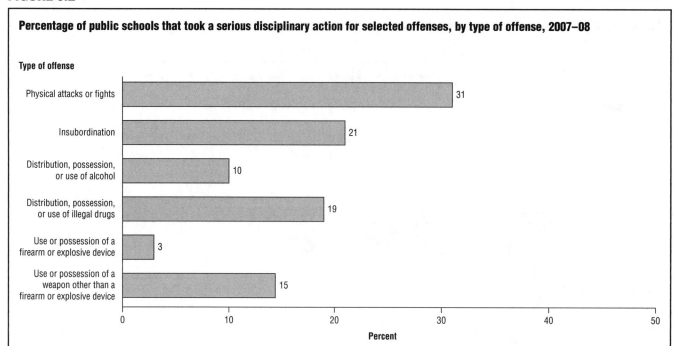

Note: Responses were provided by the principal or the person most knowledgeable about crime and safety issues at the school. Serious disciplinary actions include removals with no continuing services for at least the remainder of the school year, transfers to specialized schools for disciplinary reasons, and out-of-school suspensions lasting 5 or more days, but less than the remainder of the school year. Respondents were instructed to respond only for offenses that occured during normal school hours or when school activities or events were in session, unless the survey specified otherwise.

SOURCE: Rachel Dinkes, Jana Kemp, and Katrina Baum, "Figure 19.1. Percentage of Public Schools That Took a Serious Disciplinary Action, by Type of Offense: School Year 2007–08," in *Indicators of School Crime and Safety: 2009*, U.S. Department of Education, National Center for Education Statistics, and U.S. Department of Justice, Bureau of Justice Statistics, December 2009, http://nces.ed.gov/pubs2010/2010012.pdf (accessed October 28, 2010)

engaged in fights on school property, and more non-Hispanic African-American students (17.4%) and Hispanic students (13.5%) than non-Hispanic white students (8.6%) reported this behavior. The incidence of fighting on school grounds decreased by age in a similar pattern to physical fighting in general.

According to Eaton et al., in 2009 about 3.8% of students noted that they had been injured in a physical fight in the past 12 months—5.1% of male students and 2.2% of female students. (See Table 9.3.) Non-Hispanic African-American students (5.7%) and Hispanic students (4.7%) reported a higher percentage of injuries than did non-Hispanic white students (2.9%).

However, more students reported having experienced dating violence than having been involved in physical fights. In 2009 nearly one out of 10 (9.8%) students said they had been physically hurt by a boyfriend or girlfriend on purpose (hit, slapped, or otherwise physically hurt) one or more times in the last 12 months, including 9.3% of female students and 10.3% of male students. (See Table 9.3.) Non-Hispanic African-American students (14.3%) were the most likely to be hurt by a dating partner, followed by Hispanic students (11.5%) and non-Hispanic white students (8%). Eaton et al. find that the higher the grade level, the higher the percentage of students reported being hurt by a dating partner: 9.2% of

both ninth and 10th graders, and 10.4% of both 11th and 12th graders reported having been intentionally hurt by a dating partner in the last 12 months.

Eaton et al. also asked students if they had ever been forced to have sexual intercourse. Overall, 7.4% of students acknowledged being forced to have sexual intercourse—10.5% of female students and 4.5% of male students. (See Table 9.3.) Non-Hispanic African-American students (10%) were the most likely to report being victimized in this way, followed by Hispanic students (8.4%) and non-Hispanic white students (6.3%). Ninth graders were less likely than older students to report forced sexual intercourse. These results highlight the high level of sexual and dating violence that high school students experience.

Crimes against Teachers

Teachers sometimes fall victim to crimes at school. According to Dinkes, Kemp, and Baum, the percentage of teachers that were threatened with injury or physically attacked declined between the 1993–94 and 2007–08 school years. In 2007–08, 7% of teachers were threatened with injury by a student in their school. Teachers in city schools were more likely than teachers in other schools to be threatened with injury. Eleven percent of teachers in urban high schools were threatened in 2007–08, compared with 7% of teachers in suburban, town, and rural

FIGURE 9.3

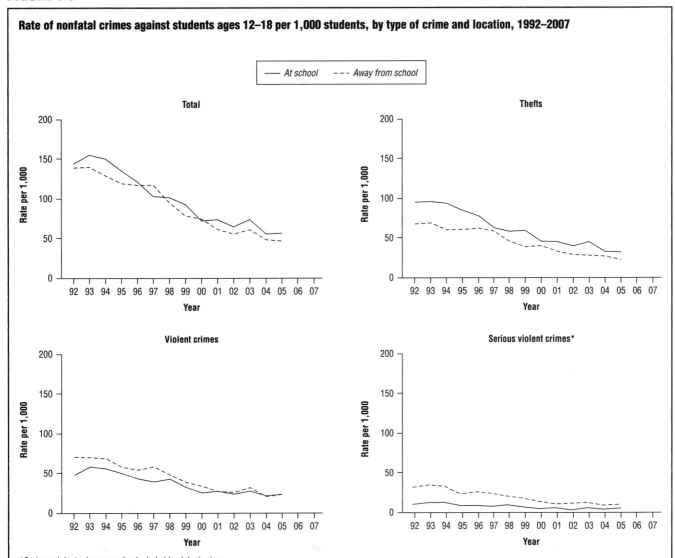

Rate of nonfatal crimes against students ages 12–18 per 1,000 students, by type of crime and location, 1992–2007

— At school   - - - Away from school

*Serious violent crimes are also included in violent crimes.

Note: There were changes in the sample design and survey methodology in the 2006 National Crime Victimization Survey (NCVS) that impacted survey estimates. Due to this redesign, 2006 data are not presented in this indicator. Data from 2007 are comparable to earlier years. Serious violent crimes include rape, sexual assault, robbery, and aggravated assault. Violent crimes include serious violent crimes and simple assault. Theft includes purse snatching, pick pocketing, all burglaries, attempted forcible entry, and all attempted and completed thefts except motor vehicle thefts. Theft does not include robbery in which threat or use of force is involved. Total crimes include violent crimes and theft. "At school" includes inside the school building, on school property, or on the way to or from school. Although *Indicators 2* and *3* present information on similar topics, the survey sources for these two indicators differ with respect to time coverage and administration.

SOURCE: Rachel Dinkes, Jana Kemp, and Katrina Baum, "Figure 2.1. Rate of Student-Reported Nonfatal Crimes against Students Ages 12–18 per 1,000 Students, by Type of Crime and Location: 1992–2007," in *Indicators of School Crime and Safety: 2009*, U.S. Department of Education, National Center for Education Statistics, and U.S. Department of Justice, Bureau of Justice Statistics, December 2009, http://nces.ed.gov/pubs2010/2010012.pdf (accessed October 28, 2010)

high schools. (See Figure 9.4.) Teachers were more likely to be threatened with injury from high school students rather than from elementary school students; however, they were more likely to be physically attacked by elementary school students.

Weapons in School

Violence at school makes students feel vulnerable and intimidated. Sometimes it makes them want to carry a weapon to school for self-protection. The Gun-Free Schools Act of 1994 required states to pass laws forcing school districts to expel any student who brings a firearm to school. Dinkes, Kemp, and Baum indicate that in 2007, 5.9% of high school students reported they had carried a weapon (a gun, knife, or club) on school property in the last 30 days, the lowest percentage since 1993. (See Table 9.4.) The percentage of students who reported carrying a weapon anywhere decreased from 22.1% in 1993 to 17.1% in 2003 before rising again; in 2007, 18% of students reported carrying a weapon. Eaton et al. state that in 2009, 17.5% of students had carried a weapon during the past 30 days, and 5.9% had carried a gun.

TABLE 9.2

Rate of student-reported nonfatal crimes against students ages 12–18 at school and rate of crimes per 1,000 students, by selected characteristics, 2007

Student or school characteristic	Number of crimes				Rate of crimes per 1,000 students			
	Total	Theft	Violent	Serious violent[a]	Total	Theft	Violent	Serious violent[a]
At school								
Total	1,510,900	826,800	684,100	118,300	57	31	26	4
Sex								
Male	798,000	402,700	395,300	94,500	58	30	29	7
Female	712,900	424,100	288,800	23,800!	56	33	22	2!
Age								
12–14	819,300	387,500	431,800	64,800	67	32	35	5
15–18	691,600	439,300	252,300	53,500	49	31	18	4
Race/ethnicity[b]								
White	969,300	523,600	445,700	55,000	62	33	28	4
Black	159,300	102,100	57,200	‡	42	27	15	‡
Hispanic	269,500	135,500	133,900	38,300!	52	26	26	7!
Other	112,800	65,500	47,300	‡	62	36	26	‡
Household income								
Less than $15,000	99,600	32,900!	66,700	‡	65	21!	43	‡
$15,000–29,999	159,900	83,000	77,000	23,300!	60	31	29	9!
$30,000–49,999	313,800	116,300	197,600	34,100!	75	28	47	8!
$50,000–74,999	285,100	156,300	128,800	16,200!	74	41	33	4!
$75,000 or more	372,800	269,300	103,600	‡	52	37	14	‡

!Interpret data with caution. Estimate based on 10 or fewer sample cases.
‡Reporting standards not met.
[a]Serious violent crimes are also included in violent crimes.
[b]Other includes Asians, Pacific Islanders, and American Indians (including Alaska Natives). Race categories exclude persons of Hispanic ethnicity.
Note: Serious violent crimes include rape, sexual assault, robbery, and aggravated assault. Violent crimes include serious violent crimes and simple assault. Theft includes purse snatching, pick pocketing, all burglaries, attempted forcible entry, and all attempted and completed thefts except motor vehicle thefts. Theft does not include robbery in which threat or use of force is involved. Total crimes include violent crimes and theft. "At school" includes inside the school building, on school property, or on the way to or from school. Detail may not sum to totals because of rounding and missing data on student characteristics. Estimates of number of crimes are rounded to the nearest 100.

SOURCE: Rachel Dinkes, Jana Kemp, and Katrina Baum, "Table 2.2. Number of Student-Reported Nonfatal Crimes against Students Ages 12–18 and Rate of Crimes per 1,000 Students at School, by Type of Crime and Selected Student and School Characteristics: 2007," in *Indicators of School Crime and Safety: 2009*, U.S. Department of Education, National Center for Education Statistics, and U.S. Department of Justice, Bureau of Justice Statistics, December 2009, http://nces.ed.gov/programs/crimeindicators/crimeindicators2009/tables/table_02_2.asp (accessed October 28, 2010)

TABLE 9.3

Percentage of high school students who engaged in violence and in behaviors resulting from violence, by sex, race and Hispanic origin, and grade, 2009

Category	In a physical fight[a]			Injured in a physical fight[b]			Dating violence[c]			Forced to have sexual intercourse[d]		
	Female %	Male %	Total %	Female %	Male %	Total %	Female %	Male %	Total %	Female %	Male %	Total %
Race/ethnicity												
White[e]	18.2	36.0	27.8	1.3	4.2	2.9	7.2	8.8	8.0	10.0	3.2	6.3
Black[e]	33.9	48.3	41.1	4.4	7.0	5.7	14.8	13.8	14.3	12.0	7.9	10.0
Hispanic	28.5	43.8	36.2	3.3	6.0	4.7	11.4	11.7	11.5	11.2	5.7	8.4
Grade												
9	27.8	45.1	37.0	2.5	5.5	4.1	9.4	9.1	9.2	9.4	4.1	6.6
10	24.8	41.2	33.5	2.7	5.2	4.1	9.0	9.3	9.2	10.6	4.0	7.1
11	20.5	36.1	28.6	2.1	5.4	3.8	9.1	11.5	10.4	11.2	5.4	8.2
12	17.0	32.5	24.9	1.4	4.2	2.9	9.5	11.4	10.4	10.8	4.9	7.8
Total	**22.9**	**39.3**	**31.5**	**2.2**	**5.1**	**3.8**	**9.3**	**10.3**	**9.8**	**10.5**	**4.5**	**7.4**

[a]One or more times during the 12 months before the survey.
[b]Injuries had to be treated by a doctor or a nurse.
[c]Hit, slapped physically hurt on purpose by their boyfriend or girlfriend during the 12 months before the survey.
[d]When they didn't want to.
[e]Non–Hispanic.

SOURCE: Adapted from Danice K. Eaton et al., "Table 10. Percentage of High School Students Who Were in a Physical Fight and Who Were Injured in a Physical Fight, by Sex, Race/Ethnicity, and Grade—United States, Youth Risk Behavior Survey, 2009," and "Table 12. Percentage of High School Students Who Experienced Dating Violence and Who Were Ever Physically Forced to Have Sexual Intercourse, by Sex, Race/Ethnicity, and Grade—United States, Youth Risk Behavior Survey, 2009," in "Youth Risk Behavior Surveillance—United States, 2009," *Morbidity and Mortality Weekly Report*, vol. 59, no. SS–5, June 4, 2010, http://www.cdc.gov/mmwr/pdf/ss/ss5905.pdf (accessed October 22, 2010)

FIGURE 9.4

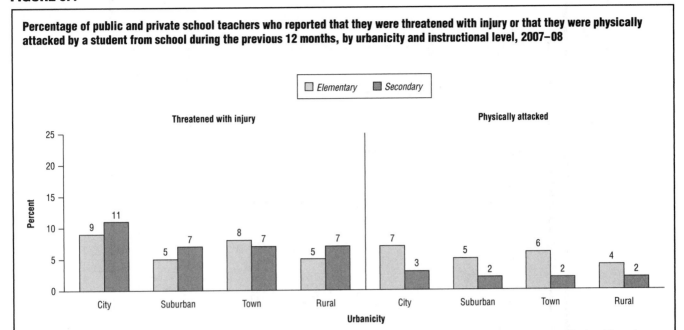

Percentage of public and private school teachers who reported that they were threatened with injury or that they were physically attacked by a student from school during the previous 12 months, by urbanicity and instructional level, 2007–08

Note: Teachers who taught only prekindergarten students are excluded. Instructional level divides teachers into elementary or secondary based on a combination of the grades taught, main teaching assignment, and the structure of the teachers' class(es).

SOURCE: Rachel Dinkes, Jana Kemp, and Katrina Baum, "Figure 5.2. Percentage of Public and Private School Teachers Who Reported That They Were Threatened with Injury or That They Were Physically Attacked by a Student from School during the Previous 12 Months, by Urbanicity and Instructional Level: School Year 2007–08," in *Indicators of School Crime and Safety: 2009*, U.S. Department of Education, National Center for Education Statistics, and U.S. Department of Justice, Bureau of Justice Statistics, December 2009, http://nces.ed.gov/pubs2010/2010012.pdf (accessed October 28, 2010)

In 2007 a much higher percentage of males (9%) than females (2.7%) reported carrying a weapon on school property. (See Table 9.4.) Males were more likely than females to carry a weapon on school property in all the years reported. Males were also more likely to carry weapons anywhere; in 2007, 28.5% of males reported having carried a weapon in the last 30 days, whereas only 7.5% of females reported this behavior.

Various reasons may explain why students are carrying fewer weapons to school. Enhanced security measures at school, such as metal detectors and locker searches, which were added in the wake of the highly publicized school shootings during the 1990s, could be partially responsible. Another reason could be the stricter punishment that is given to those who are found with a weapon in school. Many schools have adopted zero-tolerance rules, resulting in the immediate expulsion of someone who is found breaking these guidelines.

WEAPON USE ON SCHOOL PROPERTY. According to Dinkes, Kemp, and Baum, the percentage of students who reported being threatened with or injured by a weapon while at school remained fairly steady between 1993 and 2007. Approximately 7.8% of students in grades nine to 12 reported being threatened with or injured by a weapon on school property within the past 12 months in 2007. (See Table 9.5.) This figure was a slight increase from 1993, when 7.3% of students reported being threatened with or

injured by a weapon. Between 1993 and 2007 the percentage remained in the 7% to 9% range.

Male students received considerably more weapons threats and injuries in all the years surveyed between 1993 and 2007 than did female students. Among students from different ethnic and racial backgrounds, the victimization rate was highest among African-Americans (9.7%) in 2007. (See Table 9.5.) Hispanic students (8.7%) also had a fairly high victimization rate. The victimization rate of Native American or Alaskan Native students had dropped significantly from 22.1% in 2003 to 5.9% in 2007.

The youngest students were the most likely to report being threatened by or injured with a weapon. Nearly one out of 10 (9.2%) ninth graders reported being threatened with or injured by a weapon in 2007, compared with 8.4% of 10th graders, 6.8% of 11th graders, and 6.3% of 12th graders. (See Table 9.5.) Similar patterns were observed in the other years of the survey as well. It may be that younger students are viewed as more vulnerable to intimidation and therefore are more likely to be the targets of students carrying weapons.

BULLIES AND BULLYING

Most people can recall certain individuals or a group of children at school being identified as bullies. This type of behavior is not new to schools. Bullies harass certain kids they know will not fight back, including pushing

TABLE 9.4

Percentage of students in grades 9–12 who reported carrying a weapon at least 1 day during the previous 30 days, by selected student characteristics, selected years 1993–2007

Student or school characteristic	Anywhere								On school property							
	1993	1995	1997	1999	2001	2003	2005	2007	1993	1995	1997	1999	2001	2003	2005	2007
Total	22.1	20.0	18.3	17.3	17.4	17.1	18.5	18.0	11.8	9.8	8.5	6.9	6.4	6.1	6.5	5.9
Sex																
Male	34.3	31.1	27.7	28.6	29.3	26.9	29.8	28.5	17.9	14.3	12.5	11.0	10.2	8.9	10.2	9.0
Female	9.2	8.3	7.0	6.0	6.2	6.7	7.1	7.5	5.1	4.9	3.7	2.8	2.9	3.1	2.6	2.7
Race/ethnicity[a]																
White	20.6	18.9	17.0	16.4	17.9	16.7	18.7	18.2	10.9	9.0	7.8	6.4	6.1	5.5	6.1	5.3
Black	28.5	21.8	21.7	17.2	15.2	17.3	16.4	17.2	15.0	10.3	9.2	5.0	6.3	6.9	5.1	6.0
Hispanic	24.4	24.7	23.3	18.7	16.5	16.5	19.0	18.5	13.3	14.1	10.4	7.9	6.4	6.0	8.2	7.3
Asian	[b]	[b]	[b]	13.0	10.6	11.6	7.0	7.8	[b]	[b]	[b]	6.5	7.2	6.6!	2.8!	4.1
American Indian/Alaska Native	34.2	32.0	26.2	21.8	31.2	29.3	25.6	20.6	17.6!	13.0!	15.9	11.6!	16.4	12.9	7.2	7.7
Pacific Islander/Native Hawaiian	[b]	[b]	[b]	25.3	17.4	16.3!	20.0!	25.5	[b]	[b]	[b]	9.3	10.0!	4.9!	15.4!	9.5!
More than one race	[b]	[b]	[b]	22.2	25.2	29.8	26.7	19.0	[b]	[b]	[b]	11.4	13.2	13.3!	11.9	5.0
Grade																
9th	25.5	22.6	22.6	17.6	19.8	18.0	19.9	20.1	12.6	10.7	10.2	7.2	6.7	5.3	6.4	6.0
10th	21.4	21.1	17.4	18.7	16.7	15.9	19.4	18.8	11.5	10.4	7.7	6.6	6.7	6.0	6.9	5.8
11th	21.5	20.3	18.2	16.1	16.8	18.2	17.1	16.7	11.9	10.2	9.4	7.0	6.1	6.6	5.9	5.5
12th	19.9	16.1	15.4	15.9	15.1	15.5	16.9	15.5	10.8	7.6	7.0	6.2	6.1	6.4	6.7	6.0
Urbanicity																
Urban	—	—	18.7	15.8	15.3	17.0	—	—	—	—	7.0	7.2	6.0	5.6	—	—
Suburban	—	—	16.8	17.0	17.4	16.5	—	—	—	—	8.7	6.2	6.3	6.4	—	—
Rural	—	—	22.3	22.3	23.0	18.9	—	—	—	—	11.2	9.6	8.3	6.3	—	—

—Not available.

!Interpret data with caution.

[a]Race categories exclude persons of Hispanic ethnicity.

[b]The response categories for race/ethnicity changed in 1999 making comparisons of some categories with earlier years problematic. In 1993, 1995, and 1997, Asian students and Pacific Islander students were not categorized separately and students were not given the option of choosing more than one race.

Notes: "On school property" was not defined for survey respondents. The term "anywhere" is not used in the YRBS questionnaire; students are simply asked how many days they carried a weapon during the past 30 days.

SOURCE: Rachel Dinkes, Jana Kemp, and Katrina Baum, "Table 14.1. Percentage of Students in Grades 9–12 Who Reported Carrying a Weapon at Least 1 Day during the Previous 30 Days, by Location and Selected Student and School Characteristics: Various Years 1993–2007," in *Indicators of School Crime and Safety: 2009,* U.S. Department of Education, National Center for Education Statistics, and U.S. Department of Justice, Bureau of Justice Statistics, December 2009, http://nces.ed.gov/programs/crimeindicators/crimeindicators2009/tables/table_14_1.asp (accessed October 28, 2010)

TABLE 9.5

Percentage of students in grades 9–12 who reported being threatened or injured with a weapon on school property during the previous 12 months, by selected student characteristics, selected years 1993–2007

Student or school characteristic	1993	1995	1997	1999	2001	2003	2005	2007
Total	7.3	8.4	7.4	7.7	8.9	9.2	7.9	7.8
Sex								
Male	9.2	10.9	10.2	9.5	11.5	11.6	9.7	10.2
Female	5.4	5.8	4.0	5.8	6.5	6.5	6.1	5.4
Race/ethnicity[a]								
White	6.3	7.0	6.2	6.6	8.5	7.8	7.2	6.9
Black	11.2	11.0	9.9	7.6	9.3	10.9	8.1	9.7
Hispanic	8.6	12.4	9.0	9.8	8.9	9.4	9.8	8.7
Asian	(b)	(b)	(b)	7.7	11.3	11.5	4.6	7.6!
American Indian/Alaska Native	11.7	11.4!	12.5!	13.2!	15.2!	22.1	9.8	5.9
Pacific Islander/Native Hawaiian	(b)	(b)	(b)	15.6	24.8	16.3	14.5!	8.1!
More than one race	(b)	(b)	(b)	9.3	10.3	18.7	10.7	13.3
Grade								
9th	9.4	9.6	10.1	10.5	12.7	12.1	10.5	9.2
10th	7.3	9.6	7.9	8.2	9.1	9.2	8.8	8.4
11th	7.3	7.7	5.9	6.1	6.9	7.3	5.5	6.8
12th	5.5	6.7	5.8	5.1	5.3	6.3	5.8	6.3
Urbanicity								
Urban	—	—	8.7	8.0	9.2	10.6	—	—
Suburban	—	—	7.0	7.4	9.0	8.8	—	—
Rural	—	—	5.6!	8.3	8.1	8.2	—	—

—Not available.

!Interpret data with caution.

[a]Race categories exclude persons of Hispanic ethnicity.

[b]The response categories for race/ethnicity changed in 1999 making comparisons of some categories with earlier years problematic. In 1993, 1995, and 1997, Asian students and Pacific Islander students were not categorized separately and students were not given the option of choosing more than one race.

Note: "On school property" was not defined for survey respondents.

SOURCE: Rachel Dinkes, Jana Kemp, and Katrina Baum, "Table 4.1. Percentage of Students in Grades 9–12 Who Reported Being Threatened or Injured with a Weapon on School Property during the Previous 12 Months, by Selected Student and School Characteristics: Various Years, 1993–2007," in *Indicators of School Crime and Safety: 2009*, U.S. Department of Education, National Center for Education Statistics, and U.S. Department of Justice, Bureau of Justice Statistics, December 2009, http://nces.ed.gov/programs/crimeindicators/crimeindicators2009/tables/table_04_1.asp (accessed October 28, 2010)

students against lockers and taking their lunch money or other personal possessions; pulling gags in attempts to humiliate others and cause extreme embarrassment; shoving others out of their way; threatening violence or setting up derogatory websites about other students; sending threatening or insulting text messages; and disrupting class and making threatening gestures, even toward teachers. Some studies, such as Jill F. DeVoe, Sarah Kaffenberger, and Kathryn Chandler's *Student Reports of Bullying: Results from the 2001 School Crime Supplement to the National Crime Victimization Survey* (July 2005, http://nces.ed.gov/pubs2005/2005310.pdf), divide these bullying behaviors into two categories: direct and indirect. Direct bullying behaviors include physical and verbal attacks and harassment. Indirect bullying behaviors include subtle actions that might be hard for those not directly involved to recognize. These would include psychological activities, such as those listed earlier, as well as obscene gestures, hurtful facial expressions, and turning friends against each other.

In *Bullying in Schools* (May 2009, http://www.cops .usdoj.gov/files/RIC/Publications/e07063414-guide.pdf),

Rana Sampson indicates that bullying has two key components: repeated harmful acts and an imbalance of power between the victim and the perpetrator. Bullying behaviors include physical, verbal, and psychological attacks, such as assault, intimidation, spreading of rumors, destruction of property, theft, name-calling, and other behaviors. Sexual harassment, hazing, ostracism based on sexual orientation, taunting, and teasing also constitute bullying.

During the late 1990s bullying at schools became a major issue of concern for parents, educators, law enforcement officials, lawmakers, and students as increasing numbers of people perceived that bullying had become more aggressive and hurtful. In addition, a rash of school shootings shocked the nation during the 1990s. Sampson reports that many of the school shooters complained of being bullied, victimized, and harassed. They said they had grown tired of being picked on and decided to strike back.

According to Sameer Hinduja and Justin W. Patchin, in *State Cyberbullying Laws: A Brief Review of State Cyberbullying Laws and Policies* (December 2010, http://www.cyberbullying.us/Bullying_and_Cyberbullying

_Laws.pdf), 44 states and the District of Columbia had antibullying laws in 2010. Even though only six state laws included cyberbullying, 31 states had laws that prohibited electronic harassment as part of the statute. As of December 2010, no federal antibullying law had been passed.

Characteristics of Bullying

According to profiles created by various research organizations, such as "Bullying" (May 2008, http://www.aacap.org/cs/root/facts_for_families/bullying) by the American Academy of Child and Adolescent Psychiatry, bullies are most often males, although girls do engage in bullying behaviors as well. Boys are more likely to use physical and verbal abuse, frequently on a one-on-one basis. Girls typically use verbal and psychological tactics. Female bullies often refrain from one-on-one contact, preferring to work in groups. This might include circulating a "slam book" about another person, which is a notebook containing derogatory remarks about the victim written by the bullying group, or e-mailing embarrassing pictures taken by camera phones in locker rooms to a large group of girls. Male victims of bullying are typically bullied by other males, but female victims may be bullied by either male or female students.

Bullies look for situations where they can gain power over someone else through intimidation and threats. Sometimes they work alone, and other times they work in groups. Some bullies surround themselves with weaker kids who act as henchmen. Bullies seek out situations to harass others in places such as playgrounds and school hallways that are not being supervised by adults. In this way, there are no adult witnesses to either stop the act or report it to school authorities.

Sampson reports on research that shows that bullies tend to be aggressive, slightly below average in intelligence, and underperformers in school. They tend to be fairly popular and lacking in empathy for their victims. Individual risk factors include being raised in dysfunctional families and living in a household that has a low socioeconomic status. Sampson also notes that there is "a correlation between harsh physical punishments such as beatings, strict disciplinarian parents and bullying."

According to Sampson, the victims of bullies tend to be smaller and weaker than other children. The victims also tend to be fairly passive and socially awkward. Children with few friends are more at risk than other children. However, it is important to note that any student can become a victim of bullying and that the fault lies with the bully, not with the victim.

As the prevalence of bullying increases and more parents and educators grow concerned, various studies are being conducted to learn more about bullies, the victims, and the frequency of such occurrences. Rachel Dinkes,

Emily Forrest Cataldi, and Wendy Lin-Kelly state in *Indicators of School Crime and Safety: 2007* (December 2007, http://nces.ed.gov/pubs2008/2008021.pdf) that in 2005, 28.1% of 12- to 18-year-olds reported being bullied at school during the previous six months—27.1% of males and 29.2% of females. By 2007, 32.2% of students—30.6% of males and 33.7% of females—reported being bullied during the school year. (See Table 9.6.)

In 2007 white students (34.6%) reported the most problems with bullies. (See Table 9.6.) African-American students (30.9%) and Hispanic students (27.6%) reported slightly less trouble. Asian-American students (18.1%) were the least likely to report being bullied. Reports of being bullied diminished with age; 42.9% of sixth graders but only 23.5% of 12th graders reported being victimized by bullies.

Sampson indicates that victims of bullying suffer from psychological and sometimes physical distress. They tend to be absent from school more than other children and have difficulty concentrating on schoolwork. Victimization can lead to depression and low self-esteem. Victims suffer from anxiety and insomnia and contemplate suicide more than other children. Several studies, such as Farah Williams and Dewey G. Cornell's "Student Willingness to Seek Help for Threats of Violence in Middle School" (*Journal of School Violence*, vol. 5, no. 4, December 2006) and Lauren P. Ashbaugh and Dewey G. Cornell's "Sexual Harassment and Bullying Behaviors in Sixth-Graders" (*Journal of School Violence*, vol. 7, no. 2, February 2008), find that girls are more likely than boys to report and seek help for bullying.

Cyberbullying

In "Bullies Move beyond the Schoolyard: A Preliminary Look at Cyberbullying" (*Youth Violence and Juvenile Justice*, vol. 4, no. 2, April 2006), Patchin and Hinduja report that with the advent of the Internet and the increased use of cell phones among students, bullies have found a new way to taunt their victims: cyberbullying, which is also called digital bullying or Internet bullying. Instead of abusing their victims at school, on the playground, or en route to and from school, bullies are now able to taunt their victims day and night via current technology. Victims report receiving hateful and hurtful instant messages, e-mails, and text messages on their cell phones. The use of such technologies allows the perpetrators to be anonymous, if they so choose.

Some students have become the victims of hate-filled websites that discuss why the bullies and their friends do not like that certain individual. Visitors to such sites are allowed to add their insults and gossip as well. In some instances visitors have rallied to the defense of the victim and slammed the bully. Through the use of camera phones, bullies can take sensitive photos of students in locker

TABLE 9.6

Percentage of students ages 12–18 who reported being bullied at school during the school year, by location, injury, and selected student and school characteristics, 2007

| Student or school characteristic | Total | Location of bullying | | | | Students who were injured as a result of being pushed, shoved, tripped, or spit on[a] |
		Inside school	Outside on school grounds	School bus	Somewhere else	
Total	32.2	78.9	22.7	8.0	3.9	19.0
Sex						
Male	30.6	77.5	25.1	8.3	2.6	17.2
Female	33.7	80.2	20.4	7.7	5.0	21.4
Race/ethnicity[b]						
White	34.6	79.5	22.7	8.8	3.8	20.1
Black	30.9	82.2	19.1	8.2	2.4!	14.3
Hispanic	27.6	74.8	22.7	4.5	6.2	19.8
Asian	18.1	79.7	20.6!	‡	‡	‡
Other	34.6	70.0	39.4	‡	‡	19.7!
Grade						
6th	42.9	68.2	28.4	14.5	1.8!	18.0
7th	35.7	80.8	23.5	9.8	2.8!	21.9
8th	37.3	79.5	20.5	9.6	4.1	17.6
9th	30.8	83.2	18.9	5.5	3.5!	25.2
10th	28.4	77.6	22.6	7.2	6.9	16.1
11th	29.3	81.6	20.1	4.1!	4.7	15.2!
12th	23.5	79.4	28.1	3.5!	3.4!	‡
Urbanicity						
Urban	‡	‡	‡	‡	‡	‡
Suburban	‡	‡	‡	‡	‡	‡
Rural	‡	‡	‡	‡	‡	‡
Sector						
Public	32.4	78.9	22.8	8.5	4.0	19.5
Private	29.4	79.0	21.4	‡	‡	10.2!

!Interpret data with caution.
‡Reporting standards not met.
[a]Injury includes bruises or swelling; cuts, scratches, or scrapes; black eye or bloody nose; teeth chipped or knocked out; broken bones or internal injuries; knocked unconscious; or other injuries. Only students who reported that their bullying incident constituted being pushed, shoved, tripped, or spit on were asked if they suffered injuries as a result of the incident.
[b]Race categories exclude persons of Hispanic ethnicity. Other includes American Indian, Alaska Native, Pacific Islander, and more than one race.
Notes: Table was revised on June 15, 2010. "At school" includes the school building, on school property, on a school bus, or going to and from school. Location totals may sum to more than 100 because students could have been bullied in more than one location. In 2007, the unit response rate for this survey did not meet NCES statistical standards; therefore, interpret the data with caution. Due to a redesign of the methods used to measure urbanicity, estimates for 2007 locales are not shown.

SOURCE: Rachel Dinkes, Jana Kemp, and Katrina Baum, "Table 11.2. Percentage of Students Ages 12–18 Who Reported Being Bullied at School during the School Year, by Location of Bullying, Injury, and Selected Student and School Characteristics: 2007," in *Indicators of School Crime and Safety: 2009*, U.S. Department of Education, National Center for Education Statistics, and U.S. Department of Justice, Bureau of Justice Statistics, December 2009, http://nces.ed.gov/programs/crimeindicators/crimeindicators2009/tables/table_11_2.asp (accessed October 28, 2010)

rooms, in restrooms, or while being intimidated. Then the bullies pass the pictures around, either via e-mail or on websites. Researchers point out that electronic bullying can be done anywhere and does not require the bully to have any personal contact, especially eye contact, with the victim.

Hinduja and Patchin find in the fact sheet "Cyberbullying: Identification, Prevention, and Response" (2010, http://www.cyberbullying.us/Cyberbullying_Identification_Prevention_Response_Fact_Sheet.pdf) that seven different studies of lifetime cyberbullying victimization rates estimate that between 18.8% and 40.6% of children have been cyberbullied. As many as one out of five (20.1%) students admit to perpetrating cyberbullying themselves.

In one highly publicized case, 13-year-old Megan Meier committed suicide after she was cyberbullied through the social networking website MySpace. She befriended a stranger, a boy named Josh Evans, through the site. However, the Josh Evans MySpace account had been created by a group of people headed by Lori Drew, the mother of a former friend of Meier's. "Josh Evans" began sending Meier increasingly hurtful messages and posted bulletins about her. In October 2006 Meier hanged herself in her bedroom. In May 2008 a federal grand jury indicted Drew on one count of conspiracy and three counts of accessing protected computers without authorization to obtain information to inflict emotional distress. Drew was convicted in November 2008 of three misdemeanors but acquitted of felony conspiracy charges. Hinduja and Patchin report in "Bullying, Cyberbullying, and Suicide" (*Archives of Suicide Research*, vol. 14, no. 3, July 2010) that middle school students who experience bullying or cyberbullying are more likely to have suicidal thoughts or attempt suicide than are other students.

SEXTING AND CYBERBULLYING. In the fact sheet "Sexting: A Brief Guide for Educators and Parents" (2010, http://www.cyberbullying.us/Sexting_Fact_Sheet .pdf), Hinduja and Patchin report on the phenomenon of sexting, or sending sexually suggestive images over a cell phone. The researchers report on several studies that find that between 4% and 19% of youth admit to having sent sexually explicit images and between 13% and 31% of youth admit to having received them. Even though such images are generally sent in the context of a dating relationship, the recipient can easily distribute the images to others, which can have severe consequences. Hinduja and Patchin report the case of Jesse Logan, an 18-year-old girl who sent nude pictures of herself to her boyfriend. When they broke up, he forwarded the pictures to his friends. Her classmates taunted her, and two months later she committed suicide. Thirteen-year-old Hope Witsell sent a topless picture of herself to a boy she liked. After the image was forwarded to others, she endured vicious name-calling for weeks before she killed herself.

Prevention Programs

A number of U.S. schools have implemented antibullying programs that are aimed at bringing the subject out in the open. Antibullying efforts are not only geared toward bullies but also toward the students and teachers who do not do enough to stop such aggression from occurring. Some victims claim there are teachers who allow bullying to occur, even encourage it. Others say they are afraid to tell teachers because the educators will ignore it and tell the victims to toughen up. Still other victims are ashamed that they cannot stop the bullies, so they retreat into themselves and internalize it.

One successful antibullying program, the Olweus Bullying Prevention Program (October 16, 2010, http://www.clemson.edu/olweus/), teaches students, parents, and school staff to work together to address the issue. By discussing bullying and its effects, people learn the consequences of bullying on individuals and on the school environment. Rules and plans are developed and enforced. The Office of Juvenile Justice and Delinquency Prevention notes that the Olweus program is successful in elementary and middle schools. In *School-Based Programs to Reduce Bullying and Victimization* (January 2010, http://www.ncjrs.gov/pdffiles1/nij/grants/229377.pdf), David P. Farrington and Maria M. Ttofi of Cambridge University examine school-based antibullying programs (including the Olweus program) and find that the programs successfully decreased bullying and victimization by about 20%. In July 2009 the American Academy of Pediatrics stated in "Policy Statement: Role of the Pediatrician in Youth Violence Prevention" (*Pediatrics*, vol. 124, no. 1) that it endorsed the program.

HAZING

Like bullying, hazing involves humiliating people into doing something that they would not do normally. In some instances the hazing act is silly and harmless. However, in the early 21st century parents and educators have become concerned that hazings are getting more and more aggressive and violent. Such hazings, which often occur as initiations to a school or social club, are considered a "rite of passage" to some, just "horseplay" to others, and degrading and devastating to the various victims. Some athletic teams claim that hazing is done to toughen up younger players—to help them bond with the team. However, unlike bullying, hazing is often done with the consent of its victims. For example, by succumbing to peer pressure and wanting to be part of the group or clique, many students allow themselves to be subjected to humiliating acts that they do not report.

Hazings, however, can go too far and the victims can be seriously harmed. Some victims have even died. Hazings usually involve older students (veterans) initiating young classmates (newcomers) into the club. The situation can quickly turn violent when the older students gang up on the younger students, who have no idea what has been planned or what they should expect. Researchers note that students will do things in a mob situation that they would never do on their own.

Several cases of brutal hazings taking place in high school sports received significant news coverage in 2010. For example, members of a baseball team at Fletcher Public Schools in Oklahoma were exposed to severe hazing, including having substances smeared on their genitals and being forced to kiss other players. One member in particular was stripped of his clothing, tied to a tree, and urinated on. In Carmel, Indiana, a young high school basketball player was grabbed, pushed down, and assaulted on a school bus. In Idaho five members of a high school football team faced a variety of charges for hazing incidents, the most serious being sexual misconduct.

Jennifer J. Waldron and Christopher L. Kowalski report in "Crossing the Line: Rites of Passage, Team Aspects, and Ambiguity of Hazing" (*Research Quarterly for Exercise and Sport*, vol. 80, no. 2, June 2009) that between 17.4% and 36.2% of middle school, high school, and college athletes report participating in a hazing incident. However, the researchers note that these percentages are probably too low because athletes often fear retribution if they report the hazing and because athletes may not recognize the activities as hazing. Hazing was more common in aggressive contact sports, such as football and basketball, and less common in individual, noncontact sports, such as track and field and swimming.

AVOIDANCE AND FEAR

Some students continue to worry about their safety at school. Eaton et al. find that in 2009, 5% of students reported

TABLE 9.7

Percentage of high school students who did not go to school because of safety concerns, by sex, race and Hispanic origin, and grade, 2009

Category	Female %	Male %	Total %
Race/ethnicity			
White*	3.8	3.3	3.5
Black*	6.6	5.9	6.3
Hispanic	8.3	7.9	8.1
Grade			
9	6.4	5.4	5.8
10	5.3	4.6	5.0
11	5.8	4.9	5.3
12	3.3	3.4	3.4
Total	**5.3**	**4.6**	**5.0**

Note: Did not go to school because of safety concerns at least 1 day during the 30 days before the survey.
*Non-Hispanic.

SOURCE: Danice K. Eaton et al., "Table 18. Percentage of High School Students Who Did Not Go to School Because They Felt Unsafe at School or on Their Way to or from School, by Sex, Race/Ethnicity, and Grade—United States, Youth Risk Behavior Survey, 2009," in "Youth Risk Behavior Surveillance—United States, 2009," *Morbidity and Mortality Weekly Report*, vol. 59, no. SS-5, June 4, 2010, http://www.cdc.gov/mmwr/pdf/ss/ss5905.pdf (accessed October 22, 2010)

missing one or more days of school in the last 30 days because they believed it was too unsafe at school or going to and from school. (See Table 9.7.) Female students (5.3%) were slightly more likely than male students (4.6%) to report this experience. Missing school out of fear was much higher among Hispanic students (8.1%) and non-Hispanic African-American students (6.3%) than it was among non-Hispanic white students (3.5%). Younger children reported not going to school because of safety concerns more than did older children; 5.8% of ninth graders, 5% of 10th graders, 5.3% of 11th graders, and 3.4% of 12th graders reported skipping school because of safety concerns during the previous month.

Dinkes, Kemp, and Baum report that in 2007, 5.3% of students aged 12 to 18 years reported being afraid of attack or harm at school during the school year; this was down dramatically from 11.8% of students in 1995. (See Table 9.8.) In 2007 females (6%) were more likely to be afraid of harm than were males (4.6%). African-American (8.6%) and Hispanic (7.1%) students were more likely than white students (4.2%) to report being afraid of attack or harm at school. Younger students were more likely than older students to fear attack or harm at school. In 2005 urban students (10.5%) were far more likely than rural (5.1%) or suburban (4.7%) students to report being afraid of attack or harm. In 2007 fewer students were afraid of attack or harm away from school than they were at school (3.5% and 5.3%, respectively).

NO CHILD LEFT BEHIND ACT: PERSISTENTLY DANGEROUS SCHOOLS

The No Child Left Behind (NCLB) Act was passed by Congress in 2001 and signed into law by President George W. Bush (1946–) in January 2002. As a reauthorization of the Elementary and Secondary Education Act of 1965, the NCLB mandated sweeping changes to the law defining and regulating the federal government's role in kindergarten through 12th-grade education. According to the U.S. Department of Education, in "Four Pillars of NCLB" (July 1, 2004, http://www.ed.gov/nclb/overview/intro/4pillars.html), the four principles are:

- Stronger accountability for results

- Increased flexibility and local control

- Expanded options for parents

- An emphasis on teaching methods that have been proven to work

The NCLB requires schools to demonstrate "adequate yearly progress" toward statewide proficiency goals. The schools that do not make progress face corrective action and restructuring measures. Reporting of progress is public, so parents can stay informed about their school and school district. Schools that make or exceed adequate yearly progress are eligible for awards. The ultimate goal is that all children will have a quality education by the 2013–14 school year.

Unsafe School Choice Option

Among the various changes that the NCLB required was a provision mandating that states work on making schools safer. According to the Department of Education, in "Questions and Answers on No Child Left Behind" (November 17, 2004, http://www.ed.gov/nclb/freedom/safety/creating.html):

> Under Title IV of ESEA as reauthorized by the No Child Left Behind Act, states are required to establish a uniform management and reporting system to collect information on school safety and drug use among young people. The states must include incident reports by school officials and anonymous student and teacher surveys in the data they collect. This information is to be publicly reported so that parents, school officials and others who are interested have information about any violence and drug use at their schools. They can then assess the problems at their schools and work toward finding solutions. Continual monitoring and reports will track progress over time.

To hold schools accountable for ensuring student safety, the NCLB requires states to create a definition of persistently dangerous schools. States must permit students to have public school choice if their school consistently falls into this category. In addition, student victims of violent crime are also allowed public school

TABLE 9.8

Percentage of students ages 12–18 who reported being afraid of attack or harm, by location and selected student and school characteristics, selected years 1995–2007

Student or school characteristic	At school						Away from school					
	1995	1999	2001	2003	2005	2007[a]	1995	1999	2001	2003	2005	2007[a]
Total	11.8	7.3	6.4	6.1	6.4	5.3	—	5.7	4.6	5.4	5.2	3.5
Sex												
Male	10.8	6.5	6.4	5.3	6.1	4.6	—	4.1	3.7	4.0	4.6	2.4
Female	12.8	8.2	6.4	6.9	6.7	6.0	—	7.4	5.6	6.8	5.8	4.5
Race/ethnicity[b]												
White	8.1	5.0	4.9	4.1	4.6	4.2	—	4.3	3.7	3.8	4.2	2.5
Black	20.3	13.5	8.9	10.7	9.2	8.6	—	8.7	6.3	10.0	7.3	4.9
Hispanic	20.9	11.7	10.6	9.5	10.3	7.1	—	8.9	6.5	7.4	6.2	5.9
Asian	—	—	—	—	6.2!	2.3!	—	—	—	—	7.4	‡
Other	13.5	6.7	6.4	5.0	5.7	3.3!	—	5.4	6.6	3.9	3.1!	‡
Grade												
6th	14.3	10.9	10.6	10.0	9.5	9.9	—	7.8	6.3	6.8	5.6	5.9
7th	15.3	9.5	9.2	8.2	9.1	6.7	—	6.1	5.5	6.7	7.5	3.0
8th	13.0	8.1	7.6	6.3	7.1	4.6	—	5.5	4.4	5.3	5.0	3.6
9th	11.6	7.1	5.5	6.3	5.9	5.5	—	4.6	4.5	4.3	3.8	4.0
10th	11.0	7.1	5.0	4.4	5.5	5.2	—	4.8	4.2	5.3	4.7	3.0
11th	8.9	4.8	4.8	4.7	4.6	3.1	—	5.9	4.7	4.7	4.2	2.3
12th	7.8	4.8	2.9	3.7	3.3	3.1	—	6.1	3.3	4.9	5.4	3.2
Urbanicity												
Urban	18.4	11.6	9.7	9.5	10.5	‡	—	9.1	7.4	8.1	6.7	‡
Suburban	9.8	6.2	4.8	4.8	4.7	‡	—	5.0	3.8	4.4	4.6	‡
Rural	8.6	4.8	6.0	4.7	5.1	‡	—	3.0	3.0	4.0	4.7	‡
Sector												
Public	12.2	7.7	6.6	6.4	6.6	5.5	—	5.8	4.6	5.4	5.2	3.6
Private	7.3	3.6	4.6	3.0	3.8	2.5!	—	5.0	5.1	4.7	4.9	2.1!

—Not available.

!Interpret data with caution.

‡Reporting standards not met.

[a]In 2007, the reference period was the school year, whereas in prior survey years the reference period was the previous 6 months. Cognitive testing showed that estimates from 2007 are comparable to previous years.

[b]Race categories exclude persons of Hispanic ethnicity. Other includes American Indian, Alaska Native, Asian (prior to 2005), Pacific Islander, and, from 2003 onward, more than one race. Due to changes in racial/ethnic categories, comparisons of race/ethnicity across years should be made with caution.

Notes: Data for 2005 have been revised from previously published figures. "At school" includes the school building, on school property, on a school bus, and, from 2001 onward, going to and from school. For the 2001 survey, the wording was changed from "attack or harm" to "attack or threat of attack." Students were asked if they "never," "almost never," "sometimes," or "most of the time" feared attack or harm at school or away from school. Students responding "sometimes" or "most of the time" were considered fearful. Fear of attack away from school was not collected in 1995. In 2005 and 2007, the unit response rate for this survey did not meet NCES statistical standards; therefore, interpret the data with caution. Due to a redesign of the methods used to measure urbanicity, estimates for 2007 locales are not shown.

SOURCE: Rachel Dinkes, Jana Kemp, and Katrina Baum, "Table 17.1. Percentage of Students Ages 12–18 Who Reported Being Afraid of Attack or Harm, by Location and Selected Student and School Characteristics: Various Years, 1995–2007," in *Indicators of School Crime and Safety: 2009*, U.S. Department of Education, National Center for Education Statistics, and U.S. Department of Justice, Bureau of Justice Statistics, December 2009, http://nces.ed.gov/programs/crimeindicators/crimeindicators2009/tables/table_17_1.asp (accessed October 28, 2010)

choice even if the school is not considered persistently dangerous.

Underreporting of Violence and Crime at School

The National School Safety and Security Services notes in "School Crime Reporting and School Crime Underreporting" (November 26, 2009, http://www.schoolsecurity.org/trends/school_crime_reporting.html) that the unsafe school requirement of the NCLB concerns educators, parents, and police. Some believe schools will be even more hesitant to report crimes so that they will not be labeled as persistently dangerous. They suggest that by falling into this designation, these schools will undoubtedly lose enrollment and school funds. As such, schools may begin to underreport such crimes so that they maintain a clean rating.

Dinkes, Kemp, and Baum indicate that many crimes, even violent crimes, that are committed at school are not reported to the police. During the 2007–08 school year 75.5% of public schools experienced one or more violent crimes but just 37.8% reported violent crimes to the police. (See Table 9.9.) Violent incidents included physical attacks, fights with or without weapons, threats of physical violence with or without weapons, rape, sexual battery (other than rape), and robbery with or without weapons. Low-reporting trends also occurred with thefts. Even though 47.3% of public schools experienced one or more thefts, just 31% of public schools reported thefts to the police.

Proportionally, public schools were more likely to report seriously violent incidents to the police, presumably due to the gravity of such offenses. However, even

TABLE 9.9

Percentage of public schools recording and reporting incidents of crime that occurred at school, number of incidents, and the rate per 1,000 students, by type of crime, selected school years 1999–2000 through 2007–08

Type of crime	Recorded incidents						Reported incidents to police					
	1999–2000	2003–04	2005–06	2007–08			1999–2000	2003–04	2005–06	2007–08		
	Percent of schools	Percent of schools	Percent of schools	Percent of schools	Number of incidents	Rate per 1,000 students	Percent of schools	Percent of schools	Percent of schools	Percent of schools	Number of incidents	Rate per 1,000 students
Total	**86.4**	**88.5**	**85.7**	**85.5**	**2,040,800**	**42.7**	**62.5**	**65.2**	**60.9**	**62.0**	**704,200**	**14.7**
Violent incidents	71.4	81.4	77.7	75.5	1,332,400	27.9	36.0	43.6	37.7	37.8	302,600	6.3
Physical attack or fight without a weapon	63.7	76.7	74.3	72.7	812,200	17.0	25.8	35.6	29.2	28.2	171,000	3.6
Threat of physical attack without a weapon	52.2	53.0	52.2	47.8	461,900	9.7	18.9	21.0	19.7	19.5	102,100	2.1
Serious violent incidents	19.7	18.3	17.1	17.2	58,300	1.2	14.8	13.3	12.6	12.6	29,400	0.6
Rape or attempted rape	0.7	0.8	0.3	0.8	800	#	0.6	0.8	0.3	0.8	800	#
Sexual battery other than rape	2.5	3.0	2.8	2.5	3,800	0.1	2.3	2.6	2.6	2.1	2,700	0.1
Physical attack or fight with a weapon	5.2	4.0	3.0	3.0	14,000	0.3	3.9	2.8	2.2	2.1	5,400	0.1
Threat of physical attack with a weapon	11.1	8.6	8.8	9.3	20,300	0.4	8.5	6.0	5.9	5.7	9,100	0.2
Robbery with a weapon	0.5	0.6	0.4	0.4!	700!	#	0.3!	0.6	0.4	0.4!	600!	#
Robbery without a weapon	5.3	6.3	6.4	5.2	18,700	0.4	3.4	4.2	4.9	4.1	10,700	0.2
Theft*	45.6	46.0	46.0	47.3	268,900	5.6	28.5	30.5	27.9	31.0	133,800	2.8
Other incidents	72.7	64.0	68.2	67.4	439,500	9.2	52.0	50.0	50.6	48.7	267,800	5.6
Possession of a firearm/explosive device	5.5	6.1	7.2	4.7	5,300	0.1	4.5	4.9	5.5	3.6	3,900	0.1
Possession of a knife or sharp object	42.6	—	42.8	40.6	77,000	1.6	23.0	—	25.0	23.3	43,200	0.9
Distribution of illegal drugs	12.3	12.9	—	—	—	—	11.4	12.4	—	—	—	—
Possession or use of alcohol or illegal drugs	26.6	29.3	—	—	—	—	22.2	26.0	—	—	—	—
Distribution, possession, or use of illegal drugs	—	—	25.9	23.2	107,300	2.2	—	—	22.8	20.7	94,300	2.0
Distribution, possession, or use of alcohol	—	—	16.2	14.9	37,800	0.8	—	—	11.6	10.6	26,900	0.6
Sexual harassment	36.3	—	—	—	—	—	14.7	—	—	—	—	—
Vandalism	51.4	51.4	50.5	49.3	212,100	4.4	32.7	34.3	31.9	30.8	99,500	2.1

—Not available.

#Rounds to zero.

!Interpret data with caution.

*Theft/larceny includes taking things worth over $10 without personal confrontation.

Note: Responses were provided by the principal or the person most knowledgeable about crime and safety issues at the school. "At school" was defined for respondents to include activities that happen in school buildings, on school grounds, on school buses, and at places that hold school-sponsored events or activities. Respondents were instructed to include incidents that occurred before, during, or after normal school hours or when school activities or events were in session. Detail may not sum to totals because of rounding. Estimates of number of incidents are rounded to the nearest 100.

SOURCE: Rachel Dinkes, Jana Kemp, and Katrina Baum, "Table 6.1. Percentage of Public Schools Recording and Reporting Incidents of Crime, Number of Incidents, and the Rate of Crimes per 1,000 Students, by Type of Crime: Various School Years, 1999–2000 through 2007–08," in *Indicators of School Crime and Safety: 2009*, U.S. Department of Education, National Center for Education Statistics, and U.S. Department of Justice, Bureau of Justice Statistics, December 2009, http://nces.ed.gov/programs/crimeindicators2009/tables/table_06_1.asp (accessed October 28, 2010)

some serious violent crimes were not reported. During the 2007–08 school year 17.2% of public schools experienced one or more serious violent crimes and only 12.6% reported any serious violent crimes to the police. (See Table 9.9.)

CRITICISM OF "PERSISTENTLY DANGEROUS SCHOOLS": GEORGIA'S EXAMPLE. Some critics argue that the NCLB provisions that require states to define the phrase "persistently dangerous schools" allows them to underestimate the security concerns at some schools. For example, the Georgia Department of Education (GDOE) defines persistently dangerous schools in "Unsafe School Choice Option (USCO)" (2010, http://public.doe.k12.ga.us/aypnclb.aspx?PageReq= AboutUSCO). To meet the criteria, a school must meet the following conditions for three consecutive years:

At least 1 student is found by official tribunal action to have violated a school rule related to a violent criminal offense (including aggravated battery, aggravated child molestation, aggravated sexual battery, aggravated sodomy, armed robbery, arson, kidnapping, murder, rape, & voluntary manslaughter) either on campus or at a school-sanctioned event;

At least 2% of the student body or 10 students, whichever is greater, have been found to have violated school rules related to other identified criminal offenses,

including non-felony drugs, felony drugs, felony weapons, terroristic threats;

Any combination of [the above].

The conditions for being labeled a persistently dangerous school were so stringent that no schools were placed on the list until 2004. In addition, the National School Safety and Security Services reports in "School Crime Reporting and School Crime Underreporting" (November 26, 2009, http://www.schoolsecurity.org/trends/school_crime_report ing.html) that three Georgia school districts had underreported school crimes during the 2004–05 school year to evade the NCLB requirements and that one school had even failed to report a school shooting incident to the police. Heather Vogell indicates in "Zero Unsafe Schools? Officially, Yes" (*Atlanta Journal-Constitution*, March 15, 2009) that no Georgia schools were on the list of persistently dangerous schools in 2005–06, 2006–07, and 2007–08, despite the fact that across the Atlanta metro area a student brought a gun to school approximately once every three days during the 2007–08 school year. Vogell notes that "Georgia is among the states that define 'persistently dangerous' so strictly that it would take three years of extraordinarily violent crimes, or an inordinately high number of offenses such as drugs or weapons, for a school to get the designation."

CHAPTER 10
CRIME PREVENTION AND PUNISHMENT

The spike in juvenile crime during the 1990s spurred a national debate about the appropriate response to youth violence and delinquency. Should the response be wholly reactive—in other words, should a system of punishments deter crime—or should it focus on proactive measures to prevent youth crime?

While preventing violence before it happens would seem to be desirable, there is some question about the effectiveness of the strategies that are employed to do so. For example, the school environment would seem to be an ideal place to implement violence prevention programs. Hyoun-Kyoung Park-Higgerson et al. undertook an evaluation of school-based violence prevention programs and report their results in "The Evaluation of School-Based Violence Prevention Programs: A Meta-Analysis" (*Journal of School Health*, vol. 78, no. 9, September 2008). The researchers examined 26 school-based programs that were designed to reduce aggressive and violent behaviors in school-age children. Five program characteristics were considered: whether they were theory-based, characteristics of the target population, whether the program was used with all children or just some children, whether or not the program used multiple approaches, and the type of instructor. Only one program strategy—focusing on a single approach—had any effect on reducing violence, and that effect was moderate. Using multiple approaches, beginning antiviolence education at young ages, and using theory-based approaches—all considered desirable in the theoretical literature—were found to have no effect on violence reduction.

Nevertheless, Park-Higgerson et al. do not suggest that youth violence prevention programs cannot be effective; rather, they argue that more work needs to be done to identify effective interventions to stop violence before it happens. In the meantime, many responses to youth violence have emerged. Prevention efforts range from laws that hold parents responsible, to community efforts to educate youth, to curfews, to police suppression, to antigang programs. Reactive efforts range from allowing juveniles to be tried as adults for certain crimes to increased punishments. The full range of responses to youth violence are discussed in this chapter.

CRIME PREVENTION

Over the years, politicians, law enforcement officials, teachers, parents, and other concerned citizens have examined countless ideas in an effort to decrease youth violence and crime, from holding parents responsible for their children's crimes to having after-school violence prevention programs. The continuing problem of youth crime has many people devoting significant time and resources to end the cycle of violence. A variety of programs have been implemented in the area of prevention, intervention, and suppression. Efforts are ongoing to determine the effectiveness of such programs. The following sections discuss laws that have been enacted as well as a variety of prevention programs, including community prevention programs, law enforcement prevention strategies, and school-based prevention programs, to try to prevent juvenile crime.

Laws Enacted to Prevent Juvenile Crime

HOLDING PARENTS RESPONSIBLE. Civil liability laws have held parents at least partly responsible for damages caused by their children for many decades. In addition, child welfare laws included actions against those who contributed to the delinquency of a minor. By the 1990s, in response to rising juvenile crime rates, communities and states passed tougher laws about parental responsibility. In "Parent Liability Child's Act" (2010, http://www.enotes.com/everyday-law-encyclopedia/parent-liability-child-s-act), the *Encyclopedia of Everyday Law* notes that some states now hold parents of delinquent youth criminally liable. However, other less stringent parental responsibility laws are more common. Alabama, Kansas, Kentucky, and West Virginia require parents to pay court costs for their children who have been adjudicated as delinquent. Florida, Idaho, Indiana, North Carolina, and Virginia require parents to pay the costs of caring for, treating, or detaining delinquent children. Idaho, Maryland, Missouri, and Oklahoma require parents to pay restitution to the victims of their children's crimes. Nine states hold parents criminally responsible for storing a loaded firearm in a place that allows minors access to it, and other states hold parents liable if they know their child possesses a firearm and do not confiscate it.

Critics of parental liability suggest that victims are just looking for someone to blame. They assert that U.S. law usually holds people responsible for crimes only if they actively participate in the commission of such acts. They believe that if standard rules of law are practiced, the prosecutor of a case should have to prove that the parents intended to participate in a crime to be found guilty. Samantha Harvell, Belen Rodas, and Leah Hendey of Georgetown University explain in *Parental Involvement in Juvenile Justice: Prospects and Possibilities* (November 8, 2004, http://www.crocus.georgetown.edu/reports/parental.involvement.pdf) that judges and probation officers believe parents should be more involved in legal proceedings against minors because they feel the relationship between the parent and child often contributes to delinquency. However, judges and probation officers remain somewhat reluctant to use parental sanctions. In fact, Cathy Keen notes in "UF Study: Americans Give Mixed Reviews to Parental Responsibility Laws" (*University of Florida News*, March 14, 2005) that a 2005 survey found that public support for parental responsibility laws was relatively low, and Eve M. Brank and Jodi Lane of the University of Florida find in "Punishing My Parents: Juveniles' Perspectives on Parental Responsibility" (*Criminal Justice Policy Review*, vol. 19, no. 3, September 2008) that delinquent juveniles did not believe their parents should be held responsible for their crimes.

CURFEWS. To "break the cycle" of youth violence and crime, lawmakers in more than 1,000 jurisdictions have enacted curfews in various cities, towns, and rural areas across the country. According to Arlen Egley Jr. and Aline K. Major of the National Gang Center, in the fact sheet "Highlights of the 2001 National Youth Gang Survey" (April 2003, http://www.ncjrs.gov/pdffiles1/ojjdp/fs200301.pdf), 62% of jurisdictions reporting gang problems used curfews or other ordinances aimed at keeping youth from congregating at night. Of those jurisdictions, 86% argued that such laws "demonstrated at least some degree of effectiveness."

Most curfew laws work essentially the same way. They are aimed at restricting juveniles to their homes or property between the hours of 11 p.m. and 6 a.m. weekdays. Such laws usually allow juveniles to stay out a little later on weekends. Exceptions are made for youth who need to travel to and from school, attend church events, or go to work at different times. Other exceptions include family emergencies or situations when juveniles are accompanied by their parents.

Even though many people believe curfews are important in the fight against youth crime, critics of curfew ordinances argue that such laws violate the constitutional rights of children and their parents. They contend that the First, Fourth, Ninth, and 14th Amendment rights of people are endangered by curfew laws, especially the rights of free speech and association, privacy, and equal protection. Opponents also assert that no studies have proven curfew laws to be effective. In fact, most studies show that curfew laws have little effect on youth crime, such as Angie Schwartz and Lucy Wang's "Proliferating Curfew Laws Keep Kids at Home, but Fail to Curb Juvenile Crime" (*National Center for Youth Law*, vol. 26, no. 1, January–March 2005), Caterina Grovis Roman and Gretchen Moore's "Evaluation of the Youth Curfew in Prince George's County, Maryland: The Curfew's Impact on Arrests and Calls for Service" (March 11, 2003, http://www.ncjrs.gov/pdffiles1/nij/grants/200520.pdf), and Kenneth Adams's "The Effectiveness of Juvenile Curfews at Crime Prevention" (*Annals of the American Academy of Political and Social Science*, vol. 587, no. 1, May 2003). However, Patrick Kline of the University of California, Berkeley, finds in *The Impact of Juvenile Curfew Laws* (June 2010, http://www.econ.berkeley.edu/~pkline/papers/Youth%20curfews%20latest.pdf) that when he compares crime rates before and after the enactment of curfews the "curfews are effective at reducing both violent and property crimes committed by juveniles below the statutory curfew age."

Community Prevention and Intervention Programs

Prevention measures are programs aimed at keeping youth, particularly at-risk youth, from engaging in criminal behavior, joining gangs, or otherwise ending up in prison or jail. Intervention programs are designed to remove youth from gangs, criminal activities, and patterns of reckless behavior that would ultimately put the youth in prison or jail. Such programs typically include helping the individual build self-esteem, confidence, and socialization skills while offering education, recreation, and job skills assistance. Many prevention and intervention programs have seen some success with delinquent and at-risk youth. Those that succeed provide alternatives to youth and often a safe place to hang out, make new friends, and learn life skills.

THE CHICAGO AREA PROJECT. Chicago, Illinois, like Los Angeles, California, was plagued with many gangs throughout the 20th century. In an effort to deal with the gang situation on the city's streets, the Chicago Area Project (CAP) was founded in 1934—the nation's first community-based delinquency prevention program. Developed by the sociologist Clifford R. Shaw (1895–1957), the program was designed to work with delinquent youth in the poverty-stricken areas of Chicago. Project staff sought to prevent youth from joining gangs and ultimately committing crimes.

To achieve this, CAP advocates believed that improvements needed to be made to neighborhoods and communities. According to CAP, in "About Chicago Area Project" (January 2011, http://www.chicagoareaproject.org/about .html), "The agency believes that residents must be empowered through the development of community organizations so that they can act together to improve neighborhood conditions, hold institutions serving the community accountable, reduce anti-social behavior by young people, protect them from inappropriate institutionalization, and provide them with positive models for personal development." The organization emphasizes that juvenile delinquency in low-income areas is a product of social disadvantages—not a flaw of the individual child or of individuals from certain ethnic or racial backgrounds. By 2011 CAP had grown to include more than 40 affiliates and special projects.

BOYS AND GIRLS CLUBS OF AMERICA. By offering a variety of programs to help youth, the Boys and Girls Clubs of America explains in *Inspiring and Achieving Impact: 2009 Annual Report* (2010, http://www.bgca.org/whoweare/ Documents/2009_BGCA_Annual_Report-lowres.pdf) that it has worked with approximately 4.2 million children throughout the United States, Puerto Rico, the Virgin Islands, and U.S. military bases in the United States and abroad. In about 4,000 club locations, the group uses 51,000 trained, full-time staff and 186,000 program volunteers.

Law Enforcement Strategies

OFFICE OF JUVENILE JUSTICE AND DELINQUENCY PREVENTION'S COMPREHENSIVE GANG MODEL. The Office of Juvenile Justice and Delinquency Prevention (OJJDP) advocates the use of the Comprehensive Gang Model that was developed by Irving A. Spergel (1924–2010) to combat gangs. According to the National Gang Center, in *Best Practices to Address Community Gang Problems: OJJDP's Comprehensive Gang Model* (October 2010, http://www.ncjrs.gov/pdffiles1/ojjdp/231200.pdf), the model consists of five strategies that help gang members and their communities. The five strategies are:

- Mobilizing the larger community to create opportunities and service organizations for gang-involved and at-risk youth

- Mobilizing outreach workers to connect with youth involved in gangs

- Creating academic, economic, and social opportunities for at-risk and gang-involved youth

- Using gang suppression activities and holding youth involved in gangs accountable for their actions

- Helping community agencies problem-solve at a grassroots level to address gang problems

The model assumes that gang violence is a product of a breakdown in the larger community.

GANG RESISTANCE EDUCATION AND TRAINING. Hoping to reach students before they become involved in gangs and crime, uniformed police officers throughout the country visit middle schools to discuss the life consequences that are associated with such activities. The 13-part curriculum, which is offered through the Gang Resistance Education and Training (GREAT) program, was initially created in 1991 by the Phoenix (Arizona) Police Department and the Bureau of Alcohol, Tobacco, and Firearms. Because that pilot program met with success, GREAT was expanded to all 50 states and the District of Columbia. Among the topics presented are personal, resiliency, resistance, and social skills. The stated goals of the program are to help youth resist peer pressure, have positive attitudes toward law enforcement, learn ways to avoid violence, develop basic life skills, and set positive goals for the future. According to the article "G.R.E.A.T. Middle School Component" (2011, http://www.great-online.org/components/middleschool.aspx), the GREAT curriculum for seventh graders educates students about gangs, violence, drug abuse, and crime; helps students recognize their responsibilities and learn how to make good decisions; fosters communication skills; and teaches anger management skills.

The effectiveness of GREAT training became the basis for a study conducted by Finn-Aage Esbensen and D. Wayne Osgood, who published their findings in "Gang Resistance Education and Training (GREAT): Results from the National Evaluation" (*Journal of Research in Crime and Delinquency*, vol. 36, no. 2, May 1999). Program participants were said to have developed more negative opinions about gangs and more positive attitudes about police. They also reported experiencing lower rates of victimizations.

SUPPRESSION PROGRAMS. Another method intended to reduce youth crime and violence is called suppression. This tactic is used by law enforcement agencies throughout the country. Suppression usually involves a show of force, such as saturating an area with many uniformed police officers. The idea is meant to demonstrate to criminals that they are being watched and that criminal activities will not be tolerated. Suppression techniques also include sweeps, where officers sweep through an area rounding up youth and adult offenders. Some suppression programs have proven to be somewhat effective, whereas others have not. In some areas with high gang activity and violent youth crime, law enforcement personnel have tried suppression techniques. Suppression programs have been tested out in various cities, including Los Angeles, Chicago, and Houston, Texas, among others.

The Houston Police Department Gang Task Force is just one example of the many units of this type operating throughout the United States. Working in conjunction with the Mayor's Anti-Gang Office (2011, http://www.houstontx.gov/publicsafety/antigang/index.html), the task force focuses on areas with high gang activity by providing a highly visible presence in an effort to lessen gang violence and crime. Initiatives aim to target, arrest, and incarcerate gang members who are involved in criminal activities. At the same time, the Mayor's Anti-Gang Office works with communities, neighborhoods, service organizations, and schools to provide supportive services to at-risk youth, including counseling, job leads, conflict resolution, and recreation programs. The Mayor's Anti-Gang Office has also provided gang awareness training to individuals, including educators, law enforcement personnel, probation officers, and members of the public since 1994. The Mayor's Anti-Gang Office and the task force use high-tech devices, such as geomapping and tracking systems, which help staff keep track of gang locations and youth program assistance sites. Houston provides an example of how suppression can be combined with other program elements, in that the Mayor's Anti-Gang Office uses suppression techniques as one element of the OJJDP's Comprehensive Gang Model.

SCHOOL RESOURCE OFFICERS. The School Resource Officer (SRO) program is intended to improve relations between youth and police. The project, which was designed to prevent and intercept the commission of youth crime and violence, also gives students and police officers the chance to get to know one another. In some metropolitan areas children grow up with contempt for or fear of police. The SRO program works to eliminate these concerns as well as to educate students about the law and provide one-on-one mentoring.

Under the program, a police officer is assigned to a school as an SRO. The officer works to prevent crime, violence, and substance abuse; makes arrests if necessary during the commission of crimes; counsels students; and conducts classes about law enforcement and school safety. The program calls this the triad concept (police officer, educator, and counselor). To participate as an SRO, candidates must complete a specialized training program. The SRO program is credited with helping reduce youth crime in schools and in communities.

Founded in 1990, the National Association of School Resource Officers (NASRO; 2010, http://www.nasro.org/mc/page.do?sitePageId=114357&orgId=naasro) has a national membership of over 6,000 police officers. The association holds annual conferences and provides workshops for the SROs that focus on various procedures, techniques, and prevention measures.

School-Based Prevention Programs

STUDENTS AGAINST VIOLENCE EVERYWHERE. After Alex Orange was shot and killed in Charlotte, North Carolina, while trying to stop a fight in 1989, his classmates at West Charlotte High School decided to organize the group Students against Violence Everywhere (SAVE). SAVE (2010, http://www.nationalsave.org/main/statistics.php) has grown far beyond Orange's high school; in 2010 it had 1,877 chapters with over 215,000 student members. The group is active in elementary, middle, and high schools across the United States. Members have their own "colors": orange for Alex Orange and purple for peace and nonviolence.

The group focuses on violence prevention and on helping kids gain life skills, knowledge, and an understanding of the consequences of violence and crime. SAVE helps members overcome negative peer pressure situations through the development of positive peer interactions. It also plans safe activities, including cosponsorship of the National Youth Violence Prevention Campaign (2010, http://www.nyvpw.org/index.html?menu=about). During the weeklong campaign participants spend each day focused on one aspect of violence prevention. For example, the first day seeks to "promote respect and tolerance," and other days focus on anger management, conflict resolution, school and community safety, and unity.

BIG BROTHERS BIG SISTERS IN SCHOOL. The Big Brothers Big Sisters program has been serving children for over 100 years. The organization provides one-on-one mentoring services to young people (aged five to 18 years) throughout the United States. Big Brothers Big Sisters seeks to help youth perform better at school, stay clear of drugs and alcohol, improve their relationships with others, and avoid lives of crime and violence. Under the main program, a child is paired with an adult who spends time with him or her several times each month on outings, which can include sports, recreation, visits to museums or parks, and so on. Through the experience, the "Bigs" help the "Littles" develop life skills, confidence, and self-esteem.

Big Brothers Big Sisters has also developed programs for school children. Through the group's outreach program, volunteers visit schools weekly to provide one-on-one mentoring to students needing help. In addition, high school students gain experience mentoring elementary school children through the High School Bigs program. While helping older students develop skills working with children, the project helps younger children bond with teens closer to their own age and see that they, too, can grow up to lead a productive life. In *Making a Difference in Schools: The Big Brothers Big Sisters School-Based*

Mentoring Impact Study (June 2007, http://www.ppv.org/ppv/publications/assets/220_publication.pdf), Carla Herrera et al. find that children in the program demonstrate eight positive academic outcomes during their first year of being matched with a mentor, including improved overall academic performance. With longer matches, children improved their expectation to attend college.

PUNISHMENT

Juvenile Justice

Howard N. Snyder and Melissa Sickmund of the National Center for Juvenile Justice (NCJJ) indicate in *Juvenile Offenders and Victims: 2006 National Report* (March 2006, http://www.ojjdp.ncjrs.gov/ojstatbb/nr2006/downloads/NR2006.pdf) that the juvenile court generally has original jurisdiction in cases involving youth who are under the age of 18 years when the crime was committed, when the youth is arrested, or when the offender is referred to the court. In 2004, 37 states and the District of Columbia considered the oldest age for juveniles to be 17 years. Ten states (Georgia, Illinois, Louisiana, Massachusetts, Michigan, Missouri, New Hampshire, South Carolina, Texas, and Wisconsin) used the age of 16 years—meaning that youth aged 17 years are under the jurisdiction of criminal courts. In Connecticut, New York, and North Carolina, the age was set at 15 years—in other words, 16- and 17-year-olds are tried in criminal court.

When youth crime surged during the 1980s, many citizens called for changes in the juvenile justice system. Snyder and Sickmund indicate that in 2004, 47 states either changed or removed confidentiality provisions of the juvenile justice system, 45 states made it easier to transfer juveniles from the juvenile justice system to the criminal justice system, 31 states made a wider variety of sentencing options available for juveniles, 22 states passed laws that enhanced the rights of victims of juvenile crime, and new programs for juveniles were developed in most states. As a result of these changes, more juveniles are tried as adults in the criminal justice system. Codes regulating state juvenile justice systems now tend to strike a balance between prevention/treatment goals and punishment rather than focusing mainly on rehabilitation.

If the court deems that it is in the interests of the juvenile and the public, juvenile courts in some states may retain jurisdiction over juvenile offenders past the ages discussed earlier. Thus, such courts can handle juvenile offenders until they turn 20 years old in 33 states and the District of Columbia. Snyder and Sickmund note that Florida uses age 21, Kansas uses age 22, and California, Montana, Oregon, and Wisconsin use age 24 as the cutoff. Extended jurisdiction, however, may be limited by legislation to specific crimes or certain juveniles. Hence, the question of "who is considered a juvenile" does not have one consistent, standard answer. In various states exceptions can be made to the age criteria. This is done so that juveniles can be tried as adults or to provide for procedures under which a prosecutor can decide to handle an offender as a juvenile or an adult.

DOES IT WORK? The Federal Bureau of Investigation (FBI) notes in *Crime in the United States, 2009* (September 2010, http://www2.fbi.gov/ucr/cius2009/) that from 2000 to 2009 the number of juveniles arrested for murder and nonnegligent manslaughter stayed approximately the same. (See Table 10.1.) However, the number of juveniles arrested for murder and nonnegligent manslaughter had dropped since 1996. In that year 983 juveniles were arrested, whereas 656 juveniles were arrested in 2000. By 2009 the number of juveniles arrested had decreased slightly to 652. Based on these results, some public officials believe that efforts to reduce crime through adult sentencing are working. However, many experts attribute the decrease in the number of juveniles arrested for murder and nonnegligent manslaughter to expanded after-school crime prevention programs, the decline of crack cocaine and violent gangs, and big-city law enforcement efforts to crack down on illegal guns.

Despite these results, Jason J. Washburn et al. indicate in "Psychiatric Disorders among Detained Youths: A Comparison of Youths Processed in Juvenile Court and Adult Criminal Court" (*Psychiatric Services*, vol. 59, no. 9, September 2008) that decisions on whether to transfer juveniles to adult court are not blind to race, class, or gender. The researchers examine data from 1,715 youths who were arrested in Chicago and find that males, African-Americans, Hispanics, and older teens had a greater likelihood of being transferred to adult court, regardless of the type of crime.

Youth on Trial: A Developmental Perspective on Juvenile Justice (Thomas Grisso and Robert G. Schwartz, eds., 2000) discusses some of the problems in transferring juveniles to adult court. The authors note that juveniles have a harder time than adults when making "knowing and intelligent" decisions at many junctures in the criminal justice process. In particular, problems occur when waiving Miranda rights, which allow the juvenile to remain silent and talk to a lawyer before responding to questions posed by police. When a juvenile waives such rights, this can lead to much more serious consequences in adult court than in juvenile proceedings. The authors assert that "questions must be raised regarding the juvenile's judgment, decision-making capacity, and impulse control as they relate to criminal culpability" in adult proceedings. Researchers and experts in child development explain that before deciding if a youth can be held accountable as an adult for a particular offense, it is important to understand an adolescent's intellectual, social, and emotional development.

TABLE 10.1

Ten-year arrest trends, 2000–09

[8,649 agencies; 2009 estimated population 186,864,905; 2000 estimated population 172,176,040]

Offense charged[a]	Total all ages			Number of persons arrested Under 18 years of age			18 years of age and over		
	2000	2009	Percent change	2000	2009	Percent change	2000	2009	Percent change
Total[a]	**8,365,589**	**8,261,590**	**−1.2**	**1,455,216**	**1,161,830**	**−20.2**	**6,910,373**	**7,099,760**	**+2.7**
Murder and nonnegligent manslaughter	7,599	7,193	−5.3	656	652	−0.6	6,943	6,541	−5.8
Forcible rape	16,308	12,617	−22.6	2,674	1,820	−31.9	13,634	10,797	−20.8
Robbery	65,106	77,290	+18.7	16,393	19,336	+18.0	48,713	57,954	+19.0
Aggravated assault	301,315	267,314	−11.3	41,133	29,932	−27.2	260,182	237,382	−8.8
Burglary	174,741	188,781	+8.0	58,963	46,637	−20.9	115,778	142,144	+22.8
Larceny-theft	713,326	806,604	+13.1	231,759	196,863	−15.1	481,567	609,741	+26.6
Motor vehicle theft	80,109	47,473	−40.7	28,116	11,354	−59.6	51,993	36,119	−30.5
Arson	10,376	7,732	−25.5	5,584	3,615	−35.3	4,792	4,117	−14.1
Violent crime[b]	390,328	364,414	−6.6	60,856	51,740	−15.0	329,472	312,674	−5.1
Property crime[b]	978,552	1,050,590	+7.4	324,422	258,469	−20.3	654,130	792,121	+21.1
Other assaults	770,664	803,489	+4.3	142,699	135,125	−5.3	627,965	668,364	+6.4
Forgery and counterfeiting	67,233	49,992	−25.6	4,144	1,277	−69.2	63,089	48,715	−22.8
Fraud	216,666	139,935	−35.4	5,874	4,091	−30.4	210,792	135,844	−35.6
Embezzlement	12,456	11,756	−5.6	1,324	393	−70.3	11,132	11,363	+2.1
Stolen property; buying, receiving, possessing	75,471	66,304	−12.1	17,991	11,990	−33.4	57,480	54,314	−5.5
Vandalism	169,910	162,511	−4.4	71,267	55,757	−21.8	98,643	106,754	+8.2
Weapons; carrying, possessing, etc.	93,638	98,222	+4.9	22,383	20,696	−7.5	71,255	77,526	+8.8
Prostitution and commercialized vice	44,665	37,396	−16.3	729	791	+8.5	43,936	36,605	−16.7
Sex offenses (except forcible rape and prostitution)	54,150	46,628	−13.9	10,848	7,799	−28.1	43,302	38,829	−10.3
Drug abuse violations	939,138	995,708	+6.0	121,666	103,657	−14.8	817,472	892,051	+9.1
Gambling	4,568	3,359	−26.5	458	312	−31.9	4,110	3,047	−25.9
Offenses against the family and children	86,249	70,575	−18.2	4,767	2,689	−43.6	81,482	67,886	−16.7
Driving under the influence	879,666	841,869	−4.3	12,683	8,085	−36.3	866,983	833,784	−3.8
Liquor laws	406,772	340,842	−16.2	97,338	67,859	−30.3	309,434	272,983	−11.8
Drunkenness	420,017	398,412	−5.1	14,252	9,837	−31.0	405,765	388,575	−4.2
Disorderly conduct	369,207	354,032	−4.1	98,834	92,754	−6.2	270,373	261,278	−3.4
Vagrancy	16,872	16,817	−0.3	1,647	1,047	−36.4	15,225	15,770	+3.6
All other offenses (except traffic)	2,180,750	2,277,313	+4.4	252,417	196,036	−22.3	1,928,333	2,081,277	+7.9
Suspicion	3,453	1,293	−62.6	749	152	−79.7	2,704	1,141	−57.8
Curfew and loitering law violations	97,353	72,203	−25.8	97,353	72,203	−25.8	—	—	—
Runaways	91,264	59,223	−35.1	91,264	59,223	−35.1	—	—	—

[a]Does not include suspicion.
[b]Violent crimes are offenses of murder and nonnegligent manslaughter, forcible rape, robbery, and aggravated assault. Property crimes are offenses of burglary, larceny-theft, motor vehicle theft, and arson.

SOURCE: "Table 32. Ten-Year Arrest Trends: Totals, 2000–2009," in *Crime in the United States, 2009*, U.S. Department of Justice, Federal Bureau of Investigation, September 2010, http://www2.fbi.gov/ucr/cius2009/data/table_32.html (accessed October 26, 2010)

Juvenile Arrests

According to statistics maintained by the FBI, the property and violent crime arrest rates for juveniles aged 10 to 17 years began to rise during the 1980s. As recorded in the FBI's Property Crime Index and Violent Crime Index, arrests per 100,000 juveniles in that age bracket decreased for both property and violent crime between 1980 and 1983. After 1983 property crime arrests began a gradual increase, whereas violent crime arrests started to surge during the late 1980s. Around 1995 arrest rates for both property crime and violent crime began to decrease, with violent crimes seeing the greatest reduction.

Between 2000 and 2009 the number of juveniles arrested for all crimes dropped 20.2%; during this same period the number of adults arrested increased by 2.7%. (See Table 10.1.) Arrests of juveniles for some offenses declined even more drastically. For example, arrests of juveniles for motor vehicle theft dropped 59.6%; for driving under the influence, dropped 36.3%; for arson, dropped 35.3%; for forcible rape, dropped 31.9%; for drunkenness, dropped 31%; and for aggravated assault, dropped 27.2% In contrast, arrests of juveniles for prostitution actually increased by 8.5% during this period and arrests for robbery increased by 18%.

In *Crime in the United States, 2009*, the FBI reports that 8.3 million arrests were made nationwide in 2009, a decrease of 1.2% from 2000. (See Table 10.1.) In 2009, 14.1% of all people arrested were juveniles and 85.9% were adults. Adults were most often arrested for driving under the influence (866,983 arrests) and for drug abuse violations (817,472 arrests), whereas juveniles were most often arrested for larceny-theft (196,863). Adults were proportionally more likely to be arrested for violent crime than were juveniles, whereas juveniles were more likely to be arrested for property crime. In 2009, 85.8% of adults were arrested for violent crime; however, only 75.4% of adults were arrested for property crime.

ARRESTS AMONG SPECIFIC AGE GROUPS. The FBI also records in *Crime in the United States, 2009* arrest rate statistics for specific age groups: under the age of 15 years, under the age of 18 years, under the age of 21 years, and under the age of 25 years. Even though 14.1% of all people arrested were juveniles in 2009, almost half (43.6%) of all people arrested were under the age of 25 years, highlighting that crime is often perpetrated by young adults, rather than by juveniles.(See Table 10.2.) These statistics also show what crimes are more likely to be committed by juveniles as opposed to young adults. The table compares the number of arrests for these four age groups against the total number of arrests for all ages in 2009. For each offense, it presents the number of actual arrests for each age group as well as what percentage of total arrests falls within each age group.

A high percentage does not necessarily indicate a high number of arrests in a category. Instead, it means the age group was responsible for a high percentage of arrests within that category. For example, 134,610 individuals under the age of 18 years were arrested on drug abuse violations, which was 10.3% of the total arrests in that category. For comparison, 14,875 people under the age of 18 years were arrested for buying, receiving, or possessing stolen property. Even though the number of stolen property offenses was far less than the number of drug abuse violations for those under the age of 18 years, it represented 17.9% of the total arrests for stolen property. Such percentages help law enforcement personnel identify trends and patterns in juvenile crime.

Two categories that consistently had high arrest percentages among each of the four age groups presented in Table 10.2 were arson and vandalism. Two-thirds of arrests for each of these crimes (64.3% and 64.1%, respectively) were of young adults under the age of 25 years. Of the 9,509 arrests for arson in 2009, 26.1% were of youth under the age of 15 years, 44.3% were of juveniles under the age of 18 years, and 55.4% were of people under the age of 21 years. Vandalism was less associated with the youngest juveniles. Of the 212,981 people arrested for vandalism in 2009, 12.9% were under the age of 15 years, 33.6% were under the age of 18 years, and 50.1% were under the age of 21 years.

Other categories with the highest arrest percentages for those under the age of 15 years include disorderly conduct (9.3%), sex offenses, except forcible rape and prostitution (8.4%), burglary (6.9%), and larceny-theft (6.6%). (See Table 10.2.) The under-age-15 group also scored high in two other categories that are not applicable to those over the age of 18 years: curfew and loitering law violations and runaway arrests. Nearly a quarter (24.6%) of all arrests for curfew violations were of people under the age of 15 years, whereas 31.1% of arrests of runaways were of people under the age of 15 years. Arrests for murder (0.9%), fraud (0.5%), forgery and counterfeiting (0.3%), drunkenness (0.3%), embezzlement (0.2%), and prostitution (0.2%) were the least likely to be of children under the age of 15 years.

All arrests for curfew violations and for runaways were of youth under the age of 18 years. Besides arson and vandalism, arrests for disorderly conduct (25.9%), burglary (25.3%), robbery (25.1%), motor vehicle theft (24.5%), larceny-theft (24%), and carrying and possessing weapons (20.5%) were particularly likely to be of youth under the age of 18 years. (See Table 10.2.) Arrests for driving under the influence of alcohol (1%), prostitution (1.9%), drunkenness (2.4%), forgery and counterfeiting (2.5%), fraud (3.1%), and offenses against the family and children (4.1%) were the least likely to be of youth under the age of 18 years.

TABLE 10.2

Arrests of persons under 15, 18, 21, and 25 years of age, 2009

[12,371 agencies; 2009 estimated population 239,839,971]

Offense charged	Number of persons arrested					Percent of total all ages			
	Total all ages	Under 15	Under 18	Under 21	Under 25	Under 15	Under 18	Under 21	Under 25
Total	**10,741,157**	**403,671**	**1,515,586**	**3,070,768**	**4,663,319**	**3.8**	**14.1**	**28.6**	**43.6**
Murder and nonnegligent manslaughter	9,775	87	942	2,864	4,779	0.9	9.6	29.3	48.9
Forcible rape	16,442	766	2,385	4,675	6,995	4.7	14.5	28.4	42.5
Robbery	100,702	4,601	25,280	49,100	65,648	4.6	25.1	48.8	65.2
Aggravated assault	331,372	11,946	39,467	77,792	127,514	3.6	11.9	23.5	38.5
Burglary	235,226	16,173	59,432	107,897	141,939	6.9	25.3	45.9	60.3
Larceny-theft	1,060,754	70,216	254,865	441,325	580,101	6.6	24.0	41.6	54.7
Motor vehicle theft	64,169	3,094	15,724	26,983	36,154	4.8	24.5	42.0	56.3
Arson	9,509	2,479	4,216	5,269	6,116	26.1	44.3	55.4	64.3
Violent crime[a]	458,291	17,400	68,074	134,431	204,936	3.8	14.9	29.3	44.7
Property crime[a]	1,369,658	91,962	334,237	581,474	764,310	6.7	24.4	42.5	55.8
Other assaults	1,036,754	63,405	172,984	278,535	424,561	6.1	16.7	26.9	41.0
Forgery and counterfeiting	67,357	220	1,691	9,752	20,968	0.3	2.5	14.5	31.1
Fraud	162,243	835	5,014	19,993	41,743	0.5	3.1	12.3	25.7
Embezzlement	14,097	32	484	2,946	5,520	0.2	3.4	20.9	39.2
Stolen property; buying, receiving, possessing	82,944	3,250	14,875	29,731	42,557	3.9	17.9	35.8	51.3
Vandalism	212,981	27,503	71,502	106,733	136,616	12.9	33.6	50.1	64.1
Weapons; carrying, possessing, etc.	130,941	8,299	26,831	50,395	72,605	6.3	20.5	38.5	55.4
Prostitution and commercialized vice	56,640	131	1,079	7,321	15,920	0.2	1.9	12.9	28.1
Sex offenses (except forcible rape and prostitution)	60,422	5,067	10,567	17,429	24,398	8.4	17.5	28.8	40.4
Drug abuse violations	1,305,191	21,093	134,610	377,433	610,372	1.6	10.3	28.9	46.8
Gambling	8,067	156	1,395	3,114	4,331	1.9	17.3	38.6	53.7
Offenses against the family and children	87,889	1,027	3,612	9,049	19,622	1.2	4.1	10.3	22.3
Driving under the influence	1,112,384	230	10,712	99,521	300,776	*	1.0	8.9	27.0
Liquor laws	447,496	8,047	88,370	313,579	343,030	1.8	19.7	70.1	76.7
Drunkenness	471,727	1,278	11,102	52,955	127,741	0.3	2.4	11.2	27.1
Disorderly conduct	518,374	48,002	134,301	199,160	276,872	9.3	25.9	38.4	53.4
Vagrancy	26,380	521	2,151	5,615	8,306	2.0	8.2	21.3	31.5
All other offenses (except traffic)	2,946,277	60,105	258,293	607,625	1,073,879	2.0	8.8	20.6	36.4
Suspicion	1,517	47	175	450	729	3.1	11.5	29.7	48.1
Curfew and loitering law violations	89,733	22,101	89,733	89,733	89,733	24.6	100.0	100.0	100.0
Runaways	73,794	22,960	73,794	73,794	73,794	31.1	100.0	100.0	100.0

[a]Violent crimes are offenses of murder and nonnegligent manslaughter, forcible rape, robbery, and aggravated assault. Property crimes are offenses of burglary, larceny-theft, motor vehicle theft, and arson.

*Less than one-tenth of 1 percent.

SOURCE: "Table 41. Arrests: Persons under 15, 18, 21, and 25 Years of Age, 2009," in *Crime in the United States, 2009*, U.S. Department of Justice, Federal Bureau of Investigation, September 2010, http://www2.fbi.gov/ucr/cius2009/data/table_41.html (accessed October 26, 2010)

FIGURE 10.1

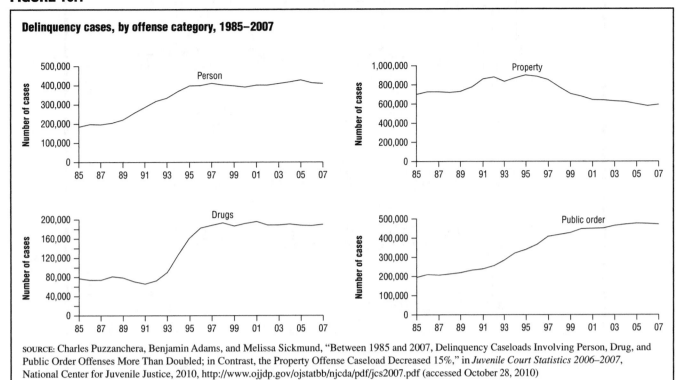

Delinquency cases, by offense category, 1985–2007

SOURCE: Charles Puzzanchera, Benjamin Adams, and Melissa Sickmund, "Between 1985 and 2007, Delinquency Caseloads Involving Person, Drug, and Public Order Offenses More Than Doubled; in Contrast, the Property Offense Caseload Decreased 15%," in *Juvenile Court Statistics 2006–2007*, National Center for Juvenile Justice, 2010, http://www.ojjdp.gov/ojstatbb/njcda/pdf/jcs2007.pdf (accessed October 28, 2010)

Despite the overall decrease in arrests of juveniles, delinquency cases handled by juvenile courts nationwide increased by 44% between 1985 and 2007. (See Figure 10.1.) Between 1997 and 2007 the number of public order offenses increased by 16% and the number of drug law violation cases increased by 1%. After big jumps between 1985 and 1997, person offenses changed very little and property offense cases decreased by 30% between 1997 and 2007.

ARRESTS BY GENDER. Between 2000 and 2009 young males were arrested in far greater numbers than young females. However, juvenile female arrest rates grew proportionately in relation to the arrests of young males, particularly in violent crime. In 2000 females represented 28% (407,526 out of a total of 1,455,216 juvenile arrests) of the juveniles arrested. (See Table 10.3.) By 2009 the percentage of juvenile arrests that was female had reached 30.5% (354,012 out of a total of 1,161,830 juvenile arrests). Even though arrests of both young males and young females decreased between 2000 and 2009, arrests of females decreased less. Arrests of males under the age of 18 years decreased by 22.9% over the decade, whereas arrests of females under the age of 18 years decreased by only 13.1%. In some categories, female arrests increased while male arrests decreased.

For example, between 2000 and 2009 juvenile male arrests for aggravated assault dropped by 28.1%, whereas juvenile female arrests dropped by only 24.4%. (See Table 10.3.) Juvenile male arrests for other assaults dropped by 10.2%, whereas juvenile female arrests increased by 5.7%. Arrests of juvenile males for larceny-theft dropped by 26.9%, whereas arrests of juvenile females for the same offenses increased by 5.2%. Arrests of juvenile males for driving under the influence decreased by 42.5%, but for juvenile females decreased by only 6%.

These male and female arrest trends among juveniles reflect to some degree changes in arrest trends among male and female adults. In *Crime in the United States, 2009*, the FBI reports that in 2009, 74.7% (6,174,287 out of a total of 8,261,590 arrests) of all arrests in the United States were of males (all ages). (See Table 10.3.) In that year 81.2% (295,890 out of a total of 364,414 arrests) of people arrested for violent crime were male, whereas 62.5% (656,186 out of a total of 1,050,590 arrests) of those arrested for property crime were male. Between 2000 and 2009 the number of arrests of males dropped by 4.9%, whereas the number of arrests of females increased by 11.4%.

According to the FBI's 10-year arrest trends, juvenile males and females engage in many of the same types of crimes. For example, the crime most frequently committed by both males and females was larceny-theft. Males were arrested 106,852 times and females were arrested 90,011 times for larceny-theft. (See Table 10.3.) However, arrested juvenile females were disproportionately charged with larceny-theft. Over a quarter (25.4%) of all juvenile females arrested were charged with larceny-theft, compared with only 13.2% of juvenile males.

TABLE 10.3

Ten-year arrest trends by sex, 2000–09

[8,649 agencies; 2009 estimated population 186,864,905; 2000 estimated population 172,176,040]

Offense charged	Male Total 2000	Male Total 2009	Male Total Percent change	Male Under 18 2000	Male Under 18 2009	Male Under 18 Percent change	Female Total 2000	Female Total 2009	Female Total Percent change	Female Under 18 2000	Female Under 18 2009	Female Under 18 Percent change
Total[a]	**6,491,372**	**6,174,287**	**−4.9**	**1,047,690**	**807,818**	**−22.9**	**1,874,217**	**2,087,303**	**+11.4**	**407,526**	**354,012**	**−13.1**
Murder and nonnegligent manslaughter	6,755	6,437	−4.7	576	599	+4.0	844	756	−10.4	80	53	−33.8
Forcible rape	16,139	12,469	−22.7	2,652	1,792	−32.4	169	148	−12.4	22	28	+27.3
Robbery	58,443	67,906	+16.2	14,861	17,342	+16.7	6,663	9,384	+40.8	1,532	1,994	+30.2
Aggravated assault	240,528	209,078	−13.1	31,550	22,685	−28.1	60,787	58,236	−4.2	9,583	7,247	−24.4
Burglary	151,244	159,017	+5.1	51,950	40,897	−21.3	23,497	29,764	+26.7	7,013	5,740	−18.2
Larceny-theft	454,947	451,750	−0.7	146,160	106,852	−26.9	258,379	354,854	+37.3	85,599	90,011	+5.2
Motor vehicle theft	67,551	38,987	−42.3	23,314	9,412	−59.6	12,558	8,486	−32.4	4,802	1,942	−59.6
Arson	8,820	6,432	−27.1	4,922	3,138	−36.2	1,556	1,300	−16.5	662	477	−27.9
Violent crime[b]	321,865	295,890	−8.1	49,639	42,418	−14.5	68,463	68,524	+0.1	11,217	9,322	−16.9
Property crime[b]	682,562	656,186	−3.9	226,346	160,299	−29.2	295,990	394,404	+33.2	98,076	98,170	+0.1
Other assaults	590,790	592,155	+0.2	98,731	88,631	−10.2	179,874	211,334	+17.5	43,968	46,494	+5.7
Forgery and counterfeiting	40,765	31,152	−23.6	2,746	889	−67.6	26,468	18,840	−28.8	1,398	388	−72.2
Fraud	116,447	78,550	−32.5	3,871	2,637	−31.9	100,219	61,385	−38.7	2,003	1,454	−27.4
Embezzlement	6,207	5,743	−7.5	686	224	−67.3	6,249	6,013	−3.8	638	169	−73.5
Stolen property; buying, receiving, possessing	62,320	52,247	−16.2	15,179	9,670	−36.3	13,151	14,057	+6.9	2,812	2,320	−17.5
Vandalism	143,680	133,421	−7.1	62,404	48,203	−22.8	26,230	29,090	+10.9	8,863	7,554	−14.8
Weapons; carrying, possessing, etc.	86,024	90,182	+4.8	20,096	18,553	−7.7	7,614	8,040	+5.6	2,287	2,143	−6.3
Prostitution and commercialized vice	18,886	11,639	−38.4	332	167	−49.7	25,779	25,757	−0.1	397	624	+57.2
Sex offenses (except forcible rape and prostitution)	50,319	42,609	−15.3	10,103	7,061	−30.1	3,831	4,019	+4.9	745	738	−0.9
Drug abuse violations	771,170	806,669	+4.6	102,909	86,857	−15.6	167,968	189,039	+12.5	18,757	16,800	−10.4
Gambling	3,984	2,877	−27.8	431	304	−29.5	584	482	−17.5	27	8	−70.4
Offenses against the family and children	67,421	53,001	−21.4	3,029	1,701	−43.8	18,828	17,574	−6.7	1,738	988	−43.2
Driving under the influence	734,872	651,424	−11.4	10,500	6,033	−42.5	144,794	190,445	+31.5	2,183	2,052	−6.0
Liquor laws	311,989	244,047	−21.8	66,585	41,879	−37.1	94,783	96,795	+2.1	30,753	25,980	−15.5
Drunkenness	363,705	331,804	−8.8	11,406	7,381	−35.3	56,312	66,608	+18.3	2,846	2,456	−13.7
Disorderly conduct	280,158	257,713	−8.0	69,814	61,616	−11.7	89,049	96,319	+8.2	29,020	31,138	+7.3
Vagrancy	13,151	13,189	+0.3	1,287	824	−36.0	3,721	3,628	−2.5	360	223	−38.1
All other offenses (except traffic)	1,720,089	1,746,701	+1.5	186,628	145,383	−22.1	460,661	530,612	+15.2	65,789	50,653	−23.0
Suspicion	2,757	958	−65.3	575	119	−79.3	696	335	−51.9	174	33	−81.0
Curfew and loitering law violations	67,275	50,288	−25.3	67,275	50,288	−25.3	30,078	21,915	−27.1	30,078	21,915	−27.1
Runaways	37,693	26,800	−28.9	37,693	26,800	−28.9	53,571	32,423	−39.5	53,571	32,423	−39.5

[a]Does not include suspicion.
[b]Violent crimes are offenses of murder and nonnegligent manslaughter, forcible rape, robbery, and aggravated assault. Property crimes are offenses of burglary, larceny-theft, motor vehicle theft, and arson.

SOURCE: "Table 33. Ten-Year Arrest Trends by Sex, 2000–2009," in *Crime in the United States, 2009*, U.S. Department of Justice, Federal Bureau of Investigation, September 2010, http://www2.fbi.gov/ucr/cius2009/data/table_33.html (accessed October 26, 2010)

Other areas with high arrest rates of both juvenile males and females include other assaults, disorderly conduct, and drug abuse violations. Young males were arrested 88,631 times on other assault charges, whereas young females were arrested 46,494 times for that offense in 2009. (See Table 10.3.) Disorderly conduct resulted in 61,616 young males and 31,138 young females under the age of 18 years being arrested, and drug abuse violations accounted for the arrests of 86,857 young males and 16,800 young females.

Other crimes most frequently committed by young males and females in 2009 included liquor law violations (41,879 arrests for males and 25,980 arrests for females) and curfew and loitering law violations (50,288 arrests for males and 21,915 arrests for females). (See Table 10.3.) Males also saw high numbers of arrests for vandalism (48,203 arrests), whereas young females were arrested 32,423 times as runaways.

Despite the high number of juvenile crimes, arrest rates for youth under the age of 18 years were down in many categories between 2000 and 2009. Young males experienced the greatest decline in the number of arrests for forgery and counterfeiting (down 67.6%), embezzlement (down 67.3%), motor vehicle theft (down 59.6%), and prostitution and commercialized vice (down 49.7%). (See Table 10.3.) During this same period young female arrest rates dropped most for embezzlement (down 73.5%), forgery and counterfeiting (down 72.2%), gambling (down 70.4%), and motor vehicle theft (down 59.6%). Arrests based on suspicion were down for both young males (down 79.3%) and young females (down 81%).

Over the decade juvenile arrests of males increased in only two categories: robbery (up 16.7%) and murder and nonnegligent manslaughter (up 4%). (See Table 10.3.) By contrast, arrests of young females were up for prostitution and commercialized vice (up 57.2%), robbery (up 30.2%), forcible rape (up 27.3%), disorderly conduct (up 7.3%), other assaults (up 5.7%), and larceny-theft (up 5.2%).

ARRESTS BY RACE. African-Americans are disproportionately arrested in the United States. The U.S. Census Bureau (June 2010, http://www.census.gov/popest/national/asrh/NC-EST2009-srh.html) estimates that in 2009, the U.S. population was 65.1% non-Hispanic white, 12.3% non-Hispanic African-American, 4.5% Asian-American, and 0.8% Native American or Alaskan Native. Hispanics, who can be of any race, represented 15.8% of the total population. In *Crime in the United States, 2009*, the FBI notes that two-thirds (69.1%) of all arrested individuals in 2009 were white (Hispanic or non-Hispanic), 28.3% were African-American, 1.4% were Native American or Alaskan Native, and 1.2% were Asian or Pacific Islander.

Arrested juveniles exhibited a similar racial distribution in 2009; 65.9% were white (Hispanic or non-Hispanic),

31.3% were African-American, 1.2% were Native American or Alaskan Native, and 1.6% were Asian or Pacific Islander. (See Table 10.4.) Among juveniles, a particularly high proportion of those arrested for driving under the influence (92%), violation of liquor laws (89.4%), drunkenness (88.5%), vandalism (78.4%), arson (76.7%), and offenses against the family and children (73.9%) were white. A particularly high proportion of those arrested for gambling (92.7%), robbery (67.3%), prostitution and commercialized vice (58.4%), murder and nonnegligent manslaughter (58%), and suspicion (57.1%) were African-American. The FBI data on arrests by race do not identify arrest rates by Hispanic origin.

DISPOSITION OF JUVENILES ARRESTED. Ann L. Pastore and Kathleen Maguire report in *Sourcebook of Criminal Justice Statistics* (2003, http://www.albany.edu/sourcebook/pdf/t4262004.pdf) that during the 1970s a change occurred in the disposition of arrested juveniles. Statistics for 1972 show that 50.8% of arrested minors were referred to juvenile court, 45% were handled within the police department and then released, and 1.3% were referred to criminal or adult court. In other words, almost half of all arrested juveniles were not formally charged with offenses in either juvenile or criminal court. Between 1972 and 2000, however, those referred to juvenile court increased to 70.8%, whereas those handled internally and then released dropped to 20.3%. The percentage of juvenile cases referred to criminal or adult court rose to 7%. By 2009 only 22.3% of juveniles arrested were released after being handled internally within the department, 67.4% were referred to juvenile court jurisdiction, and 8.8% were referred to criminal or adult court. (See Table 10.5.) Also included in this table are statistics for the percentage of juveniles referred to a welfare agency (0.5%) and those referred to another police agency (1.1%).

Juveniles in Custody

The OJJDP classifies juveniles in residential placement into three categories: committed, detained, and under a diversion agreement. According to the OJJDP (2011, http://ojjdp.ncjrs.org/ojstatbb/glossary.html), committed juveniles include those who are placed in the facility as part of a court-ordered disposition; detained juveniles include those who are held awaiting a court hearing, adjudication, disposition, or placement elsewhere; and voluntarily admitted juveniles include those in the facility who are part of a diversion agreement.

Snyder and Sickmund note that of the 109,225 juvenile offenders in residential placement overall in 2003, 74% were committed, 25% were detained, and less than 1% were under diversion agreements. The largest group, committed, was sent to residential placement by juvenile courts. Those being detained were part of a transitory population—those awaiting hearings, awaiting the disposition of their cases, or awaiting transfer to a different type of facility. It is

TABLE 10.4

Arrests of juveniles by race, 2009

[12,371 agencies; 2009 estimated population 239,839,971]

Offense charged	Arrests under 18					Percent distribution[a]				
	Total	White	Black	American Indian or Alaskan Native	Asian or Pacific Islander	Total	White	Black	American Indian or Alaskan Native	Asian or Pacific Islander
Total	**1,508,550**	**993,428**	**472,929**	**18,766**	**23,427**	**100.0**	**65.9**	**31.3**	**1.2**	**1.6**
Murder and nonnegligent manslaughter	941	380	546	8	7	100.0	40.4	58.0	0.9	0.7
Forcible rape	2,368	1,501	818	19	30	100.0	63.4	34.5	0.8	1.3
Robbery	25,226	7,854	16,968	112	292	100.0	31.1	67.3	0.4	1.2
Aggravated assault	39,341	21,790	16,694	394	463	100.0	55.4	42.4	1.0	1.2
Burglary	59,237	36,073	22,082	511	571	100.0	60.9	37.3	0.9	1.0
Larceny-theft	253,467	164,701	80,670	3,148	4,948	100.0	65.0	31.8	1.2	2.0
Motor vehicle theft	15,664	8,452	6,765	234	213	100.0	54.0	43.2	1.5	1.4
Arson	4,203	3,222	865	56	60	100.0	76.7	20.6	1.3	1.4
Violent crime[b]	67,876	31,525	35,026	533	792	100.0	46.4	51.6	0.8	1.2
Property crime[b]	332,571	212,448	110,382	3,949	5,792	100.0	63.9	33.2	1.2	1.7
Other assaults	172,000	100,872	67,420	1,849	1,859	100.0	58.6	39.2	1.1	1.1
Forgery and counterfeiting	1,687	1,120	543	9	15	100.0	66.4	32.2	0.5	0.9
Fraud	4,980	3,083	1,793	55	49	100.0	61.9	36.0	1.1	1.0
Embezzlement	481	307	160	1	13	100.0	63.8	33.3	0.2	2.7
Stolen property; buying, receiving, possessing	14,831	8,104	6,461	117	149	100.0	54.6	43.6	0.8	1.0
Vandalism	71,158	55,801	13,683	845	829	100.0	78.4	19.2	1.2	1.2
Weapons; carrying, possessing, etc.	26,666	16,190	9,938	210	328	100.0	60.7	37.3	0.8	1.2
Prostitution and commercialized vice	1,072	426	626	4	16	100.0	39.7	58.4	0.4	1.5
Sex offenses (except forcible rape and prostitution)	10,494	7,468	2,788	89	149	100.0	71.2	26.6	0.8	1.4
Drug abuse violations	134,207	97,232	34,295	1,212	1,468	100.0	72.4	25.6	0.9	1.1
Gambling	1,395	95	1,293	0	7	100.0	6.8	92.7	0.0	0.5
Offenses against the family and children	3,576	2,642	870	48	16	100.0	73.9	24.3	1.3	0.4
Driving under the influence	10,629	9,774	541	191	123	100.0	92.0	5.1	1.8	1.2
Liquor laws	87,811	78,540	5,439	2,704	1,128	100.0	89.4	6.2	3.1	1.3
Drunkenness	11,067	9,799	966	210	92	100.0	88.5	8.7	1.9	0.8
Disorderly conduct	133,674	75,946	55,295	1,362	1,071	100.0	56.8	41.4	1.0	0.8
Vagrancy	2,151	1,539	588	9	15	100.0	71.5	27.3	0.4	0.7
All other offenses (except traffic)	256,855	177,661	71,845	2,844	4,505	100.0	69.2	28.0	1.1	1.8
Suspicion	175	74	100	0	1	100.0	42.3	57.1	0.0	0.6
Curfew and loitering law violations	89,578	54,439	33,207	872	1,060	100.0	60.8	37.1	1.0	1.2
Runaways	73,616	48,343	19,670	1,653	3,950	100.0	65.7	26.7	2.2	5.4

[a]Because of rounding, the percentages may not add to 100.0.
[b]Violent crimes are offenses of murder and nonnegligent manslaughter, forcible rape, robbery, and aggravated assault. Property crimes are offenses of burglary, larceny-theft, motor vehicle theft, and arson.

SOURCE: "Table 43B. Arrests by Race, 2009," in *Crime in the United States, 2009*, U.S. Department of Justice, Federal Bureau of Investigation, September 2010, http://www.2.fbi.gov/ucr/cius2009/data/table_43.html (accessed October 26, 2010)

TABLE 10.5

Police disposition of juvenile offenders taken into custody, 2009

[2009 estimated population]

Population group		Total[a]	Handled within department and released	Referred to juvenile court jurisdiction	Referred to welfare agency	Referred to other police agency	Referred to criminal or adult court court	Number of agencies	2009 estimated population
Total agencies:	**Number**	**543,200**	**121,162**	**365,961**	**2,758**	**5,731**	**47,588**	**5,139**	**116,830,401**
	Percent[b]	**100.0**	**22.3**	**67.4**	**0.5**	**1.1**	**8.8**		
Total cities	**Number**	**461,209**	**109,243**	**308,037**	**2,175**	**5,046**	**36,708**	**4,007**	**85,067,747**
	Percent[b]	**100.0**	**23.7**	**66.8**	**0.5**	**1.1**	**8.0**		
Group I (250,000 and over)	Number	118,873	37,099	78,213	11	608	2,942	34	22,902,229
	Percent[b]	100.0	31.2	65.8	*	0.5	2.5		
Group II (100,000 to 249,999)	Number	67,487	14,463	49,091	716	965	2,252	85	12,505,038
	Percent[b]	100.0	21.4	72.7	1.1	1.4	3.3		
Group III (50,000 to 99,999)	Number	90,908	21,312	61,923	400	1,379	5,894	236	15,961,680
	Percent[b]	100.0	23.4	68.1	0.4	1.5	6.5		
Group IV (25,000 to 49,999)	Number	60,978	10,857	42,859	332	657	6,273	348	11,999,775
	Percent[b]	100.0	17.8	70.3	0.5	1.1	10.3		
Group V (10,000 to 24,999)	Number	67,593	14,093	43,038	385	655	9,422	795	12,656,463
	Percent[b]	100.0	20.8	63.7	0.6	1.0	13.9		
Group VI (under 10,000)	Number	55,370	11,419	32,913	331	782	9,925	2,509	9,042,562
	Percent[b]	100.0	20.6	59.4	0.6	1.4	17.9		
Metropolitan counties	**Number**	**63,989**	**9,139**	**45,741**	**404**	**569**	**8,136**	**579**	**23,714,860**
	Percent[b]	**100.0**	**14.3**	**71.5**	**0.6**	**0.9**	**12.7**		
Nonmetropolitan counties	**Number**	**18,002**	**2,780**	**12,183**	**179**	**116**	**2,744**	**553**	**8,047,794**
	Percent[b]	**100.0**	**15.4**	**67.7**	**1.0**	**0.6**	**15.2**		
Suburban area[c]	**Number**	**228,467**	**46,517**	**148,643**	**1,398**	**2,283**	**29,626**	**3,268**	**58,163,860**
	Percent[b]	**100.0**	**20.4**	**65.1**	**0.6**	**1.0**	**13.0**		

[a]Includes all offenses except traffic and neglect cases.
[b]Because of rounding, the percentages may not add to 100.0.
[c]Suburban areas include law enforcement agencies in cities with less than 50,000 inhabitants and county law enforcement agencies that are within a Metropolitan Statistical Area. Suburban areas exclude all metropolitan agencies associated with a principal city. The agencies associated with suburban areas also appear in other groups within this table.
*Less than one-tenth of 1 percent.

SOURCE: "Table 68. Police Disposition: Juvenile Offenders Taken into Custody, 2009," in *Crime in the United States, 2009*, U.S. Department of Justice, Federal Bureau of Investigation, September 2010, http://www2.fbi.gov/ucr/cius2009/data/table_68.html (accessed October 26, 2010)

likely that some of the detained individuals were later sent to prison or jail. People in confinement under diversion agreements entered detention voluntarily. In other words, the juvenile may have volunteered to go to a detention center to avoid going to juvenile court.

DETENTION. According to Charles Puzzanchera, Benjamin Adams, and Melissa Sickmund, in *Juvenile Court Statistics 2006–2007* (March 2010, http://www.ojjdp.gov/ojstatbb/njcda/pdf/jcs2007.pdf), approximately 22% of juveniles are put in detention as their cases are processed in juvenile court. Detention may be used if the juvenile is judged to be a threat to the community, will be at risk if returned to the community, or may not appear at an upcoming hearing if released. The researchers report that the number of delinquency cases involving detention increased by 48% between 1985 and 2007, from 247,100 to 364,600. The largest increase was for crimes against people (143%), followed by drug cases (119%), and public order cases (96%). The number of juveniles detained in property cases declined by 19% during this period. Figure 10.2 shows that the percent of juveniles who were detained for these cases fluctuated between 1985 and 2007, but did not experience much change overall.

Puzzanchera, Adams, and Sickmund find that males continued to be more likely than females to be detained, despite the increase in the use of detention for female juvenile offenders. Likewise, African-Americans made up 33% of the overall delinquency caseload in 2007, but made up 41% of those detained.

RESIDENTIAL PLACEMENT. Youths sentenced under the jurisdiction of juvenile courts could be generally confined in residential placement facilities. In 2006, 92,854 juvenile offenders were confined in public and private juvenile correctional, detention, and shelter facilities. (See Table 10.6.) Excluded from this category are juveniles in prisons and jails. Sarah Livsey, Melissa Sickmund, and Anthony Sladky of the NCJJ find in *Juvenile Residential Facility Census, 2004: Selected Findings* (January 2009, http://www.ncjrs.gov/pdffiles1/ojjdp/222721.pdf) that the number of juvenile offenders in custody decreased 7% between 2002 and 2004, probably because of the substantial decline in the number of juvenile arrests since the mid-1990s.

The OJJDP divides juvenile crimes into delinquency offenses and status offenses. Delinquency offenses are acts that are illegal regardless of the age of the perpetrator. Status offenses are acts that are illegal only for minors, such as truancy and running away. Ninety-five percent (88,137 out of a total of 92,854) of juveniles in residential placement in 2006 were delinquents. (See Table 10.6.) The other 5% were status offenders (truants from school, non-criminal ordinances and rules violators, out-of-control youths, curfew violators, and runaways). Approximately 31,704 (34.1%) juveniles in residential placement were held for offenses against people (homicide, sexual assault, robbery, and aggravated or simple assault), 23,177 (25%) were held for offenses against property (burglary, theft, auto theft, arson, or other property offenses), 15,316 (16.5%) were held for technical violations, 9,944 (10.7%) were held for public order offenses, and 7,996 (8.6%) were held for drug offenses.

FIGURE 10.2

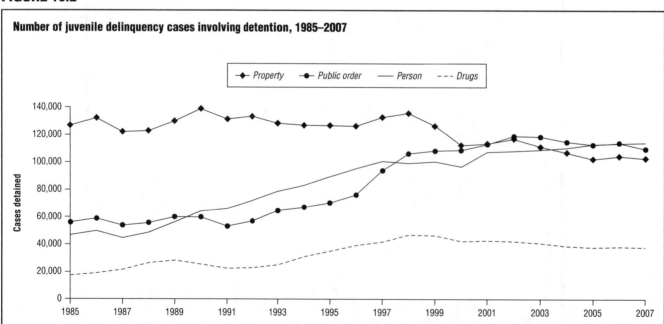

Number of juvenile delinquency cases involving detention, 1985–2007

SOURCE: Charles Puzzanchera, Benjamin Adams, and Melissa Sickmund, "The Number of Cases Involving Detention Increased Substantially between 1985 and 2007 for Person, Drug, and Public Order Offenses but Decreased for Property Offense Cases," in *Juvenile Court Statistics 2006–2007*, National Center for Juvenile Justice, 2010, http://www.ojjdp.gov/ojstatbb/njcda/pdf/jcs2007.pdf (accessed October 28, 2010)

TABLE 10.6

Juveniles in residential placement, by offense, 2006

Most serious offense	Total
Total	92,854
Delinquency	88,137
Person	**31,704**
Criminal homicide	988
Sexual assault	6,792
Robbery	6,707
Aggravated assault	7,289
Simple assault	7,308
Other person	2,620
Property	**23,177**
Burglary	9,037
Theft	4,648
Auto theft	4,650
Arson	651
Other property	4,191
Drug	**7,996**
Trafficking	1,758
Other drug	6,238
Public order	**9,944**
Weapons	3,669
Alcohol	317
Other public order	5,958
Technical violation	**15,316**
Violent Crime Index[a]	**21,776**
Property Crime Index[b]	**18,986**
Status offense	**4,717**
Running away	894
Truancy	863
Incorrigibility	1,917
Curfew violation	96
Underage drinking	524
Other status offense	423

[a]Includes criminal homicide, violent sexual assault, robbery, and aggravated assault.
[b]Includes burglary, theft, auto theft, and arson.
Note: U.S. total includes 1,466 juvenile offenders in private facilities for whom state of offense was not reported and 124 juvenile offenders in tribal facilities.

SOURCE: Melissa Sickmund, T. J. Sladky, and Wei Kang, "Detailed Offense Profile for United States, 2006," in *Census of Juveniles in Residential Placement Databook*, U.S. Department of Justice, Office of Justice Programs, Office of Juvenile Justice and Delinquency Prevention, 2008, http://www.ojjdp.ncjrs.gov/ojstatbb/cjrp/asp/State_Offense.asp (accessed October 29, 2010)

According to Melissa Sickmund, T. J. Sladky, and Wei Kang of the NCJJ, in *Census of Juveniles in Residential Placement Databook* (2008, http://www.ojjdp.ncjrs .gov/ojstatbb/cjrp/), the states with the largest number of youth under the age of 21 years in residential facilities in 2006 included California (15,240), Texas (8,247), Florida (7,302), Pennsylvania (4,323), New York (4,197), and Ohio (4,149). These six states housed 46.8% of all juveniles in residential detention. States with the smallest number included Vermont (54), Hawaii (123), and New Hampshire (189).

DEMOGRAPHICS OF THOSE IN RESIDENTIAL PLACEMENT. Sickmund, Sladky, and Kang state that in 2006 juvenile detention facilities were home to a disproportionately larger number of males (85%) than females (15%). Of the males in confinement, 35.1% had committed offenses against people and 25.9% had committed property offenses. Females were less likely to commit person offenses (28.9%) and property offenses (19.9%) than were males. Proportionally, females in detention were more likely to have committed simple assault than were males (13.4% and 6.9%, respectively), but far less likely to have committed sexual assault (0.9% and 8.5%, respectively). A larger proportion of males (10.7%) were being held for burglary than were females (4.1%). Females (14%) were substantially more likely to be held for status offenses than were males (3.5%), including incorrigibility (5.4% of females and 1.5% of males), running away (3.5% of females and 0.5% of males), and truancy (2.7% of females and 0.6% of males).

Sickmund, Sladky, and Kang also report that in 2006, 65% of juveniles in residential placement nationwide were members of minority groups. Forty percent of juvenile offenders in residential placement were African-American, 20.5% were Hispanic, 2% were Native American, and 1.2% were Asian-American. One-third (35%) of juveniles in custody were white. Minority groups were overrepresented in residential placements.

Incarcerated Juveniles

In *Prison Inmates at Midyear 2009—Statistical Tables* (June 2010, http://bjs.ojp.usdoj.gov/content/pub/pdf/pim09st .pdf), Heather C. West of the Bureau of Justice Statistics (BJS) indicates that 2,778 juveniles were held in state prison as of June 2009. (See Table 10.7.) Of the total number of juveniles in state prisons, 2,644 (95.2%) were male. Todd D. Minton of the BJS reports in *Jail Inmates at Midyear 2009—Statistical Tables* (June 2010, http:// bjs.ojp.usdoj.gov/content/pub/pdf/jim09st.pdf) that 7,220 juveniles were held in jails. (See Table 10.8.)

Christopher Hartney of the National Council on Crime and Delinquency reports in the fact sheet "Youth under Age 18 in the Adult Criminal Justice System" (June 2006, http://www.nccd-crc.org/nccd/pubs/2006may_factsheet _youthadult.pdf) that both the number of juveniles being admitted to state prisons and the proportion of people under the age of 18 years in prisons have been dropping since the mid-1990s. Nearly two-thirds (62%) of these youth have been convicted of a violent offense. However, Hartney points out that "the practice of sentencing youth as adults most seriously impacts African American, Latino, and Native American youth" and that juveniles convicted in the adult system receive little or no rehabilitative assistance and are more likely to recidivate (go back to criminal behavior) than youth convicted of similar offenses in the juvenile system.

As of January 2011, recent breakdowns of juveniles in state and federal prisons by race were not available.

TABLE 10.7

Number of inmates under age 18 held in custody in state prisons, by sex, region, and jurisdiction, 2008 and 2009

Region and jurisdiction	2008			2009		
	Total	Male	Female	Total	Male	Female
State	2,717	2,626	91	2,778	2,644	134
Northeast	676	643	33	617	584	33
Connecticut[a]	375	349	26	332	310	22
Maine	0	0	0	0	0	0
Massachusetts	3	2	1	8	5	3
New Hampshire	0	0	0	0	0	0
New Jersey[b]	19	19	0	21	21	0
New York	206	202	4	190	184	6
Pennsylvania	55	53	2	61	59	2
Rhode Island[a]	10	10	0	1	1	0
Vermont[a]	8	8	0	4	4	0
Midwest	476	458	18	499	488	11
Illinois	77	74	3	106	105	1
Indiana	63	62	1	54	54	0
Iowa	16	16	0	13	13	0
Kansas	4	3	1	5	5	0
Michigan	140	137	3	132	129	3
Minnesota	13	13	0	13	11	2
Missouri	26	25	1	31	30	1
Nebraska	15	15	0	21	19	2
North Dakota	0	0	0	0	0	0
Ohio	75	73	2	86	84	2
South Dakota[b]	0	0	0	1	1	0
Wisconsin	47	40	7	37	37	0
South	1,215	1,183	32	1,273	1,234	39
Alabama	123	123	0	118	114	4
Arkansas	17	17	0	17	17	0
Delaware[a]	25	25	0	28	28	0
Florida	301	295	6	393	384	9
Georgia	118	113	5	99	94	5
Kentucky	0	0	0	0	0	0
Louisiana[b]	26	25	1	15	14	1
Maryland	61	60	1	58	57	1
Mississippi	39	38	1	28	27	1
North Carolina[b]	186	178	8	215	206	9
Oklahoma	7	7	0	19	17	2
South Carolina	96	93	3	89	88	1
Tennessee	14	13	1	22	20	2
Texas	157	151	6	156	152	4
Virginia	45	45	0	16	16	0
West Virginia	0	0	0	0	0	0
West	350	342	8	389	338	51
Alaska[a]	10	9	1	7	7	0
Arizona	156	154	2	157	149	8
California[b]	0	0	0	0	0	0
Colorado	37	36	1	79	43	36
Hawaii[a]	0	0	0	2	2	0
Idaho	0	0	0	0	0	0
Montana	8	7	1	1	1	0
Nevada	118	115	3	118	115	3
New Mexico	1	1	0	3	3	0
Oregon	8	8	0	13	9	4
Utah	5	5	0	6	6	0
Washington[b]	3	3	0	2	2	0
Wyoming	4	4	0	1	1	0

[a]Prisons and jails form one integrated system. Data include total jail and prison populations.
[b]Counts include those held in privately–operated facilities.

SOURCE: Heather C. West, "Table 21. Reported Number of Inmates under Age 18 Held in Custody in State Prisons, by Sex, Region, and Jurisdiction, June 30, 2008 and 2009," in *Prison Inmates at Midyear 2009—Statistical Tables*, U.S. Department of Justice, Office of Justice Programs, Bureau of Justice Statistics, June 2010, http://bjs.ojp.usdoj.gov/content/pub/pdf/pim09st.pdf (accessed October 29, 2010)

However, among 24,800 (23,800 male and 1,000 female) imprisoned young adults aged 18 to 19 years in 2008, 10,700 (10,400 male and 300 female) were non-Hispanic African-American (43.1%), 6,900 (6,500 male and 400 female) were non-Hispanic white (27.8%), and 5,100 (4,900 male and 200 female) were Hispanic (20.6%). (See Table 10.9.) Of those who were aged 18 to 19 years in 2008, the rate of incarceration for non-Hispanic African-American males was 1,532 per 100,000 population; for Hispanic males, 614 per 100,000 population; and for non-Hispanic white males, 238 per

TABLE 10.8

Number of inmates in local jails, by sex, age, race and Hispanic origin, 2000 and 2005–09

Characteristic	2000	2005	2006	2007	2008	2009
Total	621,149	747,529	765,819	780,174	785,556	767,620
Sex						
Male	550,162	652,958	666,819	679,654	685,882	673,891
Female	70,987	94,571	99,000	100,520	99,673	93,729
Adults	613,534	740,770	759,717	773,341	777,852	760,400
Male	543,120	646,807	661,164	673,346	678,677	667,201
Female	70,414	93,963	98,552	99,995	99,175	93,199
Juveniles[a]	7,615	6,759	6,102	6,833	7,703	7,220
Held as adults[b]	6,126	5,750	4,835	5,649	6,410	5,847
Held as juveniles	1,489	1,009	1,268	1,184	1,294	1,373
Race/Hispanic origin[c]						
White[d]	260,500	331,000	336,500	338,200	333,300	326,500
Black/African American[d]	256,300	290,500	295,900	301,700	308,000	300,600
Hispanic/Latino	94,100	111,900	119,200	125,500	128,500	124,000
Other[d, e]	10,200	13,000	13,500	13,900	14,000	14,800
Two or more races[d]	—	1,000	700	800	1,300	1,800

Note: Detail may not sum to total due to rounding.
—Not collected.
[a]Juveniles are persons under the age of 18 at midyear.
[b]Includes juveniles who were tried or awaiting trial as adults.
[c]Estimates based on reported data adjusted for nonresponse.
[d]Excludes persons of Hispanic or Latino origin.
[e]Includes American Indians, Alaska Natives, Asians, Native Hawaiians, and other Pacific Islanders.

SOURCE: Todd D. Minton, "Table 6. Number of Inmates in Local Jails, by Characteristics, Midyear 2000 and 2005–2009," in *Jail Inmates at Midyear 2009—Statistical Tables*, U.S. Department of Justice, Office of Justice Programs, Bureau of Justice Statistics, June 2010, http://bjs.ojp.usdoj.gov/content/pub/pdf/jim09st.pdf (accessed October 29, 2010)

TABLE 10.9

Number of sentenced prisoners under State or Federal jurisdiction, by gender, race, Hispanic origin, and age, 2008

Age	Male Total[a]	Male White[b]	Male Black[b]	Male Hispanic	Female Total[a]	Female White[b]	Female Black[b]	Female Hispanic
Total[c]	1,434,800	477,500	562,800	295,800	105,300	50,700	29,100	17,300
18–19	23,800	6,500	10,400	4,900	1,000	400	300	200
20–24	208,400	59,400	85,000	48,400	11,500	5,400	3,000	2,300
25–29	246,400	66,000	102,800	60,000	16,000	7,300	4,400	3,100
30–34	238,100	70,700	96,800	54,400	18,500	8,900	5,000	3,200
35–39	226,700	75,200	90,500	45,900	20,800	9,900	5,900	3,200
40–44	202,500	75,500	77,400	35,600	17,900	8,700	5,100	2,600
45–49	136,300	53,100	51,300	22,600	10,700	5,200	3,100	1,500
50–54	75,800	31,600	27,000	12,300	5,000	2,500	1,400	700
55–59	39,100	19,000	11,900	6,200	2,100	1,300	500	300
60–64	19,200	10,700	4,700	3,000	1,000	600	200	200
65 or older	15,800	9,300	3,700	2,200	600	400	100	100

Note: Totals based on prisoners with a sentence of more than 1 year.
[a]Includes American Indians, Alaska Natives, Asians, Native Hawaiians, other Pacific Islanders, and persons identifying two or more races.
[b]Excludes persons of Hispanic or Latino origin.
[c]Includes persons under age 18.

SOURCE: William J. Sabol, Heather C. West, and Matthew Cooper, "Appendix Table 13. Estimated Number of Sentenced Prisoners under State or Federal Jurisdiction, by Gender, Race, Hispanic Origin, and Age, December 31, 2008," in *Prisoners in 2008*, U.S. department of Justice, Office of Justice Programs, Bureau of Justice Statistics, December 2009, http://bjs.ojp.usdoj.gov/content/pub/pdf/p08.pdf (accessed October 29, 2010)

100,000 population. (See Table 10.10.) Non-Hispanic African-American and Hispanic females also had higher rates of incarceration than non-Hispanic white females. Non-Hispanic African-American young adults have a much higher rate of incarceration than do non-Hispanic white juveniles and young adults.

JUVENILES IN JAIL. Between 2000 and 2009 the number of juveniles in local jails fell from 7,615 to 6,102 in 2006, before rising again to 7,220, for an overall decrease of 5.2% over the decade. (See Table 10.8.) In 2009, 5,847 (81%) juveniles in local jails were being held as adults (meaning they were either being held for trial in

TABLE 10.10

Number of sentenced prisoners under State or Federal jurisdiction per 100,000 residents, by gender, race, Hispanic origin, and age, 2008

	Male				Female			
Age	Total[a]	White[b]	Black[b]	Hispanic	Total[a]	White[b]	Black[b]	Hispanic
Total[c]	952	487	3,161	1,200	68	50	149	75
18–19	528	238	1,532	614	23	16	44	25
20–24	1,916	893	5,553	2,474	112	86	202	131
25–29	2,238	1,017	7,130	2,612	153	115	301	167
30–34	2,366	1,217	8,032	2,411	190	155	380	174
35–39	2,159	1,171	7,392	2,263	201	156	434	183
40–44	1,903	1,090	6,282	2,032	169	127	364	170
45–49	1,202	671	4,056	1,523	93	65	211	106
50–54	713	407	2,385	1,085	45	31	106	61
55–59	429	276	1,325	739	22	18	44	30
60–64	259	184	738	502	12	9	25	23
65 or older	95	69	294	186	3	2	6	4

Note: Totals based on prisoners with a sentence of more than 1 year. Rates are per 100,000 U.S. residents in each reference population group.
[a]Includes American Indians, Alaska Natives, Asians, Native Hawaiians, other Pacific Islanders, and persons identifying two or more races.
[b]Excludes persons of Hispanic or Latino origin.
[c]Includes persons under age 18.

SOURCE: William J. Sabol, Heather C. West, and Matthew Cooper, "Appendix Table 14. Estimated Rate of Sentenced Prisoners under State or Federal Jurisdiction per 100,000 U.S. Residents, by Gender, Race, Hispanic Origin, and Age, December 31, 2008," in *Prisoners in 2008*, U.S. Department of Justice, Office of Justice Programs, Bureau of Justice Statistics, December 2009, http://bjs.ojp.usdoj.gov/content/pub/pdf/p08.pdf (accessed October 29, 2010)

adult criminal court or they had been convicted as adults) and 1,373 were being held as juveniles (19%).

IMPRISONING ADULTS AND JUVENILES TOGETHER. Laurence Steinberg of Temple University argues in "Introducing the Issue" (*Future of Children*, vol. 18, no. 2, Fall 2008) that beginning in the 1990s American society experienced a "moral panic" about juvenile crime that fueled "get tough" on crime policies that treated many juvenile offenders as adults. A number of human rights organizations and juvenile justice groups point out the risks that are associated with incarcerating juveniles with adults. Among the chief concerns is that being held with hardened adult prisoners will likely cause youth offenders to become more violent, tougher, and repeat offenders. Instead of rehabilitation and education, such juveniles will be subjected to more physical and sexual abuse and violence, increasing their likelihood of showing violent tendencies when returning to society one day. In addition, youth in adult prisons and jails are vulnerable to violence.

Amnesty International notes in *Betraying the Young: Human Rights Violations against Children in the U.S. Justice System* (November 20, 1998, http://www.amnesty.org/en/library/info/AMR51/060/1998) that "young people in prison are notoriously a target of sexual and physical assault by adult inmates." Vincent Schiraldi and Jason Zeidenberg of the Center on Juvenile and Criminal Justice echo this sentiment in *The Risks Juveniles Face When They Are Incarcerated with Adults* (July 1997, http://www.cjcj.org/files/the_risks.pdf): "Young people slated to be placed in adult prisons and jails are more likely to be raped, assaulted, and commit suicide." Human rights organizations and juve-

nile justice groups also point out that juveniles are exposed to attack not only by adult inmates but also by prison guards. Reasons for this can include the juveniles' small stature, lack of confidence, and inexperience at living confined with hardened criminals. Juveniles sometimes resort to suicide because they may give in to despair more quickly.

However, Steinberg argues that at the end of the first decade of the 21st century get-tough policies were softening "as politicians and the public [came] to regret the high economic costs and ineffectiveness of the punitive reforms and the harshness of the sanctions." Elizabeth S. Scott and Laurence Steinberg find in "Adolescent Development and the Regulation of Youth Crime" (*Future of Children*, vol. 18, no. 2, Fall 2008) that by 2008 the justice system was once again recognizing that age and maturity level needed to be taken into account when calculating punishment for crimes. The researchers suggest that most juveniles who commit crimes are "adolescence-limited" offenders who will mature out of their criminal tendencies; however, contact with a harsh, adult corrections system can push juveniles into adult criminality. Instead, Scott and Steinberg indicate that successful programs "seek to provide young offenders with supportive social contexts and authoritative adult figures and to help them acquire the skills necessary to change problem behavior and attain psychosocial maturity."

Other surveys support the idea that get-tough attitudes appear to be changing. The survey "New NCCD Poll Shows Public Strongly Favors Youth Rehabilitation and Treatment" (February 7, 2007, http://www.nccd-crc.org/nccd/pubs/zogbyPR0207.pdf), which was conducted by

Zogby International for the National Council on Crime and Delinquency, finds that the American public supports rehabilitation and treatment for young people, not prosecution in adult criminal courts or incarceration in adult jails or prisons. Nine out of 10 people surveyed believed this approach might help prevent crime in the future, and seven out of 10 believed imprisoning juveniles in adult facilities would increase the likelihood that they would commit future crimes. Most people believed that youth should not be automatically transferred to adult court, but that such transfers should be handled on an individual basis.

Children and the Death Penalty

Until 2005 convicted criminals could be executed for crimes they committed as juveniles. Victor L. Streib of Ohio Northern University reports in *The Juvenile Death Penalty Today: Death Sentences and Executions for Juvenile Crimes, January 1, 1973–February 28, 2005* (October 7, 2005, http://www.law.onu.edu/faculty_staff/ faculty_profiles/coursematerials/streib/juvdeath.pdf) that between 1973 and 2005, 22 offenders were executed for crimes they committed when they were younger than 18 years old. The U.S. Supreme Court has considered many cases concerning the practice of executing offenders for crimes they committed as children. In *Eddings v. Oklahoma* (455 U.S. 104 [1982]), the court found that a juvenile's mental and emotional development should be considered as a mitigating factor when deciding whether to apply the death penalty, noting that adolescents are less mature and responsible than adults and not as able to consider long-range consequences of their actions. In this case, the court reversed the death sentence of a 16-year-old who had been tried as an adult.

Subsequent Supreme Court rulings have further limited the application of the death penalty in cases involving juveniles. In *Thompson v. Oklahoma* (487 U.S. 815 [1988]), the court found that applying the death sentence to an offender who had been 15 years old at the time of the murder was cruel and unusual punishment, concluding that the death penalty could not be applied to offenders who were younger than 16 years old. However, the following year the court found in *Stanford v. Kentucky* (492 U.S. 361) that applying the death penalty to offenders who were aged 16 or 17 years at the time of the crime was not cruel and unusual punishment.

The court was asked to reconsider this decision in 2005. In *Roper v. Simmons* (543 U.S. 551), the court set aside the death sentence of Christopher Simmons by a vote of five to four, concluding that the "Eighth and Fourteenth Amendments forbid imposition of the death penalty on offenders who were under the age of 18 when their crimes were committed." Snyder and Sickmund note that few states applied death penalty provisions to juveniles at the time of the *Roper* decision, even though 20 states allowed juveniles to be sentenced to death under the law.

IMPORTANT NAMES
AND ADDRESSES

Advocates for Youth
2000 M St. NW, Ste. 750
Washington, DC 20036
(202) 419-3420
FAX: (202) 419-1448
URL: http://www.advocatesforyouth.org/

**American Academy of Child and
Adolescent Psychiatry**
3615 Wisconsin Ave., NW
Washington, DC 20016-3007
(202) 966-7300
FAX: (202) 966-2891
URL: http://www.aacap.org/

Boys and Girls Clubs of America
1275 Peachtree St. NE
Atlanta, GA 30309-3506
(404) 487-5700
E-mail: info@bgca.org
URL: http://www.bgca.org/

Child Trends
4301 Connecticut Ave. NW, Ste. 350
Washington, DC 20008
(202) 572-6000
FAX: (202) 362-8420
URL: http://www.childtrends.org/

Children's Defense Fund
25 E St. NW
Washington, DC 20001
1-800-233-1200
E-mail: cdfinfo@childrensdefense.org
URL: http://www.childrensdefense.org/

CLASP
1200 18th St. NW, Ste. 200
Washington, DC 20036
(202) 906-8000
FAX: (202) 842-2885
URL: http://www.clasp.org/

College Board
45 Columbus Ave.
1-866-630-9305
New York, NY 10023-6917
URL: http://www.collegeboard.com/

Cyberbullying Research Center
E-mail: info@cyberbullying.us
URL: http://www.cyberbullying.us/

Feeding America
35 E. Wacker Dr., Ste. 2000
Chicago, IL 60601
1-800-771-2303
FAX: (312) 263-5626
URL: http://www.feedingamerica.org/

Guttmacher Institute
1301 Connecticut Ave. NW, Ste. 700
Washington, DC 20036
(202) 296-4012
1-877-823-0262
FAX: (202) 223-5756
URL: http://www.guttmacher.org/

Kaiser Family Foundation
2400 Sand Hill Rd.
Menlo Park, CA 94025
(650) 854-9400
FAX: (650) 854-4800
URL: http://www.kff.org/

Monitoring the Future
Survey Research Center
1355 ISR Bldg.
PO Box 1248
Ann Arbor, MI 48106
(734) 764-8365
URL: http://monitoringthefuture.org/

**National Association of
Child Care Resource and
Referral Agencies**
1515 N. Courthouse Rd., 11th Floor
Arlington, VA 22201
(703) 341-4100
FAX: (703) 341-4101
URL: http://www.naccrra.org/

**National Association of School
Resource Officers**
2020 Valleydale Rd., Ste. 207A
Hoover, AL 35244
1-888-316-2776
FAX: (205) 536-9255
URL: http://www.nasro.org/

**National Campaign to Prevent Teen and
Unplanned Pregnancy**
1776 Massachusetts Ave. NW, Ste. 200
Washington, DC 20036
(202) 478-8500
FAX: (202) 478-8588
URL: http://www.thenationalcampaign.org/

National Center for Children in Poverty
215 W. 125th St., Third Floor
New York, NY 10027
(646) 284-9600
FAX: (646) 284-9623
E-mail: info@nccp.org
URL: http://www.nccp.org/

**National Center for Missing and
Exploited Children**
Charles B. Wang International Children's
Building
699 Prince St.
Alexandria, VA 22314-3175
(703) 224-2150
1-800-843-5678
FAX: (703) 224-2122
URL: http://www.missingkids.com/

National Center for Victims of Crime
2000 M St. NW, Ste. 480
Washington, DC 20036
(202) 467-8700
FAX: (202) 467-8701
URL: http://www.ncvc.org/

National Crime Prevention Council
2001 Jefferson Davis Highway, Ste. 901
Arlington, VA 22202-4801
(202) 466-6272
FAX: (202) 296-1356
URL: http://www.ncpc.org/

National Gang Center
Institute for Intergovernmental Research
PO Box 12729
Tallahassee, FL 32317
(850) 385-0600
FAX: (850) 386-5356
E-mail: information@nationalgangcenter.gov
URL: http://www.nationalgangcenter.gov/

National Institute on
Drug Abuse
National Institutes of Health
6001 Executive Blvd., Rm. 5213
Bethesda, MD 20892-9561
(301) 443-1124
E-mail: information@nida.nih.gov
URL: http://www.nida.nih.gov/

STRYVE
URL: http://www.safeyouth.gov/

Urban Institute
2100 M St. NW
Washington, DC 20037
(202) 833-7200
URL: http://www.urban.org/

RESOURCES

Many U.S. government agencies publish timely information on their programs and on the U.S. population. The U.S. Census Bureau publishes statistics on American life in its *Current Population Reports*, including *Income, Poverty, and Health Insurance Coverage in the United States: 2009* (Carmen DeNavas-Walt, Bernadette D. Proctor, and Jessica C. Smith, September 2010), *Families and Living Arrangements* (January 2009), *America's Families and Living Arrangements* (Rose M. Kreider and Diana B. Elliott, September 2009), *Custodial Mothers and Fathers and Their Child Support: 2007* (Timothy S. Grall, November 2009), and *Who's Minding the Kids? Child Care Arrangements: Spring 2005/Summer 2006* (Lynda Laughlin, August 2010). The Census Bureau also provides information on nationwide population projections by age, race, Hispanic origin, and sex.

The Federal Interagency Forum on Child and Family Statistics, in *America's Children in Brief: Key National Indicators of Well-Being, 2010* (July 2010), provided invaluable data on many aspects of children's health and well-being. The U.S. Department of Health and Human Services (HHS) provided a wide assortment of statistical data, including *Indicators of Welfare Dependence, Annual Report to Congress, 2008* (Gil Crouse, Susan Hauan, and Annette Waters Rogers, December 2008). The HHS's Administration for Children and Families publishes *The AFCARS Report* (July 2010), which provides information on foster care and adoption.

The Centers for Disease Control and Prevention (CDC) issues the *Morbidity and Mortality Weekly Report*, which focuses on various aspects of death and disease. The CDC's "Youth Risk Behavior Surveillance—United States, 2009" (Danice K. Eaton et al., June 2010) was the source of survey information on risk behaviors among U.S. high school students. The CDC is also a leading source of HIV/AIDS statistics with its annual *HIV Surveillance Report: Diagnoses of HIV Infection and AIDS in the United States and Dependent Areas, 2008* (June 2010).

Child Health USA 2010 (October 2010), published by the Maternal and Child Health Bureau, reports the health status and needs of American children. *Child Maltreatment 2008* (2010) by the Administration for Children, Youth, and Families counts cases of child abuse that were reported to state child protective agencies. The Administration for Children and Families provided data on child support collections.

The Social Security Administration's Office of Policy offered helpful statistics on children receiving Supplemental Security Income. The Bureau of Labor Statistics, which is part of the U.S. Department of Labor, provided data on employment and unemployment in "Employment Characteristics of Families—2009" (May 2010).

The *National Vital Statistics Reports*, which is published by the National Center for Health Statistics (NCHS), provided statistics on births and infant mortality. The NCHS also published *Health, United States, 2009* (February 2010), which gives invaluable data on many health conditions, birthrates, fertility rates, and life expectancy.

The U.S. Department of Agriculture provided estimates of expenditures on children from birth through age 17. Its Center for Nutrition Policy and Promotion calculates how much it costs to raise a child in *Expenditures on Children by Families, 2009* (Mark Lino, June 2010). The Department of Agricultural also published "Characteristics of Supplemental Nutrition Assistance Program Households: Fiscal Year 2009" (Joshua Leftin, Andrew Gothro, and Esa Eslami, October 2010) and statistics on the national school lunch program.

The National Center for Education Statistics, which is part of the U.S. Department of Education, published *Digest of Education Statistics, 2009* (Thomas D. Snyder and Sally A. Dillow, April 2010), *Projections of Education Statistics to 2018* (William J. Hussar and Tabitha M. Bailey, September 2009), and *The Condition of Education 2008*

(Michael Planty et al., June 2008), which provided important statistics on education in the United States. The NCES collaborated with the Bureau of Justice Statistics to publish *Indicators of School Crime and Safety: 2009* (Rachel Dinkes, Jana Kemp, and Katrina Baum, December 2009).

The Bureau of Justice Statistics provided other important information on juvenile crime and victimization in *Criminal Victimization, 2009* (Jennifer L. Truman and Michael R. Rand, October 2010), *Prisoners in 2008* (William J. Sabol, Heather C. West, and Matthew Cooper, December 2009), *Prison Inmates at Midyear 2009—Statistical Tables* (Heather C. West, June 2010), *Jail Inmates at Midyear 2009—Statistical Tables* (Todd D. Minton, June 2010), and *Criminal Victimization in the United States, 2007 Statistical Tables* (February 2010). The Federal Bureau of Investigation's *Crime in the United States, 2009* (September 2010) covers crime and victimization.

The Office of Juvenile Justice and Delinquency Prevention (OJJDP) of the U.S. Department of Justice was a valuable resource of information about youth violence, crime, and gangs in the United States. Various sources of the OJJDP provided important data that helped in the compilation of this book. These included "Highlights of the 2008 National Youth Gang Survey" (Arlen Egley Jr., James C. Howell, and John P. Moore, March 2010) and *Census of Juveniles in Residential Placement Databook* (Melissa Sickmund, T. J. Sladky, and Wei Kang, 2008). The annual reports of the National Youth Gang Survey, which is prepared by the OJJDP, were also helpful.

The National Center for Children in Poverty provided information on children in low-income households. The Guttmacher Institute provided information on abortion rates among teenagers in the journal *Perspectives on Sexual and Reproductive Health*. The National Association of Child Care Resource and Referral Agencies provided information on the cost of child care in all 50 states in *Parents and the High Cost of Child Care: 2010 Update* (August 2010).

INDEX

Page references in italics refer to photographs. References with the letter t following them indicate the presence of a table. The letter f indicates a figure. If more than one table or figure appears on a particular page, the exact item number for the table or figure being referenced is provided.

A

AAP. *See* American Academy of Pediatrics

Abductions
family, 106–108
nonfamily, 108
problem of, 105–106

Abiola, Sara, 75

Abma, Joyce, 79–80

Abortion
legal abortions/abortion ratios, 78t
by teenagers, 76, 77

"Abortion among Young Women and Subsequent Life Outcomes" (Fergusson, Boden, & Horwood), 76

"About Chicago Area Project" (Chicago Area Project), 149

"About the Omnibus Autism Proceeding" (Health Resources and Services Administration), 45

Abstinence
HPV vaccine and, 75
impact on teens, 79

"Abstinence and Abstinence-Only Education: A Review of U.S. Policies and Programs" (Santelli et al.), 79

Abuse. *See* Child abuse/neglect

"Abuse Experiences in a Community Sample of Young Adults: Relations with Psychiatric Disorders, Sexual Risk Behaviors, and Sexually Transmitted Diseases" (Tubman et al.), 72

ACF. *See* Administration for Children and Families

Acquired immunodeficiency syndrome (AIDS)
abstinence programs and, 79
in children, 54–56
in children younger than 13, diagnoses of, 56t
high school students who were ever taught in school about AIDS/HIV, 71t
sex education in schools, 79–80

ACT (American College Test), 95–96

ACT Profile Report—National (ACT), 95, 96

"ACT Scores Dip, but More Students Meet College Benchmarks" (Associated Press), 95

ACYF (Administration for Children, Youth, and Families), 104–105

Adams, Benjamin, 160

Adams, Gina, 38–39

Adams, Kenneth, 148

Addresses/names, of organizations, 167–168

ADHD (attention deficit hyperactivity disorder), 58–59

Administration for Children and Families (ACF)
on child support, 29
on cost of TANF, 22–23
Head Start program of, 42, 88

Administration for Children, Youth, and Families (ACYF), 104–105

Adolescence, definition of, 1

"Adolescent Development and the Regulation of Youth Crime" (Scott & Steinberg), 164

"Adolescent Girls' Perceptions of the Timing of Their Sexual Initiation: 'Too Young' or 'Just Right'?" (Cotton et al.), 70

"Adolescent Sexual Behaviors at Varying Levels of Substance Use Frequency" (Floyd & Latimer), 71

"Adolescent Sexual Risk: Factors Predicting Condom Use across the Stages of Change" (Grossman et al.), 73

Adolescents
abortions/abortion ratios, legal, 78t
birthrates for teenagers by age, 75f
births to unmarried women, by age, 76t
childhood deaths, 61–62, 65–67
contraceptive use, 72–73, 73t
date crime victims, 104
death penalty and, 165
drug/alcohol/tobacco use by, 59–60
early sexual activity, 69–72
employment of, 29–31
HIV/AIDS and, 54, 56
homeless, 49, 51
homosexuality and, 77, 79
obesity, percentage of high school students who were obese/overweight, by sex, race/Hispanic origin, grade, 54t
overweight/obese, 52–54
sex education, grade when teenagers aged 15–19 first received, 81f
sex education, percentage of teenagers aged 15–19 who received, 80f
sexual intercourse, high school students who drank alcohol/used drugs before last, and who were ever taught in school about AIDS/HIV, 71t
sexual intercourse, percentage of high school students who ever had, who had for first time before age 13, 70t
sexually transmitted diseases, 73–75
sexually transmitted diseases, rates of per 100,000 adolescents/young adults, by age, race/Hispanic origin, 74f
STD/pregnancy prevention programs for teens, 79–80
suicide and, 65–67
teen abortion, 77
teen childbearing trends, 75–77
unmarried teen birthrates, 9
See also Crime prevention/punishment; Crime/victimization, juvenile; High school students

schools, unreported crimes at, 144
on violent deaths in schools, 129
on weapons in school, 135, 143
Kentucky, Stanford v., 165
Kernell, David, 103
Kitts, Robert Li, 66–67
Klebold, Dylan, 129–131
Kline, Patrick, 148
Klitsch, Michael, 76
Kochanek, Kenneth D., 109
Kowalski, Christopher L., 142
Kreider, Rose M., 12
Kunkel, Dale, 70–71

L

Lancet (newspaper), 45
Lane, Jodi, 148
Larceny-theft
juvenile arrests by gender, 155
juvenile arrests for, 153
UCR statistics on, 101–102
Latchkey kids, 35
Latimer, William W., 71
Laughlin, Lynda, 35
Law enforcement
disposition of juveniles arrested, 157
juvenile crime prevention strategies, 149–150
police disposition of juvenile offenders taken into custody, 159*t*
See also Police
Laws, to prevent juvenile crime, 147–148
Layton, Lyndsey, 52
"Lead, Chemicals Found in Toys Despite Stricter Law" (Layton), 52
Lead poisoning, 51–52
Leftin, Joshua, 26
Legislation and international treaties
Adoption and Safe Families Act of 1997, 13, 14
American Recovery and Reinvestment Act of 2009, 26, 86
Balanced Budget Act, 48
Child Support Recovery Act of 1992, 29
Children's Health Insurance Program Reauthorization Act, 48
Economic Opportunity Act of 1964, 88
Education of the Handicapped Act, 90, 93
Elementary and Secondary Education Act, 35, 143
Family and Medical Leave Act, 33, 42
Gun-Free-Schools Act, 135
Individuals with Disabilities Education Act, 93
Individuals with Disabilities Education Improvement Act, 93
McKinney-Vento Homeless Assistance Act of 1987, 49, 93, 95
McKinney-Vento Homeless Education Assistance Improvements Act of 2001, 95

Missing Children's Assistance Act, 105–106
No Child Left Behind Act, 35, 83–86, 143–144, 146
Personal Responsibility and Work Opportunity Reconciliation Act, 29, 40
Pregnancy Discrimination Act, 33
Social Security Act, 79
Lesbian adolescents, 77, 79
Lescano, Celia M., 73
Levy, Harold O., 120
Lindhorst, Taryn, 108
Lin-Kelly, Wendy, 140
Littleton, Colorado, 130
Living arrangements of children
by age, 12*f*
children living with grandparents by presence of parents, race/Hispanic origin, 13*f*
children under age 18, by presence of married parents in household and race/Hispanic origin, 11*t*
foster care/adoption, 13–15
grandparents, 12–13
homeless children, 49
nontraditional families, 11–12
parent/child situations, all, by type, race, Hispanic origin of householder, 9*t*
single-parent families, 9–11
young adults, 15–16
young adults living at home, 17*t*
Livingston, Gretchen, 4
Livsey, Sarah, 160
Lizotte, Alan J., 77
Loeber, Rolf, 121–122
Logan, Jesse, 142
"Long-Term Consequences for Teens with Older Sexual Partners" (Schelar, Ryan, & Manlove), 72
"The Long-Term Effects of Parental Alienation on Adult Children: A Qualitative Research Study" (Baker), 56–57
"Long-Term Health Correlates of Timing of Sexual Debut: Results for a National U.S. Study" (Sandfort et al.), 69
Low-income families, 41–42
See also Poverty
Lui, Christina, 121
Lynch, James P., 123, 125

M

Magee, Lara Leanne, 72
Maguire, Kathleen, 157
Major, Aline K.
on curfews, 148
on gangs, 118, 122–123
Making a Difference in Schools: The Big Brothers Big Sisters School-Based Mentoring Impact Study (Herrera et al.), 150–151

Males
bullying and, 140
taking SAT, 96
weapons in schools, statistics on, 137
See also Boys; Fathers; Gender
Mancha, Brent E., 71
Manlove, Jennifer
on children of teen mothers, 76–77
on condom use, 73
on voluntary/nonvoluntary sexual experiences, 72
Mara Salvatrucha (MS 13), 122
Marijuana
high school students who drank alcohol/used marijuana, 59*t*
sexual activity and, 71
use by high school students, 59
Marriage
children under age 18, by presence of married parents in household and race/Hispanic origin, 11*t*
employment status of population, by sex, marital status, presence/age of own children under age 18, 34*t*
mental health issues in children from conflict in, 56–57
nontraditional families, 11–12
single-parent families, 9–11
working mothers and, 33–34
young adults living at home and, 15–16
Martin, Joyce A.
on age of first-time mothers, 33
on births to unmarried women, 9
on teen childbearing trends, 75–76
Martinez, Gladys, 79–80
Martino, Steven C., 70
Maternal and Child Health Bureau
on HPV vaccine, 75
on STDs, 73–74
Maternity Leave and Employment Patterns, 1961–1995 (Smith, Downs, & O'Connell), 33
Mattel (toy maker), 52
Mayor's Anti-Gang Office, 150
McBride, Cami K., 69
McDevitt, Caitlin, 96
McDonald, Dale, 90
McKinney-Vento Homeless Assistance Act of 1987
education requirements, 93, 95
report on homeless children, 49
McKinney-Vento Homeless Education Assistance Improvements Act of 2001, 95
Measles, mumps, and rubella (MMR), 43, 45–46
Media, teen concepts of sexuality and, 70–71
Medicaid, 48
Meier, Megan, 141
Mello, Michelle M., 75
"Menacing or Mimicking? Realities of Youth Gangs" (Howell), 119, 120

National Association for Regulatory Administration, 39–40

National Association of Child Care Resource and Referral Agencies (NACCRRA), 41, 167

National Association of School Resource Officers (NASRO), 150, 167

National Campaign to Prevent Teen and Unplanned Pregnancy, 167

National Center for Children in Poverty, 167

National Center for Education Statistics (NCES)
Condition of Education 2010, 84
on homeschooling, 95
on preprimary schools, 87–88

National Center for Health Statistics (NCHS)
on infant mortality, 60–61
on physician visits, 46
on teenage pregnancy, 76

National Center for Juvenile Justice (NCJJ)
on juvenile justice, 151
on residential placement, 160, 161

National Center for Missing and Exploited Children, 106, 167

National Center for Social Statistics, 13

National Center for Victims of Crime, 167

National Council on Crime and Delinquency, 165

National Crime Prevention Council, 167

National Crime Victimization Survey (NCVS), 99, 132

National Directory of New Hires, 29

National Education Association (NEA), 85

National Education Goals Panel, 83

National Gang Center (NGC)
on Comprehensive Gang Model, 149
contact information, 168
"National Youth Gang Survey Analysis," 117

National Gang Intelligence Center (NGIC)
on gang use of technology, 120
National Gang Threat Assessment 2009, 118, 126

National Gang Threat Assessment 2009 (NGIC)
on gang use of technology, 120
on gangs and organized crime, 126
on modern street gangs, 118
on spread of gangs, 122

National Highway Traffic Safety Administration, 62, 65

National Household Education Survey, 95

National Incidence Studies of Missing, Abducted, Runaway, and Thrownaway Children (NISMART), 105

National Institute of Child Health and Human Development (NICHD), 40–41, 61

National Institute on Drug Abuse, National Institutes of Health, 168

National Population Estimates—Characteristics (U.S. Census Bureau), 13

National School Lunch Program, total participation in, 27, 30t

National School Safety and Security Services, 144, 146

National Survey of Family Growth, 71–72, 80

National Vaccine Injury Compensation Program (VICP), 44, 45

National Victim Assistance Academy Textbook (DOJ), 123

National Youth Gang Survey (NYGS), 117

"National Youth Gang Survey Analysis" (NGC), 117

"National Youth Gang Survey Trends from 1996 to 2000" (Egley, Howell, & Major), 118

Native Americans and Alaskan Natives
arrests by race, 157
birth/fertility rates for, 1, 4
college test results for, 96
in foster care, 13
gang membership among, 122–123
HIV/AIDS and, 56
infant mortality and, 60
juveniles in residential placement, 161
sexually transmitted diseases and, 74, 74f
sudden infant death syndrome and, 61
teen childbearing trends, 76
weapons at school and, 137

Native Mob (gang), 122–123

NCES. *See* National Center for Education Statistics

NCHS. *See* National Center for Health Statistics

NCJJ. *See* National Center for Juvenile Justice

NCLB Act. *See* No Child Left Behind (NCLB) Act

NCVS (National Crime Victimization Survey), 99, 132

NEA (National Education Association), 85

Neglect. *See* Child abuse/neglect

Neural tube defects, 43

A New Era of Responsibility: Renewing America's Promise (White House), 79

"New NCCD Poll Shows Public Strongly Favors Youth Rehabilitation and Treatment" (National Council on Crime and Delinquency), 164–165

New York Times (newspaper), 45

"Next Round Begins for No Child Left Behind" (Paulson), 83

NGC. *See* National Gang Center

NGIC. *See* National Gang Intelligence Center

NICHD (National Institute of Child Health and Human Development), 40–41, 61

The NICHD Study of Early Child Care and Youth Development: Findings for Children up to Age 4 1/2 Years (NICHD), 41

"Nine States and the District of Columbia Win Second Round Race to the Top Grants" (U.S. Department of Education), 86

Ninth Amendment, 148

NISMART (National Incidence Studies of Missing, Abducted, Runaway, and Thrownaway Children), 105

No Child Left Behind (NCLB) Act
charter schools, 85–86
overview of, 83
persistently dangerous schools, 143–144, 146
proficiency testing, 84–85
provisions for safe schools, 143
school accountability in, 83–84
21st CCLC under, 35
voucher controversy, 85

"No Child Left Behind: How to Give It a Passing Grade" (West), 83

Nonfamily Abducted Children: National Estimates and Characteristics (Hammer, Finkelhor, & Sedlak), 108

Nonfamily households, rise in, 6, 8

Nonfatal crimes
in schools, 132, 134–135, 137
against students ages 12–18, 135f

Nonnegligent manslaughter, 151

Nonstandard hours, child care during, 41

Nontraditional families, 11–12

Nord, Mark, 51

Nutrition programs
school, 27
Special Supplemental Nutrition Program for Women, Infants, and Children, 26–27
Supplemental Nutrition Assistance Program, 25–26

NYGS (National Youth Gang Survey), 117

O

Obama, Barack
Children's Health Insurance Program Reauthorization Act, 48
education reform of, 83–84
Race to the Top Fund, 86
sex education and, 79
TANF block grant extension and, 23

"Obama: Revise No Child Left Behind Law" (Anderson), 83–84

O'Connell, Martin, 33

O'Donnell, Christina E., 118

Offenders, juvenile
computer crime, 102–103
drug use, illegal, 103–104
homicide, 101
overview of, 100
rape, 101
relationship to victim, 109–110
robbery/burglary/larceny-theft, 101–102
youth violence, risk factors for, 100–101